P.C.P. SERIES IN ACCOUNTING AND FINANCE

Consulting Editor: Michael J. Sherer

The aim of this series is to publish lively and readable textbooks for university, polytechnic and professional students, and important, up-to-date reference books for researchers, managers and practising accountants. All the authors have been commissioned because of their specialist knowledge of their subjects and their established reputations as lecturers and researchers. All the major topics in accounting and finance will be included, but the series will give special emphasis to recent developments in the subjects and to issues of continuing debate and controversy.

INTRODUCTION TO ACCOUNTING

INTRODUCTION TO ACCOUNTING

J.R. EDWARDS, *Reader in Accounting*
and
H.J. MELLETT, *Lecturer in Accounting*

Cardiff Business School

P·C·P
Paul Chapman
Publishing Ltd

First published 1989

Paul Chapman Publishing Ltd.
144 Liverpool Road
London N1 1LA

British Library Cataloguing in Publication Data

Edwards, J.R. (John Richard), *1946–*
  Introduction to accounting.
  1. Accounting
  I. Title   II. Mellett, H.J. (Howard J.)
  657

ISBN 1–85396–020–9

Typeset by Inforum Ltd, Portsmouth
Printed and bound by Athenaeum Press Ltd, Newcastle upon Tyne
B C D E F G   5 4 3 2 1

Contents

Series editor's preface

These days it is not only students of accountancy who require a good under-standing of the principles and techniques of accounting. Increasingly, under-graduate and professional students from other disciplines are finding that accounting is included in one or more of their course components. For business studies undergraduates and postgraduate MBA students accounting is one of the core subjects of the degree. Accounting is also a popular optional course for economics and social science students and, more recently, a basic knowledge of accounting has become a requirement for many engineering students.

It is no easy task to write an introductory textbook on accounting that can satisfy the study needs of such a diverse group. It is particularly difficult to write an accounting book that introduces the techniques of double entry book-keeping to enable students to prepare balance sheets and profit and loss accounts, and that discusses critically the main problems of accounting measurement.

It is, therefore, with great pleasure that I welcome the addition of *Introduction to Accounting* by Dick Edwards and Howard Mellett to the Accounting and Finance Series. They have written a highly readable and informative introduction to the subject but they have not shied away from a thoughtful and critical evaluation of some of the traditional concepts and practices adopted by the accountancy profession. For example, by devoting separate chapters to the valuation of assets and the measurement of profit, the authors make the key point that in fact accounting profit can be determined using two quite distinct methods. Profit can be determined as the difference between two balance sheets, after allowing for changes in capital, or by matching the appropriate costs against the related revenue in the profit and loss account for the period. Both methods are acceptable in principle and in practice, but they can and often do produce quite different profit figures.

Introduction to Accounting also emphasizes how important it is for the user to understand and interpret correctly the various financial statements prepared by accountants. Today's students need to understand how the balance sheet, the profit and loss account and the source and application of funds statement are prepared and how they interrelate. In addition, the authors pay particular attention to the interpretation of the monetary amounts contained in all these financial statements. They emphasize that the calculation of standard financial ratios is simply the starting point for a full investigation of the economic and financial performance of a business enterprise.

An introductory textbook cannot cover all aspects of accounting and the emphasis of this book is on financial accounting and financial reporting. Nevertheless, the importance of accounting information in managerial decisions is recognized and separate chapters deal with the measurement of relevant costs and revenues for different decisions and the use of computerized spreadsheets as an aid to budgeting and financial planning.

In today's world of complex financial transactions it is important for most students, and not just those specializing in accountancy, to have a basic understanding of accounting. *Introduction to Accounting* is likely to become one of the standard introductory textbooks on accounting over the next few years for all students who wish to acquire such an understanding.

Michael Sherer

Preface

Recent years have seen an increasing interest in the study of accounting both as a subject in its own right and as an adjunct to other disciplines, such as engineering and medicine. This trend reflects recognition of the fact that the financial aspects of human enterprise cannot be ignored; the activities of almost any undertaking have financial consequences which should be measured and controlled, and this requires the involvement of someone versed in the appropriate techniques. However, it must be remembered that the operation of an accounting system is itself neutral, and the financial information produced has to be interpreted and its relevance weighed, alongside other considerations, before decisions are made. This process requires that the users of accounting information understand what lies behind it and the extent of its uses and limitations.

The authors have produced this book to provide an introduction to accounting which embraces both the basic techniques and the underlying theoretical concepts and shows how these are applied in various circumstances. It is designed to meet the needs of both the non-specialist and those intending to qualify, in due course, as accountants. To meet these objectives the text is fully illustrated with worked examples and, for reinforcement, the text contains chapter-end questions of varying complexity. The solutions to these questions are given in the appendix at the end of the book. To enable students to develop further their technical skills, a companion workbook is available which contains numerous questions taken from the papers of the following examining bodies: Royal Society of Arts; Association of Accounting Technicians; London Chamber of Commerce and Industry; the Chartered Association of Certified Accountants; and the Institute of Chartered Secretaries and Administrators. In all cases the solutions have been prepared by the authors, who accept full responsibility for any errors.

The book has been designed to be read in chapter order, and readers are advised to follow this. The first three chapters introduce the subject, the balance sheet, and the calculation of profit as an increase in the value of an enterprise. Chapter 4 examines one of the most basic records, that of cash received and paid, and shows how its contents are converted into a comprehensive set of accounting statements. Chapters 5 to 7 cover the accounting process based on the double entry system of book keeping from the initial record of each transaction through to the production of a final report. By this stage the reader should have grasped the underlying techniques, and Chapter 8 discusses the more subjective areas of asset valuation and profit measurement. Chapters 9 and 10 consider the application of accounting theory and techniques to specific forms of enterprise, namely partnerships and limited companies, while Chapter 11 covers the use of techniques in certain specialized areas. Chapters 11 to 14 deal with the interpretation of financial data and its application to decision-making. Chapter 15 examines the role of computers in accounting.

The authors wish to thank those professional bodies which have allowed the use of their examination material as examples, and those companies from whose published accounts illustrative figures have been taken. We are grateful to the Chartered Institute of Bankers for permission to include extracts from *Introduction to Accountancy for Banking Students* written by the same authors and published by the Institute.

1
The Framework of Accounting

THE ACCOUNTING PROCESS

Accounting is a data-processing system that has been vividly described as the 'language of business'. It may be defined as a system for recording and reporting business transactions, in financial terms, to interested parties who use this information as the basis for performance assessment, decision-making and control.

The various stages in the accounting and decision-making process are presented diagrammatically in Figure 1.1. It can be seen that the accounting process contains two basic elements, namely recording business transactions (stages 1–5) and reporting financial information to enable decisions to be taken (stages 6–10). These are interrelated since accounting records form the basis for accounting reports.

The accounting process begins with an economic event, such as the receipt of goods from a supplier. An originating document or voucher is then made out to record the movement of goods, services or cash into, within or out of a business. It is important that the document is made out immediately, since any delay increases the risk of an error that can undermine the entire accounting process. The term 'garbage in, garbage out' has been coined to describe the effect, on the information system, of starting with incorrect data.

Documents and vouchers quite naturally originate in many different departments of a company, but copies of all of them are sent to the accounts department where they are summarized, analysed, and then entered in the books of account. Periodically, at least once a year, but probably more often, the balances are extracted from the ledger accounts and assembled in a 'trial balance'. This is used as the basis for preparing the final accounts, which consists of a profit and loss account and a balance sheet. These accounting statements are then made available to both management and a variety of 'external' users (see later in this chapter) to help them reach better informed decisions than would otherwise have been possible – for example, the financial statements prepared for a well-known company, such as John Menzies, may indicate that good progress has been made over the last year. On this basis, an individual might decide to purchase some of the company's shares. That individual will use financial statements subsequently published by John

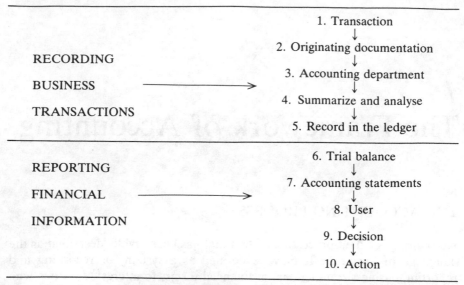

RECORDING

BUSINESS

TRANSACTIONS

1. Transaction
↓
2. Originating documentation
↓
3. Accounting department
↓
4. Summarize and analyse
↓
5. Record in the ledger

REPORTING

FINANCIAL

INFORMATION

6. Trial balance
↓
7. Accounting statements
↓
8. User
↓
9. Decision
↓
10. Action

Figure 1.1   Accounting and decision-making process

Menzies to judge whether the performance has come up to expectations and whether to retain the shareholding, add to it or sell the shares.

The profit and loss account and balances sheet of John Menzies for 1987, are given in Figure 1.2.

SUPPLIERS OF ACCOUNTING INFORMATION

Suppliers of accounting information include the following business units operating in the *private* sector of the economy. They are listed in no particular order of priority:

1. *Sole traders* These are businesses that have a single owner who also takes all the major managerial decisions. Operations are usually on a small scale, and typical examples are an electrician, the local newsagent and the milkman. The main reason why accounts are prepared for the sole trader is to help establish the amount of income tax due to the Inland Revenue. He or she makes little use of accounting statements for business decisions that he or she instead bases on knowledge obtained as a result of direct contact with all aspects of business activity.

2. *Partnerships* These exist where two or more individuals join together to undertake some form of business activity. The partners share between them ownership of the business and the obligation to manage its operations. Professional people, such as accountants, solicitors and doctors, commonly organize their business activities in the form of partnerships. Accounting

John Menzies
1 9 8 7

GROUP PROFIT AND LOSS ACCOUNT

	Notes	1987 £m	1986 £m
Turnover	2	595.7	546.9
Net operating costs	3	573.0	527.4
Profit on ordinary activities before taxation		22.7	19.5
Taxation	7	8.7	8.4
Profit for the financial period		14.0	11.1
Dividends	8	2.7	2.4
Profit retained		11.3	8.7

GROUP BALANCE SHEET

	Notes	1987 £m	1986 £m
Fixed assets			
Tangible assets	10	44.8	38.8
Investments	11	1.2	1.1
		46.0	39.9
Current assets			
Stocks		38.5	34.3
Debtors	12	59.3	49.5
Cash at bank and in hand		18.2	11.5
		116.0	95.3
Creditors: amounts due within one year			
Bank loans and overdrafts		1.1	0.8
Other	13	96.2	82.6
Net current assets		18.7	11.9
Total assets less current liabilities		64.7	51.8
Creditors: amounts due after more than one year			
Taxation		8.8	4.6
Finance debt	14	1.4	1.6
Other		1.2	—
Provisions for liabilities and charges			
Deferred taxation	15	1.8	1.5
		51.5	44.1
Capital and reserves			
Called-up share capital	16	15.6	15.6
Reserves			
Revaluation reserve	17	3.7	3.7
Other reserves	17	1.1	1.3
Profit and loss account		31.1	23.5
		51.5	44.1

Figure 1.2   Profit and loss account and balance sheet of John Menzies, 1987

statements are required as a basis for allocating profits between the partners and, again, for agreeing tax liabilities with the Inland Revenue.

3. *Clubs and societies* There are, in Britain, many thousands of clubs and societies organized for recreational, educational, religious, charitable and other purposes. Members invariably pay an annual subscription and management powers are delegated to a committee elected by the members. The final accounts prepared for (usually large) societies, formed by registering with the Registrar of Friendly Societies, are often controlled by statute. For the local club or society, the form of the accounts is either laid down in the internal rules and regulations or decided at the whim of the treasurer. Conventional accounting procedures are sometimes ignored in a small organization. Reasons for this are lack of expertise, the meagre quantity of assets belonging to the organization and the fact that the accounts are of interest only to the members.

4. *Limited companies* A limited company is formed by registering, under the Companies Act, with the Registrar of Companies and complying with certain formalities. The company may be private, indicated by the letters Ltd at the end of its name, or public, in which case the designatory letters are plc. The main significance of the distinction is that only the latter can make an issue of shares to the general public. In the case of public companies there is the further distinction between quoted companies, whose shares are traded on the stock exchange, and unquoted companies. In general, public companies are larger than private companies and quoted companies larger than unquoted.

   The directors of all limited companies are under a legal obligation to prepare and publish accounts, at least once in every year, which comply with the requirements of the Companies Act. (It should be noted that there are also in existence a small number of unlimited companies – for example, this method of incorporation is sometimes used by professional firms who are not allowed to have limited liability but want the tax advantages of being a company.)

   A limited company may, alternatively, be formed by means of either a private Act of Parliament or a royal charter. These are called statutory and chartered companies respectively. The form of their accounts may be regulated by the charter or statute. In addition, it is normal practice to comply with the general requirements of the Companies Acts.

Reporting units in the *public* sector include local authorities, nationalized industries, state colleges and the health service. These are outside the scope of this book, although many of the accounting techniques they employ are exactly the same as those used by organizations in the private sector.

FINANCIAL ACCOUNTING AND MANAGEMENT ACCOUNTING COMPARED

A conventional division of accounting is into financial accounting and management accounting. The former is concerned with the provision of accounting information for external user groups while the latter concentrates on the provision of information for management. The principal accounting statements – the balance sheet and the profit and loss account – are of interest to internal and external users but, when presented to the latter, they will normally be in a condensed form. It will be noticed that the final accounts of John Menzies (Figure 1.2) summarize on a single sheet the financial effect of millions of individual transactions. For example, the balance sheet reports total assets of £162 million (fixed assets £46 million + current assets £116 million) divided into just five categories: tangible assets (£44.8 million), investments (£1.2 million), stocks (£38.5 million), debtors (£59.3 million) and cash at bank and in hand (£18.2 million).

The main factor affecting the amount of detail contained in the accounts is the requirements of the user group. In general, external users wish to assess the overall performance of the entity and an enormous amount of detail is inappropriate both because it is of little interest and because it is likely to obscure the important trends. It is mainly for this reason that information is presented in a highly-summarized form. A further reason is that the disclosure of too much detail might be used by competitors to analyse the company's strengths and weaknesses.

Financial statements prepared for management contain much more detail. The explanation for this difference may be found in the types of decision to be taken. Shareholders base their decision to sell shares, retain their investment or buy more shares, mainly on the level of reported profit and dividends declared. Management, in contrast, is keenly interested in the costs and revenues that make up the profit figure. This is because they are responsible for taking the following kinds of decisions which influence *individual items* of revenue and expenditure: whether to expand or contract production; whether to substitute one material for another, or one type of worker for another; whether to replace labour-intensive production methods by machinery; whether to acquire property instead of renting it; and which type of power supply to use. In many instances reports must be specially prepared to help reach these decisions, and appraisal techniques have been developed to help the management process. After the decisions have been made, the outcome is monitored to see the extent to which expectations have been fulfilled.

This book introduces accounting techniques that form the basis for both branches of accounting – financial and management – although individual chapters or sections of chapters focus on specialist aspects of each. Chapters 2–8 deal, in detail, with the calculation of profit, the valuation of assets and the preparation of the profit and loss account and balance sheet. As has already been explained, these documents are widely used by both internal and external consumers of accounting information. Chapters 9–11 cover the preparation of certain specialized accounting techniques and identify the distinctive features of final accounts prepared for partnerships and limited companies. Chapters 12 and 13 explain how the information contained in the accounts may be analysed and interpreted to help both internal and external users decide how to commit resources at their disposal. Chapter 14 contains an introduction to some of the important accounting techniques used by management for resource allocation decisions. Chapter 15 examines the implication of computerization for the accounting process.

EXTERNAL USERS OF ACCOUNTING INFORMATION

In 1975 the accounting profession published a discussion document, called *The Corporate Report*, in an attempt to stimulate interest in the scope and aims of financial reports in the light of modern needs and conditions. The following seven user groups were identified as having a reasonable claim to corporate financial information:

1. The equity investor group made up of existing and potential shareholders.
2. The loan creditor group made up of present and potential holders of debentures and loan stock, and providers of short-term loans and finance.
3. The employee group made up of existing, potential and past employees.
4. The adviser group made up of financial analysts and journalists, economists, statisticians, researchers, trade unions, stockbrokers and credit-rating agencies.
5. The business contact group made up of customers, suppliers, competitors, business rivals, and those interested in mergers, amalgamations and take-overs.
6. The government, particularly the tax authorities, departments and agencies concerned with the supervision of commerce and industry, and local authorities.
7. The public, including taxpayers, ratepayers, consumers and other community and special interest groups such as political parties, consumer and environmental protection societies and regional pressure groups.

Each of the above groups has a common interest in company accounts, but they use financial information as the basis for quite different decisions. For instance, shareholders require assistance to help reach share-trading decisions, i.e. whether to retain their present investment, increase it or sell. Employees require financial information to help assess employment prospects and also for the purpose of collective bargaining. Suppliers require accounting information to decide whether to advance credit to a potential customer. Loan creditors, such as the bank, need accounting information to help decide whether to make an initial advance, and to monitor progress and the ability of the customer to repay the amount due at the end of the loan period. A marked deterioration in the company's financial position might well cause the bank to call in the loan before the financial position deteriorates even further.

There are significant variations in the quantity of financial information made available to each of these groups. This results from differential legal requirements, voluntary decisions by management to make financial information available to particular users and the ability of certain individuals to insist on additional disclosures.

PRINCIPAL ACCOUNTING STATEMENTS

The two main accounting statements, the profit and loss account and the balance sheet, are now introduced in a little more detail.

The profit and loss account

Revenues are generated and costs are incurred as the result of undertaking business activity. These revenues and costs are summarized in the profit and loss account, which may be prepared to cover a week, a month, a year or any other chosen interval. Provided total revenue exceeds total expenditure a profit is earned; in the converse situation a loss is suffered.

The published profit and loss account of John Menzies (Figure 1.2) covers the twelve months to 31 January 1987. The account starts with turnover and, from this figure, is deducted net operating costs to arrive at profit before tax. Tax payable to the Inland Revenue and dividends due to shareholders are then subtracted to produce the retained profit for the year. Full details of each of these items is given in notes 2, 3, 7 and 8 to the accounts (not reproduced).

The advantages of the profit and loss account are that it sets out the following information: whether a profit has been earned; how much profit has been earned; how the profit figure has been arrived at; and how the profit is appropriated between taxation, dividends and the amount retained for reinvestment.

The balance sheet

This sets out the financial position of the business at a chosen point in time. It is the date to which the profit and loss account is made up. The most common accounting dates are the calendar year end (31 December) and the tax year end (31 March).

An obvious difference between the profit and loss account and balance sheet is that, whereas the former reports inflows and outflows of resources over a period of time, the latter sets out the assets and liabilities at a particular point in time. It is for this reason that the balance sheet has been likened to a financial photograph of a business. Like all photographs, the position just before or just afterwards may be entirely different. This provides scope for management to undertake cosmetic exercises that present the company's position in the best possible light. For example, it might borrow money just before the year end in order to inflate the cash balance and make repayment on the first day of the next accounting period. Such devices are called 'window dressing' and it is part of the auditor's job to ensure that decision-makers are not misled by the adoption of such procedures.

The balance sheet of John Menzie's shows fixed assets of £46 million and current assets of £116 million. Moving down the balance sheet a range of liabilities are then deducted made up of creditors due for payment within one year and those due for payment in more than one year's time and deferred taxation. The 'net' asset figure is £51.5 million. The remainder of the statement shows how these assets have been financed by shareholders in the form of capital and reserves.

The aim of a business is to make a profit and, if this objective is achieved, the financial position of the business improves and the assets increase. Certainly this is happening at John Menzies where the shareholders' interest at the end of January 1987 amounts to £51.5 million compared with £44.1 million a year earlier.

The preparation of the balance sheet is examined in Chapters 2 and 3, and readers are introduced to the profit and loss account in Chapter 4.

2
The Balance Sheet

THE ENTITY CONCEPT

In Chapter 1 we saw that there are three main forms of trading organization (clubs and societies don't usually trade) within the private sector of the economy – the sole trader, the partnership and the limited company. There are two important differences between sole traders and partnerships (sometimes referred to as 'firms') on the one hand and limited companies on the other.

1. *The relationship between ownership and management* In the case of firms, the owner or owners also run the business, whereas in the case of the limited company there may well be a significant separation between the ownership and managerial functions. This is particularly likely in the case of the public limited company where the bulk of the finance is provided by the general public.
2. *The owner's liability for business debts* Sole traders and partners normally have unlimited liability for the debts of their firm, whereas the shareholders of limited companies are not required to contribute beyond the amount originally paid for shares issued by the company.

The latter distinction is significant when a business runs into financial difficulties. In the case of firms, the creditors claim first against the business assets but, if these are insufficient to satisfy the amounts due, creditors can then claim against the owner's personal wealth. In an extreme situation, the owner of a bankrupt firm could be forced to sell his or her home and all other personal belongings to meet demands from the firm's creditors. (It is to avoid this outcome that a person in business sometimes transfers the ownership of personal assets to his or her spouse.) This contrasts with the relative position of investors and creditors of a limited company, where any deficiency of business assets compared with liabilities at the date of liquidation is borne by the creditors.

Company law, therefore, regards a limited company as a separate legal entity. The creditor contracts with the company and can claim only against its assets. No such legal distinction is recognized where the business is carried on by a sole trader or by partners. *The position in accountancy is quite different*. It is always assumed, for accounting purposes, that the business entity has an existence separate and distinct from owners, managers or any other individuals with whom it comes into contact during the course of its trading activities. The assumption of a separate existence, usually referred to as the *entity concept*, requires a careful distinction to be drawn between business affairs and personal transactions. One of the reasons for requiring this distinction to be made is that it facilitates performance assessment. A sole trader forms a business in the hope that it will earn him or her a satisfactory profit and, to discover whether this objective has been achieved, profit must be calculated on the basis of only business transactions.

Illustration 2.1

On 1 January 19X1 Mr Old was made redundant and received £30,000 in compensation. He used the cash as follows:

(a) Purchased a sports car – £19,500.
(b) Arranged the redecoration of his house – £1,000.
(c) Paid off his personal overdraft – £3,500.
(d) Decided to form a business called Old Ventures and, as a first step, opened a business bank account and paid in £6,000.

To comply with the entity concept it is necessary to distinguish between Mr Old's personal transactions and the business transactions of Old Ventures. An examination of the above information shows (a), (b) and (c) to be personal transactions and (d) to be a business transaction.

Readers should now work Question 2.1 at the end of the chapter. In all cases readers should work the question *and only then compare their answer with the solution provided in the appendix at the end of the book.*

REPORTING CAPITAL IN THE BALANCE SHEET

Because the business is regarded as a separate accounting entity, all business transactions must be recorded *twice*: *first*, to show the effect of the transaction on the assets belonging to the business; and *second*, to show the effect of the transaction on the relationship between the business, on the one hand, and providers of finance on the other.

Applying this rule to transaction (d) in Illustration 2.1 we find that its effect is as follows:

Effect on business assets:	Assets increase from zero to £6,000 as the result of the injection of cash.
Effect on relationship with providers of finance:	The business now owes Mr Old £6,000.

The financial effect of this transaction may be presented in a balance sheet in the following manner:

Illustration 2.2

Balance Sheet of Old Ventures at 1 January 19X1

Assets	£	Sources of finance	£
Cash at bank	6,000	Capital: Mr Old	6,000

The left side of the balance sheet shows that the assets belonging to the business consist of cash amounting to £6,000. The right side of the balance sheet shows that Mr Old is owed £6,000. Put another way, the right-hand side shows that Mr Old has made an investment of £6,000 in the business. This is called his capital. Readers should note that there is numerical equality between the two sides of the balance sheet. This must always be the case. Assets belonging to the business are not conjured out of 'thin air' and must have been financed in some way or another. The corresponding finance is shown on the right side of the balance sheet and the following fundamental equation continues throughout the life of the business:

$$\text{Assets} = \text{Sources of finance.}$$

We may therefore describe the balance sheet as a financial statement that shows on the one side the assets belonging to the business and on the other side the way in which those assets have been financed.

Two obvious differences should be noted between the above balance sheet and that given for John Menzies in Chapter 1, Figure 1.2:

1. The balance sheet of John Menzies contains much more information. This is because it has been in business for many years, and the balance sheet reports the accumulated financial effect of literally millions of transactions undertaken between the date of formation and 31 January 1987. Old Ventures, by way of contrast, has only just been formed and has undertaken a single transaction.
2. The balance sheet of John Menzies is presented in vertical format with the assets listed *above* the sources of finance. The balance sheet of Old Ventures is presented in horizontal format with assets on the left and sources of finance on the right. Either presentation is perfectly legal.

RAISING FURTHER FINANCE

Before a business commences operations, sufficient finance should be raised to support the planned level of activity. Too many businesses begin their lives with insufficient cash resources and most of them fail before they get off the ground. At best, the early years of the firm's life is marked by a continuous shortage of cash and much of management's time is taken up coping with cash-flow problems rather than being directed towards the development of profitable trading activities.

Mr Old has made a personal investment of £6,000 in Old Ventures (see Illustration 2.2), and we will assume that he has estimated that a total initial investment of £10,000 is required to finance the planned level of business operations. He is £4,000 short and is likely to explore a number of avenues in the endeavour to obtain this sum and to place the business on a sound financial footing. One possibility is to borrow from family, friends or the bank; another is to seek government aid; and a third might involve acquiring some of the business assets on hire purchase. We will assume that Mr Old convinces his bank manager that there are sound prospects for Old Ventures and on 2 January the bank lends him £4,000. The effect of the transaction is as follows:

Effect on business assets:	Cash increases by £4,000.
Effect on relationship with providers of finance:	Indebtedness to bank increases from zero to £4,000.

The revised balance sheet becomes as follows.

Illustration 2.3

Balance Sheet of Old Ventures at 2 January 19X1

Assets	£	Sources of finance	£
Cash at bank	10,000	Capital	6,000
		Loan from bank	4,000
	10,000		10,000

The equality between assets and sources of finance is retained with the increase in business assets financed by the bank loan. There are now, however, two different types of finance. The amount advanced by Mr Old, his capital, is a permanent investment that will not usually be withdrawn until the business is wound up, whereas the amount advanced by the bank is a liability that must be repaid in due course. The relationship Assets = Sources of finance, therefore, needs to be extended, as follows, by dividing the sources of finance into its two component parts:

$$\text{Assets} = \text{Capital} + \text{Liabilities}.$$

which may be abbreviated to

$$A = C + L.$$

Readers should test their understanding of this relationship by working Question 2.2 at the end of this chapter.

THE INVESTMENT DECISION

It is the job of management to employ profitably the resources that have been placed at its disposal, and to carry out this function many decisions have to be made. These result in a continuous flow of cash and other assets into, through and out of the business. Accounting statements, amongst which the balance sheet is one of the most important, are prepared at regular intervals to enable management to monitor the results of their decisions and to gauge the extent to which they are achieving the objective of profit maximization. In the case of Old Ventures, Mr Old, when performing his managerial role, must decide how to employ the cash available to the business, i.e. he must make an *investment decision*. Mr Old decides to go into business as an antique dealer and purchases a small warehouse for cash, £7,000, on 10 January 19X1. On the same day he acquired various relics, second-hand goods and memorabilia (this is called his *stock-in-trade*) for cash, £2,500. The effect of these transactions is as follows:

Effect on business assets: Premises increase by £7,000,
Stock-in-trade increases by £2,500.
Cash at bank reduces by £9,500.

Effect on relationship
with outsiders: Zero.

Illustration 2.4

Balance Sheet of Old Ventures at 10 January 19X1

Assets	£	Sources of finance	£
Premises	7,000	Capital	6,000
Stocks*	2,500	Loan from bank	4,000
Cash at bank	500		
	10,000		10,000

Note
* This is the commonly used abbreviation for stock-in-trade.

Illustration 2.4 sets out the revised financial position of Old Ventures at 10 January. No additional sources of finance have been raised and the right-hand side of the balance sheet remains unchanged. The effect of the investment decision is merely to cause a reallocation of resources between business assets.

Before Old Ventures is ready to commence trading, Mr Old must make sure that his display of antiques is sufficiently extensive to attract customers into his warehouse. Let us assume that a further consignment of furniture, costing

£2,000, is required for this purpose. The above balance sheet shows that the company has insufficient cash available for this purpose and an additional source of finance must be obtained. In practice, very few businesses operate entirely on the cash basis. Instead, a proportion – often a high proportion – of purchases and sales are made on credit, i.e. a period of time elapses between the dates that goods are supplied and paid for. Normally businesses take the maximum period of credit allowed because, during this time, stock is financed by suppliers rather than by the firm itself. The period of credit allowed by suppliers varies a great deal but thirty days is most common.

Old Ventures takes delivery of furniture costing £2,000 on 11 January 19X1. The supplier allows thirty days credit. The effect of the transaction is as follows:

Effect on business assets:	Stock-in-trade increases by £2,000.
Effect on relationship with outsiders:	Trade creditors increase by £2,000.

Illustration 2.5

Balance Sheet of Old Ventures at 11 January 19X1

Assets	£	Sources of finance	£
Premises	7,000	Capital	6,000
Stocks	4,500	Loan from bank	4,000
Cash at bank	500	Trade creditors	2,000
	12,000		12,000

The above balance sheet shows that the firm now owns assets totalling £12,000 made up of premises, stocks and cash at bank. The finance has been obtained from three sources: ownership, the bank and suppliers who are described as trade creditors for balance sheet purposes. The investment made by the owners is normally permanent, while the loan is likely to be the subject of a formal agreement that covers such matters as the repayment date and the rate of interest payable. Trade creditors expect to be repaid in accordance with the normal practice of the particular trade, in this case thirty days. An important feature of trade credit is that it is a renewable source of finance in the sense that, provided the firm pays money currently owed, it will be able to acquire further supplies on credit, thereby maintaining a constant level of indebtedness.

Readers should now work Question 2.3 at the end of the chapter.

BUSINESS DEVELOPMENT

Old Ventures is now ready to start trading. Mr Old established the business in the expectation that it would earn profits, and stocks must therefore be sold for sums sufficiently in excess of cost to convince Mr Old that his capital is efficiently employed and would not yield a larger return if invested elsewhere.

On 12 January Old Ventures sells antiques costing £2,000 to Rustic Relics (a nearby antique shop) for £3,500, payment to be made by the end of the month. Ignoring interest charges and other operating costs, a profit of *£1,500* (sales price £3,500 minus cost £2,000) has been earned that accrues to Mr Old and is added to his capital to show that the value of his investment in the business has increased. The effect of the transaction is as follows:

Effect on business assets:	Stock-in-trade decreases by £2,000. Trade debtors increase by £3,500.
Effect on relationship with outsiders:	Capital increases by £1,500.

Illustration 2.6

Balance Sheet of Old Ventures at 12 January 19X1

Assets	£	Sources of finance	£
Premises	7,000	Capital	6,000
Stocks	2,500	Add: Profit	1,500
Trade debtors	3,500		
Cash at bank	500		7,500
		Loan from bank	4,000
		Trade creditors	2,000
	13,500		13,500

The total assets of Old Ventures (an alternative description is *gross assets*) have increased from £12,000 in Illustration 2.5, to £13,500 in Illustration 2.6. This is because one asset (stock) costing £2,000 has been replaced by a new asset (trade debtors) worth £3,500. A similar increase occurs in the sources of finance as the result of adding the profit earned to Mr Old's initial capital investment. It should be noticed that profit is recognized despite the fact that the price paid by the customer has not yet been received in cash. This bring us to a second assumption made by accountants when preparing accounting statements, namely, the *realization concept* (considered further in Chapter 4). This concept assumes that profit is earned or realized *when the sale takes place*, and the justification for this treatment is that Old Ventures now possesses a more valuable asset, since the £3,500 is a legally enforceable debt. The trading cycle is completed by Old Ventures collecting £3,500 from Rustic Relics on 31 January 19X1 and paying £2,000 to its supplier on 8 February 19X1, thirty days after the goods were supplied. The effect of these transactions are as follows:

Effect on business assets:

Trade debtors decrease
by £3,500.
Cash increases by £3,500.
Cash decreases by £2,000.

Effect on relationship
with outsiders:

Trade creditors decrease by £2,000.

Illustration 2.7

Balance Sheet of Old Ventures at 8 February 19X1

Assets	£	Sources of finance	£
Premises	7,000	Capital	6,000
Stocks	2,500	Add: Profit	1,500
Cash at bank	2,000		
			7,500
		Loan from bank	4,000
	11,500		11,500

Readers should now work Question 2.4 at the end of this chapter.

THE TRADING CYCLE

The single trading cycle for Old Ventures, examined above, is now complete, and can be expressed in the form of a diagram as in Figure 2.1.

Balance Sheet of Old Ventures at 8 February 19X1

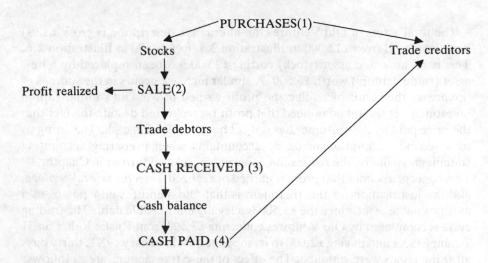

Figure 2.1   The trading cycle

The cycle consists of the following four stages:

Stage 1   The purchase of goods on credit that gives rise to balance sheet entries for trade creditors and stock.

Stage 2   The sale of stock results in a profit being realized or a loss incurred. At this stage some of the stock is replaced by trade debtors in the balance sheet.

Stage 3   The collection of trade debts. This produces a change in the composition of the firm's assets, from debtors to cash.

Stage 4   The payment of the amounts due to suppliers. This causes a reduction in cash and the removal of trade creditors from the balance sheet.

A comparison of the position before (Illustration 2.4) and after (Illustration 2.7) completion of the trading cycle shows just two differences: cash has risen by £1,500 and the owner's capital investment has increased by a similar amount to reflect profit earned.

The trading cycle examined above is obviously a simplified version of what happens in practice. A company does not complete one cycle before commencing another, but is involved in a continuous series of overlapping business transactions. The purchases cycle consists of ordering goods, receiving them into stock as an asset and paying for them by means of a cash outflow, while the sales cycle consists of making a sale, parting with the stocks sold as an asset outflow and collecting the money due from the customer to produce a cash inflow. Therefore, even before one creditor is paid another is created and debtors are turned over in a similar manner. It is the responsibility of management to ensure that all these flows are adequately controlled and recorded. Thus no payment should be made without ensuring that the related goods or services have in fact been received, and no goods should be allowed to leave the firm except in exchange for cash or by the creation of a debt. In the latter case there must be adequate follow up to ensure that the cash is subsequently collected.

A simplified version of the trading cycle occurs when purchases and/or sales are made for cash. There are just two stages: stage 1, the purchase of goods, involves the exchange of cash for stocks; stage 2, the sale of goods, involves the exchange of stock for cash of a greater or lesser value, with the amount of the difference recorded as a profit or a loss.

REPORTING CHANGES IN OWNER'S CAPITAL

The capital section of the balance sheet records the indebtedness of the business to its owner. This indebtedness is initially created by ownership advancing money to the business, but the amount changes over time – for example, a profit increases the indebtedness, whereas a loss reduces the value of the owner's capital investment. The capital section also reports all other transactions between the business and its owner – for instance, it reports any additional capital investment made by the owner during the life of the business, and also the regular withdrawals of cash and goods made for personal use. The manner in which these matters are reported is shown in Illustration 2.8. Because we are only interested in changes in capital, the remainder of the balance sheet is omitted.

Illustration 2.8

C. Newman started in business on 1 January 19X1 and paid £2,000 into his business bank account. On 30 June he transferred to the business his car valued at £1,400. Each week he withdrew £60 from the business in cash. The accounts prepared for 19X1 showed that his business had earned a profit of £4,000 during the year.

Extracts from Balance Sheet at 31 December 19X1

	£
Opening capital, 1 January 19X1	2,000
Add: Additional capital investment	1,400
Profit for 19X1	4,100
	7,500
Less: Drawings (£60 × 52)	3,120
Closing capital, 31 December 19X1	4,380*

Note
* The closing capital for 19X1 is the opening capital for 19X2.

The owner does not normally wait until profit is calculated before making withdrawals. He or she is often dependent on the business for his or her livelihood and profits are withdrawn, for personal use, as they are earned during the year. Where profits exceed drawings, as is the case in Illustration 2.8, the surplus of £980 (profit £4,100 minus drawings £3,120) is retained in the business and increases the owner's capital by an equivalent amount. These extra resources may be used to finance an expansion in the level of business operations. Illustration 2.8 also demonstrates the fact that capital may be introduced in the form of assets other than cash. The motor vehicle, transferred to the business, by Newman, appears as an asset in the balance sheet, and is matched by a corresponding increase in the value of his capital investment. Similarly, drawings may be made in a non-cash form (e.g. the family of a farmer is likely to consume some of the farm produce) though this has not happened in the above illustration.

Readers should now work Question 2.5 at the end of the chapter.

ASSETS = CAPITAL + LIABILITIES: A FURTHER ILLUSTRATION

In the case of Old Ventures we saw that the equality between sources of finance and assets was maintained throughout the trading cycle and, because all assets must be financed in some manner or other, we can be confident that this equality will continue throughout the firm's life. In this context there are four basic categories of business transaction:

1. Where an increase in an asset is matched by a corresponding increase in a source of finance – for example, cash increases as the result of extra capital being invested by the owner.
2. Where an increase in a source of finance is matched by a decrease in a different source of finance – for example, a loan raised from the bank to enable trade creditors to be paid the amount due to them.
3. Where a reduction in an asset is matched by a reduction in a source of finance – for example, cash is used to pay trade creditors.
4. Where an increase in an asset is matched by a reduction in a different asset – for example, a new motor vehicle purchased for cash.

A complication occurs in the case of a transaction involving the sale of goods, since this gives rise to a profit or a loss that must also be recorded. For example, assume an item of stock that cost £80 is sold on credit for £100. In the balance sheet stock is replaced by debtors, i.e. a category 4 transaction takes place. In addition a category 1 transaction occurs, because the higher value of debtors, £20, gives rise to a profit that must be added to the owner's capital.

Example 2.1

Examine separately the effect of each of the following transactions on the relationship $A = C + L$:

1. The owner of a business received a legacy of £2,000 and paid it into his business bank account.
2. Machinery costing £3,000 is purchased for cash.
3. Stock-in-trade is purchased on credit for £800.
4. A business computer is purchased for £5,000 and is financed by a loan from a friend.
5. Trade debts amounting to £750 are collected from customers.
6. Stock-in-trade costing £1,000 is sold for £1,400.
7. A supplier is paid £220 due to him.
8. Stock-in-trade is purchased for cash, £350.
9. A filing cabinet is purchased for £60 by increasing an existing bank overdraft.
10. The owner of a business drew a cheque for £100 on his business bank account to meet private expenses.

You should present your answer in the following form:

Transaction	Assets	=	Capital	+	Liabilities
	£		£		£
1	+2,000	=	+2,000		0
2	+3,000	=	0		0
	−3,000				

Note

In transaction 2, the machinery acquired increases assets by £3,000 but the payment reduces assets by the same amount. The net effect is zero.

Solution

Transaction	Assets	=	Capital	+	Liabilities
	£		£		£
1	+2,000	=	+2,000		0
2	+3,000	=	0		0
	−3,000				
3	+800	=	0		+800
4	+5,000	=	0		+5,000
5	−750	=	0		0
	+750				
6	−1,000	=	+400		0
	+1,400				
7	−220	=	0		−220
8	+350	=	0		0
	−350				
9	+60	=	0		+60
10	−100	=	−100		0

Readers should now work Question 2.6 at the end of this chapter.

CLASSIFICATION OF ASSETS AND SOURCES OF FINANCE

Assets

Business assets may be defined as resources owned by an entity that have the potential for providing it with future economic benefits in the sense that they help to generate future cash inflows or reduce future cash outflows. The fact that a business asset exists, however, does not necessarily mean that it will be reported in the balance sheet. For this to be done, the asset must satisfy the further requirement that the benefit it provides can be measured or quantified, in money terms, with a reasonable degree of precision. This rule is called the *money measurement concept*. For example, stock-in-trade is reported as a business asset because it is owned by the firm, it has an identifiable monetary value (its cost) and it is expected to produce an at least equivalent cash benefit to the firm when it is sold. Expenditure incurred on training staff, on the other hand, presents a more difficult problem. While it is possible to identify the amount of the expenditure, it is not possible to forecast with a high degree of certainty whether the firm will benefit from the expenditure. Employees may be poorly motivated and fail to improve their competence as the result of attending training courses. In addition, they may leave the firm and take their new expertise elsewhere. Because of this uncertainty concerning the likely extent of any future benefit, such expenditure is not reported as a business asset but is instead written off against profit as it is incurred.

Assets reported in the balance sheet are divided into two categories:

1. *Current assets* These are defined as assets that are held for resale, conversion into cash or are cash itself. There are three main types of current assets: stock-in-trade, trade debtors and cash. A *temporary* investment of funds in the shares of a quoted company or government securities should also be classified as a current asset. A characteristic of current assets is that the balances are constantly changing as the result of business operations and, in earlier times, the evocative term 'circulating assets' was used to describe these items.
2. *Fixed assets* These are assets a firm purchases and retains to help carry on the business. It is not intended to sell fixed assets in the ordinary course of business and it is expected that the bulk of their value will be used up as the result of contributing to trading activities. Examples of fixed assets are premises, plant, machinery, furniture and motor vehicles. A characteristic of fixed assets is that they usually remain in the business for long periods of time and will only be sold or scrapped when they are of no further use.

It is important for readers to realize that it is possible to classify an asset as current or fixed only by examining the reason why it was purchased, i.e. was it purchased for resale or retention? Assets purchased by one company for resale may be purchased by another for retention. For example, a garage purchases motor vehicles for resale while a manufacturing concern acquires them as fixed assets to be used by sales representatives.

Assets are reported in the balance sheet in the order of increasing liquidity, i.e. the list starts with the items least likely to be turned into cash and ends with the items expected to be converted into cash in the near future. A typical balance sheet presentation of assets is given in the left-hand column of Figure 2.2.

	£	£		£	£
Fixed assets			Capital		179,000
Land and buldings		75,000			
Plant and machinery		49,000	*Non-current liabilities*		
Motor vehicles		21,500	Loans repayable 19X8		50,000
		145,500			
Current assets			*Current liabilities*		
Stock-in-trade	145,700		Trade creditors	170,000	
Trade debtors	143,700		Expense creditors	1,900	
Investments	2,600		Bank overdraft	36,700	208,600
Cash in hand	100	292,100			
		437,600			437,600

Figure 2.2   Balance Sheet of the Nut and Bolt Engineering Company at 31 December 19X1

Sources of finance

We have seen that sources of finance are divided into the capital invested by the owners and the liabilities due to non-ownership groups. These liabilities may be further classified into current liabilities, defined as amounts repayable within twelve months of the balance sheet date, and non-current liabilities. Typical examples of current liabilities are a bank overdraft, amounts owing to suppliers of stock in trade and creditors for miscellaneous services. Any loans repayable within the following year are also listed under current liabilities. The only loan outstanding in the case of Nut and Bolt Engineering (Figure 2.2) is not repayable for another seven years (in 19X8) and is therefore classified as a non-current liability and positioned between the capital section and current liabilities in the balance sheet.

We can see from Figure 2.2 that sources of finance are arranged in order of permanence, with the most permanent sources at the top and amounts repayable (or potentially repayable) in the near future at the bottom of the balance sheet. Most sources of finance are easily classified into one or other of the three categories, but certain items cause a little more difficulty. For example, the terms of a bank loan may provide for an advance of £100,000 repayable by five equal annual instalments of £20,000. In these circumstances the liability must be divided into two parts, with the next instalment repayable, of £20,000, shown as a current liability and the balance reported as a non-current liability. Therefore, at the end of the first year, £20,000 is reported as a current liability and £80,000 as a non-current liability.

As accounting is a device for communicating relevant financial information to interested parties, it is important that the information reported should not only be technically accurate but also be presented in an orderly fashion so that it can be readily understood by owners, managers and others who wish to assess progress. The balance sheet of the Nut and Bolt Engineering Company is drafted in a manner that helps to achieve this objective. It is divided into five sections and, for each of these, an appropriate description is given and sub-heading provided. Users of accounting statements are therefore able to see, at a glance, the amount of finance provided by the owners, the volume of long-term loans and the quantity of short-term finance. The statement also shows how the total finance has been allocated between fixed and current assets. If a firm is to be financially stable, it is normally important for long-term investments in fixed assets to be financed substantially by the owners and for current assets to be sufficient to meet current liabilities falling due over the next twelve months. A well-prepared balance sheet enables these and other forms of financial analysis, examined in Chapters 12 and 13, to be efficiently carried out.

Readers should now work Questions 2.7–2.9 at the end of this chapter.

VALUATION OF ASSETS

The balance sheet contains a list of assets belonging to the company and, for each category, a value is given. For example, a freehold property may be shown in the balance sheet at £50,000. What does this value represent? If a lay person was asked this question, it is quite likely that he or she would say 'It is what the asset is worth'. This seem reasonable on the face of it, but it leads to the further questions, such as 'Worth to whom, when, and for what purpose?'

There are four possible methods for valuing assets, although we will see that only one of these normally finds favour with the accountant. The four methods are as follows:

1. *Historical cost* The asset is valued at its original purchase price.
2. *Replacement cost* The asset is valued at the amount it would cost the business to buy the asset at the balance sheet date.
3. *Realizable value* This is the price at which the asset could be sold at the balance sheet date. It differs from replacement cost as anyone who has ever attempted to sell, say, a second-hand motor vehicle will know.
4. *Present value* This is a little more complicated and is the present value of cash expected to be generated, in the future, as a result of owning a particular asset. These estimated cash flows are then discounted, at a rate of interest, to take account of the fact that £1 receivable, say, in one year's time is worth rather less than £1 receivable immediately.

The appropriate method of valuation depends on the purpose for which it is required. If the company is contemplating the acquisition of an asset, purchase price is most relevant. The replacement cost of an asset is likely to be of interest if the existing asset is worn out. Realizable value is relevant if there is an intention to sell the asset in the near future, while the present value calculation should be made if the asset is to continue in use for some time generating a stream of cash flows stretching into the future.

In general, assets are shown in company accounts at their historical cost less, in the case of fixed assets, a reduction to reflect wear and tear (depreciation) that has occurred since the acquisition took place. At first glance this is a little surprising. The analysis in the preceding paragraph shows that, although historical cost is of interest at the date of the initial purchase, it is the other valuation methods, particularly market price and present value, that are likely to be more relevant when a balance sheet is prepared at some subsequent date. Why is historical cost so popular? Perhaps the main reason is because this figure is readily available. Most assets are purchased on credit and are entered in the books at their historical cost so as to provide a record of the amount to be paid to the supplier at some future date. Once the figure is in the books it is simply convenient to use it for the purpose of preparing the balance sheet.

Many people believe that this is not a sufficient justification for continuing to use historical cost. For example, it seems quite ridiculous to report a share investment in the balance sheet at £7,000 – the price paid ten years ago – if the shares could today be sold for, say, £25,000. But this is what is done. A further reason for this, apparently, curious choice is the difficulty of obtaining a more relevant estimate of value. If the shares are quoted on the stock exchange it would be relatively easy to obtain their current market price from the *Stock*

Exchange Daily Official List. However, this figure is only relevant if there is an intention to sell the securities at once. If the asset is to be retained indefinitely, the more relevant figure is present value. As indicated earlier this must be calculated on the basis of future cash flows – dividends and sales proceeds – which it is, of course, impossible to forecast with any degree of accuracy. In the case of most business assets – for example, land, buildings, plant, machinery and unquoted shares – it is even very difficult to get an accurate figure for current market price.

It is therefore clear that historical cost is used, not so much because it is relevant, but because the data is readily available. This limitation should be borne in mind when assessing the usefulness of information appearing in the accounts.

Example 2.2

Lexington owns a fleet of cars that are rented to customers. One of the cars, B634 HAB, was purchased a couple of years ago for £7,000. The company has discovered that it could purchase a car in similar condition, today, for £5,000 from the local distributor. Cars no longer needed by Lexington are usually sold to employees or their families. It is estimated that B634 HAB would now sell for £3,800.

The company's intention is to retain the vehicle as part of its fleet for one year. It will be rented to a single customer for an annual rental of £2,000, payable in arrears. The car will then be immediately sold for £3,000.

Assume the rental arises at the end of the year and that future cash flows have to be discounted at 10 per cent in order to convert them into an equivalent present value.

Required

Valuations of the car on the following bases:

(a) historical cost;
(b) replacement cost;
(c) realizable value; and
(d) present value.

Solution

(a) *Historical cost* £7,000, less a deduction for wear and tear or depreciation suffered since the date of purchase.
(b) *Replacement cost* £5,000.
(c) *Realizable value* £3,800.
(d) *Present value*

$$\text{Rentals, £2,000} \times \frac{1^*}{1.1} = \quad 1,818$$

$$\text{Sales proceeds, £3,000} \times \frac{1^*}{1.1} = \quad \frac{2,727}{4,545}$$

Note
* The effect of this fraction is to discount the future cash flows to an equivalent present value using an interest rate of 10 per cent. Looked at another way, £4,545 invested at 10 per cent for one year increases to £5,000 (£4, 545 × 1.1), which is the cash expected to be received if the asset is retained for use within the business.

QUESTIONS

2.1   Indicate which of the following transactions relate to Clive's business as a newsagent and which are his personal transactions:

1. £50 win on premium bonds owned by Clive.
2. £100 paid for the following advertisement on a hoarding at the local football ground: 'Clive's for all the up-to-date news'.
3. Payment to the newspaper wholesaler, £1,260.
4. Sale of unsold newspapers to a local fish-and-chip shop.
5. Purchase of a new car for family use, although it will be used each morning to collect papers from suppliers.

2.2   John decides to start up in business on 1 April 19X2, and pays £4,000 from his private bank account into a newly-opened business bank account. On 2 April 19X2 John's father loans the firm £600 to help with the new venture, and this amount is paid immediately into the business bank account. On 4 April the firm borrows £150 from John's friend, Peter. This amount is kept in the form of 'ready cash' to meet small business expenses.

Required

Balance sheets for John's business after the transactions on:

(a) 1 April,
(b) 2 April,
(c) 4 April.

2.3   Roger starts up in business on 1 September with a capital of £1,200 which he pays into his business bank account on that day. The bank agrees to provide him with a business overdraft facility of £1,500 for the first three months. The following business transactions take place:

2 September   A machine is bought, on three months credit, from Plant Suppliers Ltd for £750. £1,000 is borrowed from the Endridge Local Authority, which is keen to encourage this type of enterprise.
3 September   £1,820 is paid for a second-hand machine. Stock is purchased, for cash, £420.
4 September   Stock is purchased, on credit, for £215.

Required

Balance sheets for Roger's business following the transactions on:

(a) 1 September,
(b) 2 September,
(c) 3 September,
(d) 4 September.

2.4   The following balance sheet was prepared for Jeff's business at 1 October 19X5. The firm has an overdraft facility of £700.

Balance Sheet

	£		£
Machinery	2,200	Capital	5,300
Stocks	2,870		
Debtors	800	Trade creditors	690
Cash at bank	120		
	5,990		5,990

Jeff enters into the following transactions:

2 October   Sells goods that cost £120 for £200, cash. Sells goods that cost £240 for £315, on credit.
3 October   Collects £150 from customers. Purchases stock for £190, on credit.
4 October   Pays trade creditors £75. Purchases a machine for £600, cash.

Required

Balance sheets for Jeff's business following the transactions on:

(a) 2 October,
(b) 3 October,
(c) 4 October.

2.5 (a)   Prepare the balance sheet of Daley from the following list of assets and liabilities at 31 December 19X1:

	£
Cash	1,750
Stock	5,250
Owed by customers	3,340
Owed to suppliers	2,890
Business premises	9,000
Loan from Weakly	3,000

(b) Prepare the balance sheet of Daley's business at the end of each of the first seven days of January taking account of the following transactions:

January 19X2
1. Purchased, on credit, a typewriter for office use, £500.
2. Received £190 from a customer.
3. Paid a supplier £670.
4. Purchased stock, on credit, £260.
5. Sold goods that had cost £350 for £530 cash.
6. Repaid Weekly £1,000 of the balance due to him (ignore interest).
7. Withdrew stock costing £100 for private use.

2.6   Prepare balance sheets to determine the amount missing from each of the
following lists of balances at 31 December 19X1:

	A £	B £	C £	D £	E £	F £
Capital at 1 January 19X1	2,500	2,000	3,000	4,000	3,800	?
Profit for 19X1	1,000	3,200	?	5,700	2,300	7,000
Drawings during 19X1	800	3,000	1,000	4,900	?	4,500
Current liabilities	750	?	600	1,300	1,700	2,100
Fixed assets	1,800	1,750	2,800	?	3,700	8,500
Current assets	?	850	1,200	1,900	1,600	3,500

2.7   Review your understanding of the following concepts and terms discussed
in this chapter by writing a short explanation of each of them:

1. Accountancy.
2. Entity concept.
3. Balance sheet.
4. Realization concept.
5. Trade credit.
6. Trading cycle, credit transactions.
7. C+L=A.
8. Owner's capital.
9. Money measurement concept.
10. Fixed assets.
11. Current assets.
12. Current liabilities.
13. Gross assets.

2.8   For a fish-and-chip shop, indicate which of the following items are current
liabilities, which are current assets and which are fixed assets:

1. Microwave oven.
2. 2,000 kilos of King Edward potatoes.
3. Cash register.
4. Amount owing to the Fat Fishy Company Ltd.
5. Capital investment of Mr V. Greasy, owner.
6. Mrs Greasy's pearl knecklace and gold wristwatch.

7. 250 mackerel.
8. Loan from V. Greasy's father, repayable in two years' time.
9. Last instalment due, in one month's time, on the microwave oven acquired on hire purchase.
10. Shop rented from a property company.

For items not classified as current liabilities or current assets or fixed assets, describe how they would be reported in the balance sheet, if at all.

2.9   The following list of balances relate to the business of C. Forest at 31 December 19X3:

	£
Plant and machinery	26,500
Stock in trade	14,200
Loan repayable June 19X4	2,500
Capital of C. Forest at 1 January 19X3	52,380
Trade creditors	10,600
Trade debtors	14,100
Cash-in-hand	270
Bank overdraft	3,940
Profit for 19X3	12,600
Owner's drawings during 19X3	10,950
Loan repayable 19X9	9,000
Leasehold premises	25,000

Required

The balance sheet of C. Forest's business at 31 December 19X3 *presented in good style.*

3
Profit Calculated as the Increase in Capital

PROFITABLE ACTIVITY

The maximization of profit has been traditionally regarded as the principal factor motivating the individual to invest in a business venture. In recent years, however, businessmen and women have often appeared reluctant to justify business activity in quite so direct a manner. This is in many ways a healthy development that demonstrates an increasing awareness of the fact that business organizations, particularly the very large ones, have responsibilities other than to produce an adequate return for their investors. A list of the responsibilities acknowledged by business people today can be obtained by examining the corporate objectives declared by company chairmen in their annual reports to shareholders. These often include a wide range of items, amongst which earning a profit appears to be accorded no particular priority. Identified corporate goals include such matters as an increase in the market share, the improvement of product quality, a contented work force, pollution free production processes, the maximization of exports and survival.

It is difficult to say whether these aims are each of equal importance, but probably they are not. One view is that profit maximization is the main objective, and the other stated objectives have as their central purpose to contribute, either directly or indirectly, to the long-run achievement of that principal aim. This view may attach rather too much significance to profit, but widespread agreement that profit is an essential product of business activity in Great Britain can safely be assumed.

There are basically two competing claims on the profits generated by business activity:

1. *Withdrawals* The owner requires a satisfactory return on his or her investment in the form of drawings or dividends. An inadequate return will cause
   him or her to close down the business and invest his or her money elsewhere.
2. *Reinvestment* The second claim on profit arises from the fact that retained
   profits are a major source of finance for business expansion. For example,
   the balance sheet of Unilever plc at 31 December 1986 shows share capital as

£180 million, whereas retained profits amount to £3,590 million, i.e. nearly eighteen times more. The retention of profits increases the value of the owner's investment in the business, of course, and should produce higher profits and dividends in the future.

When trading conditions are difficult there may be insufficient profits to finance expansion or even to pay a return on the owner's investment. In these circumstances management must look elsewhere for the finance required for a continuation of business activity. This is not a situation that can persist indefinitely; just as consistent profitability generates the resources necessary for a healthy business, equally a succession of losses gradually deprives a company of the finance needed to support a continuation of business activity. Failure to achieve an adequate level of profitability eventually results in the cessation of business activities. It is part of the accounting function to help management guard against such an outcome by enabling it to monitor progress and ensure that resources are efficiently employed.

PROFIT AND CHANGES IN GROSS ASSETS

In Chapter 2, attention was drawn to the fact that, where management organizes business activity in an efficient manner and a profit is earned, gross assets increase by a similar amount. This relationship was illustrated by means of a series of balance sheets setting out the financial development of a firm called Old Ventures. Readers should now revise their understanding of the link between profit and the level of business assets by working the following example.

Example 3.1

Balance Sheet of Larch at 31 December 19X1

Assets	£	£	Sources of finance	£
Fixed assets			Capital	2,000
Plant and machinery		1,600	Current liabilities	
Current assets			Trade creditors	700
Stocks	600			
Trade debtors	300			
Cash	200	1,100		
		2,700		2,700

On 1 January 19X2 Larch sold stock (cost price £140) on credit for £220.

Required

The balance sheet of Larch following the transaction on 1 January 19X2.

Solution

Balance Sheet of Larch at 1 January 19X2

Assets	£	£	Sources of finance	£
Fixed assets			Capital	2,000
Plant and machinery		1,600	Add: Net profit (220 − 140)	80
Current assets				———
Stocks (600 − 140)	460			2,080
Trade debtors (300 + 220)	520		*Current liabilities*	
Cash	200	1,180	Trade creditors	700
	———	———		———
		2,780		2,780

A comparison of the two balance sheets shows that the financial effects of the single trading transaction undertaken by Larch are as follows:

1. Gross assets have increased from £2,700 to £2,780 as the result of stock costing £140 being replaced by a debt due from a customer of £220.
2. Total sources of finance have increased by the same amount as the result of adding the profit realized, of £80, to Larch's opening capital.

BALANCE SHEET PRESENTATION: VERTICAL FORMAT

The balance sheets used, so far, have usually been presented in what is conventionally described as the horizontal format, with assets on the left and sources of finance on the right. Since the early 1960s industry has gradually discarded the horizontal format in favour of the vertical format, e.g. the accounts of John Menzies reproduced in Chapter 1, Figure 1.2. The vertical presentation is further illustrated (Example 3.2) by re-arranging the information taken from Larch's balance sheets in Example 3.1.

Example 3.2

Vertical presentation of the balance sheets of Larch

	1 Jan. 19X2 £	£	31 Dec. 19X1 £	£
Fixed assets				
Plant and machinery		1,600		1,600
Current assets				
Stocks	460		600	
Trade debtors	520		300	
Cash	200		200	
	1,180		1,100	
Less: Current liabilities				
Trade creditors	700		700	
Working capital		480		400
		2,080		2,000
Financed by:				
Capital				
Opening capital		2,000		
Add: Net profit		80		
Closing capital		2,080		2,000

The main advantage of the vertical presentation is that it is easier to compare the position of a business at a series of accounting dates. The above illustration gives the position at just two dates, but a columnar presentation dealing with five or even ten accounting dates poses no particular difficulty. It is then a relatively easy matter to glance across the series of figures to discover relevant changes and overall trends. Such an analysis might show that large amounts of money are being spent each year on fixed assets, suggesting a policy of rapid expansion. By way of contrast, a continuous decline in the balance of cash, perhaps converting into a substantial overdraft, suggests that the company is suffering from increasing cash difficulties.

A second advantage of the vertical presentation is that it contains an item of useful information that does not appear in the horizontal balance sheet, namely working capital. This is the balancing figure obtained by deducting current liabilities from current assets. A financially stable business is one that is able to meet its debts as they fall due for payment, and an adequate balance of working capital is an essential requirement if this desirable state of affairs is to exist. It is not possible to specify a figure for working capital that all firms should try to maintain. Much will depend on individual circumstances, such as the size of the firm, the speed with which creditors are paid, stocks are sold and cash is collected from customers. Nevertheless managers, shareholders, creditors and other users of accounting statements normally hold firm views concerning what can be regarded as an acceptable balance for a particular business. Working capital is examined further in Chapter 12.

PROFITS, LOSSES AND CHANGES IN NET ASSETS

The vertical balance sheet contains the same basic financial information as does the horizontal balance sheet, since the facts are in no way altered by adopting a different method of presentation. Similarly, the overall financial relationship between sources of finance and assets, expressed in the formula $A = C + L$ (Assets = Capital + Liabilities) remains unchanged. The revised presentation does, however, focus attention on a different aspects of the relationship between the three magnitudes, since it emphasizes the fact that capital is equal to gross assets minus liabilities, i.e:

$$A - L = C$$

In practice, the term 'gross assets minus liabilities' is normally shortened to 'net assets'. We can therefore say that capital equals net assets. Indeed these are two descriptions of the same financial total; the only difference is the way in which the figure is calculated. Capital is computed by taking the owner's opening investment, adding profit earned and deducting withdrawals for private use to give his or her closing investment at a particular date. Net assets, on the other hand, are computed by adding together the values of the various assets owned at the balance sheet date, and then deducting the amount of finance obtained from suppliers and other creditors. Since assets are, by definition, financed either from capital or from liabilities, the balance that remains must necessarily be equal, in value, to the owner's investment.

Example 3.1 reminded us that profit produces an equivalent increase in the gross assets of a firm; the profit of £80 resulted in gross assets increasing from £2,700 to £2,780. The presentation of the same data in the form of a vertical balance sheet (see Example 3.2) draws attention to the fact that profit also results in an equivalent increase in *net* assets; these are up from £2,000 to £2,080. Where a firm suffers a loss, net assets and, therefore, the owner's capital, are reduced by the amount of the loss. These circumstances are illustrated in Example 3.3.

Example 3.3

The following balance sheet is prepared in respect of Elm at 31 December 19X1.

Balance Sheet of Elm at 31 December 19X1

Assets	£	£	Sources of finance	£
Fixed assets			Capital	7,600
Plant and machinery		4,000	*Current liabilities*	
Current assets			Trade creditors	1,200
Stocks	1,900			
Trade debtors	2,200			
Cash	700	4,800		
		8,800		8,800

On 1 January 19X2 Elm sold, on credit for £480, goods that cost £600 some weeks ago.

Required

(a) Calculations of:
  (i)   Elm's net assets at 31 December 19X1;
  (ii) The profit or loss arising on the 1 January sale;
  (iii) Elm's capital investment on 1 January after the above transaction; and
  (iv) Elm's net assets on 1 January after the above transaction.
(b) Elm's balance sheet at 1 January 19X2, presented in vertical format.

Solution

			£
(a) (i)	Assets		8,800
	Less: Liabilities		1,200
	Net assets		7,600
(ii)	Cost of stock		600
	Less: Sales proceeds		480
	Loss		120
(iii)	Capital at 31 December		7,600
	Less: Loss		120
	Capital at 1 January		7,480
(iv)	*Assets*		
	Plant and machinery		4,000
	Stock (£1,900 − £600)		1,300
	Trade debtors (£2,200 + £480)		2,680
	Cash		700
			8,680
	Liabilities		
	Trade creditors		1,200
	Net Assets		7,480

(b)   **Balance Sheet of Elm at 1 January 19X2**

	£	£
Fixed assets		
Plant and machinery		4,000
Current assets		
Stocks	1,300	
Trade debtors	2,680	
Cash	700	
	4,680	
Less: Current liabilities		
Trade creditors	1,200	
Working capital		3,480
		7,480
Capital		
Opening capital		7,600
Less: Net loss (£600 − £480)		120
Closing capital		7,480

We can therefore conclude from the above examples that

$$\text{Profit} = \text{Increase in net assets (or capital);}$$
$$\text{Loss} = \text{Decrease in net assets (or capital).}$$

An awareness of the relationship between profits, losses and changes in net assets is fundamental to a sound understanding of the financial effects of business activity. The relevant connections between the various financial magnitudes can be expressed diagrammatically as shown in Figure 3.1.

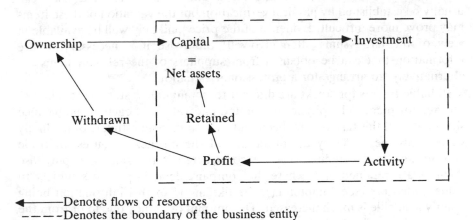

Denotes flows of resources
Denotes the boundary of the business entity

Figure 3.1   Connections between financial magnitudes

The ownership group invests capital that is used to acquire business assets. These assets form the basis for business activity subsequently undertaken in order to generate profit. Some of the profit is likely to be withdrawn by the owners (sole traders and partnerships) or paid out to them as dividends (limited companies). The remainder is retained and this results in an increased volume of net assets to be used for trading purposes during the following accounting period. The re-investment takes place in the expectation that the greater volume of net assets will enable a higher profit to be earned.

Readers should now work Question 3.1 at the end of this chapter.

PROFIT MEASURED BY CAPITAL CHANGES

It sometimes happens that the accountant is faced with the task of measuring profit despite the fact that no record exists of business transactions undertaken during the accounting period under review, for example, because the records have been lost or destroyed by fire. In these circumstances it is *not* possible to calculate profit by comparing the cost of goods sold with their selling price, as in the previous examples worked. Instead the calculation must be based on the fundamental fact, established earlier in this chapter, that profit produces an equivalent increase in net assets or owner's capital, i.e.

Net profit* = Closing capital − Opening capital; or
Net profit* = Increase in capital.

Note
* If opening capital exceeds closing capital, the result of the calculation is a negative figure and this means that a loss has been suffered.

The accountant, when faced with the job of calculating profit based on capital changes, must first take steps to establish the proprietor's investment at the beginning and end of the period. This process usually involves a significant element of estimation and judgement, particularly in relation to assets owned at the earlier of the two accounting dates. The existence of fixed assets can usually be established by physical verification but the valuation of these items may prove more difficult. Evidence of the price paid may well be available in view of the large sums often involved; otherwise it is necessary to use information that can be obtained from suppliers of the relevant items or, alternatively, to arrange for a professional valuation.

Reliable figures for stocks are difficult to obtain unless steps were taken to arrange for them to be physically counted and valued at each of the balance sheet dates. If this task has not been undertaken then an estimate of the likely values must be made by the proprietor of the business. Figures for trade debtors and trade creditors can be constructed if the sales and purchase invoices are retained and, where the company deals in products subject to value added tax (see Chapter 11), the likelihood of this information being readily available is much increased. The amount of money due to or from the bank can be established by an examination of the relevant bank statements. The measurement of profit by capital changes is illustrated in Example 3.4.

Example 3.4

The following information is provided relating to the affairs of James who trades in fashionable garments from rented property:

Assets and liabilities	31 Dec. 19X1 £	31 Dec. 19x2 £
Motor vehicles	1,800	1,350
Fixtures and fittings	450	820
Stocks	1,060	1,610
Trade creditors	730	810
Trade debtors	240	300
Bank overdraft	920	760
Cash in hand	40	50

Required

(a) Calculations of James's capital investment in the business at the end of 19X1 and 19X2.
(b) A calculation of the profit earned by James during 19X2.
(c) The balance sheet of James's business at 31 December 19X2, presented in horizontal format.

Solution

(a) Capital is calculated at each date by deducting liabilities from assets.

Statements of assets, liabilities and capital at 31 December

	£	19X1 £	£	19X2 £
Assets				
Motor vehicles		1,800		1,350
Fixtures and fittings		450		820
Stocks		1,060		1,610
Trade debtors		240		300
Cash in hand		40		50
		3,590		4,130
Less: Liabilities				
Trade creditors	730		810	
Bank overdraft	920	1,650	760	1,570
Capital		1,940		2,560

(b) Profit is calculated based on the increase in capital.

	£
Closing capital	2,560
Less: Opening capital	1,940
Profit	620

(c) **Balance Sheet at 31 December 19X2**

	£	£		£	£
Fixed assets			Opening capital		1,940
Motor vehicles		1,350	Add: Net profit		620
Fixtures and fittings		820			
			Closing capital		2,560
		2,170			
Current assets			*Current liabilities*		
Stocks	1,610		Trade creditors	810	
Trade debtors	300		Bank overdraft	760	1,570
Cash in hand	50	1,960			
		4,130			4,130

Readers should now work Question 3.2 at the end of the chapter.

CAPITAL INJECTIONS AND WITHDRAWALS

There are two categories of business transaction which cause capital to increase or decrease during an accounting period:

1. transactions which produce a profit or a loss
2. transactions involving the injection or withdrawal of capital by the owners.

The previous section of this chapter demonstrated the measurement of profit by capital changes assuming that there are no capital injections or withdrawals. This assumption is now dropped. Where capital injections or withdrawals occur, their financial effects must be isolated if profit is to be measured accurately. This is because, although an investment or withdrawal of funds causes capital and, therefore, net assets to increase or decrease, these changes have not come about as the result of trading activity and therefore give rise to neither a profit nor a loss. The following adjustments must therefore be made:

1. *Drawings* These reduce closing capital but, because they are not a business expense, they must be *added back* to the increase in capital arrived at by deducting opening capital from closing capital.

2. *Capital injections* These increase closing capital but they are not business profits and so their effect must be eliminated by *deducting* the amount of the additional investment from the increase in capital arrived at by deducting opening capital from closing capital.

The calculation of profit therefore becomes:

Profit = Increase in capital + Drawings − Capital introduced.

Example 3.5

Assume the same assets and liabilities as are given in Example 3.4. In addition you discover that James withdrew cash totalling £1,000 to meet living expenses during 19X2, while on 1 August he paid into his business bank account the first prize of £200 won in his golf club's raffle.

Required

(a) A calculation of the corrected profit earned by James during 19X2.
(b) The capital section of James's balance sheet at 31 December 19X2.

Solution

(a) Profit is calculated, based on the increase in capital, as follows:

	£
Closing capital	2,560
Less: Opening capital	1,940
Increase in capital	620
Add: Drawings	1,000
Less: Capital introduced	(200)
Profit	1,420

Note
The assets and liabilities remain the same as in Example 3.4, and so the increase in capital is unchanged at £620 (£2,560 − £1,940). However, account must be taken of the two 'non-trading' transactions that have affected the value of closing capital and caused a net reduction of £800 (cash withdrawals of £1,000 partly compensated by a capital injection of £200). This amount must be added back to the observed increase in capital to produce a 'true' profit figure of £1,420.

(b) **Balance Sheet extract 31 December 19X2**

Capital section	£
Opening capital	1,940
Add: Capital introduced	200
Net profit	1,420
	3,560
Less: Drawings	1,000
	2,560

Note:
The balance sheet now contains a full and accurate statement of transactions affecting the owner's capital during the year. It shows that James made an additional capital investment of £200, that he made personal withdrawals of £1,000 and that a profit figure of £1,420 (not £620) should be used as the basis for assessing the firm's performance and as a starting point for computing tax payable.

An injection of additional capital by the owner is an unusual event and is normally quite easy to identify. Sources of extra capital might include a legacy or gambling winnings or the sale of a non-business asset belonging to the proprietor. Drawings are usually more difficult to calculate as they may well vary from week to week and comprise both cash and stock-in-trade, the latter being particularly likely in the case of a retail business. In the absence of a reliable record of withdrawals, a careful estimate is required from the proprietor. The various matters discussed in this chapter are incorporated in Example 3.6.

Example 3.6

The following information is provided relating to the affairs of John, who owns a tobacconist, confectionery and newspaper kiosk:

Assets and liabilities	1 Jan. 19X3	31 Dec. 19X3
	£	£
Kiosk	2,000	2,000
Stocks of tobacco and confectionery	450	600
Trade creditors	250	320
Bank balance	160	940
Cash in hand	20	30

During 19X3 John received a legacy of £800 that was paid into his business bank account. Cash drawings are estimated at £200 per week and, in addition, John took from the business goods worth £150 for his own use during the year.

Required

(a) A calculation of the profit earned by John during 19X3.
(b) The balance sheet of John's business at 31 December 19X3, presented in vertical format.

Solution

(a) (i) Calculation of capital by deducting liabilities from assets:

Statement of Assets, Liabilities and Capital at:

	1 Jan. 19X3 £	31 Dec. 19X3 £
Assets		
Kiosk	2,000	2,000
Stocks	450	600
Bank balance	160	940
Cash in hand	20	30
	2,630	3,570
Liabilities		
Trade creditors	250	320
Capital	2,380	3,250

(ii) Calculation of profit on the basis of the increase in capital:

	£
Closing capital	3,250
Less: Opening capital	2,380
Increase in capital	870
Add: Drawings	10,550 W1
Less: Capital introduced	(800)
Net profit	10,620

W1 drawings:	Cash, £200 × 52 =	£10,400
	Goods	150
		10,550

(b) **Balance Sheet at 31 December 19X3**

Assets	£	£
Fixed assets		
Kiosk		2,000
Current assets		
Stocks	600	
Bank balance	940	
Cash in hand	30	
	1,570	
Less: Current liabilities		
Trade creditors	320	
Working capital		1,250
		3,250
Capital		
Opening capital		2,380
Add: Capital introduced		800
Profit		10,620
		13,800
Less: Drawings –cash	10,400	
– goods	150	10,550
		3,250

The procedure for calculating profit, described above, is also used by the Inland Revenue where existing business records are unreliable but profit needs to be estimated because the taxpayer is believed to have understated his or her income in his or her tax return. In such cases, the major area of dispute is usually the level of drawings that have been made. The taxpayer will attempt to argue that they have been fairly modest, whereas the Inland Revenue will endeavour to demonstrate that much larger drawings *must* have been made to support the taxpayer's observed life style. When the amount of the profit understatement has been computed, tax due will be calculated and penalties and interest added. The level of the penalty will depend, a great deal, on the co-operation received from the taxpayer since the initial discovery of the deception.

Readers should now work Questions 3.3 and 3.4 at the end of this chapter.

QUESTIONS

3.1   The following balance sheet relates to the affairs of Columbus who works for the government and also buys and sells second-hand cars. The balance sheet of his second-hand car business is as follows:

Balance Sheet at 31 December 19X1

	£	£		£
Fixed assets		2,000	Capital	6,500
Current assets			*Current liabilities*	
Stock of cars	2,700		Trade creditors	200
Debtors	1,000			
Bank	1,000	4,700		
		6,700		6,700

Transactions undertaken in January 19X2:

1. Columbus collects the £1,000 owing in respect of the second-hand car sold in December 19X1.
2. Columbus wins £500 on the football pools and pays the proceeds into his business bank account.
3. Columbus sells for £1,200 a car that was in stock on 31 December 19X1 at a value of £1,300.
4. Columbus withdraws £50 for private use.
5. Columbus purchases a friend's car for £150, and promises to pay him in February.
6. Columbus purchases a new machine for £700 and pays in cash.

Required

(a) Give the totals for gross assets, net assets and working capital based on the figures in the above balance sheet.
(b) Taking each of the transactions listed above separately, give their effect (increase or decrease) on:
 (i)   profit,
 (ii) net assets,
 (iii) gross assets, and
 (iv) working capital.

3.2   The balance sheet of Paul at 30 June 19X3 is as follows:

Balance Sheet at 30 June 19X3

	£	£		£	£
Fixed assets		7,500	Capital		10,330
Current assets			*Current liabilities*		
Stock	3,280		Trade creditors	1,220	
Debtors	1,750	5,030	Bank overdraft	980	2,200
		12,530			12,530

During the year to 30 June 19X3, Paul received a loan of £3,000 from a friend. The loan is interest free and repayable at the end of 19X6. On 1 December 19X3 Paul purchased fixed assets costing £2,350. At 30 June 19X4, trade creditors amounted to £1,890, stock was valued at £4,270 and debtors amounted to £1,450. In addition Paul had £570 in his bank account and cash in hand of £30.

Required

(a) A calculation of Paul's capital investment in the business at 30 June 19X4.
(b) A calculation of the profit earned by Paul's business during the year to 30 June 19X4.
(c) The balance sheet of Paul's business at 30 June 19X4, presented in vertical format.

3.3   The following information is obtained in connection with the business of G. Haze, a trader:

	31 December 19X3 £	31 December 19X4 £
Fixed assets at book value	9,000	see below
Stocks	2,650	3,710
Trade debtors	5,200	5,600
Trade creditors	1,710	1,210
Bank balance (overdraft)	(360)	50

During 19X4 motor vehicles were purchased at a cost of £3,144, part of which was met by G. Haze trading in his private motor car at an agreed valuation of £600. Cash drawings made by G. Haze amounted to £150 per week and, in addition, stocks valued at £300 were taken during the year for personal use.

Required

(a) A calculation of the profit earned by G. Haze's business during 19X4.
(b) The balance sheet of the firm at 31 December 19X4 presented in the horizontal format.

3.4   The following table shows the cumulative effects of a succession of separate transactions on the assets and liabilities of a business:

| Transaction | | A | B | C | D | E | F | G | H | I |
Assets	£000	£000	£000	£000	£000	£000	£000	£000	£000	£000
Land and buildings	500	500	535	535	535	535	535	535	535	535
Equipment	230	230	230	230	230	230	230	200	200	200
Stocks	113	140	140	120	120	120	120	120	119	119
Trade debtors	143	143	143	173	160	158	158	158	158	158
Prepaid expenses	27	27	27	27	27	27	27	27	27	27
Cash at bank	37	37	37	37	50	50	42	63	63	63
Cash on hand	9	9	9	9	9	9	9	9	9	3
	1,059	1,086	1,121	1,131	1,131	1,129	1,121	1,112	1,111	1,105
Liabilities										
Capital	730	730	730	740	740	738	733	724	723	717
Loan	120	120	155	155	155	155	155	155	155	155
Trade creditors	168	195	195	195	195	195	195	195	195	195
Accrued expenses	41	41	41	41	41	41	38	38	38	38
	1,059	1,086	1,121	1,131	1,131	1,129	1,121	1,112	1,111	1,105

Required

Identify clearly and as fully as you can what transaction has taken place in each case. Give *two* possible explanations for transaction I. Do not copy out the table but use the reference letter for each transaction.

(20 marks)

(AAT, Basic Accounting, December 1986)

4
The Preparation of Accounts from Cash Records

ACCOUNTING SYSTEMS AND INFORMATION REQUIREMENTS

For the unincorporated enterprise, the complexity of the accounting system for recording and reporting business transactions depends mainly on the size of the organization. (The position is different in the case of a limited company that, irrespective of its size, is legally required to keep formal accounting records.) The large number of transactions undertaken each day, in the case of a substantial business concern, requires a sophisticated accounting system for the dual purposes of *control* and *assessment*. In the small firm the accounting system is usually far more rudimentary, since effective protection of valuable resources is achieved through the owner's close personal contact with all aspects of the firm's business activities. Control is enhanced if the firm's most vulnerable assets, e.g. the cash balance and the bank account, are under the direct control of the owner. Other resources, e.g. stocks, which may be in the custody of trusted personnel, nevertheless remain under the close scrutiny of the proprietor.

Neither is it necessary, in the small firm, to employ formal reporting procedures as a basis for performance assessment. Trade creditors and customers are likely to be relatively small, in number, and any difficulties associated with the supply of or demand for the firm's products should come quickly to the attention of a diligent proprietor. Similarly, in the absence of a significant level of capital expenditure, changes in the bank balance are likely to provide a fairly reliable indication of progress; the function of accounting reports, in these circumstances, is simply to provide a basis for agreeing tax liabilities with the Inland Revenue and, where there are a number of proprietors, as a means of allocating profit between the partners. Although an increase in the scale of a firm's activities implies the need for a more formal system of accounting, it does not necessarily follow that transactions will be recorded daily in accordance with the system of double entry described in Chapter 6. It is essential that accounting systems be judged in terms of their usefulness, and a decision to invest the time and money required to operate a complex system must be justified in terms of the benefits it produces.

There is a certain minimum range of financial information that must be made available, however, to enable the accountant to prepare both a trading and profit and loss account, which gives a detailed list of business revenues and expenditures arising during the year (see p. 49 of this chapter), and a balance sheet. The information required consists of:

1. assets at the beginning and at the end of the year;
2. liabilities at the beginning and at the end of the year; and
3. cash receipts and payments during the year.

The steps that must be taken to obtain details of assets and liabilities are discussed in Chapter 3. This information is used to compile the closing balance sheet and also the opening balance sheet unless this statement was prepared at the end of the previous year. Details of cash transactions are required as the starting point for preparing the trading and profit and loss. The business bank statements fulfil an essential role in this context, since they contain a wide range of reliable information concerning cash transactions undertaken during the year. There is, of course, usually a large number of bank statements and the analysis of these documents is a lengthy process, particularly because the statements provide few details. For example, the only information usually given in respect of cheque payments is the amount and the cheque number, while in the case of receipts only a brief description, indicating the source of the lodgement, is provided. It is, therefore, important for cheque books and paying in books to be retained so that an accurate description of the various items appearing on the bank statements can be constructed. Details must also be obtained of any cash transactions that have *not* gone through the bank. This information may be recorded in a 'petty' cash book (see Chapter 5); alternatively, it may be possible to build up the relevant figures from files of cash receipts and payments. In examination questions the analysis work has generally been done, and figures for receipts and payments are given in a summary

Cash transactions, year to 31 December 19X1

Receipts	£	Payments	£
Opening balance of cash	510	Payments to suppliers	17,380
Sale of goods	23,750	Wages	2,560
		Rent and rates	840
		Lighting and heating	620
		General expenses	375
			21,775
		Closing balance of cash	2,485
	24,260		24,260

Figure 4.1 Summary of figures for receipts and payments

form similar to that given in Figure 4.1. The receipts side of the summary shows cash from customers of £23,750 that, when added to the sum available at the start, £510, means that cash totalling £24,260 came available to the business at some stage during 19X1. From this total, cash payments of £21,775 must be deducted, leaving a cash balance at the year end of £2,485.

Provided the rudimentary financial facts referred to in this section can be assembled, it is possible to prepare a full set of final accounts. The process, described as the preparation of accounts from cash records, is examined in this chapter.

THE MATCHING CONCEPT: PROFIT = REVENUE − EXPENSES

Chapter 3 demonstrated how profit can be measured in the absence of detailed information concerning trading transactions undertaken during a particular accounting period, i.e. it is computed by identifying the change in capital between the beginning and the end of the year. Where there exists an adequate accounting record of transactions undertaken, *during the year*, profit is instead computed in accordance with the *matching concept*, i.e. the accountant measures profit by comparing or 'matching' the total cost of the many trading transactions undertaken during an accounting period with the total revenues arising therefrom.

Example 4.1

Mex Cars Ltd is a motor vehicle distributor that prepares its accounts on the calendar year basis. Ten cars are purchased during 19X1 for £4,500 each and sold for £6,000 each.

Required

Calculate profit by matching revenues with expenditures.

Solution

	£
Revenue:	
Proceeds from sale of cars (£6,000 × 10)	60,000
Less: Expenditure:	
Cost of cars sold (£4,500 × 10)	45,000
Profit	15,000

GROSS PROFIT AND NET PROFIT

The balance of profit, which is arrived at by matching sales proceeds with the actual costs of goods sold, is called *gross profit*. In practice many other costs are also incurred, such as salaries paid to employees, commissions paid to salesmen, rent and rates for the showroom and office accommodation, and the numerous incidental expenses such as telephone costs, stationery, etc. Since these outlays are incurred to help generate sales revenue, they must also be deducted to leave a final balance called *net profit*. Revenues and expenditures are matched against one another in the *trading account and the profit and loss account* (usually abbreviated to trading and profit and loss account), and a common method of presenting this accounting statement is given in Figure 4.2.

The gross profit is calculated in the trading account and the remaining expenses are deducted in the profit and loss account. It might occur to readers that the calculation of profit on the basis of changes in capital is a rather more straightforward process than by comparing revenue with expenditure. The accumulation of figures for sales revenue and the many items of expenditure incurred during the year is a far more laborious and time-consuming task than the identification of figures for capital at just two dates: the beginning and end of the accounting period. Part of the justification for the extra work is that trading transactions entered into during an accounting period are recorded, not only to enable profit to be measured, but also to facilitate effective control over inflows and outflows of cash and goods, e.g. to ensure that cash is collected from customers and that employees are paid the amounts due to them.

Detailed accounting records also enable management to make a more useful

Trading and Profit and Loss Account, Mex Cars Ltd, year to 31 December 19X1

Expenditure	£	Revenue	£
Cost of cars sold	45,000	Sales	60,000
Gross profit	15,000		
	60,000		60,000
Salaries	6,200	Gross profit	15,000
Commissions	600		
Rent and rates	1,400		
Lighting and heating	250		
Telephone	150		
Postage and stationery	220		
Advertising	370		
General expenses	500		
	9,690		
Net profit	5,310		
	15,000		15,000

Figure 4.2   Trading account and profit and loss account

calculation of profit because, although the end result is the same, the preparation of a trading and profit and loss account produces the following advantages. First, it contains a comprehensive statement of *how* the net profit balance has been achieved. Second, it is a valuable means for assessing performance, e.g. by comparing this year's gross profit and expenses with results achieved last year, and for reaching decisions concerning the future allocation of resources.

THE PROBLEM OF PERIODIC PROFIT CALCULATION

The frequency with which the profit and loss account and balance sheet are prepared varies depending on the circumstances of the particular business. As a minimum, however, accounts must be prepared once a year – limited companies are legally required to prepare annual accounts for publication, while sole traders and partnerships are obliged to prepare annual accounts for tax purposes. To provide the information needed to take day-to-day decisions designed to achieve the most effective use of available resources, management requires more frequent calculations of profit, and the preparation of quarterly or even monthly management accounts is a common feature within commerce and industry today.

The calculation of periodic profit causes difficulties because business activity is continuous. For example, a business may last for ten years but, for accounting purposes, it must be split into at least ten accounting periods, each lasting one year. Many transactions cause no difficulty because they can be easily identified with a particular accounting period. For example, assuming accounts are prepared on the calendar year basis, an item of stock purchased and paid for in January 19X1 and sold for cash in February 19X1 must clearly be taken into account in computing the profit for 19X1. Problems arise with transactions that *overlap* the end of one accounting period and the beginning of another. Consider the following facts assuming a 31 December accounting date:

1. Stocks delivered to a customer in December 19X1 but not paid for until January 19X2.
2. Stocks purchased and paid for in November 19X1 but not sold until March 19X2.
3. Rates paid on 1 October 19X1 for the six months to 31 March 19X2.
4. Machinery purchased and paid for in 19X1, which is expected to last for eight years.

The problem of deciding whether these transactions give rise to revenues and expenditures in 19X1 or 19X2 or another accounting period is solved by the accountant making certain assumptions and applying a range of accounting conventions to the factual information generated by the accounting system. These procedures are examined in the following sections.

THE IDENTIFICATION OF REVENUE: THE REALIZATION CONCEPT

Revenue is obtained from the sale of goods purchased in the case of a trading organization, from the sale of goods manufactured in the case of an industrial concern and from the supply of services in the case of a service industry. For accounting purposes, revenue is assumed to arise at the point of sale. In the case of a cash sale this is when the goods or services are supplied in exchange for cash; in the case of a credit sale, it occurs when the goods or services have been supplied and the sales invoice delivered to the customer. The assumption that revenue, and therefore profit, arises when the sale takes place is called the *realization concept* and it is a good illustration of how accounting procedures are based on generally agreed conventions rather than indisputable facts.

For example, consider the case of a manufacturer of motor vehicles where demand exceeds supply. A great deal of work goes into building the car and, when completed, little more needs to be done to earn the profit. Demand exceeds supply and so delivery to a motor vehicle distributor is likely to take place fairly soon to satisfy consumer requirements. No profit is recognized during production, however, and the motor vehicle remains in the books at cost until the sale takes place. This procedure demonstrates the rather cautious approach towards profit measurement the accountant generally adopts.

It might be argued that, during the course of the production process, profit is gradually being earned that should be recognized in the accounts, but the accountant prefers to wait until the expected profit is validated by a sale. This view is taken partly because it would be difficult to decide how much extra value to recognize at any interim stage and partly because it is considered imprudent to anticipate sales that may not occur. At the other extreme it might be argued that, in the case of a credit sale, it would be even safer to wait until the cash is actually collected before recognizing a profit. But although the accountant rightly has the reputation of being cautious, he or she is not that cautious. The goods have been supplied and, in exchange, the business has a legally enforceable debt against the customer. The collection of cash will in most cases be a mere formality and no further delay in the recognition of revenue is thought to be justified (the complication of bad debts is examined in Chapter 7).

Example 4.2

On 1 January Jubilee Ltd received an order for an 'indestructible' aluminium pallet. The pallet was priced in the company's catalogue at £5,000. The pallet was manufactured during the week ended 6 January and production costs totalling £2,000 were incurred. At close of business, on 6 January, the pallet was transferred to the company's warehouse and held in stock until 15 January when it was dispatched to the customer. Cash, £5,000, was collected from the customer on 12 February 19X1.

Required

Calculate (a) the value recognized in the accounts, and (b) the profit recognized in the accounts at each of the following stages of the transaction:

  (i) receipt of order;
 (ii) production of pallet;
(iii) transfer of pallet to stock;
(iv) dispatch of pallet to customer; and
 (v) collection of cash.

Solution

Stage	Value recognized £	Profit recognized £
(i) Receipt of order	–	–
(ii) Production of pallet	2,000	–
(iii) Pallet to stock	2,000	–
(iv) Dispatch (sale)	5,000	3,000
(v) Collection of cash	5,000	–

Note
Profit is recognized when the pallet is dispatched to the customer. No additional profit is recognized when cash is collected. The only amendment to the accounts made at this date is that a debtor of £5,000 is replaced by cash of a similar amount.

Calculating sales from records of cash receipts

The sales figure is calculated by taking the figure for cash received from customers during the year, deducting opening debtors and adding closing debtors. The purpose of the calculation is to convert the figure for cash received into the figure for goods or services supplied.

Example 4.3

During 19X1, John received £17,500 from customers in respect of credit sales. At 1 January 19X1, his trade debtors amounted to £3,600 and at 31 December 19X1 they were £4,720.

Required

The calculation of sales for 19X1.

Solution

Calculation of sales:	£
Cash received in respect of credit sales	17,500
Less: Opening trade debtors	3,600
	13,900
Add: Closing trade debtors	4,720
Sales	18,620

Of the £17,500 received during the year, £3,600 was collected from customers to whom goods were sold in 19X0 and that would have been reported as revenue in the trading account for that year. The balance, £13,900, represents cash received in respect of sales actually made *during* 19X1. To this must be added closing debtors for goods sold during 19X1, but not yet paid for, to produce the sales figure of £18,620.

The rule to remember is therefore:

Sales = Cash received from customers − Opening debtors + Closing debtors.

MATCHING EXPENDITURE WITH REVENUE: THE BENEFIT PRINCIPLE

The first step in the calculation of profit for the year is to compute revenue; the second step involves identifying the expenditures that must be matched against revenue. The basic test is 'Which accounting period benefits from the expenditure?' If the answer is the current accounting period then the expenditure is charged against revenue for the current year. If the answer is a future accounting period, then the expenditure must be carried forward as an asset in the balance sheet and charged against the revenue of the future accounting period that benefits. If the answer is both the current period and one or more future periods, an apportionment must be made. This process, which bases the charge on *benefits received* during the year, rather than payments made during the year, is called the *accruals concept*. The application of this concept to specific business facts is examined next.

Accounting for stock

The calculation of the figure for cost of goods sold, to be matched with sales revenue for the purpose of computing gross profit, involves two steps:

1. *Calculate purchases* The procedure is analogous to that followed when computing sales, and may be summarized using the following formula:

Purchases = Cash paid to suppliers − Opening creditors + Closing creditors.

2. *Calculate cost of goods sold* It is unusual for all the goods purchased during the year to be sold by the end of the year. The items that remain in stock, at the year end, should be deducted from purchases and carried forward, in the balance sheet, to the following accounting period that will benefit from their sale. In a similar manner, stocks brought forward from the previous year and sold during the current accounting period must be added to purchases and matched with the current year's sales proceeds. The calculation that must be memorized in this case is:

Cost of goods sold = Opening stock + Purchases − Closing stock.

Example 4.4

James made payments by cheque to suppliers of goods on credit amounting to £27,300 during 19X2. In addition, he made cash purchases of £1,600. Trade creditors at 1 January 19X2 and 31 December 19X2 amounted respectively to £4,750 and £6,100. Opening stocks were £10,250, while closing stocks amounted to £9,640.

Required

Calculate (a) purchases and (b) cost of goods sold for 19X2.

Solution

(a) Calculation of purchases:

	£
Cash paid to suppliers:	
Credit purchases	27,300
Cash purchases	1,600
	28,900
Less: Opening creditors	4,750
	24,150
Add: Closing creditors	6,100
Purchases	30,250

(b) Calculation of cost of goods sold:

	£
Opening stock	10,250
Add: Purchases	30,250
	40,500
Less: Closing stock	9,640
Cost of goods sold	30,860

The calculations discussed and illustrated above are central to the measurement of profit by matching revenue with expenditure. Readers should test their understanding of these calculations by working Example 4.5.

Example 4.5

The following information is provided relating to Peter's business for 19X3:

	£
Cash collected from customers in respect of:	
Credit sales	41,750
Cash sales	12,350
Payments to suppliers	36,590

Balances at	1 January £	31 December £
Trade debtors	12,650	11,780
Trade creditors	6,540	8,270
Stock	9,150	9,730

Required

(a) Calculations for 19X3 of:
   (i)   receipts from customers,
   (ii)   sales,
   (iii) purchases, and
   (iv)   cost of goods sold.
(b) The trading account of Peter's business for 19X3.

Solution

(a) (i)   Cash collected in respect of:

	£
Credit sales	41,750
Cash sales	12,350
Receipts from customers	54,100

(ii) Receipts from customers	54,100
Less: Opening debtors	(12,650)
Add: Closing debtors	11,780
Sales:	53,230

(iii) Payments to suppliers	36,590
Less: Opening creditors	(6,540)
Add: Closing creditors	8,270
Purchases	38,320

(iv) Opening stock	9,150
Add: Purchases	38,320
Less: Closing stock	(9,730)
Cost of goods sold	37,740

(b)

Trading Account for 19X3

	£			£
Opening stock	9,150	Sales		53,230
Add: Purchases	38,320			
Less: Closing stock	(9,730)			
Cost of good sold	37,740			
Gross profit	15,490			
	53,230			53,230

Note
Readers should note that it is conventional practice to show the calculation of cost of goods sold on the face of the trading account, but not the calculations of purchases and sales.

Accounting for services: accruals and prepayments

When preparing accounts from cash records, it is also necessary to adjust cash payments for services rendered to the company, so that the amount charged in the profit and loss account reflects the cost of benefits actually consumed during the year.

For certain services, payments are made before the associated benefits are received, i.e. the payment is made *in advance*. In the case of rent and rates, advance payments are made for the right to occupy the property for a fixed future period of time. Where the period of occupation covers the end of one accounting year and the beginning of another, an arithmetic apportionment of the amount paid must be made between the two consecutive accounting periods. For example, if a rental of £600 is paid on 1 April 19X1 for the forthcoming twelve months, and the accounts are made up on the calendar year basis, nine months (or three-quarters) of the total benefit is received during 19X1 and three months (or one-quarter) of the benefit is received during 19X2. Therefore, ¾ × £600 = £450 is charged against revenue arising during 19X1 and ¼ × £600 = £150 is carried forward in the balance sheet as an asset; it is called 'prepaid expense' and is charged against revenue arising during 19X2.

The majority of expenses are, however, paid *in arrears*, mainly because the amount charged depends on the extent to which the service has been utilized. Examples are electricity charges, telephone charges (except the rental) and the wage bill. In these cases it is necessary to raise an 'accrual', at the end of the accounting period, representing the value of the benefit received but not yet paid for. The amount of the accrual may be estimated on the basis of past experience. Alternatively, where the bill is received by the time the accounts are prepared, an apportionment may be made in the manner described in the previous paragraph. This does not necessarily produce strictly accurate results because the service will not have been utilized at an even rate throughout the period under consideration. However, the error is unlikely to be significant, and the extra work and cost involved in obtaining a more precise apportionment would not be justified. The amount accrued is charged against revenue in the profit and loss account and carried forward in the balance sheet as a current liability under the heading 'accrued expense'.

Example 4.6

The following information is provided relating to Mark's business for 19X4:

Payments during the year for:	£	
Rates	500	
Telephone	375	

Balances at	1 Jan.	31 Dec.
	£	£
Rates paid in advance	100	125
Telephone charges outstanding	50	62

Required

Calculations of the amount to be charged against revenue for 19X4 in respect of (a) rates (b) telephone.

Solution

£

(a) Rates:

	£
Payments during 19X4	500
Add: Amount prepaid at 1 January 19X4	100*
	600
Less: Amount paid at 31 December 19X4	125
Charge for the year	475

Note
* This amount was paid in 19X3, but relates to the occupation of the premises during 19X4 and must be carried forward and charged against revenue arising during 19X4.

(b) Telephone:

	£
Payments 19X4	375
Less: Amount accrued at 1 January 19X4	50†
	325
Add: Amount accrued at 31 December 19X4	62
	387

Note
† This amount was paid in 19X4, but relates to services received during 19X3; therefore it will have been charged against revenue arising during 19X3.

Accounting for depreciation of fixed assets

Fixed assets are usually paid for at the date of acquisition, or soon afterwards, but they are expected to *benefit* the firm for many years. For example, a motor vehicle might last five years, a machine ten years and a building fifty years or more. It would therefore be unreasonable to burden revenue arising during the year that the asset is acquired with its entire cost. At the same time, most fixed assets have a limited useful life, and it would be equally wrong to keep these items indefinitely in the books at cost.

The term accountants use to describe the fall in the value of a fixed asset between the date it is acquired and the date it is sold or scrapped is 'depreciation'. It may be defined as the fall in the value of a fixed asset due to the passage of time, usage or obsolescence. This reduction in value is acknowledged, in the accounts, by making an annual charge designed to spread the loss over the periods that are expected to benefit from using the asset. There are many different methods of charging depreciation, and we will concentrate here on the one that is most common and easy to apply for illustration purposes, namely the straight-line method (sometimes called the equal instalment method). This method assumes that each accounting period receives the same amount of benefit from using the asset and the total decline in its value is therefore spread equally over the period of ownership. The formula used to calculate the depreciation charge for one year is as follows:

$$\text{Straight-line depreciation} = \frac{\text{Original cost} - \text{Estimated disposal value}}{\text{Estimated life}}$$

Example 4.7

Paul purchased a machine for £130,000 on 1 January 19X1. It is estimated that the machine will have a useful life of six years and then be sold for £10,000.

Required

(a) Calculate the straight-line depreciation charge for each of the years 19X1–X6, for inclusion in the profit and loss account; and
(b) calculate the book value of the machine at the end of each of the years 19X1–X6, to be reported in the balance sheet.

Solution

(a) Depreciation charge $= \dfrac{£130,000 - £10,000}{6} = £20,000$ per annum.

(b)
Balance Sheet extracts, 31 December

	19X1 £000	19X2 £000	19X3 £000	19X4 £000	19X5 £000	19X6 £000
Fixed assets						
Machine at cost	130	130	130	130	130	130
Less: Accumulated depreciation	20	40	60	80	100	120
	110	90	70	50	30	10

The effect of charging depreciation is that the balance sheet value of the machine is gradually reduced to its disposal value. If everything works out as planned, on 31 December 19X6 the written down value of the machine, £10,000, will be removed from the balance sheet and replaced by cash of an equal value. Events may not progress quite so smoothly, and it may turn out that the estimates on which the calculation was based prove to be wrong, i.e. the machine might not last for six years or sell for £10,000 at the end of its useful life. These complications are considered in Chapters 7 and 8.

THE PREPARATION OF ACCOUNTS FROM CASH RECORDS: A WORKED EXAMPLE

The preparation of accounts from cash records involves the following four steps:

Step 1   Prepare an opening balance sheet, sometimes called the 'statement of affairs'. This shows the proprietor's opening capital, which is needed when preparing the year-end balance sheet.

Step 2   Calculate revenues and expenditures for inclusion in the trading and profit and loss account.

Step 3   Prepare the trading and profit and loss account.

Step 4   Prepare the closing balance sheet.

Example 4.8

William is a trader who has carried on business for a number of years. In the past a friend has prepared accounts that were sufficient to enable William to agree his tax liabilities. William's friend has now left the country and is therefore unable to help. William maintains separate files of invoices received from suppliers and issued to customers.

The following summary has been prepared from William's paying-in books, cheque books and bank statements for 19X2:

Bank Summary

	£		£
Cash sales	39,640	Opening balance	3,520
Proceeds from credit sales	18,500	Payments to suppliers	31,910
Sale of furniture	250	Rates	2,800
		Personal drawings	6,500
		Wages for part-time staff	5,930
		General expenses	3,180
		Vehicle	4,000
		Closing balance	550
	58,390		58,390

The following additional information has been obtained from the files of invoices and other books and records of William:

1. William has paid all sales proceeds into his bank except for £200 that was used to pay additional part-time staff over the busy Christmas period.
2. Assets and liabilities at 31 December, based on an analysis of the invoice files, and from discussions with William, were as follows:

	19X1	*19X2*
	£	*£*
Premises at cost	6,600	6,600
Furniture at book value	3,000	Note 3
Stocks	4,250	5,760
Trade creditors	4,630	4,920
Trade debtors	2,140	2,320
Rates paid in advance	180	200
General expenses accrued	320	290

3. During the year furniture with a book value of £300, on 1 January 19X2, was sold for £250.
4. William charges depreciation at 10 per cent on the book value of furniture owned at the end of the year.
5. The vehicle was purchased on 1 July 19X2 and is to be written off over five years assuming a resale value of £1,000 at the end of that period. Ignore depreciation of premises.

Required

The trading and profit and loss account of William's business for the year ended 31 December 19X2 and the balance sheet at that date.

Solution

This question is answered by following the four steps outlined at the beginning of this section.

Step 1

Balance Sheet at 1 January 19X2

	£	£
Fixed assets		
Premises		6,600
Furniture		3,000
		9,600
Current assets		
Stocks	4,250	
Trade debtors	2,140	
Prepaid expenses	180	
	6,570	
Less: Current liabilities		
Trade creditors	4,630	
Accrued expenses	320	
Bank overdraft	3,520	
	8,470	
Working capital		(1,900)
Capital		7,700

Step 2

Workings

W1   Sales:

	£
Paid into bank:	
Cash sales	39,640
Credit sales	18,500
Proceeds not paid in	200
Total cash received	58,340
Less: Opening debtors	(2,140)
Add: Closing debtors	2,320
	58,520

W2   Purchases:

Payments to suppliers	31,910
Less: Opening creditors	(4,630)
Add: Closing creditors	4,920
	32,200

W3   Rates:

Paid during year	2,800
Add: Opening advance payment	180
Less: Closing advance payment	(200)
	2,780

W4   General expenses:

Paid during year	3,180
Less: Opening accrual	(320)
Add: Closing accrual	290
	3,150

W5   Wages:

Paid by cheque	5,930
Paid in cash	200
	6,130

W6   Loss on furniture sale:

Book value	300
Sales proceeds	250
	50

W7   Depreciation of furniture:
$$(£3,000 - £300) \times 10\% = £270.$$

W8   Depreciation of vehicle:
$$(£4,000 - £1,000) \div 5 \times \tfrac{1}{2} \, * = £300.$$

Note
* The vehicle has only been owned for six months.

Step 3

Trading and Profit and Loss Account for 19X2

	£				£	
Purchases	32,200	W2	Sales		58,520	W1
Add: Opening stock	4,250					
Less: Closing stock	(5,760)					
Cost of goods sold	30,690					
Gross profit	27,830					
	58,520				58,520	
Rates	2,780	W3	Gross profit		27,830	
General expenses	3,150	W4				
Wages	6,130	W5				
Loss on sale of furniture	50	W6				
Depreciation:						
furniture	270	W7				
vehicle	300	W8				
	12,680					
Net profit	15,150					
	27,830				27,830	

Step 4

Balance Sheet at 31 December 19X2

	£	£		£	£
Fixed assets			Opening capital		7,700
Premises at cost		6,600	Add: Net profit		15,150
Furniture	2,700		Less: Drawings		(6,500)
Less: Depreciation	270	2,430			16,350
Vehicle at cost	4,000		*Current liabilities*		
Less: Depreciation	300	3,700	Trade creditors	4,920	
		12,730	General expenses	290	5,210
Current assets					
Stocks	5,760				
Trade debtors	2,320				
Prepaid rates	200				
Bank	550	8,830			
		21,560			21,560

Trading and profit and loss account presented in vertical format

Chapter 3 drew attention to the fact that today, the balance sheet is usually presented in the vertical format rather than the horizontal format. The same is the case with the trading and profit and loss account. The reasons are similar: the layout is thought to be more easily comprehended by the non-accountant; it is possible to present a number of years results on a single sheet; and comparison of results between years is made much easier. The trading and profit and loss account of William is now reproduced in Figure 4.3 in vertical format for the purpose of illustration. In exam questions, instructions to use either the horizontal format or vertical format must be complied with but, where no instruction is given, either presentation may be followed.

Readers should now work Questions 4.1, 4.2 and 4.3 at the end of this chapter.

	£	£
Sales		58,520
Less: Purchases	32,200	
Add: Opening stock	4,250	
Less: Closing stock	(5,760)	
Cost of goods sold		30,690
Gross profit		27,830
Less: Rates	2,780	
General expenses	3,150	
Wages	6,130	
Loss on sale of furniture	50	
Depreciation:		
furniture	270	
vehicle	300	12,680
Net profit		15,150

Figure 4.3   Trading and profit and loss account of William for 19X2

CLUBS AND SOCIETIES

Clubs and societies are a common feature of most local communities. Such organizations are often formed as the result of a group of individuals, possessing a common interest, voluntarily joining together with the objective of providing a social facility otherwise not available. For instance, most towns have their own tennis club, parent–teachers' association and children's playgroup. Such clubs and societies are usually described as *non-profit making organizations* whose objectives are to further recreational, educational or religious activities. This description is a little misleading. Many clubs and societies expect to generate an excess of income over expenditure but, unlike commercial concerns, this is not their principal objective. Furthermore, any profit that does arise is not distributed to members but is instead viewed as a source of finance for facilities required to extend their activities. These facts should be clearly spelled out in the rules governing the activities of the club or society. Provided this is done, the organization is exempted from taxation.

The scale of the activities undertaken by many, though by no means all, clubs and societies is relatively small. The officers of these organizations, namely the chairman, secretary, treasurer, etc. are unpaid volunteers. For these reasons a comprehensive accounting system is unlikely to exist. Indeed, in the majority of clubs and societies, the accounting system is unlikely to consist of more than a record of receipts and payments during the year. At the year end, a decision must be taken concerning the form the final accounts should take. Perhaps because of the absence of necessary expertise, and also perhaps because there is little demand for accounting information from the members, the treasurer may simply prepare a 'receipts and payments account' for the year. This is an analysed list of total cash coming into and going out of the club during the year; no attempt is made to take account of debts and liabilities outstanding at the balance sheet date and no balance sheet is prepared. This form of account may be satisfactory for the very small club or society, but is totally inadequate for the larger organization where there exist valuable assets or substantial outstanding liabilities (perhaps because a bank loan has been raised to build a new squash court) of which the members should be made aware. For the larger organizations, the accounts must be prepared in accordance with the *accruals concept*, and the procedure then followed is almost exactly the same as that described for industrial and commercial concerns earlier in this chapter.

Accounting terms used by clubs and societies

The only distinction, of any significance, between properly prepared final accounts of clubs and societies, on the one hand, and those of industrial and commercial concerns, on the other, is that different terms are used to describe

Industrial and commercial concerns	Club/ society	Comment
Profit and loss account	Income and expenditure account	These differences reflect the fact that clubs and societies are not profit oriented. When computing income and expenditure, however, the accruals concept is usually applied in exactly the same way as when calculating figures for inclusion in the profit and loss account
Net profit/ net loss	Surplus/ deficit	
Capital	Accumulated fund	The term capital denotes a proprietorial interest that does not exist in clubs and societies, e.g. if a member resigns he or she has no right to reclaim his or her joining fee

Table 4.1   Differences in terms used by clubs and societies

certain essentially similar financial magnitudes. The main differences are as shown in Table 4.1.

Readers should now work Question 4.4 at the end of this chapter.

Subscriptions and entry fees

A main source of revenue for clubs and societies is the subscriptions received from members, but it is often considered inappropriate to apply the full force of the accruals concept to this item. At the end of an accounting period, there are usually subscriptions that remain unpaid for that year and subscriptions received in advance for the following year. Strict application of the accruals concept requires subscriptions outstanding to be credited to income and treated as a debt due to the club. This treatment is rarely followed in practice, although there may be no doubt that an individual has made use of the club's facilities during the year. The fact that his or her subscription remains unpaid at the year end is a fairly clear indication that it will never be collected. The former member has probably now left the club and the amount outstanding would be insufficient to justify the costs of any legal action needed to achieve its recovery. In accordance with the accruals concept, however, subscriptions received in advance should be shown as a liability in the balance sheet and treated as income of the following accounting period.

Example 4.9

At the end of 19X2 subscriptions outstanding amounted to £300 and subscriptions received in advance for 19X3 amounted to £90. During 19X3 subscriptions received amounted to £5,400. This included the £300 outstanding at the end of 19X2 and £120 in advance for 19X4. Subscriptions outstanding at the end of 19X3 amounted to £500.

Required

Calculate the amount to be credited to the income and expenditure account for 19X3 assuming that subscriptions are accounted for on (a) the cash basis, (b) the accruals basis and (c) the prudent basis.

Solution

		£
(a) Cash basis		5,400
(b) Accruals basis:		
Cash received in 19X3		5,400
Add:	Received in 19X2 for 19X3	90
	Outstanding at end of 19X3	500
		5,990
Less:	Outstanding at end of 19X2	(300)
	Received in 19X3 for 19X4	(120)
		5,570

(c) Prudent basis (subscriptions outstanding ignored):   £
     Cash received in 19X3

	£
Cash received in 19X3	5,400
Add: Received in 19X2 for 19X3	90
	5,490
Less: Received in 19X3 for 19X4	(120)
	5,370

Many clubs charge new members an entry fee. These receipts may be credited either to income or direct to the accumulated fund. Either treatment is acceptable, but the method chosen should be applied consistently from year to year with the amount involved clearly disclosed. Life membership fees may also be accounted for in a variety of ways. There are three main alternatives:

1. Credit to the accumulated fund.
2. Credit in full to the income and expenditure account in the year received.
3. Credit initially to a life membership account, and transfer the fee to the income and expenditure account, in instalments, over an agreed number of years.

The third alternative is theoretically superior, since it attempts to relate income to the periods when the member uses the club's facilities, but it is also the most time-consuming accounting treatment.

Identifying the results of separate activities

It is always important, when deciding what form the annual accounts should take, to consider carefully the information that is likely to be of interest to the recipients of these reports. For this reason the accounts should be designed to reflect the particular nature of the organization's activities. It is quite usual for clubs and societies to have a number of spheres of interest. For instance, a recreation club may provide facilities for lawn tennis, squash, table tennis, bowls, rugby and cricket. It is usually considered useful to identify the contribution of each section, whether positive or negative, to the overall finances of the club. This information is not, however, necessarily required as a basis for deciding to extend or discontinue particular facilities. It must be remembered that it is the aim of clubs to provide recreational facilities, not to make a profit.

However, the extent to which the profitable sections can subsidize the unprofitable is not unlimited and, if a succession of poor results reflects a decline in the demand for a particular sport, the facility may have to be withdrawn in the interests of the club members as a whole. More likely, significant deficits in certain areas will be interpreted as evidence of the need to revise subscriptions upwards. For these reasons a separate income and expenditure account should be prepared for each section, and the balances transferred to a general income and expenditure account where they will be combined with any unallocated items of income and expenditure arising from the club's activities.

Many clubs provide bar facilities at which drinks and perhaps tobacco and refreshments are sold and, where this occurs, the relevant items of income and expenditure are collected together in the bar trading account. The balance of this account, whether a profit or a loss, is also transferred to the general income and expenditure account.

In the case of industrial and commercial organizations, separate identification of the results of different product lines in order to show whether they are operating at a profit or a loss is a principal basis for management decisions on whether to expand or close down an area of activity. The information made available for the purpose of this type of management decision is examined in Chapter 9. Readers should now attempt Question 4.5 at the end of this chapter.

QUESTIONS

The preparation of accounts from incomplete records involves fundamental accounting procedures that must be mastered before readers can expect to make progress in their accounting studies. It is for this reason that questions testing students' understanding of these procedures are extremely common in examinations. Such questions often follow a pattern similar to William (Example 4.8 in this chapter), and solutions should consist of the same four steps recommended for answering that question. Questions 4.1, 4.4 and 4.5 are of this type. Some variation is of course possible, and the remaining two questions in this section include certain innovations. The opening balance sheet is provided in Question 4.2 so that only steps 2, 3 and 4 need to be processed. Question 4.3 is a revision question that deals with matters covered in Chapter 3 as well as the present chapter.

4.1   Stoll, a trader, pays all his business takings into his bank account. All business payments are made by cheque. The following is a summary of his bank account for the year 19X5.

Bank Summary

	£		£
Balance 1 January 19X5	480	Trade creditors	24,800
Received from debtors	31,560	General expenses	2,524
		Rent	300
		Drawings	3,600
		Balance 31 December 19X5	816
	32,040		32,040

The following information is obtained from the available records:

	31 Dec.19X4 £	31 Dec.19X5 £
Debtors for goods sold	1,900	2,344
Trade creditors	1,630	1,930
Stock	2,040	1,848
Furniture and fittings:		
at cost less depreciation	400	360

Required

(a) Calculate the balance of Stoll's capital at 31 December 19X4.
(b) Prepare the trading and profit and loss account for the year 19X5 and the balance sheet at 31 December 19X5. Present these accounting statements in vertical format.

4.2   Bennett commenced business as a retail trader at the beginning of 19X0. He maintains no formal system of ledger accounts for recording business transactions. An accountant was called in during 19X2 to prepare accounts for 19X1, in order to enable tax liabilities to be agreed. The following balance sheet was prepared as at 1 January 19X1:

Balance Sheet, 1 January 19X1

	£		£
Motor vehicles at cost	10,000	Capital	8,720
Less: Accumulated		Loan at 15%	2,000
depreciation	2,000	Creditors	850
	———	Accrued expenses	260
	8,000	Bank overdraft	2,030
Stock	3,750		
Debtors	1,060		
Prepaid expenses	400		
Bank deposit account	650		
	———		———
	13,860		13,860

The following information is provided regarding 19X1:

1. An analysis of the business bank accounts provided the following information:

Receipts	£	Payments	£
Cash sales	32,100	Paid to suppliers	20,850
Proceeds from credit sales	7,560	General expenses	7,560
Legacy from relative	2,650	Drawings	12,500
Bank interest received	50	Motor vehicle	4,000
	———		———
	42,360		44,910

2. During the year, a new motor vehicle was purchased for £4,000; Bennett depreciates vehicles at the rate of 20 per cent on cost.
3. Debtors outstanding at the end of 19X1 amounted to £1,840, none of which was considered to be bad or doubtful.
4. Amounts due to suppliers at the end of 19X1 totalled £1,140 and stock was valued at £4,600.
5. Accruals and prepayments of general expenses, at the end of 19X1, amounted to £310 and £520 respectively.

Required

The trading and profit and loss account of Bennett's business for 19X1 and the balance sheet at 31 December 19X1.

4.3   The following is the balance sheet of Stondon, a trader, at 31 December 19X2:

Balance Sheet

	£		£
Furniture and fittings	800	Capital	7,940
Stock	5,384		
Trade debtors	4,162	Trade creditors	3,294
Balance at bank	888		
	11,234		11,234

In January 19X3 Stondon sold certain private investments for £4,200; he purchased a motor van for business use for £3,000 and paid the balance of the proceeds into his business bank account.

At 31 December 19X3, trade debtors amounted to £4,124, stock in trade was valued at £6,891 and trade creditors amounted to £3,586. Stondon's business bank account was overdrawn by £782. His drawings during 19X3 were £12,840.

The total of running expenses charged to the profit and loss account for the year 19X3 amounted to £14,420. This total included £500 for depreciation of the motor van.

Stondon's gross profit is at the rate of 25 per cent of selling price for all goods sold during 19X3.

Required

(a) Prepare Stondon's balance sheet at 31 December 19X3.
(b) Calculate Stondon's net profit for 19X3 on the basis of changes in capital.
(c) Reconstruct the trading and profit and loss account of Stondon's business for the year 19X3.

Note
Ignore depreciation of furniture and fittings.

4.4 The following details are extracted from the books of the Fellowship Club:

Balances at	31 Dec.19X7 £	31 Dec.19X8 £
Bar stock	8,200	11,936
Creditors for bar supplies	4,080	4,568
Creditors for expenses	160	248

Summary of Bank Account for 19X8

	£		£
Balance 1 January 19X8	13,280	Bar purchases	80,760
Subscriptions received	12,400	Salaries	16,840
Bar sales	107,600	Rent of club premises	2,800
Interest on investments	4,160	Rates	2,000
		General expenses	5,360
		Cost of new investments	26,000
		Balance 31 December 19X8	3,680
	137,440		137,440

On 1 January 19X8 the club held temporary investments it had purchased for £49,200, and the furniture in use was valued at £30,400. The club is building up its investments to enable it to purchase its own clubhouse in due course. Depreciation should be charged on the furniture at the rate of 10 per cent per annum on the opening value.

Required

(a) A bar trading account for 19X8.
(b) A general income and expenditure account for 19X8.
(c) A balance sheet as at 31 December 19X8.

4.5 The Ridlingham Recreation Club consists of a tennis section and a rugby section. The following information has been obtained relating to the position of the club on 1 January 19X1:

	£
Clubhouse at cost	38,000
Creditors for bar purchases	3,720
Creditors for general expenses	500
Tennis courts at cost (£40,000), less depreciation to date	24,000
Furniture and equipment at book value	5,000
Bar stocks	4,400
Bank balance	1,500

The club's bank statements for 19X1 have been analysed and the following summary prepared:

Bank Account, 19X1

	£		£
Balance 1 January	1,500	New tennis court	16,000
Ten-year membership	12,000	Repairs to tennis courts	2,520
Other subscriptions: Tennis	6,400	Prizes for tennis tournaments	140
Rugby	1,300	Rugby kit	900
Tennis tournament entry fees	240	Rental of rugby pitch	400
Bar sales	69,660	Rates on clubhouse	1,100
Collections at rugby matches	180	Payments for bar supplies	48,400
Tennis court fees	5,700	Wages of bar steward	7,800
		General expenses	17,300
		Balance 31 December	2,420
	96,980		96,980

You discover that all cash received is paid into the club bank account and all payments are made by cheque.

During the year a new tennis court was built that was first used on 1 July 19X1. In order to help pay for the new court, ten-year memberships were offered for sale, at the beginning of the first year, at £400 each.

At 31 December 19X1 creditors for bar purchases and general expenses amount to £4,300 and £640 respectively. Bar stocks are valued at £5,280. It is the club's policy to write off the cost of the tennis courts over a ten-year period. Furniture is depreciated at 10 per cent on the balance at the year end. For the purpose of the accounts the rugby kit is considered to possess a nil value.

Required

(a) The bar trading account and a general income and expenditure account for 19X1. The general income and expenditure account should show the net surplus or deficit arising separately from the tennis section and the rugby section.

(b) The balance sheet at 31 December 19X1.

5
The Double Entry System
I: The Initial Record of
Transactions

INTRODUCTION

Accounting reports are based on summarized information, and are accurate only if the initial record of the individual transactions is correct. The operation of a company results in numerous individual transactions taking place; in the case of large companies there is likely to be a massive volume of these. Inflows and outflows of goods, services and cash occur, and it is the responsibility of management to ensure that there is an efficient system of accounting. This system must be designed both to record and control individual transactions and to enable the production of summarized results in the form of accounting reports. For example, a retail shop that makes a large number of relatively small sales must have controls to ensure that all items that leave the shop are paid for and that all cash received is recorded; summaries showing the total value of sales, possibly analysed by product, are then produced for management so that the shop's progress can be monitored. This chapter covers the detailed recording of the separate items in such a way as to provide an adequate foundation for the rest of the accounting process.

CASH FLOWS

Control of cash receipts and payments is obviously of particular importance to the company as resources that are in the form of cash are vulnerable to misappropriation; the cash book, in which all receipts and payments are recorded, is the central element of this control. The objective is to ensure that all cash due to the company is received and retained until its subsequent, properly authorized, disbursement takes place. A simple way to establish this control is to ensure that:

1. all cash receipts are recorded as they are received;

2. all cash receipts are paid with little delay into the company's bank account; and

3. only senior personnel are permitted to authorize the bank to make payments from the bank.

One result of using a bank account is to create an additional source of information on cash flows since all the entries in the cash book have a corresponding entry in the statement of account, which is provided periodically by the bank. (The importance of this is discussed later in this chapter.) The initial record of cash receipts is usually in the form of a memorandum list that should be prepared at the point and time of receipt. The necessary documentation is completed as each sale is made when the goods are exchanged directly for cash, as is the case with a retail shop, or at some other point where goods are sold on credit and the cash received some time after the sale. For example, if it is usual for cheques to be received in the post, a reliable employee should be made responsible for opening all letters, removing and listing the cheques enclosed and passing them to the cashier for prompt payment into the bank. The inclusion of a number of different people in this line of control reduces the possibility of undetected theft since the list produced by the person responsible for opening the post is independent of, and can be checked with, the sum accounted for by the cashier. On the payments side, it must be ensured that only a limited number of senior people are authorized to sign documents, such as cheques and standing order mandates, which are accepted by the bank as instructions to pay sums of money out of the account. The official signing the document – for example, the cheque – should require evidence to warrant its completion, such as a valid invoice received from a supplier. In this example, the invoice should be referenced to the cash payment and retained so that the transaction's validity can, if required, be subsequently verified. This involves a system of cross-referencing, with the payment recorded in the cash book cross-referenced to a supplier's account in which the liability has been recorded on the previous receipt of a valid invoice.

The cash account

The cash account is used to record the inflows and outflows of cash and is kept in an accounting record called the cash book. The account consists of two lists of figures, one of which gives details of cash receipts and the other cash payments; in accordance with the rules of double entry book keeping (explained in detail in Chapter 6), the receipts are known as 'debits' and are placed on the left-hand page of the cash book, while payments are recorded on the right-hand page and are termed 'credits'. (The terms debit and credit are often abbreviated to 'dr' and 'cr' respectively.) A period of time, such as a week or a month, is covered by the lists and, as well as the cash flows that take place during the period, the opening cash position is included so that the closing balance of cash can be determined. If the company starts the period with cash in hand, the amount is entered at the top of the cash received (debit) column, while an overdraft is entered at the top of the payments (credit) column.

To find the closing balance of cash, the account is 'balanced'. This is done by finding the difference between the total values of debits and credits. The closing balance of one period, known as the 'balance carried down', is the opening balance for the following period, when it is termed the 'balance brought down'; this balance appears in the company's balance sheet.

Example 5.1

Wire Ltd balances its cash book each week, and at the end of week 8 of 19X7 held cash of £782. During week 9 the following receipts and payments took place:

		£
Receipts:	Sales	5,769
	Loan from Newbank plc	2,000
Payments:	Purchase of goods for resale	3,150
	Wages	790
	Rent	126
	Advertising	75
	Delivery van	3,500

Required

Prepare the cash account for week 9 of Wire Ltd as it would appear in the company's cash book and show the balance carried forward to week 10.

Solution

Cash Account

Cash in = Receipts (Debit)		£	*Cash out = Payments (Credit)*		£
Week 9	Balance brought down	782	Week 9	Purchases	3,150
	Sales	5,769		Wages	790
	Loan	2,000		Rent	126
				Advertising	75
				Van	3,500
					7,641
				Balance carried down	910
		8,551			8,551
Week 10	Balance brought down	910			

Notes

1. Although the £910 is a debit balance, i.e. the debit items exceed credit items by this amount, it is conventionally added to the list of credits so that the two columns add up to

£8,551. The surplus is then brought down as the opening balance for week 10. As, in this case, the balance brought down is on the debit side of the account, it is a debit balance; credit balances are those brought down on the credit side of the account.
2. The terms 'balance carried down' and 'balance brought down' are often abbreviated to 'balance b/d' and 'balance c/d' respectively.

Readers should now work Question 5.1 at the end of this chapter to test their understanding of the preparation of the cash account.

The bank reconciliation

A company's cash account should contain exactly the same receipts and payments as pass through its bank account. A valuable check on the accuracy of the cash account is provided by the routine preparation of the bank reconciliation statement that agrees the cash account's balance with the bank statement. To provide additional control, the reconciliation should ideally be prepared or checked by an official of the company who is otherwise independent of the control and recording of the flows of cash.

The bank reconciliation statement is prepared by comparing items in the cash account with those in the bank statement. Entries that appear in both during the period under examination are checked off, but usually these records, although covering the same period of time, do not correspond exactly. This is the result of some or all of the following:

1. *Payments in the cash account not on the bank statement* These mainly result from the fact that there is a delay between the issue of a cheque, at which time it is entered in the cash account, and its clearance by the bank, when it appears on the bank statement.
2. *Receipts in the cash account not on the bank statement* A company may enter the cash received each day in the cash account, but pay it into the bank the following day, or even allow it to accumulate for a short period of time. This causes a lapse of time between the cash account record and the bank statement entry. For security reasons, the delay should be kept to a minimum.
3. *Payments on the statements not in the cash account* Some payments, such as those for bank charges, are generated by the bank. The company may know that they have been paid only when a statement has been received, and they would not have been previously entered in the cash book. Other items that fall into this category are payments made by standing order and direct debits.
4. *Receipts on the statement not in the cash book.* It is common nowadays for sums to be paid directly into the recipient's bank account, and sometimes they are identifiable only when the statement is received.

Items 1 and 2 above are merely timing differences and, although appearing in the bank reconciliation, require no further entry in the cash account. Items 3 and 4, however, are additional items that, if valid, should be entered in the cash account when the statement is received.

The procedure for preparing a bank reconciliation statement is to take the entries in the cash account for a certain period of time and mark off in both records those that also appear on the bank statement for the same period. Any items left unmarked must be examined and classified into types 1, 2, 3 and 4. Items of types 3 and 4 are entered in the cash account from which the balance is then extracted. This balance will still differ from that shown on the bank statement if there are any items of types 1 and 2, and so a memorandum statement is drawn up that adjusts the balance on the statement for these items, after which it should agree with that shown on the cash account.

Example 5.2

The following information relates to Check Ltd for the month of March:

Cash Account

Receipts (debit)		£	Payments (credit)		£
March			March		
1	Balance b/d	1,000		Cheques issued:	
9	Receipts paid into bank	350	4	No. 11	150
16	Receipts paid into bank	200	9	No. 12	225
23	Receipts paid into bank	475	15	No. 13	75
30	Receipts paid into bank	150	22	No. 14	445
			30	No. 15	160
			31	No. 16	330
			31	Balance c/d	790
		2,175			2,175

Bank statement

		Debit £	Credit £	Balance £
March				
1	Balance brought forward			1,000Cr.
6	Cheque No. 11	150		850
11	Lodgement		350	1,200
	Cheque No. 12	225		975
17	Cheque No. 13	75		900
18	Lodgement		200	1,100
24	Cheque No. 14	445		655
25	Lodgement		475	1,130
	Standing order	60		1,070
26	Direct credit		50	1,120
31	Bank charges	100		1,020
	Balance carried forward			1,020Cr.

Note
As the bank statement is prepared from the point of view of the bank, payments made by the company are shown as debits and deposits with the bank as credits, i.e. the terms are the opposite way round compared with the cash account in the company's books.

Required

(a) Make the necessary adjustments to the cash account for the month of March.
(b) Prepare the bank reconciliation statement at the end of March.

Solution

When the entries in the cash account are checked with those on the statement, the following differences are found:

1. Payments in the cash account not on the bank statement:
   Cheque No. 15   £160
   Cheque No. 16   £330
2. Receipts in the cash account not on the bank statement:
   Lodgement   £150
3. Payments on the bank statement not in the cash account:
   Standing order £60
   Bank charges   £100
4. Receipts on the bank statement not in the cash account:
   Direct credit   £50

Items 3 and 4 are used to complete the cash account, and items 1 and 2 appear in the bank reconciliation statement.

(a) **Completion of the cash account for March**

	Receipts (debit)			Payments (credit)	
March		£	March		£
31	Balance b/d	790	31	Standing order	60
31	Direct credit	50	31	Bank charges	100
			31	Balance c/d	680
		840			840

(b) **Bank reconciliation statement at 31 March**

	£	£
Balance per bank statement		1,020
Less: Outstanding cheques:		
No. 15	160	
No. 16	330	
		490
		530
Plus: Outstanding lodgement		150
Balance as per cash account		680

Notes
1. Subsequent bank statements should be checked to ensure that all outstanding items are cleared without undue delay.
2. It is possible for banks to make mistakes. Any unexplained entry on the bank statement should be queried as it may have been entered in the company's account in error. Until a satisfactory explanation is obtained, such items should be shown as part of the reconciliation statement and not entered in the cash book.

Readers should now attempt Question 5.2 at the end of this chapter to test their understanding of the preparation of the bank reconciliation statement.

The double column cash book

It was stated above that all cash receipts should be paid into the firm's bank account without delay, and that all disbursements should be made from the bank account. Although this is a very good rule to observe in practice, there are occasions when it is not applied, especially in the case of small businesses. In these circumstances it is particularly important to ensure that all cash flows are recorded so that none is overlooked – for example, a trader may make sales of £100 for cash and out of the proceeds pay wages of £30 and motor expenses of £5 before banking the residual £65. It is incorrect merely to record in the books of the firm the lodgement of £65 in respect of sales, since this ignores the receipt of the additional £35, which was paid out on wages and motor expenses. The effect of the omission would be to understate sales, wages and motor expenses.

Where sums are paid out of cash takings before they are banked, it is necessary to maintain two cash accounts, one to deal with the flows of cash that take place through the bank account, called the 'cash-at-bank account', and one to deal with other cash flows, called the 'cash-in-hand account'. Transfers between the two accounts are made in the usual way, so that, for example, when cash is banked a payment is entered in the cash-in-hand account and a receipt recorded in the cash-at-bank account. Although it is possible to maintain two completely separate accounts, it is usual in these circumstances to modify the traditional cash-book format and use what is known as a double column cash book.

Example 5.3

Glue Ltd undertook the following transactions between 1 and 10 June:

Date	Details	£
June		
1	Cash balance in hand	50
1	Balance at bank	200
3	Received from cash sales	1,275
4	Cash paid into bank	1,000
7	Pay wages in cash	100
8	Make cash purchases	200
9	Draw cash from bank	300
10	Pay for purchases by cheque	150
10	Pay rent in cash	175

Required

Prepare the double column cash book to record the above transactions, carrying down the balances on 10 June.

Solution

Double Column Cash Book

	Receipts (debits)				Payments (credits)		
Date	Detail	Cash in hand	Cash at bank	Date	Detail	Cash in hand	Cash at bank
		£	£			£	£
June				June			
1	Balance b/d	50	200	4	Cash to bank	1,000	
3	Sales	1,275		7	Wages	100	
4	Cash paid in		1,000	8	Purchases	200	
9	Cash from			9	Cash		
	from bank	300			withdrawn		300
				10	Purchases		150
				10	Rent	175	
				10	Balances c/d	150	750
		1,625	1,200			1,625	1,200
10	Balances b/d	150	750				

Note that the accounts shown above comply with the usual convention that debits are recorded on the left and credits on the right, but it differs from the usual format as there are two columns on each side, one to record the flows of cash into the business and the manner of its disposition, while the other contains details of the cash flows that take place through the bank account. The opening balances are respectively cash in hand and at the bank on 1 June, and the first transaction increases cash held by £1,275, which is debited in the cash column to represent a cash receipt. Of this cash, £1,000 is paid into the bank on June 4. Cash in hand is credited with this amount to show that the payment was made out of cash, while the bank is debited to show the corresponding receipt. Conversely, when cash is drawn from the bank to be used for cash payments, cash at bank is credited and the cash-in-hand column debited.

Readers should now work Question 5.3 at the end of this chapter.

The analysed cash book

To enable accounting reports to be prepared it is necessary to ascertain why particular cash flows have taken place. For example, cash from sales and the receipt of a loan are both recorded as cash inflows, but the former is an element in the calculation of profit while the latter is entered in the balance sheet as a liability. A simple way to break down cash flows into their constituent parts is to maintain an analysed cash book. This has columns not only for cash inflows and outflows, but also further columns for different types of flows. When a type of receipt or payment occurs on a regular basis, such as payments for goods or wages, a separate column is devoted to this category of transaction; infrequent transactions are entered in a sundry, or ledger, column. An advantage of the use of an analysed cash book is that the nature of each item must be ascertained at the time it is recorded; errors are more likely to occur if there is delay in this process, due, for example, to lapse of memory.

Example 5.4

The following cash transactions were undertaken by Thorn & Co.:

Day	Receipts		£	Payments	£
1	Sales		250	Purchases of stock	125
2	Sales		300	Wages	76
3	Sales		270	Purchases of stock	150
4	Sales		315	Wages	79
4	Loan		150	Rent	50
4				Purchase of fixed assets	200

Required

Prepare the company's analysed cash book to record the above transactions.

Solution

Cash account

		Receipts side (debit)		
Day	Detail	Total £	Sales £	Sundry £
1	Sales	250	250	
2	Sales	300	300	
3	Sales	270	270	
4	Sales	315	315	
	Loan	150		150
		1,285	1,135	150

				Payments side (credit)		
Day	Detail	Total	Purchases of stock	Wages	Rent	Sundry
		£	£	£	£	£
1	Purchases of stock	125	125			
2	Wages	76		76		
3	Purchases of stock	150	150			
4	Wages	79		79		
	Rent	50			50	
	Purchase of fixed assets	200				200
		680	275	155	50	200

The fact that the aggregate of the totals in the analysis columns is equal to the total of the 'Total' column provides a useful check of arithmetical accuracy.

Readers should now work Question 5.4 at the end of this chapter.

The petty cash account

All businesses have to meet small incidental expenses in the course of operating and, as it is often inconvenient to pay these by cheque, it is usual to maintain a petty cash float. The normal procedure is to adopt the 'Imprest' system, which uses a fixed sum as a float from which money is paid in return for a properly authorized petty cash voucher. The size of the float should be sufficient to cover the normal level of disbursements during the length of time between replenishments. At regular intervals the petty cashier exchanges the petty cash vouchers for a cheque equal to their total value, which is then used to restore the fund to its designated amount. An advantage of using this system is that at any time the cash in hand plus that represented by vouchers should total the amount of the initial float. This facilities spot checks by an appropriate official.

Although petty cash expenditure, by definition, covers only relatively small amounts, it is still necessary to ensure that it is properly controlled and accounted for. The use of the Imprest system gives control, and to ensure that a proper record exists it is usual to maintain a petty cash book, in which the details of the receipts and payments of petty cash are entered. The petty cash book also acts as the petty cash account. Example 5.5 shows entries in a petty cash account recording the transactions of an Imprest petty cash fund of £50.

Example 5.5

Petty cash account

Receipts (debit)			Payments (credit)					
Date			Date	Voucher no.	Total	Postage	Travel	Cleaning
June		£	June		£	£	£	£
1	Balance b/d	12	4	11	10		10	
3	Bank	38	11	12	7			7
			18	13	5	5		
			24	14	8		8	
			29	15	4	4		
					—	—	—	—
					34	9	18	7
			30	Balance c/d	16	—	—	—
		—			—			
		50			50			
		—			—			
July								
1	Balance b/d	16						
2	Bank	34						

The opening balance of £12 shows that expenditure of £38 has been made in the previous period and should be represented by vouchers to support the amount of cash drawn from the bank. The debit entry in the petty cash account of £38 shows the receipt of cash and will correspond with a credit in the cash-at-bank account from which the payment is made. The fund stands at £50 immediately after reimbursement. Withdrawals of cash are entered as payments on the credit side of the book in the cash column and this has the effect of reducing the petty cash balance. Analysis columns are used to provide a summary of the amount spent for each purpose. Vouchers 11 to 15 account for £34, and this sum is drawn from the bank to replenish the fund at the beginning of July.

Question 5.5 at the end of this chapter should now be worked.

FLOWS OF GOODS AND SERVICES

Accounts are designed to reflect the economic activity that takes place during a period of time, and this is not accurately shown by simply reporting cash movements. This is because it is usual for sales and purchases to be made on credit and, in these circumstances, the movement of goods is not immediately accompanied by equivalent transfers of cash. Companies must, therefore, keep records of inflows and outflows of goods and services as well as for flows of cash. For example, the fact that goods have been purchased on credit must be reported, even if they have not been paid for.

One reason for making a record of flows of goods and services is because control is needed to ensure that cash is subsequently collected from credit customers and that suppliers are paid on time. This section deals with the initial record of economic events – the control of debtors and creditors is dealt with in Chapter 6.

Day books

In its simplest form a day book is a list of sales or purchases that have taken place on credit with the name of the customer or supplier entered next to each item. The total of each list gives the value of purchases or sales that have taken place during a period of time.

To make certain that all sales are recorded, steps should be taken to ensure that a sales invoice is made out each time goods are supplied. A number of copies of the sales invoice are normally required, one of which goes to the customer and another to the accounts section as the basis for entering the transaction in the sales day book. A final control, such as pre-numbering, should be used to ensure that copies of all invoices are entered in the day book; any missing numbers should be investigated.

The purchases day book is written up on the basis of invoices received from suppliers. To ensure that payment is made only for goods received, a record should be kept of goods delivered to the company against which the invoice can be checked. The record of goods received is cancelled after checking the invoice to prevent the possibility of paying twice for one delivery. The invoice should also be matched with its originating order to make sure that goods delivered are actually required by the company. An invoice not supported by both evidence of receipt of the goods and a purchase order should be investigated and not passed for entry in the books until there is sufficient proof that it relates to a valid transaction. Invoices for services, such as cleaning, should be supported by an order or contract and passed for payment only by an authorized official.

To produce final accounts and provide management with relevant information, the inflows and outflows of goods and services must be broken down, and this is achieved by adding analysis columns to the day books, as was done in the case of the cash book. The analysis headings are determined on the basis of which aspects of the organization are to be monitored. Excessive detail impairs comprehension and so too many headings should not be used. On the other hand, significant matters may be masked if the headings are too broad. Management needs to identify areas of strength and weakness, and this is achieved if, for example, sales and purchases are analysed by type of product, and the department or branch in which they originate.

Example 5.6

House Ltd owns a shop that consists of two distinct departments, one selling bricks and the other mortar. All purchases are made on credit and management requires reports that show the individual results of each department.

Required

Prepare from the following details the purchases day book in a manner that provides the information needed by management:

Purchases: 1 March from Builder Ltd – bricks £100; mortar £75
(supplied on one invoice)
2 March from Cement Ltd – mortar £50
3 March from Jerry Ltd – bricks £65

Solution

Purchases day book

Date	Supplier	Total	Bricks	Mortar
March		£	£	£
1	Builder Ltd	175	100	75
2	Cement Ltd	50		50
3	Jerry Ltd	65	65	
		290	165	125

The use of day books is not restricted to purchases and sales – they can be used for any routine transactions, such as the return of goods from customers or to suppliers. In all cases appropriate controls must be established to ensure that only valid entries are made in the records.

Readers should now work Question 5.6 at the end of this chapter to test their understanding of the preparation of day books.

QUESTIONS

5.1   Mr Wall decided to set up in business as a sole trader on 1 January 19X1. He opened a business bank account into which he pays all the takings and from which he pays all business costs. His transactions for January 19X1 were as follows:

(a) Pay £5,000 into the bank as capital on 1 January.
(b) Buy for cash a second-hand delivery van for £4,000 on 2 January.
(c) Pay one month's rent on premises £100 on 3 January.
(d) Sell goods for £2,250 cash during the month.
(e) Collect £450 from debtors and pay £2,500 to creditors during the month.
(f) Withdraw £110 on 15 January.
(g) Pay insurance for one year, from 1 January 19X1 of £120 on the 30 January.

Required

Write up the cash account for January 19X1.

5.2   At the close of business on 31 May 1985, the bank statement of Amos Jones, a sole trader, showed that his balance with the bank amounted to £1,960. This does not agree with the bank balance according to his cash book, and the following transactions account for the difference:

(a)   On 31 May the bank allowed Jones interest amounting to £76, but this had not yet been entered in the cash book.
(b)   During May 1985 the bank had paid on behalf of Jones, under a banker's standing order, the rent of his business premises amounting to £110. This had not been entered in the cash book.
(c)   On 31 May, William Smith, a *debtor* of Jones, paid direct to Jones' account with his bankers the sum of £89, but this had not yet appeared in the cash book.
(d)   During May, Jones had drawn several cheques but, at the close of business on 31 May 1985, the following three cheques had not yet been presented for payment: £21, £44 and £39.

Required

Commencing with the bank statement balance of £1,960, prepare the bank reconciliation statement of Amos Jones as at 31 May 1985, ending with the correct bank balance as shown in his cash book.

(LCC, Book-keeping, summer, 1985)

5.3   Ray Gunne set up in business on 1 January 19X3. The firm's transactions for the first week of January 19X3 were as follows:

(a)   Pay capital of £10,000 into the bank.
(b)   Buy premises for £8,000 and equipment for £2,750 – both paid by cheque.
(c)   Borrow £5,000 from Gunne's brother. He provided this sum in cash of which £4,000 was used to buy a delivery van and £750 was paid into the bank.
(d)   Buy trading stock: £3,000 by cheque and £1,000 for cash.
(e)   Make cash sales of £5,500.
(f)   Pay wages of £100 in cash.
(g)   Take cash drawings of £150.
(h)   Pay rates by cheque of £250.
(i)   Pay £4,250 of cash into the bank.

Required

Prepare the double column cash book of Gunne's business for the first week of

January 19X3 and carry down the balances at the end of the week.

5.4   At the start of a trading week the cash account of Laser Ltd showed that the company was £6,510 overdrawn. During the week the company undertook the following cash transactions:

Day	Receipts	£	Payments	£
1	Sales	1,790	Purchases	2,250
2	Sales	2,190	Wages	380
3	Sales	1,250		
3	Sale of fixed asset	1,000		
4	Sales	3,720	Interest on loan	400
5	Sales	1,540	Purchases	3,140
6	Sales	2,710	Wages	450

Required

Prepare the analysed cash book of Laser Ltd to record the above information and carry down the balance at the end of the week.

5.5 James Walton is a sole trader who keeps his petty cash on the Imprest System – the Imprest amount being £50. At the start of business on 1 October 1985, the petty cash in hand was £3.75.

Walton's petty cash transactions for the month of October 1985 were as follows:

1 October	Petty cash restored to Imprest amount
4 October	Wages paid – £11.60
5 October	Stamps purchased – £3.94
8 October	Stationery purchased – £4.09
11 October	Stamps purchased – £2
18 October	Wages paid –£12.93
21 October	Paid to F. Smith, a creditor – £3.42
24 October	Stationery purchased – £4.66
28 October	Stamps purchased – £3.80

Required

Draw up Walton's petty cash book for the month of October 1985, carry down the balance on 31 October 1985, and restore the petty cash to the Imprest amount on 1 November 1985.

Note
Your analysis columns should be Wages, Postage, Stationery and Ledger.

(LCC, Book-keeping, autumn, 1985)

5.6   Office Ltd owns a shop that sells typewriters and also repairs office equipment. The following credit sales took place:

Day 1   Sold a typewriter for £300 and stationery for £75 to Gum Ltd.
         Repaired Glue Ltd's typewriter for £100.
Day 2   Sold stationery to Stick Ltd for £70.
Day 3   Sold a typewriter to Fast Ltd for £450.
         Repaired Stick Ltd's typewriter for £50.

Required

Prepare an analysed sales day book for Office Ltd to record the above transactions. The results of each separate activity are to be ascertained.

6
The Double Entry System II: Ledger Accounts and the Trial Balance

INTRODUCTION

The previous chapter explained the manner in which the primary records of flows of goods, services and cash are compiled. This chapter examines how the information on inflows and outflows is recorded by means of the system of double entry book-keeping, thereby enabling control to be exercised and the conversion of prime data into accounting reports.

THE INTERLOCKING EFFECT OF TRANSACTIONS

In Chapter 2 the impact on the balance sheet of a number of transactions was examined. Assets remained equal in value to sources of finance after each transaction, and the relationship

$$A(\text{assets}) = C(\text{capital}) + L(\text{liabilities})$$

remains true in all circumstances. The interlocking effect of transactions is fundamental to the system of double entry book-keeping, and is now given further consideration.

To maintain the relationship $A = C + L$, each transaction must have two equal, but opposite effects. The alternatives are shown in Figure 6.1. A single transaction can affect any of the items listed as *Effect 1* and be paired with any item from the *Effect 2* list. The interlocking effect means that the total value of either of the two impacts must be the same as that of the other.

Figure 6.1 covers changes in assets, liabilities and capital; it can be extended to include revenues and expenses. Items of revenue and expense are recorded separately – the impact of an expense is to decrease capital, and so it is recorded as an effect 1, while revenue increases capital and so is an effect 2. The effects of

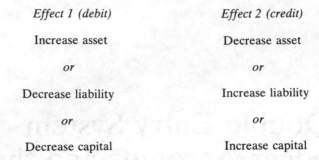

Effect 1 (debit)	Effect 2 (credit)
Increase asset	Decrease asset
or	or
Decrease liability	Increase liability
or	or
Decrease capital	Increase capital

Figure 6.1   Alternative effects on relationship A = C + L

revenues and expenses are compared to calculate the firm's net profit or loss. A net profit is then added to capital and any net loss is deducted from it. Figure 6.2 extends Figure 6.1 to include revenues and expenses. A practical application of the interlocking effect is given in Illustration 6.1.

Effect 1 (debit)	Effect 2 (credit)
Increase asset	Decrease asset
or	or
Decrease liability	Increase liability
or	or
Decrease capital	Increase capital
or	or
Increase expense	Decrease expense
or	or
Decrease revenue	Increase revenue

Figure 6.2   Figure 6.1. extended to include revenues and expenses

Illustration 6.1

The following transactions were undertaken by Bernard Egin, a sole trader, when starting his business:

Transaction number	Description	Value £
1	Introduce cash as capital	1,000
2	Raise a loan for cash	500
3	Buy plant for cash	1,000
4	Buy stock for cash	250

Transaction number	Description	Value
5	Buy stock on credit	350
6a	Sell stock on credit	550
6b	Cost of stock sold	350
7	Collect cash from creditors	550
8	Pay cash to creditors	350
9	Pay cash for general expenses	80

The twofold effect of each of these transactions is as follows:

Transaction number	Value £	Effect 1 (debit)	Effect 2 (credit)
1	1,000	+Asset (cash)	+Capital
2	500	+Asset (cash)	+Loan
3	1,000	+Asset (plant)	−Asset
4	250	+Asset (stock)	−Asset (cash)
5	350	+Asset (stock)	+Liability
6a*	550	+Asset (debtor)	+Revenue
6b*	350	+Expense	−Asset (stock)
7	550	+Asset (cash)	−Asset (debtor)
8	350	−Liability	−Asset (cash)
9	80	+General expenses	−Asset (cash)

Note
* Trading transactions 6a and 6b have the combined effect of producing a gross profit of £200 from which general expenses of £80 (item 9) are deducted to leave a net profit of £120. The net profit is added to capital when the balance sheet is prepared.

Both effect 1 and effect 2 have the same value and so their combined impact on the relationship $C + L = A$ is to leave it in balance. For example, transaction 1 adds £1,000 to each side, while transaction 3 both adds and subtracts £1,000 from the same side; the asset cash is exchanged for the asset plant. Readers should now revise their understanding of the relationship $A = C + L$ by preparing the balance sheet of Egin as it appears after each individual transaction has been completed.

The dual effect of each transaction has given rise to the system of *double entry book-keeping*, under which each transaction is recorded twice: its effect 1 is recorded as a debit and its effect 2 is a credit. The equality between debits and credits holds true even if more than two elements are affected by a single deal. For example, a customer buys and takes away goods for £250. The price is settled by an immediate cash payment of £100, and an agreement to pay the remaining £150 in one month's time. The facts to be recorded at the time of sale together with their impact are as follows:

	Value £	Effect 1	Effect 2
Sales	250		250 + Revenue (sales)
Cash received	100	100 + Asset (cash)	
Creation of debtor	150	150 + Asset (debtor)	
		250	250

There is a credit of £250 and total debits of £250; equality has been sustained.

LEDGER ACCOUNTS

The practical operation of a set of double entry books to record transactions involves the use of a separate record for each type of revenue, expenditure, asset and liability. Each record is named according to the item to which it relates, and is known as an 'account', for example, each company maintains a cash account, as described in Chapter 5, in which all inflows and outflows of cash are recorded. The guiding principle that must be followed when designing a system of accounts is that it must provide the information needed to prepare the accounting statements, which comprise at least a trading and profit and loss account and a balance sheet. The complete set of accounts kept by a firm is called its 'ledger', and this term is also used to refer to particular groups of the accounts, such as the 'debtors' ledger' and the 'nominal ledger'.

'T' accounts

The ledger accounts in which business transactions are recorded are known as 'T' accounts, a name derived from each account's appearance, as is apparent from the following examples. The T account represents an open ledger and has two sides – the left is used to record debits and the right credits. An example, containing no accounting entries, is shown in Figure 6.3.

Debit	Credit
£	£

Figure 6.3   A 'T' account

We can now return to the transactions of Bernard Egin given in Illustration 6.1. The first was the introduction into his firm of capital in the form of cash of £1,000. The two accounts needed to record this transaction are 'cash' and 'capital'; cash, an asset, is increased by an inflow of £1,000 and so is debited with this sum, while capital, the liability to ownership, is increased by £1,000 and the account is credited. The accounts appear as follows when the transaction has been entered:

Cash Account

Debit	Credit
£	£
Capital 1,000	

Capital Account

Debit	Credit
£	£
	Cash 1,000

Note that a system of cross-reference is used whereby, in each account, the location of the corresponding entry is named. Thus, for this transaction, the credit entry corresponding to the debit entry in the cash account can easily be traced to the capital account. This referencing is necessary as the separate accounts would not necessarily be adjacent to each other in the ledger.

Example 6.1

The transactions undertaken by B. Egin, given in Illustration 6.1, are reproduced for ease of reference:

Transaction number	Description	Value £
1	Introduce cash as capital	1,000
2	Raise a loan for cash	500
3	Buy plant for cash	1,000
4	Buy stock for cash	250
5	Buy stock on credit	350
6a	Sell stock on credit	550
6b	Cost of stock sold	350
7	Collect cash from debtors	550
8	Pay cash to creditors	350
9	Pay general expenses in cash	80

Required

Record the transactions of B. Egin in a set of T accounts. Insert the transaction number before each item. (The impact of each item is given in Illustration 6.1 above.)

Solution

Cash Account

	Debit	£		Credit	£
1	Capital	1,000	3	Plant	1,000
2	Loan	500	4	Stock	250
7	Debtor	550	8	Creditor	350
			9	General expenses	80

Capital Account

	Debit	£		Credit	£
			1	Cash	1,000

Loan Account

	Debit	£		Credit	£
			2	Cash	500

Plant Account

	Debit			Credit	
		£			£
3	Cash	1,000			

Stock Account

	Debit			Credit	
		£			£
4	Cash	250	6b	Cost of goods sold	350
5	Creditors	350			

Creditors Account

	Debit			Credit	
		£			£
8	Cash	350	5	Stock	350

Debtors Account

	Debit			Credit	
		£			£
6a	Sales	550	7	Cash	550

Sales Account

	Debit			Credit	
		£			£
			6a	Debtor	550

Cost of goods sold*

	Debit			Credit	
		£			£
6b	Stock	350			

General expenses Account

	Debit			Credit	
		£			£
9	Cash	80			

Note
*In this example, the asset 'stock' is converted to the expense 'cost of goods sold' at the time of sale. In practice, the cost of goods sold is found by preparing a trading account in which purchases are adjusted for opening and closing stocks. See Chapter 7 for the explanation of how to achieve this using double entry techniques.

At the end of the accounting period, the accountant prepares the profit and loss account and balance sheet and, at this stage, it is necessary first to balance each of the accounts in the manner described in Chapter 5. The balances on the accounts that relate to items of revenue and expense are then transferred to the trading and profit and loss accounts where the net result of trading is calculated; the balances remaining, together with the net result of trading, are then used to compile the balance sheet.

Example 6.2

Required

(a) List the balances from the ledger accounts in Example 6.1 in two columns, one for debit balances and one for credit balances.
(b) Prepare B. Egin's trading and profit and loss accounts and balance sheet from the balances listed in answer to part (a).

Solution

(a)

	Debit £	Credit £
Cash	370	
Capital		1,000
Loan		500
Plant	1,000	
Stock	250	
Sales		550
Cost of goods sold	350	
General expenses	80	
	2,050	2,050

Notes
1. There are no debtors or creditors as, in this instance, their inflows and outflows are exactly equal in value and so cancel each other out.
2. The debit balances are equal in value to the credit balances; this provides a check of accuracy, the importance of which is discussed later in this chapter.

(b) Trading and Profit and Loss Account

	£
Sales	550
Less: Cost of goods sold	350
Gross profit	200
Less: General expenses	80
Net profit	120

Balance Sheet of Bernard Egin

	£			£	£
Capital			*Fixed assets*		
At start of period	0		Plant		1,000
Introduced	1,000		*Current assets*		
Profit for period	120		Stock	250	
	———		Cash	370	
	1,120			———	
Loan	500				620
	———				———
	1,620				1,620
	———				———

The balances carried forward in the sales, cost of goods sold and general expenses accounts are zero. The transactions that were entered in them relate to a period of time; at the end of the period the accounts are cleared to the trading and profit and loss account and appear as follows:

Sales Account

	£		£
Transfer to trading account	550	Balance b/d	550

Cost of goods sold Account

	£		£
Balance b/d	350	Transfer to trading account	350

General expenses Account

	£		£
Balance b/d	80	Transfer to profit and loss account	80

Once the balances on all the accounts cleared to the trading and profit and loss account have reverted to zero, these accounts are ready to accumulate information for the next period. The assets and liabilities shown in the balance sheet are carried forward to the next accounting period in their individual accounts where they are adjusted for any changes which then occur.

Alternative formats for ledger accounts

The advent of machine and, more recently, computer-based systems of accounting have resulted in a move away from the T-account format, although all of the rules of double entry are still complied with. There are a number of possible alternatives, for example, there may be separate columns for debits and credits or the transactions in an account may be listed with credits identified by an asterisk. One rule that must be observed is that, irrespective of the method used to distinguish debits from credits, it must be consistently applied. Figure 6.4 lists three ways for recording the same information in a mechanized or computerized cash account.

	1		2	3		
	Debit £	Credit £	£	Debit £	Credit £	Balance £
Opening balance	500		500DR			500DR
Cash from sales	1,250		1,250DR	1,250		
Cash for purchases		1,000	1,000CR		1,000	
Closing balance	750		750DR			750DR

Figure 6.4   Three ways of recording in a mechanized or computerized cash account

The ledger in practice

Accounts can be classified into the types shown in Figure 6.5. Personal accounts are those that record the relationship between the entity and outsiders, such as debtors, creditors and investors. There should be a separate account for each individual who owes money to or is owed money by the company so that it can be established how much to demand or pay respectively.

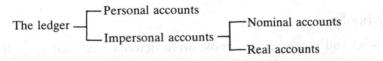

Figure 6.5   Classification of accounts

Impersonal accounts are either nominal accounts or real accounts:

Nominal accounts contain all of the items that are transferred to the trading and profit and loss account and so include such items as sales, purchases, wages and expenses.

Real accounts are used for the non-personal assets of the company, such as cash, stock and fixed assets.

Personal accounts should be first classified according to general type such as trade debtors, trade creditors, debenture holders and capital. Normally total, or control, accounts are maintained in the main ledger for each of these classes, and subsidiary, or memorandum, ledgers kept for individual details (see later in this chapter). Some of the real accounts can be treated in the same way, so that while the main ledger contains such general accounts as plant and machinery and stock, they are backed up by a register of plant and machinery or stock records to show the detail that comprises their total value.

The decision as to which nominal accounts to use should be based on a compromise between providing information that is of little use, because it is too general, or alternatively giving too much detail. The exact selection is based on the type of activity the business undertakes and the items management wishes to monitor and control, but in general the rule applies that accounts should be opened in respect of all items that are likely to be material (see Chapter 8). For example, it would not be deemed important in normal circumstances to identify individually the costs of petrol and motor insurance since they are both consequent upon running a vehicle and are reported under the heading 'motor expenses'. The income derived from sales made in the normal course of trade, however, should be distinguished from the proceeds of the sale of fixed assets. A failure to distinguish between them would mask the sources of revenue and would be seriously misleading if, for example, a large amount had been derived from the sale of a surplus piece of land that had been held as a fixed asset.

BOOKS OF PRIME ENTRY

It is unwieldy to attempt to enter each individual flow of cash, goods or services in the accounts ledger. To overcome this problem each transaction is entered, in the first instance, in a 'book of prime entry'. The initial record of transactions is made in either a day book, the cash book or the journal; each of these is now considered in turn.

Day books

The sales and purchases day books were described in Chapter 5. It is also advisable to use day books for any type of transaction that occurs frequently, such as the return of goods sold from customers who decide not to keep them (returns inwards) and the return of goods purchased to suppliers (returns outwards). Day books are used to summarize the flows of goods and services into and out of the company in order to generate entries for the appropriate ledger accounts. The sales day book must produce:

1. the value of debtors created from sales to be debited to the debtors account; and
2. the value of credit sales to be credited in the sales account, possibly analysed according to type of sale.

The purchases day book creates:

1. the total to be credited to the creditors account; and
2. the values to be debited to the various expense and asset accounts.

For example, the following are the totals from a purchases day book:

Total	Goods for resale	Stationery	Motor van (fixed asset)
£	£	£	£
18,450	11,500	500	6,450

The totals of the analysis columns add up to the total value, and are entered in the following ledger accounts:

	Debit	Credit
	£	£
Goods for resale (increase asset)	11,500	
Stationery (expense)	500	
Motor van (increase asset)	6,450	
Creditors (increase liability)		18,450
	18,450	18,450

There should be clear cross-referencing between the books of prime entry and the accounts so that the trail can be retraced if necessary. A note should be made in the day book of the account, and its location, to which the figures are posted. The entry in the accounts should refer to the source of the figure, preferably also stating the page in the book of prime entry on which it can be found.

The cash book and discounts

The cash book, unlike the day books, is itself a ledger account; it is therefore necessary only to complete the corresponding double entry for the transactions it contains. At the end of the accounting period the cash book is balanced and the result entered in the balance sheet. Again, only the analysis totals need to be posted and not each separate transaction. For example, the following are the totals from an analysed cash book:

Cash Book

Receipts			Payments			
Total	Debtors	Cash sale	Total	Wages	Creditors	Rent
£	£	£	£	£	£	£
5,000	3,500	1,500	4,000	1,000	2,500	500

The total of cash received, £5,000, is already debited in the ledger as the result of including it in the total column of the cash book, and so the double entry is completed by making the following credit entries:

	£	
Sales (revenue)	1,500	(credit)
Debtors (reduce asset)	3,500	(credit)

The entries to complete the record of the effect of cash payments are:

	£	
Wages (expense)	1,000	(debit)
Creditors (reduce liability)	2,500	(debit)
Rent (expense)	500	(debit)

The cash balance of £1,000 (£5,000 debit − £4,000 credit) is entered in the balance sheet as a current asset.

The petty cash book (see Chapter 5) is also part of the double entry accounts, and is operated in the same way as the main cash book. The totals of its analysis columns are posted to the ledger accounts, and its balance is entered in the balance sheet.

The full value of each sale made on credit is entered in the debtors account, and in some cases this may be cleared by the receipt of cash together with the grant of a discount for prompt payment, that is, the cash received is less than the value of the debt. To remove the full amount of indebtedness shown in the debtors account it is necessary to credit the account with the value of the discount; the corresponding debit is to the 'discounts allowed account' in which all such discounts are accumulated. The balance on this account is transferred to the profit and loss account when the periodic accounting reports are prepared. If, alternatively, the company takes a discount offered by a supplier, the creditors account is debited and the 'discounts received account' is credited; the balance on the latter account is income and is credited to the profit and loss account. Where, as is the case with discounts given for purchasing large quantities, the discount is received as a reduction in price, that is, a trade discount, no entry in the discount column is needed as the amount invoiced is reduced by the discount. The procedure for recording discounts for prompt payment is illustrated in Example 6.3.

Example 6.3

Seller sells goods on credit to Buyer for £500. A discount of 4 per cent may be taken if the debt is settled within ten days.

Required

On the assumption that the discount is taken, prepare:

(a)   the debtor and discount accounts in Seller's books; and
(b)   the creditor and discount accounts in Buyer's books.

Solution

(a) The books of Seller:

Debtor Account

	£		£
Sales	500	Cash	480
		Discounts allowed	20
	500		500

Discounts Allowed Account

	£		£
Debtor	20		

(b) The books of Buyer:

Creditor Account

	£		£
Cash	480	Purchases	500
Discounts received	20		
	500		500

Discounts Received Account

	£		£
		Creditor	20

It is quite likely that a large number of discounts will be received and allowed during an accounting period. To save time, each transaction is not recorded separately; instead, discounts allowed and received are accumulated in the cash book and transferred to the ledger at the end of the period. Example 6.4 shows how this method is operated. It should be noted that the cash book record of discounts is purely memorandum.

Example 6.4

Disco owes £400 to Dancer and £760 to Tapper. He is owed £540 by Jumper and £880 by Runner. Prepare the cash book for Disco on the assumption that all of the above debts are settled subject to a 5 per cent prompt payment discount.

Solution

Cash Book – Disco

	Discount allowed	Cash		Discount received	Cash
	£	£		£	£
Jumper – debtor	27	513	Dancer – creditor	20	380
Runner – debtor	44	836	Tapper – creditor	38	722
	—	——		—	——
	71	1,349		58	1,102

The cash received of £1,349 is credited to the debtors account and the £1,102 cash paid is debited to the creditors account; this completes the double entry in both cases. Since the columns in which the discounts are recorded are only memorandum, it is necessary to make both debit and credit entries in respect of their contents. The total of discounts allowed, £71, is debited to the discounts allowed account and credited to the debtors account while the £58 of discounts received is debited to the creditors account and credited to discounts received. In all cases the value of the discount plus the amount of cash flow is equal to the total amount of indebtedness.

It is useful to keep the discounts received and discounts allowed in separate accounts, rather than to net them, so that the cost of granting discounts and the benefit of taking them can be easily identified and their impact assessed. If discounts allowed rise in value, the question should be asked whether the terms are too generous, and the benefits of taking discounts must be weighed against the alternative advantages of retaining the cash in the business for a longer period of time.

The three-column cash book

Chapter 5 covered the operation of a double- or two-column cash book in which separate columns are used to record the flows of cash in hand and cash at bank. It is possible to add an extra column to create a three-column cash book; the additional column is used to record discounts allowed and received in the manner explained above. The use of a three-column cash book is shown in Example 6.5.

Example 6.5

Henry York is a sole trader who keeps records of his cash and bank transactions in a three-column cash book. His transactions for the month of March 1986 were as follows:

March
1   Cash in hand £100. Cash at bank £5,672.
4   York received from W. Abbot a cheque for £246 that was paid directly into the bank.

March (cont.)

6   Paid wages in cash £39.
8   Sold goods for cash £152.
10   Received cheque from G. Smart for £315, in full settlement of a debt of £344; this was paid directly into the bank.
11   Paid sundry expenses in cash £73.
14   Purchased goods by cheque £406.
18   Paid J. Sanders a cheque of £185 in full settlement of a debt of £201.
23   Withdrew £100 from the bank for office purposes.
24   Paid wages in cash £39.
26   Sold goods for cash £94.
28   Paid salaries by cheque £230.
31   Retained in office cash amounting to £150 and paid the remainder into the bank.

Required

(a)   Enter the above transactions in the three-column cash book of Henry York.
(b)   Balance the cash book at 31 March 1986 and bring down the balances.

(LCCI, Book-Keeping, summer, 1986)

(See p. 104 for solution.)

The journal

There are a few transactions not entered in the cash or day books, and these are instead initially entered in the 'journal'. The use of a journal ensures that every entry in the ledger first passes through a book of prime entry, which fully explains the nature of the transaction. Each entry in the journal should be authorized to ensure that no unsanctioned changes are made in the ledger. Journal entries are likely to be relatively small in number, and include such items as the following:

1. *Transfers* These occur when it is necessary to transfer value from one account to another, for example, to correct a mistake made in the original posting that placed the entry in the wrong account.
2. *Adjustments* The original entry may be made in the correct account in the light of prevailing knowledge, but circumstances may change and require a further entry. For example, a debtor is created when a credit sale is made but if, at a later date, it becomes apparent that the money will not be collected, the debt must be written off by transfer to the bad debts account, since it no longer represents an asset. (Bad debts are considered further in Chapter 7.)
3. *Closing entries* Adjusting entries must be made at the accounting date to enable the periodic accounts to be drawn up. (These are dealt with in Chapter 7.)

Solution (to Example 6.5)

Henry York Cash Book

Debit side

	Details	Discount allowed £	Cash in hand £	Cash at bank £
March				
1	Balance b/d		100	5,672
4	W Abbot			246
8	Sales		152	
10	G. Smart	29		315
23	Bank		100	
26	Sales		94	
31	Cash			145
		29	446	6,378
April				
1	Balance b/d		150	5,441

Credit side

	Details	Discount received £	Cash in hand £	Cash at bank £
March				
6	Wages		39	
11	Sundry expenses		73	
14	Purchases			406
18	J. Sanders	16		185
23	Cash			100
24	Wages		39	
28	Salaries		145	
31	Bank			230
31	Balance c/d		150	5,457
		16	446	6,378

The debit and credit entry for each transaction is entered in the journal together with a brief narrative to explain its purpose. Example 6.6 shows some specimen entries.

Example 6.6

A. Jones, a trader, wishes to record the following in his firm's ledger:

(a) The correction of a wrong posting that entered the purchase of a fixed asset costing £1,000 in the purchase of goods for resale account.
(b) The accrual of rent due for three months of £50.
(c) The introduction by A. Jones of capital in the form of a fixed asset worth £2,500.

Required

Prepare the journal entries to enter the above facts in the firm's ledger accounts.

Solution

The journal entries are as follows:

A. Jones – Journal

	Debit (DR*) £	Credit (CR*) £
(a) Fixed assets	1,000	
Purchases		1,000
Narrative: Transfer to fixed assets of incorrect posting		
(b) Rent	50	
Landlord		50
Narrative: Rent due for three months		
(c) Fixed assets	2,500	
A. Jones – Capital		2,500
Narrative: Introduction of capital in the form of a fixed asset		

Note
* 'DR' and 'CR' are usual abbreviations for the words 'debit' and 'credit' respectively.

Although for practical purposes, the use of the journal is restricted to those cases where there is no other appropriate book of prime entry, it is theoretically possible to record all entries in journal form, and an exercise on these lines provides a useful way for examiners to test students' understanding of double entry accounting without calling for the preparation of a full set of T accounts. For example, the transactions of Bernard Egin given in Illustration 6.1 can be recorded in journal form:

Bernard Egin – Journal

Transaction Number		Debit	Credit
		£	£
1.	Cash	1,000	
	Capital		1,000
	Receipt of capital in the form of cash		
2.	Cash	500	
	Loan		500
	Loan raised		
3.	Plant	1,000	
	Cash		1,000
	Purchase of plant for cash		
4.	Stock	250	
	Cash		250
	Purchase of stock for cash		
5.	Stock	350	
	Creditor		350
	Purchase of stock on credit		
6(a)	Debtor	550	
&(b)	Sales		550
	Cost of goods sold	350	
	Stock		350
	Sale of goods on credit		
7.	Cash	550	
	Debtors		550
	Collection of cash from debtors		
8.	Creditors	350	
	Cash		350
	Payment of cash to creditors		
9.	General expenses	80	
	Cash		80
	Payment of general expenses in cash		

These entries can be checked to the T accounts in Example 6.1.

CONTROL ACCOUNTS FOR DEBTORS AND CREDITORS

Businesses require two types of information about debtors and creditors:

1. Their total values must be made available both to provide a record of the total amount due to and by the company and to provide the figures for inclusion in the balance sheet.

2. The amount owed to each individual creditor and by each debtor is needed for day-to-day control; the correct amount must be paid or claimed in each case.

The required information is produced by maintaining two records – in the main double entry ledger 'control' or 'total' accounts are kept, which provide the overall values of debtors and creditors, while memorandum debtors and creditors ledgers contain a separate account for each individual debtor and creditor. (The debtors ledger is also referred to as the sales ledger and the creditors ledger is also known as the purchase ledger.) The debtors and creditors ledgers are referred to as 'memorandum' as they are subsidiary to, and do not form part of, the main double entry system.

Records of debtors and creditors

The memorandum accounts for debtors and creditors are written up from the day books and cash book using the entries for each separate transaction. The control accounts in the double entry ledger are compiled using totals from the books of prime entry. Example 6.7 shows the operation of this system for sales; the same method is applicable to purchases.

Example 6.7

Use the following information to prepare (a) a single-column sales day book; (b) the cash book (receipts side only); (c) the debtors control account; and (d) the individual memorandum debtor accounts.

Customer	Balance 1 March	Sales during March	Goods returned	Cash received	Discounts
	£	£	£	£	£
Page	100	150	–	98	2
Book	125	130	10	79	1
Volume	150	160	–	150	–
	375				

Solution

(a) **Sales day book**

	£
Page	150
Book	130
Volume	160
	440

The total figure for credit sales is credited to the credit sales account and debited to the sales ledger control account. The individual transactions are debited to the individual memorandum debtor accounts.

(b) Cash book (debit side)

	Cash £	Discounts £
Page	98	2
Book	79	1
Volume	150	—
	327	3

The total figure for cash received is credited to the sales ledger control account; the individual amounts are credited to the memorandum debtor accounts. The total discount figure is credited to the sales ledger control account; the individual amounts are credited to the individual memorandum debtor accounts.

(c) Sales Ledger (Debtor) Control Account

	£		£
Balance b/d	375	Cash book	327
Sales day book	440	Discounts allowed	3
		Returns inwards	10
		Balance c/d	475
	815		815

(d) Page Account

	£		£
Balance b/d	100	Cash	98
Sales day book	150	Discounts allowed	2
		Balance c/d	150
	250		250

Book Account

	£		£
Balance b/d	125	Cash	79
Sales day book	130	Discounts allowed	1
		Returns inwards	10
		Balance c/d	165
	255		255

Volume Account

	£		£
Balance b/d	150	Cash	150
Sales day book	160	Balance c/d	160
	310		310

Reconciling the control account

The use of control accounts for customers and suppliers reduces the number of entries in the main ledger and enables a cross-check to be performed. The total of the balances on the individual memorandum accounts should agree with the single balance of the control account. Agreement on these lines based on the figures in Example 6.7 is:

	£
Balances from individual accounts:	
Page	150
Book	165
Volume	160
Balance as per control account	475

The maintenance of the memorandum debtors and creditors ledgers can be delegated to a responsible person who has no access to the main ledger, which is likely to contain many confidential entries. Where this system is operated, the personnel in charge of the debtors and creditors ledgers should periodically supply a list of balances to the official responsible for the control accounts, who can then check that the totals agree. Any difference must be investigated, but there is the possibility that the totals may agree despite the fact that an error has been made, for example, an invoice may have been posted to the wrong debtor account. However, such an error should be identified when the incorrect amount is demanded from a customer who has been wrongly charged for the goods in question.

Example 6.8

A list of the balances on the memorandum individual personal accounts in a company's sales ledger at 31 December 19X6 had a total of £305,640. This did not agree with the balance on the sales ledger control account at that date of £325,000. The following errors were discovered:

1. A sales invoice of £12,900, included in the sales day book, had not been posted to the personal account in the sales ledger.

2. Discounts allowed to customers of £1,260 had been credited to the individual accounts in the sales ledger, but no other entries had been made in the books.
3. The returns inwards day book had been wrongly totalled; it was over-cast by £3,000.
4. A sales invoice of £9,400 had been entirely omitted from the books.
5. A debit balance of £7,400 on the personal account of a customer had been included in the list of balances as £4,700.
6. The balance on a customer's account in the sales ledger of £5,500 had been omitted from the list of balances.

Required

(a) Write up the control account to correct it for those errors by which it is affected.
(b) Revise the total value of the list of balances in respect of those errors by which it is affected.

Solution

(a) **Sales Ledger Control Account**

19X6		£	19X6		£
31 Dec.	Balance b/d	325,000	31 Dec.	Discounts allowed (2)	1,260
	Returns inwards (3)	3,000		Balance c/d	336,140
	Sales (4)	9,400			
		337,400			337,400

(b)

	£
Value of list of balances	305,640
Invoice not in memorandum account (1)	12,900
Invoice omitted (4)	9,400
Balance wrongly extracted (7,400−4,700) (5)	2,700
Balance omitted (6)	5,500
Correct value of debtors	336,140

Note
The same closing balance now appears in the control account and the list of balances; the results obtained from the two separate sources of information have therefore been reconciled.

The control account is likely to include the following entries in addition to those for sales, cash and discounts:

1. *Credit balances on the debtors ledger and debit balances on the creditors ledger* For example, if a customer overpays, the account in the debtors ledger will be a credit. These balances should be carried down separately in the control account and added to creditors in the balance sheet.
2. *Bad debts* Some debtors are unable to pay, and the amounts they owe are known as bad debts. These balances must be removed from debtors, by a journal entry, as they no longer represent an asset.
3. *Settlement by contra* A firm may both buy from and sell to another company; this gives rise to a debtor account and creditor account in the same name. The balances on the two accounts may be set off, and the net balance settled for cash.
4. *Interest on overdue debts* When a debtor is very slow to pay, a firm may, by agreement, charge interest on the debt; this is added to the amount owed.
5. *Returns* Goods may be returned either to or by the company; the related debt must be cancelled.

Example 6.9

Singer Ltd maintains memorandum debtors and creditors ledgers in which the individual accounts of customers and suppliers are kept. The following information relates to 19X1:

	£
Debit balances on debtors control account 1 January 19X1	66,300
Credit balances on creditors control account 1 January 19X1	50,600
Sundry credit balances on debtors ledger 1 January 19X1	724
Goods purchased on credit	257,919
Goods sold on credit	323,614
Cash received from debtors	299,149
Cash paid to creditors	210,522
Discounts received	2,663
Discounts allowed	2,930
Cash purchases	3,627
Cash sales	5,922
Bad debts written off	3,651
Interest charged on overdue debtor accounts	277
Returns outwards	2,926
Returns inwards	2,805
Accounts settled by contra between debtor and creditor ledgers	1,106
Sundry credit balances on debtors ledger 31 December 19X1	815
Sundry debit balances on creditors ledger 31 December 19X1	698

Required

Prepare the debtors control account and the creditors control account as they would appear in the company's ledger at 31 December 19X1.

Solution

Debtors (Sales Ledger) Control Account

19X1		£	19X1		£
1 Jan.	Balance b/d	66,300	1 Jan.	Balance b/d	724
	Sales	323,614		Cash	299,149
	Interest	277		Discounts allowed	2,930
31 Dec.	Balance c/d	815		Bad debts	3,651
				Returns inwards	2,805
				Contra – creditors	1,106
			31 Dec.	Balance c/d	80,641
		391,006			391,006
19X2			19X2		
1 Jan.	Balance b/d	80,641	1 Jan.	Balance b/d	815

Creditors (Purchase Ledger) Control Account

19X1		£	19X1		£
	Cash	210,522	1 Jan.	Balance b/d	50,600
	Discounts received	2,663		Purchases	257,919
	Returns outwards	2,926	31 Dec.	Balance c/d	698
	Contra debtors	1,106			
31 Dec.	Balance c/d	92,000			
		309,217			309,217
19X2			19X2		
1 Jan.	Balance b/d	698	1 Jan.	Balance b/d	92,000

Note
The cash sales and cash purchases do not appear in the control accounts. They do not affect the recorded value of debtors or creditors.

Reconciliation with suppliers' statements

Monthly statements should be sent to customers reminding them of the amount due and requesting payment. The customer can then compare this document with the information contained in his or her own ledger. The balances on the statement and in the customers' books are unlikely to be the same, for example, the customer may not have received certain goods appearing on the statement, and so a reconciliation must be prepared. In the same way, the company should receive details of their account from suppliers, and these should be checked with the creditors account in the company's books. This procedure is similar to the preparation of the bank reconciliation (dealt with in Chapter 5) and is illustrated in Example 6.10.

Example 6.10

Included in the creditors ledger of J. Cross – a shop-keeper – is the following account, which disclosed that the amount owing to one of his suppliers at 31 May 1984 was £472.13.

Creditors Ledger
Nala Merchandising Company

1984			£	1984			£
May	18	Purchases returns	36.67	May 1		Balance b/d	862.07
	27	Purchases returns	18.15	16		Purchases	439.85
	27	Adjustment		25		Purchases	464.45
		(overcharge)	5.80	25		Adjustment	
	31	Discount received	24.94			(undercharge)	13.48
	31	Bank	1,222.16				
	31	Balance c/d	472.13				
			£1,779.85				£1,779.85

		June 1	Balance b/d	472.13

In the first week of June 1984, J. Cross received a statement (shown below) from the supplier, which showed an amount owing of £2,424.53.

J. Cross
in account with
Nala Merchandising Company
Statement of Account

			Debit	Credit	
1984			£	£	£
May	1	BCE			1,538.70 Dr.
	3	DISC		13.40	1,525.30 Dr.
		CHQ		634.11	891.19 Dr.
	5	ALLCE		29.12	862.07 Dr.
	7	GDS	256.72		1,118.79 Dr.
	10	GDS	108.33		1,227.12 Dr.
	11	GDS	74.80		1,301.92 Dr.
	14	ADJ	13.48		1,315.40 Dr.
	18	GDS	162.55		1,477.95 Dr.
	23	GDS	301.90		1,779.85 Dr.
	25	ALLCE		36.67	1,743.18 Dr.
	28	GDS	134.07		1,877.25 Dr.
	29	GDS	251.12		2,128.37 Dr.
	30	GDS	204.80		2,333.17 Dr.
	31	GDS	91.36		2,424.53 Dr.
	31	BCE			2,424.53 Dr.

Abbreviations
BCE = Balance;   CHQ = Cheque;   GDS = Goods;   ALLCE = Allowance;
DISC = Discount; ADJ = Adjustment.

Required

Prepare a statement reconciling the closing balance on the supplier's account in the creditors' ledger with the closing balance shown on the statement of account submitted by the supplier.

(CACA, Level 1 Accounting, December, 1984)

Solution

	£	£
Balance per creditors ledger		472.13
Add items on statement not in account:		
May 28 Goods	134.07	
May 29 Goods	251.12	
May 30 Goods	204.80	
May 31 Goods	91.36	
		681.35
		1,153.48
Add items in account not on statement:		
May 31 Paid	1,222.16	
May 31 Discount	24.94	
May 27 Goods returned	18.15	
May 27 Overcharge	5.80	
		1,271.05
Balance per statement		2,424.53

Notes
1. The opening balance on the supplier's account in the creditors ledger and the statement balance on 5 May are the same, and so at that point the records are in agreement.
2. Some purchases are combined for entry in the supplier's account: the purchases entered on May 16 of £439.85 consist of the statement entries of May 7 (£256.72), 10 (£108.33) and 11 (£74.80); the purchases entered on May 25 of £464.45 consist of the statement entries of May 18 (£162.55) and 23 (£301.90).

THE TRIAL BALANCE

A set of books maintained in accordance with the double entry method provides a comprehensive and appropriately analysed record of all the transactions undertaken by an entity. This record not only enables the day-to-day control of such items as debtors and creditors, but also provides the basis from which the final accounting statements, namely the trading and profit and loss account and balance sheet, are prepared.

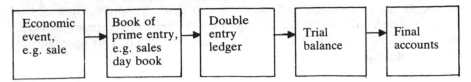

| Economic event, e.g. sale | → | Book of prime entry, e.g. sales day book | → | Double entry ledger | → | Trial balance | → | Final accounts |

Figure 6.6 Process by which an economic event becomes part of final accounting statement

The process by which an economic event becomes included in the final accounting statement is as shown in Figure 6.6. It can be seen that the stage prior to the production of the statements from the ledger (covered in Chapter 7) is the preparation of a trial balance. This is a list of all the balances remaining at the end of the accounting period on the many accounts contained in the main ledger; the balances are entered in separate columns according to whether they are debit balances or credit balances. The two columns should possess the same total value since each entry in the books consists of a debit and a credit of equal value and, as described earlier in this chapter, leaves the relationship $C + L = A$ in balance. Although it was not described as such, Example 6.2 part (a) shows the trial balance of Bernard Egin.

Readers should now work Questions 6.1 to 6.6 at the end of this chapter.

The fact that the trial balance shows equal totals for both debit and credit balances does not necessarily mean that it is correct, since there are some errors that are not revealed by an imbalance. These are as follows:

1. *Error of principle* An entry may be made in the wrong account, for example, wages may be debited to purchases.
2. *Duplication* Both the debits and credits for a transaction could be entered in the accounts twice.
3. *Omissions* A transaction may be omitted altogether.
4. *Compensatory errors* There may be two or more errors, the effects of which cancel each other out.
5. *Error in the original entry* An incorrect figure may be used as the basis for the double entry record.

The suspense account

The trial balance, when it is first extracted, does not always balance, and it is then obvious that some error has been made. The first step to discover the mistake is to review all the balances to ensure that they have been extracted correctly from the books. The next step is to check that subsidiary memorandum ledgers, for such items as debtors and creditors, have been reconciled with their control accounts. Any discrepancy would indicate a likely area in which the error is to be found. Finally, if the difference is material enough to make its discovery essential, a more thorough checking of the records of prime entry to the ledger must be carried out. So as not to delay the preparation of the accounts, a difference on the trial balance may be placed in a suspense account, which is cleared after investigations have been completed. This procedure is shown in Example 6.11.

Example 6.11

The trial balance of Wrong at 31 December, as first compiled, contained total debits of £197,500 and total credits of £210,000. The difference of £12,500 was placed to the debit of a suspense account to balance the trial balance. Subsequent investigation revealed the following errors:

1. The balance from the cash book of £3,750 had not been entered in the trial balance.
2. The debtors balance had been wrongly recorded as £71,560 instead of £75,160.
3. A fixed asset purchased for £10,000 had been credited to the fixed asset account instead of being debited.
4. The previous year's profit of £14,850 had not been added to the profit and loss account balance brought forward.

Required

Prepare the suspense account to record the correction of the errors.

Solution

Suspense Account

	£		£
Difference on trial balance	12,500	Cash (1)	3,750
Profit and loss account (4)	14,850	Debtors (2)	3,600
		Fixed assets (3)	20,000
	27,350		27,350

Note

The suspense account now has no value left on it, and the double entry is completed within the trial balance with the following effects:

1. Cash of £3,750 appears as an asset.
2. Debtors are increased by £3,600, to their correct value of £75,160.
3. The incorrect entry in the fixed asset account of £10,000 is cancelled and the correct debit entry of £10,000 is substituted. Note that the total effect of this error was to understate fixed assets by £20,000.

4. The profit and loss account balance is increased by £14,850, being the previous year's profit omitted.

ADVANTAGES OF DOUBLE ENTRY

The double entry system is very flexible. In this chapter reference has been made to books of account and pages within these books. The records could, in practice, be kept on separate cards or be produced as computer print-outs. Whichever method of operation is employed, however, the benefits derived from the use of double entry are as follows:

1. It enables all types of transactions undertaken by the business, which can be expressed in monetary terms, to be recorded. Provided an economic event has a measurable financial impact, it can be entered into the double entry framework.
2. It enables large numbers of transactions to be recorded in an orderly manner; similar transactions are grouped together.
3. Economic events are recorded both from the personal point of view (that is, their impact on the relationship between the entity and outsiders) and also from their impersonal aspect (that is, their effect on the company itself in terms of assets owned, revenue and expenses).
4. The debits entered to record a particular transaction must be of equal value to the credits. This equality enables a trial balance to be prepared that gives an initial check on the arithmetical accuracy of the records, although there are errors that are not revealed.
5. The trial balance, an end product of the double entry system, is the basis for the preparation of the trading and profit and loss account and balance sheet. The former of these gives an indication of the return made by the entity on the resources invested in it, while the latter presents a picture of the extent to which management has carried out its custodial duties in the form of a statement of the financial position.

Readers should now work Questions 6.7 to 6.10 at the end of this chapter.

QUESTIONS

Questions 6.1 to 6.6 trace the transactions of a business from the opening balances of the accounting period through to the closing trial balance. The remaining questions test other aspects covered in this chapter.

6.1   The following are the balances on the accounts of Radio on 1 January:

Credit balances

	£	£
Capital		8,500
Trade creditors:		
Tele	2,300	
Trany	1,000	
Valve	1,300	
		4,600
		13,100

Debit balances

	£	£
Plant and machinery at written-down value		4,500
Stock		2,700
Debtors:		
Vision	2,500	
Sister	1,500	
Batty	1,200	
		5,200
Cash		700
		13,100

Required

Prepare the journal entries to record the opening balances in Radio's books on
1 January.

6.2   During January, Radio undertook the following transactions:

Credit transactions with customers during January

Customer	Sales	Returns inwards	Cash received	Prompt payment Discount
	£	£	£	£
Vision	7,000	300	6,350	50
Sister	4,000	–	3,500	40
Batty	2,700	200	2,600	25
Flat	200	–	–	–
Broke	300	–	–	–

Credit transactions with suppliers during January

Supplier	Detail	Purchases	Returns outwards	Cash paid	Prompt payment discount
		£	£	£	£
Tele	Goods for resale	3,000	—	2,950	55
Trany	Goods for resale	2,000	100	1,950	35
Valve	Goods for resale	2,400	150	2,200	20
Garage	Motor expenses	100	—	—	—
Paper	Office supplies	50	—	—	—

Other cash transactions during January:

Payee	Detail	£
Plantmax	Purchase of plant	1,000
Cash	Wages	1,500
Accom.	Rent for 6 months to 30 June	600
Supplies	Office expenses	250
Garage	Motor expenses	300

£100 was received from Scrap for machinery that was disposed of.

Required

Enter this information in the books of prime entry, i.e. the day books and cash book.

6.3   Use the information in Questions 6.1 and 6.2 to prepare the ledger accounts, other than cash, in Radio's main ledger.

6.4   Use the information in Questions 6.1 and 6.2 to prepare the memorandum debtors and creditors ledger.

6.5   Use the information in Questions 6.3 and 6.4 to prepare reconciliations of the purchases and sales ledger accounts with their memorandum ledgers.

6.6   Prepare Radio's trial balance from the accounts produced in Questions 6.2 and 6.3.

6.7   (a) Define and distinguish, with examples, the following three classifications of ledger accounts:
   (i)   Real accounts.
   (ii)   Personal accounts.
   (iii) Nominal accounts.

(b) Give the appropriate classification for each of the following account balances:
   (i)   Fixed assets at cost, £10,000.
   (ii)   Wages paid, £700.

(iii)   Discounts received, £1,400.

(iv)   Balance due from Double Ltd, £1,500.

6.8   Explain how the accountant makes use of the trial balance.

6.9   The following particulars have been extracted from the books of a trading concern for the year ended 30 September 19X5:

		£
1.	Sales ledger debit balances at 1 October 19X4	102,300
2.	Sales ledger credit balances at 1 October 19X4	340
3.	Credit sales	630,800
4.	Cash sales	140,100
5.	Cash received from debtors	498,660
6.	Returns outwards	8,300
7.	Returns inwards	2,700
8.	Discounts received	15,200
9.	Discounts allowed	11,790
10.	Accounts settled by contra to purchase ledger	5,200
11.	Bad debts written off	3,950
12.	Sales ledger credit balances 30 September 19X5	510

Required

Prepare the sales ledger control account for the year to 30 September 19X5.

6.10   Ian Error has produced a trial balance for his business for the year to 30 September 19X2 that does not balance, and the error has been placed in a suspense account. An examination of the company's books reveals the following errors:

(a) An invoice from Zed amounting to £1,000, for goods purchased, has been omitted from the purchase day book and posted direct to the purchase account in the nominal ledger and to Zed's account in the memorandum purchase ledger. It has not been included in the creditors control account in the trial balance.

(b) The sales day book has been undercast by £2,400.

(c) Discounts allowed for the month of June amounting to £4,890 have not been debited to the ledger.

(d) Goods received from Wye on 30 June 19X2, which cost £24,100, have been included in the stock but the invoice has not yet been received and entered in the books.

(e) A cheque for £1,920 received from Exe, a debtor, has been debited to cash and credited to the sales account in the nominal ledger.

Required

(i)   Prepare the journal entries to correct these errors.

(ii)   Prepare a statement that shows the effect of the corrections on the company's profit for the year.

(iii)   Calculate the difference between the sides of the trial balance that was placed to suspense account.

7
The Double Entry System III: Periodic Accounting Reports

PERIODIC ACCOUNTS

The preparation of accounting statements should be a routine procedure as they are regularly needed by management, ownership and other interested parties, such as debenture holders, to monitor the progress and position of the company. The principal accounting statements used for these purposes are the trading and profit and loss account and the balance sheet. It is normal to prepare these statements at least once a year to comply with legal and taxation requirements, but they can be produced more frequently if required. Their usefulness depends, first, on the ability of the recipients to base decisions on them and, second, on the time lags between the occurrence of events, their financial effects being reported and decisions taken. If decisions are delayed because of a lack of financial information, then opportunties may be missed, possibly with disastrous consequences. For this reason management, and sometimes other interested parties, are provided with statements more fre- quently than once a year, usually monthly, but possibly even more often. For example, when losses are being made it is important to realize this fact at an early stage; this is helped by the frequent and prompt production of a profit and loss account. The first evidence that losses are being incurred may otherwise be the collapse of the company, an eventuality that might have been avoided if the losses had been identified earlier and remedial action taken.

The procedures described in Chapters 5 and 6 provide the foundations of the accounting process as they are used to record the flows of cash, goods and services and provide a summary of these flows in the form of the trial balance. This chapter deals with the adjustments necessary to the information contained in the trial balance to enable the production of the trading and profit and loss account and balance sheet.

ADJUSTMENTS TO THE TRIAL BALANCE

Adjustments to the trial balance are necessary because the transactions in the ledger accounts do not reflect precisely the economic events that have occurred during the period covered by the accounting statements. Adjustments are therefore needed to take account of the following:

1. *Timing differences* These occur when an item recorded in the books during an accounting period has significance for the business not only in that accounting period but also in previous or subsequent ones. In these circumstances an adjustment must be made to distribute the item accordingly. For example, the purchase of a fixed asset is initially recorded at cost in the year of purchase, but it is necessary to apportion this cost over the years that derive benefit from the expenditure. (For a fuller explanation, see Chapter 8.) Timing differences also operate in the opposite direction. For example, there may be an interval between the receipt of goods and the arrival of the related invoice. (For a fuller explanation, see later in this chapter.)
2. *Incomplete information* The entries in the books may not reflect all the economic changes that must be reported, since some events are not supported by a documented flow of value on which a day book entry is based. For example, a debtor may be unable to pay the sum due to the company, or a machine may be scrapped unsold (see later in this chapter). The routine documentation procedures for a sale or purchase do not apply in these cases, and care must be taken to ensure that allowance has been made for them when the accounts are prepared. The accountant must be satisfied that all the items that relate to the period under review have been included and also that all items that are not relevant have been excluded.

The adjustments made to the trial balance must comply with the rules of double entry – each must comprise a debit and a credit of equal value. The implementation of the adjustments that routinely arise when periodic accounts are prepared are examined in this chapter; the principles of valuation on which the adjustments are based are dealt with in Chapter 8.

STOCKS (INVENTORIES)

Profit is measured by comparing the value of sales for a period of time with their related costs, and so it is necessary to determine the value of goods consumed in the manner described in Chapter 4. Companies may hold many different types of stock, such as raw materials, work in progress and finished goods, and the general equation to find the cost of items consumed is:

$$\text{Cost of goods consumed} = \frac{\text{Opening}}{\text{stock}} + \frac{\text{Inflow of}}{\text{goods}} - \frac{\text{Closing}}{\text{stock}}$$

Care must be taken to ensure that all inflows of goods are included. Any items received prior to the accounting date and included in stock, but which have not been entered as purchases as they have not yet been invoiced, must be identified. An adjustment in the form of an accrual is then made, which increases the value of purchases (debit) and is shown as a liability in the balance sheet (credit); for a fuller explanation, see the section on prepayments and accruals in this chapter.

In a system of double entry accounting, unless continuous inventory control as described in Chapter 8 is used, it is usual to enter the opening stock in one account and to accumulate in another account, called purchases, the cost of all acquisitions made during the accounting period. The effect of this procedure is that the trial balance contains separate balances for opening stock and purchases; these provide two of the three elements in the formula given above. The missing element is the figure for closing stock, and this is usually determined by means of a physical stock-take to find the quantities of each type of stock, which are then valued.

To find the cost of goods sold in the trading account the values of opening stock and purchases contained in the trial balance are transferred to the debit of this account. The accounting entry to record closing stock in the final accounts must then be made:

Debit	Credit	With
Stock account	Trading account	Value of closing stock

The closing balance on the stock account appears as an asset in the balance sheet and is subsequently included as opening stock in the trading account for the following accounting period.

Example 7.1 involves the preparation of final accounts from the trial balance where an adjustment has to be made for closing stock.

Example 7.1

The trial balance of Button, a sole trader, at 31 December 19X4 was:

	£	£
Capital		10,000
Drawings	10,000	
Sales		75,500
Purchases	45,250	
Stock 1 January 19X4	6,750	
Debtors	4,300	
Creditors		3,200
Cash	1,125	
Delivery costs	875	
Wages	11,225	
Sundry expenses	3,000	
Freehold premises	6,175	
	88,700	88,700

The stock at 31 December 19X4 was £7,150.

Required

Prepare the Trading and Profit and Loss Account of Button for the year to 31 December 19X4 and a Balance Sheet at that date. The accounts should be presented in vertical format.

Solution

Trading and Profit and Loss Account Year to 31 December 19X4

	£	£
Sales		75,500
Stock 1 January	6,750	
Purchases	45,250	
Stock 31 December	(7,150)	
Cost of goods sold		44,850
Gross profit		30,650
Wages	11,225	
Delivery costs	875	
Sundry expenses	3,000	
		15,100
Net profit		15,550

Balance Sheet at 31 December 19X4

Fixed assets	£	£
Freehold premises		6,175
Current assets		
Stock	7,150	
Debtors	4,300	
Cash	1,125	
	12,575	
Current liabilities		
Creditors	3,200	
		9,375
		15,550
Capital		
At 1 January		10,000
Profit for 19X4		15,550
		25,550
Drawings		10,000
		15,550

Readers should now attempt Question 7.1 at the end of this chapter.

DEPRECIATION

Fixed assets and their related accumulated depreciation are recorded in the double entry ledger by using an account for each type of fixed asset at cost and another for each type of fixed asset's accumulated depreciation. The number of accounts to be opened depends on the nature of the business, but usually separate accounts for land and buildings, plant and machinery, motor vehicles and furniture and fittings suffice. Further accounts can be used if appropriate, for example, computer equipment or assets out on hire may have a value significant enough to warrant separate identification. The totals of these accounts should be backed up by detailed analysis in a fixed asset register so that the individual assets can be identified.

When the trial balance is extracted it contains for each type of fixed asset, as a debit, the cost and, as a credit, the accumulated balance of depreciation brought forward at the start of the accounting period. The value of the depreciation charge for the period for each class of asset has then to be calculated, and the amounts are debited to the profit and loss account and credited to the accounts containing the opening balances of accumulated depreciation. (The calculation of the depreciation charge is dealt with in Chapter 8.) The debit balance on each of the fixed assets (at cost) accounts is entered in the balance sheet, and from it the credit balance on the related accumulated depreciation account is deducted to give the written-down value, that is, the portion of cost not yet written off and therefore carried forward to the next accounting period. It is helpful to the users of the accounts if both the total cost and the total related depreciation are shown in the balance sheet, rather than just the net figure; this procedure indicates how much of the value has been used up and, therefore, how long it is likely to be before replacement becomes necessary. In the case of a limited company, such disclosure is a legal requirement.

Example 7.2

The following information relates to the machinery owned by Clip Ltd:

	£
At cost, 1 January 19X1	65,000
Accumulated depreciation at 1 January 19X1	25,000
Acquired during 19X1	10,000
Depreciation charge for 19X1	8,000

Required

(a) Prepare the ledger accounts for 19X1 to record the above information.
(b) Show the balance sheet extract for machinery at 31 December 19X1.

Solution

(a) Machinery at Cost Account

			£				£
1 Jan. 19X1	Balance b/d		65,000	31 Dec. 19X1	Balance c/d		75,000
19X1	Purchases		10,000				
			75,000				75,000

Accumulated Depreciation Account – Machinery

			£				£
31 Dec. 19X1	Balance b/d		33,000	1 Jan. 19X1	Balance b/d		25,000
				31 Dec. 19X1	Profit and		
					loss account		8,000
			33,000				33,000

(b) Balance Sheet Extract 31 December 19X1

	£	£
Machinery at cost	75,000	
Less: Depreciation	33,000	
		42,000

Readers should now attempt Questions 7.2 and 7.3 at the end of this chapter. The former question tests the entries for fixed assets and depreciation in the books of account, and the latter puts them in the context of preparing the final accounts from the trial balance.

DISPOSAL OF FIXED ASSETS

When a fixed asset is disposed of, its cost and related depreciation must be eliminated from the books and any profit or loss on disposal calculated. Any proceeds from disposal must not be included in the company's sales figure as they do not relate to routine trading activity. Instead, the proceeds are credited in a disposal of fixed assets account, the balance on which appears as a credit entry in the trial balance. The calculation of the profit or loss arising on disposal may then be made in the disposal of fixed assets account using the following entries:

Account debited	Account credited	With
Disposal of fixed assets	Fixed assets at cost	Historical cost of the asset
Accumulated depreciation	Disposal of fixed assets	Accumulated depreciation on the asset

Example 7.3

In 19X3 Case Ltd sold for £6,500 cash a piece of machinery that had cost the company £25,000. At the time of sale, the accumulated depreciation on the asset was £20,000.

Required

Prepare the disposal of fixed assets account to record the sale of the machinery.

Solution

Disposal of Fixed Assets Account

	£		£
Machinery at cost	25,000	Cash	6,500
Profit on sale*	1,500	Accumulated depreciation	20,000
	26,500		26,500

Note
*Balancing figure credited to the profit and loss account.

Sometimes a disposal of fixed assets account is not maintained during the year and instead any proceeds are credited to the fixed assets at cost account. This happens especially where a 'trading-in' allowance is received, for example, when changing motor vehicles, as a reduction in the amount paid for the new asset. In these circumstances, the proceeds or trading-in allowance must be transferred to the disposal account by the following entry:

Account debited	*Account credited*	*With*
Fixed assets at cost	Disposal of fixed assets	Proceeds of disposal or trading-in allowance

Instead of making the appropriate entries in a disposal of fixed assets account, the profit or loss on the disposal of an individual asset may alternatively be calculated by using the following formula:

$$\text{Proceeds on disposal} - \left[\text{Historical cost} - \text{Accumulated depreciation}\right] = \text{Profit/Loss on disposal}$$

Questions can be framed so that any one element from this equation is unknown and has to be found as the balancing figure after the others have been determined and entered.

Example 7.4

Shed Ltd bought a fixed asset for £10,000 in 19X1, which was sold for £6,250 in 19X5 to give a profit on disposal of £1,250.

Required

(a) Calculate the accumulated depreciation that had been charged on the asset up to the time it was sold.
(b) Explain why, when the amount of profit on disposal is known, it is necessary to calculate the depreciation figure.

Solution

(a)

> £6,250 (Proceeds) − (£10,000 (cost) − Accumulated depreciation)
>   = £1,250 (profit)

∴. £6,250 − £10,000 + Accumulated depreciation
    = £1,250

∴. Accumulated depreciation = £10,000 − £6,250 + £1,250
    = £5,000.

(b) It is necessary to know the value of accumulated depreciation as, when an asset is disposed of, all the related entries in the books must be removed. This is done by using double entry procedures to complete a disposal of fixed assets account:

Disposal of Fixed Assets Account

	£		£
Fixed assets at cost	10,000	Proceeds	6,250
Profit on disposal	1,250	Accumulated depreciation	5,000
	11,250		11,250

When a fully-depreciated asset is scrapped, and no proceeds are received, its cost and accumulated depreciation must be eliminated from the books. This is achieved by the entries:

Account debited	Account credited	With
Accumulated depreciation	Fixed assets at cost	Historical cost of asset scrapped

Readers should now work Question 7.4 at the end of this chapter, which tests all the aspects of asset disposal described in this section.

PREPAYMENTS AND ACCRUALS

A business makes a number of payments that give it a right to enjoy certain benefits over a period of time. Some of these payments, such as rates on the occupation of property, are paid in advance of the receipt of the benefit and give rise to a prepayment, while others, such as for the consumption of gas or electricity, are made in arrears and create accruals. The accruals concept, as explained in Chapter 4, is applied, and so, unless the period of time covered by these payments coincides exactly with the accounting period, an adjustment is needed to take account of the asset created where payments are made in advance, and the liability that arises when benefits are paid for in arrears. The value of accruals and prepayments for items that relate to a period of time is found by apportioning the cost on a time basis.

Prepayments

The entries in the accounts to record a prepayment are:

Account debited	Account credited	With
Prepayment	Expense	Value of prepayment

The credit of the prepayment in the expense account reduces the expense, and the prepayment is shown in the balance sheet as a current asset. In practice, the prepayment may be carried down in the expense account to which it relates. This is illustrated in Example 7.5.

Example 7.5

Gelco Ltd makes up its accounts to 31 December, and made the following cash payments in respect of rates:

Year	Month	Payment
		£
19X0	October	900
19X1	April	1,000
19X1	October	1,000

The payments for rates relate to the six-month period starting with the month in which they are paid.

Required

Prepare the rates account for 19X1.

Solution

Rates Account

		£			£
1 Jan. 19X1	Balance b/d	450	31 Dec. 19X1 Balance c/d		500
April	Cash	1,000		Profit and loss	
October	Cash	1,000		account	1,950
		2,450			2,450
1 Jan.19X2	Balance b/d	500			

The balance brought down at the start of the year is half of the payment of £900 made in October 19X0 and covers January, February and March 19X1. The balance of £500 carried down at the end of 19X1 is an asset since it pays in advance for the first three months of 19X2 and will appear as a current asset in the balance sheet at 31 December 19X1. The transfer to the profit and loss account is found as a balancing figure once all the other entires have been made. The balance brought down on 1 January 19X2 will be charged against profit as an expense in 19X2, even though payment was made in 19X1.

Accruals

The entries in the accounts to record an accrual are:

Account debited	Account credited	With
Expense	Accruals	Value of accrual

The accrual increases the expense figure charged in the profit and loss account (debit) and is included as a current liability in the balance sheet (credit). In practice, the accrual may be carried down in the expense account to which it relates. This is illustrated in Example 7.6.

Example 7.6

Gelco Ltd makes up its accounts to 31 December, and made the following payments in respect of electricity:

Year	Month	Payment £
19X0	October	400
19X1	January	600
19X1	April	630
19X1	July	400
19X1	October	500
19X2	January	750

The payments are for electricity consumed during the three months immediately prior to the months in which they are made.

Required

Record the above transactions in the company's electricity account for 19X1 and 19X2.

Solution

Electricity Account

19X1		£			£
January	Cash	600	1 Jan. 19X1	Balance b/d	600
April	Cash	630	31 Dec. 19X1	Profit and loss	
July	Cash	400		account	2,280
October	Cash	500			
31 Dec. 19X1	Balance c/d	750			
		2,880			2,880
19X2			1 Jan. 19X2	Balance b/d	750
January	Cash	750			

The credit balance of £600 brought down would have appeared in the balance sheet at 31 December 19X0 as a liability and relates to the electricity consumed in the last three months of 19X0. It can be seen that it is cancelled by the actual cash payment made in January 19X1 since at that point the balance on the account is zero. The same reasoning relates to the £750 carried down at the end of 19X1.

Readers should now attempt Question 7.5 at the end of this chapter.

BAD DEBTS

When a company makes sales on credit there is a possibility that some of the customers will not be able to pay their debts, with the result that bad debts are suffered. Although known bad debts may be written off during the year, it is usual to review carefully the list of debtors outstanding when the annual accounts are prepared and write off any additional bad debts. The fact that a debt is likely to prove bad becomes apparent when a great deal of time has elapsed since the goods were supplied and no cash has been received despite repeated efforts to collect the amount outstanding. This emphasizes the importance of monitoring debtors on a routine basis so that, when the terms for payment are exceeded, further supplies can be stopped; such action encourages the customer to pay the amount owed and also minimizes the loss if the debt should prove to be bad. When it becomes apparent that the full amount of the debt will not be received from the debtor, it is necessary to remove the value of the irrecoverable debt from the total debtors account and record the loss. The double entry to achieve this is:

Account debited	Account credited	With
Bad debts	Debtors control	Value of bad debt

The amount is also credited to the individual personal account of the debtor in the memorandum debtors ledger. The balance on the bad debts account appears as a debit balance in the trial balance, and is written off to the profit and loss account when the annual accounts are prepared since it represents the loss of an asset and, therefore, is an expense.

In addition, a company may know, from experience, that a stable proportion of the debts outstanding at the balance sheet date will prove to be bad, although it is not possible to tell in advance which specific debts will remain unpaid. Prudence suggests that, in these circumstances, an allowance should be made for the likely bad debts contained in the value of debtors outstanding at the year end by the introduction of a provision for doubtful debts. When the amount to be allowed for has been determined, the provision is created by a debit to the doubtful debts account with the corresponding credit to a provision for doubtful debts account; this credit balance is offset against the value of debtors in the balance sheet to show the net amount that is expected to be collected. The fact that this provision is general, or non-specific, means that no consequential adjustments are made in the debtor's individual memorandum personal accounts.

Once a provision has been created, it appears as a credit balance in the trial balance prepared at the end of the subsequent accounting period, and it is necessary only to adjust its value from year to year, rather than charge annually the full required value. This is because the provision created at the end of one year is carried forward to the next, and any debts that in fact prove bad are debited to the bad debts account and then written off to the profit and loss account. The double entry to record adjustments for doubtful debts is:

Account debited	Account credited	With
Doubtful debts	Doubtful debt provision	Increase in provision
Doubtful debt provision	Profit and loss	Decrease in provision

Example 7.7

The following balances appeared in the books of Fifth Ltd at the end of 19X1:

	Debit £	Credit £
Bad debts written off during 19X1	950	
Provision for doubtful debts brought forward		900
Debtors control account	125,000	

It is decided, after a review of the debtors' balances at the end of the year, to write off a further £1,000 of bad debts and create a provision of 1 per cent of the value of the remainder for doubtful debts.

Required

Write up the T accounts to deal with these matters and show the appropriate extracts from the profit and loss account and balance sheet.

Solution

Bad Debts Account

		£			£
19X1	Debtors	950	31 Dec. 19X1	Profit and loss	1,950
31 Dec. 19X1	Debtors	1,000			
		1,950			1,950

Debtors Control Account

		£			£
31 Dec. 19X1	Balance	125,000	31 Dec. 19X1	Bad debts	1,000
			31 Dec. 19X1	Balance c/d	124,000
		125,000			125,000

Provision for Doubtful Debts Account

		£			£
31 Dec. 19X1	Balance c/d	1,240*	31 Dec. 19X1	Balance b/d	900
			31 Dec. 19X1	Doubtful debts	340
		1,240			1,240

Note
* 1% of £124,000 = £1,240.

Doubtful Debts Account

		£			£
31 Dec. 19X1	Provision for doubtful debts	340	31 Dec. 19X1	Profit and loss	340

Profit and Loss Account (extract)

	£	£
Bad debts	1,950	
Doubtful debts	340	
		2,290

Balance Sheet (extract)

	£	£
Debtors	124,000	
Less: Provision for doubtful debts	1,240	
		122,760

Notes
1. The bad debts of £950 have already been written off the value of debtors and so no further adjustment to the debtors control account is required in respect of this loss.
2. All bad debts arising during 19X1 have been written off against profit. It is therefore necessary only to increase the provision to the revised value, that is, by £340 to £1,240. In some cases the review of debtor balances results in a reduction of the provision and hence a credit to the profit and loss account.

Readers should now work Question 7.6 at the end of the chapter, which tests the book entries related to bad debts, and Question 7.7, which revises the preparation of final accounts from the trial balance with some additional adjustments.

THE ADJUSTED TRIAL BALANCE

The adjustments made to the trial balance when the trading and profit and loss account are prepared must be carried out in a systematic manner that complies with double entry procedures. Examples 7.8 shows how this can be done.

Example 7.8

The following trial balance was extracted from the books of T. Jones on 31 December 19X5:

	£	£
Sales		100,000
Purchases	50,000	
Stock – 1 January	10,000	
Rent	5,000	
Wages	12,000	
Electricity	1,500	
Debtors	9,000	
Trade creditors		8,000
Cash	1,000	
Fixed assets at cost	34,000	
Accumulated depreciation – 1 January		13,000
Other expenses	6,000	
Capital – 1 January		17,000
Drawings	9,500	
	138,000	138,000

The following addition information is provided:

1. Goods that cost £1,000 were received during 19X5 and were included in closing stock. No invoice was included in purchases for them in 19X5.
2. Rent of £500 is prepaid.
3. Electricity of £350 is accrued.
4. The depreciation charge for the year is £6,000.
5. Jones took stock for his own use that cost £450. No entry was made in the books in respect of this.
6. The closing stock is £12,000.
7. Bad debts of £150 are to be written off.
8. A provision for doubtful debts of £100 is to be created.

Required

(a) Prepare the adjusted trial balance of T. Jones as at 31 December 19X5.
(b) Prepare the trading and profit and loss account of T. Jones for the year to 31 December 19X5 and the balance sheet as at that date.

Solution (Example 7.8 (a))

Adjusted trial balance

	Original trial balance at 31 Dec. 19X5 £ Dr.	£ Cr.	Adjustments £ Dr.	£ Cr.	Trading and profit and loss account £ Dr.	£ Cr.	Balance sheet £ Dr.	£ Cr.
Sales		100,000				100,000		
Purchases	50,000		1,000 (1)	450 (5)	50,550			
Stock	10,000		12,000 (6)	12,000 (6)	10,000	12,000	12,000	
Rent	5,000			500 (2)	4,500			
Wages	12,000				12,000			
Electricity	1,500		350 (3)		1,850			
Debtors	9,000			150 (7)			8,850	
Creditors		8,000		1,000 (1)				9,000
Cash	1,000						1,000	
Fixed assets at cost	34,000						34,000	
Accumulated depreciation 1 January		13,000		6,000 (4)	6,000			19,000
Other expenses	6,000				6,000			
Capital 1 January		17,000						17,000
Drawings	9,500		450 (5)				9,950	
Accruals				350 (3)				350
Prepayments			500 (2)				500	

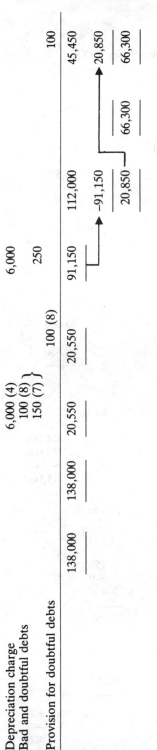

Depreciation charge	6,000 (4)			6,000			
Bad and doubtful debts	100 (8) 150 (7) }			250			
Provision for doubtful debts		100 (8)					100
	138,000	138,000	20,550	20,550	91,150	112,000	45,450
					−91,150	20,850	20,850
						66,300	66,300

Notes

1. The adjustment columns show the debit and credit entries needed to give effect to the additional information. The number in brackets by such figures refers to the note in the question on which it is based.
2. The opening balance of each line is taken, adjusted, and then entered in the final trial balance.
3. The fact that the two adjustment columns have the same total shows that the double entry rules have been complied with.
4. The final trial balance is separated into the trading and profit and loss account and the balance sheet. This is to aid the preparation of the final accounts. The proof of the trial balance in this format is that each section has an equal, but opposite, difference. This is the profit figure.
5. The accrual of £1,000 for the goods received but not invoiced at the year end represents a trade creditor and so is added to the existing balance of £8,000.

Solution (Example 7.8(b))

Trading and Profit and Loss Account Year to 31 December 19X5

	£	£
Sales		100,000
Opening stock	10,000	
Purchases	50,550	
Closing stock	(12,000)	
Cost of goods sold		48,550
Gross profit		51,450
Rent	4,500	
Wages	12,000	
Electricity	1,850	
Other expenses	6,000	
Depreciation	6,000	
Bad and doubtful debts	250	
		30,600
Net profit		20,850

Balance Sheet at 31 December 19X5

	£	£	£
Fixed assets			
Fixed assets at cost			34,000
Less: Accumulated depreciation			19,000
			15,000
Current Assets			
Stock		12,000	
Debtors	8,850		
Less: Provision for doubtful debts	100		
		8,750	
Prepayment		500	
Cash		1,000	
		22,250	
Current liabilities			
Creditors	9,000		
Accruals	350		
		9,350	
Working capital			12,900
			27,900

Capital	£
Balance at 1 January	17,000
Profit for year	20,850
	37,850
Less: Drawings	9,950
	27,900

An adjusted trial balance, as used in Example 7.8, should be completed for inclusion in a set of permanent working papers when final accounts are prepared in practice. In examinations it is often too time consuming to prepare this but, with practice, this process can be avoided. The important requirement is that students should adopt a systematic approach so as to ensure that all necessary adjustments are properly made. One useful technique is to note the double entry effects of all the adjustments to the trial balance on the question paper. The adjusted balances are then used to prepare the final accounts. This approach is now illustrated in Example 7.9, which uses the data given in Example 7.8 for T. Jones. The notes on the trial balance, which would in practice be made by hand, are shown in italics, and the final accounts include notes on how the figures have been calculated.

Example 7.9

The following trial balance was extracted from the books of T. Jones on 31 December 19X5 and shows, in italics, the adjustments needed to prepare the final accounts:

	£			£	
Sales				100,000	
Purchases	50,000	*+1,000*	*−450*		
Stock – 1 January	10,000				
Rent	5,000	*−500*			
Wages	12,000				
Electricity	1,500	*+350*			
Debtors	9,000	*−150*			
Trade creditors				8,000	*+1,000*
Cash	1,000				
Fixed assets at cost	34,000				
Accumulated depreciation –					
1 January				13,000	*+6,000*
Other expenses	6,000				
Capital – 1 January				17,000	
Drawings	9,500	*+450*			
	138,000			138,000	
Prepayments	*500*				
Accruals				*350*	
Depreciation	*6,000*				
Bad debts	*150*				
Doubtful debt provision	*100*			*100*	

The additional information on which the adjustments (in italics) are based is given in Example 7.8.

Care must be taken to include workings with the answer submitted to ensure that the examiner understands how the figures were derived. In this example, the workings are given in brackets on the face of the accounts:

Trading and Profit and Loss Account Year to 31 December 19X5

	£	£
Sales		100,000
Opening stock	10,000	
Purchases (50,000+1,000−450)	50,550	
Closing stock	(12,000)	
Cost of goods sold		48,550
Gross profit		51,450
Rent (5,000−500)	4,500	
Wages	12,000	
Electricity (1,500+350)	1,850	
Other expenses	6,000	
Depreciation	6,000	
Bad and doubtful debts (100+150)	250	
		30,600
Net profit		20,850

Balance Sheet at 31 December 19X5

	£	£	£
Fixed assets			
Fixed assets at cost			34,000
Less: Accumulated depreciation			
(13,000+6,000)			19,000
			15,000
Current assets			
Stock		12,000	
Debtors (9,000−150)	8,850		
Less: Provision for doubtful debts	100	8,750	
		500	
		1,000	
Prepayment			
Cash		22,250	
Current liabilities			
Creditors (8,000+1,000)	9,000		
Accruals	350	9,350	

	£
Working capital	12,900
	27,900

Capital	
Balance at 1 January	17,000
Profit for year	20,850
	37,850
less: Drawings (9,500+450)	9,950
	27,900

Errors may come to light during the examination of the books that takes place when the periodic accounts are prepared. The correction of these errors must be made in accordance with the double entry techniques described in this chapter. This aspect of preparing final accounts is tested in Question 7.8 at the end of this chapter, which readers should now work.

QUESTIONS

7.1   The trial balance of Finis, a sole trader, at 31 December 19X4, was:

	£ Debit	£ Credit
Sales		130,000
Returns inwards	250	
Stock at 1 January 19X4	15,000	
Returns outwards		150
Purchases	80,000	
Capital at 1 January 19X4		27,600
Cash at bank	3,100	
Debtors	15,400	
Creditors		5,000
Premises	8,000	
Wages	17,300	
Discounts received		300
Rents and rates	3,000	
Delivery costs	2,750	
Cash withdrawn by Finis	12,000	
Heat and light	3,500	
Sundry expenses	2,750	
	163,050	163,050

Note
The value of stock at 31 December 19X4 was £17,750.

Required

(a) State the location in the final accounts of each item in the trial balance, i.e. whether it is entered in the trading account, the profit and loss account or the balance sheet.

(b) Prepare the trading and profit and loss account of Finis for the year to 31 December 19X4 and a balance sheet at that date.

7.2   Tip Ltd was established and started trading on 1 January 19X1 and draws up its accounts to 31 December each year. Its purchases and disposals of fixed assets over the subsequent three years were as follows:

Asset	Date of purchase	Cost £	Date of disposal	Proceeds on disposal £
A	1 January 19X1	5,000	—	—
B	1 January 19X1	2,500	1 January 19X3	900
C	1 January 19X3	7,000	—	—

Required

Use this data to:

(a) prepare the fixed assets at cost, accumulated depreciation and disposal of fixed assets accounts based on straight line depreciation of 20 per cent per year for 19X1, 19X2 and 19X3; and
(b) show the fixed asset extracts from the balance sheets at the end of each year.

7.3   The following is the trial balance of Push, a sole trader, at 30 June 19X7:

	£	£
Capital		30,350
Sales		108,920
Purchases	72,190	
Drawings	12,350	
Debtors	7,350	
Creditors		6,220
Cash	1,710	
Stock	9,470	
Plant and machinery at cost	35,000	
Accumulated depreciation at 1 July 19X6		12,500
Rent	1,000	
Wages	14,330	
Other costs	4,590	
	157,990	157,990

Notes
1. The value of stock at 30 June 19X7 was £9,960.
2. The depreciation charge for the year to 30 June 19X7 was £3,000.

Required

Prepare the trading and profit and loss account of Push for the year to 30 June 19X7 and the balance sheet at that date.

7.4 At 31 December 19X3 the trial balance of Damp Ltd contained the following balances in respect of motor vehicles:

	Debit £	Credit £
Motor vehicles at cost	127,000	
Accumulated depreciation at 1 January 19X3		76,000
Disposal of motor vehicles		1,600

You ascertain that during 19X3 the following occurred:

1. A delivery van, which was fully depreciated and had cost £2,000, was scrapped. No proceeds were received.
2. A car that cost £5,000, on which accumulated depreciation was £3,000, had been traded in for a new model with a full cost of £8,000. A trade-in allowance of £1,500 was received, and only the net cost of the new car, £6,500, has been entered in the books.
3. A car that cost £4,000 and had a written down value of £1,250 was sold for £1,600 (credited to the disposals account).
4. A delivery van was sold for £2,500. This vehicle had cost £10,000 and a loss of £750 was made on its sale. The proceeds have been credited to the fixed asset account.
5. The depreciation charge for the year is £25,000.

Required

(a) Prepare the motor vehicles at cost account, motor vehicles accumulated depreciation account and disposal of motor vehicles account for 19X3 to show the effect of the above information and the transfer to the profit and loss account.
(b) Show the extract for motor vehicles that would appear in the company's balance sheet at 31 December 19X3.

7.5   Prepac Ltd prepared its accounts to 31 December. The following facts relate to 19X8:

	£
Balance on insurance account 1 January	450 (Dr.)
Balance on electricity account 1 January	300 (Cr.)
Balance on rates account 1 January	290 (Dr.)
Balance on gas account 1 January	600 (Cr.)
February – pay for electricity consumed during quarter to 31 January	900
March – pay for gas consumed during quarter to 28 February	850
– pay rates for the half year to 30 September	780
May – pay for electricity consumed during quarter to 30 April	820
June – pay for gas consumed during quarter to 31 May	840
– pay insurance for the year to 30 June 19X9	1,020
August – pay for electricity consumed during quarter to 31 July	690
September – pay for gas consumed during quarter to 31 August	610
– pay rates for 6 months to 31 March 19X9	780
November – pay for electricity consumed during quarter to 31 October	550
December – pay for gas consumed during quarter to 30 November	960
Electricity consumed in November and December 19X8	390
Gas consumed in December 19X8	680

Required

Prepare the insurance account, electricity account, rates account and gas account for 19X8 as they appear in the books of Prepac Ltd and showing clearly in each case the transfer to profit and loss account.

7.6   At 31 December 19X0 the following balances were shown in the books of E. Rider Ltd:

	£
Sales control account	156,937 (Dr.)
Provision for doubtful debts	2,600 (Cr.)
Bad debts	750 (Dr.)

The list of debtors contained balances that were considered to be bad or doubtful as indicated in the 'remarks' column of the schedule below:

Schedule of bad and doubtful debts, 31 December 19X0

Customer	Account number	Account balance	Remarks
B. Clyde	C6	£560	Irrecoverable
S. Wars	W2	£680	In liquidation. At least 50p in the £ is anticipated, but full recovery is a possibility
M. Poppins	P4	£227	Irrecoverable
M. Express	E9	£390	This debt is doubtful to the extent of 20%
M. Ash	A1	£240	A provision of £80 is to be made against this debt

The general provision for doubtful debts in respect of debts other than those dealt with individually above is to be raised to £3,750.

Required

(a) Prepare the sales ledger control account, bad debts account, doubtful debts account and provision for doubtful debts account as they appear after recording the above transactions.
(b) Show the balance sheet extract for debtors at 31 December 19X0.

7.7   The following trial balance was extracted from the books of Dellboy, a retail trader, at 31 December 19X6:

	£	£
Capital account		193,894
Freehold land and buildings at cost	114,000	
Motor vans at cost	37,500	
Provision for depreciation on motor vans at 1 January 19X6		15,450
Purchases	164,770	
Sales		234,481
Rent and rates	3,000	
General expenses	7,263	
Wages	26,649	
Bad debts	693	
Provision for doubtful debts at 1 January 19X6		876
Drawings	18,000	
Debtors and creditors	20,911	13,006
Stock in trade at 1 January 19X6	32,193	
Bank balance	32,728	
	457,707	457,707

You are given the following additional information:

1. Wages outstanding at 31 December 19X6 amounted to £271.
2. The provision for doubtful debts is to be increased by £104.
3. Stock in trade at 31 December 19X6 was £34,671.
4. Rent and rates amounting to £300 were paid in advance at 31 December 19X6.
5. During 19X6 Dellboy took stock costing £1,250 for his own use. No entry has been made in the books in respect of this.
6. During 19X6 a motor van, which had cost £2,500 and had a written-down value of £1,000, was sold for £1,500. No entry had been made in the books to record this, other than to credit the cash received to the motor vehicles account.
7. The depreciation charge for the year is £7,000.

Required

A trading and profit and loss account for the year 19X6 and a balance sheet as at 31 December 19X6.

7.8　During the preparation of the accounts from the books of S. Top, a sole trader, for the year to 30 June 19X7, the following items were found:

1. Included in the repairs to machinery account was £2,750, which was paid on 29 June 19X7 and was for the purchase of a new lathe.
2. Manufacturing wages account included £350 paid to an employee for time spent repairing a machine.
3. A debt of £1,290 due from J. Jones was included in debtors, but in fact was irrecoverable.
4. The rates on S. Top's private house of £200 had been paid by the business and charged to the rates account.
5. Goods worth £1,500 had been received into stock on 30 June and included in the value of stock for accounts purposes. No entry had been made in the books to record this purchase.
6. An old machine that had cost £1,000 and was fully depreciated had been scrapped during the year. This fact had not been recorded in the books.
7. S. Top had taken stock to the value of £150 for his own use during the year. No entry appeared in the books in respect of this usage.
8. A payment of £125 for delivery of goods to customers had been entered in the purchases account.

Required

(a) Prepare the journal entries to record the adjustments.
(b) Prepare a statement to show the effect of these adjustments on the profit for the year to 30 June 19X7.

8
Asset Valuation, Profit Measurement and the Underlying Accounting Concepts

ASSET VALUATION AND PROFIT MEASUREMENT

The level of profit reported in the accounts depends on the amounts at which assets, listed in the balance sheet, are valued. Any error made when valuing assets has a corresponding effect on the level of reported profit and, therefore, reduces its usefulness as a basis for assessing performance. For example, if closing stock is overvalued by £1,000, the figure for cost of goods sold is understated and reported profit overstated by this amount. Great care should therefore be taken when calculating asset values for inclusion in the accounts. The procedures that are followed, in practice, are examined below.

TANGIBLE FIXED ASSETS

Fixed assets are reported in the balance sheet at cost less accumulated depreciation. The identification of cost and the calculation of the depreciation charge are considered below.

Calculating cost

The expenditure incurred by a business must be accounted for as *either* capital expenditure *or* revenue expenditure. The basic test applied to distinguish between the two types of expenditure is the effect that the outlay has on the company's long-run ability to earn profits. If it is enhanced, the expenditure is capital whereas, if the expenditure merely enables the business to continue to operate at its existing level, it is revenue. The distinction is of crucial import-ance because it affects how the expenditure is reported in the profit and loss account and balance sheet. Capital expenditure on fixed assets is recorded in the balance sheet at cost, and is subsequently charged against revenue over the period of years that benefit from the use of the asset. Revenue expenditure, on the other hand, is normally charged against revenue arising during the period when the cost is incurred. A proper classification is important, otherwise the reported balances for profit and net assets will be incorrectly stated and wrong conclusions may be reached regarding the performance and position of the firm. The effects of misallocations are shown in Figure 8.1.

	Effect on	
	Profit	*Net assets*
Capital expenditure wrongly allocated to revenue	Understated	Understated
Revenue expenditure wrongly allocated to capital	Overstated	Overstated

Figure 8.1   Effect of wrongly allocating expenditure to capital or revenue

Most items of expenditure are easily classified as capital or revenue, but there are some 'grey areas' where judgement is needed to help make a proper allocation in the light of all the available facts. The cost of fixed assets acquired or built by the firm itself, to form the basis for business activity, is clearly capital expenditure. Difficulties arise in connection with expenditure incidental to the acquisition of the fixed asset and expenditure on fixed assets currently in use. The following rules should be followed to achieve a proper allocation:

1. Expenditure incurred in getting a new fixed asset ready for business use is a capital expense. This includes, for example, any transport costs, import duties and solicitors' fees. In addition, costs incurred in modifying existing premises to accommodate a new fixed asset should also be capitalized.
2. Expenditure on an existing fixed asset that enhances its value to the business, e.g. by increasing its capacity, effectiveness or useful life, should be capitalized.
3. Expenditure on an existing fixed asset intended to make good wear and tear and keep it in satisfactory working order is a revenue expense. Where the expenditure contains an element of improvement, as well as repair, an apportionment between capital expenditure and revenue expenditure must be made.

Example 8.1

Indicate for each of the following items whether it is capital or revenue expenditure:

1. Legal expenses incurred when acquiring a new building.
2. Giving the factory a fresh coat of paint.

3. Repacing 200 tiles on a roof damaged by a gale.
4. Expenditure incurred demolishing part of a wall to make room for a recently purchased machine.
5. Replacing wooden office windows by double-glazed metal windows.
6. Installing a system of ventilation in the factory.

Solution

1. *Capital* This is part of the cost of acquiring the new asset.
2. *Revenue* This makes good wear and tear.
3. *Revenue* This merely restores the roof to its pre-gale condition.
4. *Capital* This is part of the cost of bringing the fixed asset into use.
5. *Part capital/part revenue* The new windows should be more effective in eliminating draughts and making the office sound proof.
6. *Capital* Working conditions and employee performance should improve.

Readers should now work Questions 8.1. and 8.2 at the end of this chapter.

Depreciation methods

Depreciation is charged in the accounts to reflect the fact that the business has benefited from using fixed assets that, as a result, have declined in value. The pattern of benefit that arises differs from one type of fixed asset to another. For example, some fixed assets produce a greater benefit in the early years of ownership, when the asset is more efficient, whereas others make a fairly steady contribution over their entire useful life. There are a number of different methods of charging depreciation and management should choose the one that most closely reflects the forecast pattern of benefits receivable.

Straight-line (equal instalment) method

Under this method the difference between original cost and ultimate disposal value is spread equally over the asset's estimated useful life. This method is described and illustrated in Chapter 4, and has been used in all previous examples and questions requiring a charge to be calculated. The method assumes that each accounting period benefits to an equal extent from using the fixed asset, and the annual charge is calculated on the basis of the following formula:

$$\frac{\text{Original cost} - \text{Estimated disposal value}}{\text{Estimated useful life}}$$

An attraction of this method is that it is easy to apply once the initial estimates have been made and, for this reason, it is widely used in Great Britain.

Example 8.2

On 1 January 19X1 a manufacturing company acquired a new lathe for £23,000. It is estimated to have a useful life of four years during which time it will produce 100,000 units of output: 50,000 units in 19X1; 10,000 units in 19X2; 10,000 units in 19X3; and 30,000 units in 19X4. The lathe is expected to be sold for £3,000 at the end of four years.

The annual straight-line charge is calculated as follows:

$$\text{Depreciation charge} = \frac{£23,000 - £3,000}{4}$$

$$= £5,000$$

Reducing (declining) balance method

This is the second most popular method. A depreciation rate is decided upon and then applied to the *net* book value (original cost less accumulated depreciation) of the asset brought forward at the beginning of each accounting period. The charge is highest in year 1 and then falls, each year, because the depreciation rate is applied to a declining balance. The rate is usually given in examinations but, where it is not provided, it may be calculated using the following formula:

$$\text{Depreciation rate} = \left(1 - \sqrt[n]{\frac{s}{c}}\right) \times 100$$

where: n is the expected useful life
s is the expected scrap value
c the original cost.

Applying this formula to the facts provided in Example 8.2 gives the following results:

$$\text{Depreciation rate} = \left(1 - \sqrt[4]{\frac{3,000}{23,000}}\right) \times 100$$

$$= 39.9\%$$

Depreciation charges, 19X1–19X4

	£
Original cost	23,000
19X1 depreciation charge, £23,000 × 39.9%	9,177
Net book value at 31 December 19X1	13,823
19X2 depreciation charge, £13,823 × 39.9%	5,515
Net book value at 31 December 19X2	8,308
19X3 depreciation charge, £8,308 × 39.9%	3,315
Net book value at 31 December 19X3	4,993
19X4 depreciation charge, £4,993 × 39.9%	1,993
Net book value at 31 December 19X4	3,000

It should be noticed that the charge for 19X1 (£9,177) is over four times higher than the charge for 19X4 (£1,993). Clearly, the method is appropriate only when the bulk of the benefit arises early on. An argument sometimes put forward for this method (and the sum of the digits method, see below) is that repair and maintenance costs normally increase as a fixed asset becomes older and the reducing balance basis therefore helps to ensure that the total annual charge (depreciation + maintenance) remains steady over the asset's useful life.

Sum of the digits method

This method also produces larger charges in the early years, but the differences that occur are less dramatic than with the reducing balance method. Each year of the asset's life is represented by a digit, beginning with 1, and the depreciation charge for each year is calculated by applying the following formula:

$$\frac{\text{Original cost} - \text{Estimated disposal value}}{\text{Sum of the year's digits}} \times \frac{\text{Number of years' life remaining}}{\text{at beginning of year}}$$

Applying the formula to the facts provided in Example 8.2 gives the following results:

Depreciation charge:

$$19X1 = \frac{£20,000}{(1+2+3+4)} \times 4 = £8,000$$

$$19X2 = \frac{£20,000}{(1+2+3+4)} \times 3 = £6,000$$

$$19X3 = \frac{£20,000}{(1+2+3+4)} \times 2 = £4,000$$

$$19X4 = \frac{£20,000}{(1+2+3+4)} \times 1 = £2,000$$

The units of service method

This method relates the charge to the extent the asset is used during an accounting period. For this purpose usage may be measured on the basis either of the number of units produced or the number of hours in service. The formula used to calculate the annual charge is as follows:

$$\frac{\text{Original cost} - \text{Estimated disposal value}}{\text{Total estimated number of units (hours)}} \times \begin{array}{l}\text{Number of units}\\\text{(hours) in use.}\end{array}$$

Applying the formula to the facts provided in Example 8.2 produces the following results:

Depreciation charge: 19X1 = $\dfrac{20,000}{100,000} \times 50,000 = £10,000$

19X2 = $\dfrac{20,000}{100,000} \times 10,000 = £2,000$

19X3 = $\dfrac{20,000}{100,000} \times 10,000 = £2,000$

19X4 = $\dfrac{20,000}{100,000} \times 30,000 = £6,000$

This depreciation method is considered to be the most rational because it produces a variable charge that depends on the level of activity. The lathe is capable of producing 100,000 units, of which 50,000 are produced in 19X1. Half of the total benefit provided by the asset arises in 19X1 and half of its net cost to the business (£20,000 × ½) should therefore be charged against revenue arising during that year. Only the units of service method produces this result. In the following year, 19X2, when 10,000 units are produced, one-tenth of the asset's net cost, i.e. £2,000, is charged against revenue. The disadvantage of this method is the difficulty of estimating the units of service that a fixed asset will provide, and it is not widely used.

Comparing the methods

The charges made under each of the four methods are as follows:

	19X1 £	19X2 £	19X3 £	19X4 £	Total £
Straight line	5,000	5,000	5,000	5,000	20,000
Reducing balance	9,177	5,515	3,315	1,993	20,000
Sum of the digits	8,000	6,000	4,000	2,000	20,000
Units of service	10,000	2,000	2,000	6,000	20,000

It can be seen that the pattern of charges differs a great deal depending on the method used. For example, the highest charge arises in 19X1 from using the units of service method, in 19X2 from using the sum of the digits method, in 19X3 from using the straight-line method and in 19X4 again from using the units of service method. Within particular years the difference is also marked. For example, in 19X1 the units of service method produces a charge that is twice as high as under the straight-line method. Looked at another way, reported profit for 19X1 is £5,000 more if the straight-line basis is used. This shows that great care should be taken when choosing the depreciation method as this can have a substantial effect on the level of reported profit. The choice is rarely easy, however, as the depreciation policy must be decided upon when the asset is acquired and management does not know, at that stage, the precise benefit that will arise in each future accounting period. The decision is, therefore, to some extent arbitrary and, if an error is made, profit will be either under- or overstated.

Readers should now work Question 8.3 at the end of this chapter.

Estimation errors

In addition to the difficulty of selecting the most appropriate method, there is the problem of making accurate estimates of the useful life of the fixed asset, measured in terms of years or output, and its disposal value at the end of that period. Care should be exercised when making these estimates as errors produce an incorrect charge for depreciation and a consequent understatement or overstatement of profit.

Example 8.3

A machine is purchased for £60,000 on 1 January 19X1. It is estimated that the machine will last for five years and then have a zero disposal value. Management believes that each accounting period will benefit equally from the use of the machine and the straight-line method of depreciation is therefore considered appropriate.

Required

(a) Calculate the depreciation charge to be made each year, 19X1–X5.
(b) Assuming it turns out that all management's estimates are correct, except that it totally misjudges the second-hand demand for the machine, which eventually sells for £20,000, calculate the depreciation charge that *would* have been made each year if the disposal value had been accurately estimated.

Solution

(a) Depreciation charge $= \dfrac{£60,000}{5} = £12,000.$

(b) Depreciation charge $= \dfrac{£60,000-£20,000}{5} = £8,000.$

Because the disposal value was wrongly estimated, the annual charge is overstated and profit is understated by £4,000 during each of the five years of ownership. This is balanced by crediting £20,000 to the profit and loss account when the fixed asset, by this time completely written off, is sold for that figure. Where the profit on sale of a fixed asset is abnormally large, as in this case, the amount should be separately disclosed in the accounts so that users do not assume that the highly favourable results are derived from normal business operations.

INTANGIBLE FIXED ASSETS

Business assets may be classified as either tangible or intangible. Both categories of asset are valuable because they help the business to earn a profit. The most common examples of tangible assets are stocks and fixed assets. The main types of intangible assets are goodwill and research and development expenditure.

Goodwill

Goodwill arises as the result of business connections built up over a period of time. It was described as follows by Lord MacNaughton in CIR v. Muller (1901), A.C. 217:

> It is the benefit and advantage of the good name, reputation and connection of a business. It is the attractive force which brings in custom. It is the one thing which distinguishes an old established business from a new business at its first start.

Goodwill may be classified into 'purchased goodwill', which arises on the acquisition of an existing business, and 'non-purchased goodwill', which has been created but has no value and which has been evidenced by an arm's length transaction.

Purchased Goodwill This is calculated as the difference between the price paid for the business as a whole and the aggregate of the 'fair' (current) values of its various identifiable assets – both tangible and intangible.

Example 8.4

Ted Anthony who had been in business for many years decided to retire and sold his business assets, other than cash and debtors, to William Jones for £30,000. The tangible assets transferred consisted of premises worth £20,000, machinery worth £3,500 and stocks valued at £2,500.

Required

Calculate the value of goodwill arising on the sale of Ted Anthony's business to William Jones.

Note
William Jones took over none of the creditors or other liabilities of Ted Anthony.

Solution

	£	£
Purchase price		30,000
Less: Tangible assets		
Premises	20,000	
Machinery	3,500	
Stock	2,500	26,000
Goodwill		4,000

The total value of the tangible assets is £26,000, and we can therefore conclude that William Jones was willing to pay an extra £4,000 to cover the goodwill built up by Ted Anthony over the years.

In the above example, goodwill is the 'balancing' figure which results from comparing the agreed purchase price with the total value of the tangible assets acquired. The price paid for goodwill is initially recorded in the books of the acquiring company at cost, but goodwill does not last forever, e.g. the range of customers supplied gradually changes and those 'taken over' with the business eventually leave. Goodwill must therefore be written off either immediately against reserves, or gradually against profits over the estimated useful life of the asset. The latter approach is theoretically more sound as it complies with the accruals concept by attempting to match costs with revenues. Immediate write off is often the option selected, however, because it is favoured by Statement of Standard Accounting Practice (SSAP) 22, entitled Accounting for Goodwill, and because of the great difficulty of estimating the likely future life of this particular asset. A further advantage of immediate write-off is that it enables the business to report, in the future, higher profits than would otherwise be possible.

Non-purchased goodwill Goodwill is built up gradually over the years and, when a business person 'sells up', he or she expects the buyer to pay a price which covers the value of this asset. In these circumstances it is useful to prepare a valuation as a basis for negotiations. The following are two examples of the methods which may be used.

1. *Weighted average profits basis* Goodwill may be valued as a multiple of past profits. For this purpose a number of years' profits may be averaged and 'weights' attached to the profits arising each year.

Example 8.5

The profits of a partnership for the last three years are as follows: 19X1, £20,000; 19X2, £26,000; and 19X3, £31,000.

Required

Calculate goodwill on the basis of 1.5 times the weighted average profits of the last three years, using weights of 3 for the most recent year, 2 for the previous year and 1 for the earliest year.

Solution

Weighted average profits are calculated as follows:

Year	Weight	Profits	Total
		£	£
19X1	1	20,000	20,000
19X2	2	26,000	52,000
19X3	3	31,000	93,000
	─		
Total	6		165,000
	─		

Weighted average = $\dfrac{£165,000}{6}$ = £27,500

Goodwill = £27,500 × 1.5 = £41,250

2. *Super profit basis.* This method seeks to identify the additional profit earned by a firm because of the existence of goodwill. It then values the goodwill by attaching a capital value to the expected *future* stream of 'super profit.'

Example 8.6

Leake Ltd has earned profits averaging £20,000 per annum in recent years. It is estimated that £17,000 represents a reasonable return on the existing tangible assets.

	£
Actual profit	20,000
Normal profit	17,000
Super profit	3,000

The amount a buyer is willing to pay for the 'super profit' depends on what is considered a reasonable rate of return on intangible assets in this line of business. If a return of 20 per cent is considered reasonable, goodwill is worth:

$$\text{Goodwill} = £3,000 \times \frac{100}{20} = £15,000,$$

i.e. at a 20 per cent rate of interest, £15,000 must be invested to give an annual return of £3,000.

Both of the above approaches enable goodwill to be valued, but it does not necessarily follow that a buyer will be willing to pay either of these amounts or that the seller will accept them. The price actually paid for goodwill depends on negotiation between these two parties, and the main use of the above calculations is that they produce measures of value which can be referred to during discussions.

SSAP 22 categorically states that only purchased goodwill should be recognized in the accounts. The main reason for excluding non-purchased goodwill is that its value is subject to wide fluctuation due to both internal and external circumstances, making any assessment of its worth highly subjective and problematic. It is probably the right conclusion.

Readers should now work Question 8.4 at the end of this chapter.

Research and development expenditure (R & D)

Research is undertaken to discover new products and processes and to improve those products and processes already in existence. The development stage involves the conversion of these ideas into marketable products or services. In large organizations, separate departments are established to undertake these kinds of activities. The record-keeping system normally provides for the accumulation of research and development costs in a separate ledger account. The appropriate accounting treatment of such expenditure, at the end of an accounting period, has been the subject of debate for many years.

Because R & D is undertaken to help a company generate higher revenues in the future, it is reasonable to argue that it represents an asset that should be capitalized and written off against related revenues when they arise. Indeed, the proper application of the accruals concept would seem to require this procedure to be followed. In practice, companies are legally required to write off research expenditure immediately it is incurred, and also development expenditure unless a number of stringent conditions are met. These include requirements that development work should be reasonably well advanced, that the development costs can be accurately identified and that there exists a strong demand for the product.

The reason for the cautious accounting treatment of R & D expenditure is the difficulty of establishing whether a future benefit is likely to occur, and in one particularly well-known case R & D was heavily overvalued and investors and creditors totally misled. The case involved Rolls Royce, which collapsed in 1971 despite the fact that it had reported satisfactory profits and paid healthy dividends for many years. The company's problems were concealed by the capitalization of large amounts of R & D expenditure that were valueless and should have been written off. A more prudent, and realistic, treatment of this expenditure would have brought the company's difficulties to the attention of the investing public at a much earlier stage.

STOCK VALUATION METHODS

For a trading organization, stock consists of goods purchased but not sold at the end of the accounting period whereas, for a manufacturer, the term covers raw materials, work-in-progress and finished goods awaiting sale. In the service industry, the caption work-in-progress is used to cover the cost of services supplied but not yet billed. For many businesses stock is a large proportion of gross assets. The 1986 accounts of Vickers plc, for example, included stock amounting to £172,100,000, and this represented 31 per cent of its total assets.

The calculation of the figure for stock involves two steps: first, the physical quantities of stocks must be established; and, second, these physical quantities must be valued.

The quantity of stock on hand is usually established by a physical count after close of business at the end of the accounting period. Because of the import-ance of the 'stock count', stock-taking procedures should be worked out well in advance and the exercise undertaken in a systematic manner by reliable employees who are fully aware of their responsibilities. In these circumstances the likelihood of error, as the result of items being mis-described, counted twice or completely omitted, is reduced to a minimum. It is also necessary for management to take steps to ensure that all goods sold and invoiced to customers on the last day of the accounting period have been dispatched from the premises by the time the count takes place. Failure to ensure this happens may mean that profit is substantially overstated as the result of including certain items in *both* sales for the year and the year-end stock figure. For similar reasons management operates controls designed to ensure that all goods on the premises, and included in stock, are recorded in the books as purchases made during the year.

The way in which the quantities of stock are valued is now examined.

The basic rule

The fundamental rule is that stock would be valued at 'the *lower* of cost and net realizable value'. Readers will be broadly familiar with what is meant by cost (examined further in the section on calculating cost in this chapter), but the term 'net realizable value' (NVR) is met here for the first time. Basically, NRV is the market selling price of stock less any further costs to be incurred in its sale or disposal by the firm.

Example 8.7

The following information is provided relating to a vehicle held in stock by Thornhill Carsales Ltd:

	£
Cost	3,700
Market selling price	5,000

Salesmen are paid a commission of 2 per cent on market selling price, and it is the company's policy to allow the customer a full tank of petrol at an estimated cost of £20.

Required

Calculate the net realizable value of the vehicle.

Solution

	£	£
Net realizable value:		
Market selling price		5,000
Less: Further costs – Commission	100	
– Petrol	20	120
		4,880

NRV normally exceeds cost in a profitable concern, as is the case in the above example – NRV (£4,880) exceeds cost (£3,700) by £1,180. Sometimes NRV is below cost. For example, where an existing model of car is to be replaced, the firm will be anxious to clear its 'old' stock before it becomes unsaleable, and is likely to accept a low price.

Example 8.8

The following information is provided for three vehicles held in stock by Reliable Cars Ltd:

Vehicle	Cost	NRV
	£	£
A	5,400	6,200
B	5,200	8,500
C	7,100	6,200

Required

Calculate the value of Reliable Cars Ltd's stock for the purpose of its accounts.

Solution

Vehicle	Cost	NRV	Value for the accounts lower of cost and NRV
	£	£	£
A	5,400	6,200	5,400 (cost)
B	5,200	8,500	5,200 (cost)
C	7,100	6,200	6,200 (NRV)
	17,700	20,900	16,800

The total cost of the three vehicles is £17,700, compared with a total NRV of £20,900, i.e. total NRV exceeds total cost. It is to ensure that the fall in value of vehicle C is not ignored that the test is applied to each vehicle separately. Where the comparison between the cost and net realizable value of stock on an individual items' basis would be excessively time-consuming, for example, because of the large number of items involved, groups of similar items of stock may be compared.

Most of a company's stock is usually valued at cost, with a small number of items reduced to net realizable value either because they are damaged or because they are no longer popular with customers.

Readers should now work Question 8.5 at the end of this chapter.

Calculating cost

The calculation of the cost of stock is a straightforward matter in the case of a trading organization, and normally consists of the price paid to the supplier plus delivery charges (sometimes described as 'carriage inwards') where these are not included in the purchase price. The calculation is more difficult for a manufacturing organization because, in these businesses, cost consists of the price paid for raw materials *plus* the processing costs incurred to convert these materials into finished goods. This raises the question, 'Which processing costs should be included?' Clearly the wages paid to employees working with the materials should be included as part of the cost of the finished item, but what about the wages paid to supervisors and other essential manufacturing costs such as lighting and heating, rent and rates of the factory and depreciation of the machinery? In practice one of the following two procedures is followed:

1. Include only those costs that can be traced directly to the item manufactured. This is called the 'marginal (or prime) cost basis', and the costs included are normally materials costs and the wages paid to those employees directly involved in processing the materials.
2. Include all manufacturing costs, i.e. marginal costs plus a fair proportion of other manufacturing expenses, called 'manufacturing overheads', such as depreciation and factory rent and rates. This is called the 'total cost basis'.

The total cost figure for stock therefore exceeds the marginal cost figure by the amount of the fixed manufacturing overhead costs.

Example 8.9

The following data are provided relating to the manufacture of Nexo for the month of January 19X1:

	£
Raw materials used (£5 per unit)	6,000
Wages paid to staff directly involved in manufacture	8,400
Salary paid to supervisor	850
Rent and rates	420
Light and heat	670
Depreciation of machinery	460

During January 1,200 items were manufactured of which 1,000 were sold. There was no opening stock and no work-in-progress at the beginning or end of the month. Closing stock consists of 200 completed items.

Required

Valuations of closing stock on the:

(a) marginal cost basis;
(b) total cost basis.

Solution

(a) Marginal costs basis:

		£
Direct manufacturing costs: Raw materials		6,000
Labour		8,400
		14,400

Marginal cost per unit manufactured, £14,400/1,200 =		12
Marginal cost of unsold stock, £12 × 200 =		2,400

(b) Total cost basis:

		£	£
Direct manufacturing costs			14,400
Manufacturing overheads: Salary	850		
Rent and rates	420		
Light and heat	670		
Depreciation	460	2,400	
		16,800	

Total cost per unit manufactured, £16,800/1,200 =	14
Total cost of stock, £14 × 200 =	2,800

The total cost basis produces a cost per unit that is £2 more (£14 −£12). This results from the inclusion of a proportion of manufacturing overheads that amount, in total, to £2,400, or £2,400/1,200 = £2 per unit manufactured.

A company must be able to cover all its costs if it is to survive and flourish in the long run and, for this reason, companies are required to use the total cost basis when valuing stock for inclusion in the accounts published for external use. For internal reporting purposes, however, either total costs or marginal costs can be used and management may well regard the latter as the more relevant basis for *short-run* business decisions. For example, a business operating below its full productive capacity may find it worth while to accept orders at prices below total costs, provided marginal costs are covered, since overhead costs will be incurred anyway.

First in first out (FIFO) and last in first out (LIFO)

We saw in Chapter 4 that profit is calculated by matching costs with revenues arising during an accounting period. The difficulty, in the case of stocks, is to decide which costs to match with sales revenue in view of the large number of items acquired. It is theoretically possible to identify the actual items sold and, where a firm deals in a relatively small number of high-value items that can be easily identified, for example, cars, this procedure is followed in practice. Where there are a large number of transactions, however, the heavy additional cost involved in keeping such detailed records rules out this option. Instead the matching process is facilitated by making one of a number of arbitrary *assumptions* concerning the flow of goods into and out of the business. Two of the most common assumptions are as follows:

1. *First in first out (FIF0)* This assumes that the first items purchased are the first items sold. The items assumed to be in stock are therefore the most recent acquisitions.
2. *Last in first out (LIFO)* This assumes that the last items purchased are the first sold. The items assumed to be in stock are therefore likely to have been purchased months or even years ago.

Example 8.10

The following information is provided for Frame Ltd for 19X2:

	£
Opening stock, 200 units at £5 each	1,000
Purchases during 19X2, 1,000 units at £6 each	6,000
Sales during 19X2, 900 units at £10 each	9,000
Closing stock, 300 units	

Required

Calculate the value of Frame's closing stock using:
   (a) FIFO; and
   (b) LIFO.

Solution

	£
(a) FIFO, 300 units at £6	1,800

Note
The 900 items sold are assumed to be made up of the opening stock of 200 units, plus 700 units purchased during the year. Closing stock, therefore, consists of the remaining 300 units purchased during the year and are therefore valued at £6 each.

	£
(b) LIFO: 200 units at £5	1,000
100 units at £6	600
	1,600

Note
The 900 items sold are assumed to have been made entirely from purchases during the year. Closing stock is, therefore, assumed to consist of the opening stock of 200 units, plus the 100 units purchased during the year that were not sold.

Perpetual inventory

In the previous section the total number of items sold was deducted from the total number of items that came available for sale during the accounting period (i.e. opening stock + purchases), and the balance that remained was valued at latest purchase prices, under FIFO, and earliest purchase prices under LIFO. This is called the 'periodic basis' for matching stocks sold with those available for sale.

Many large companies operate a system of perpetual inventory. In such circumstances the stock records contain details of quantities, and sometimes also values, of the various types of stock on hand throughout the year. This enables the *transaction basis* to be used for matching stocks sold with those available for sale, i.e. each batch of goods dispatched is matched with stock on hand at that point in time, using FIFO or LIFO, as appropriate. Other advantages that result from the maintenance of detailed records are as follows:

1. They provide an element of control by showing the quantity of goods that *should* be in stock at a particular point in time. Any discrepancies compared with *actual* holdings can then be investigated.
2. Steps can be taken, in good time, to replenish stocks when they fall to a pre-determined minimum level.
3. Stock values are readily available for the purpose of management accounts, which are perhaps prepared monthly, and the annual accounts published for external use. At least once a year, however, and perhaps more often, it is necessary to have a physical stock-take to check the accuracy of the stock records.

Example 8.11

The following purchases and sales are made by Trader Ltd during the first two weeks of January 19X1. There are no opening stocks.

		Purchases		Sales	
		Units	Price per unit £	Units	Price per unit £
January	1	100	7	10	9
	2			20	9
	5			50	9
	7	75	8		
	10			20	9
	12			50	10
		175		150	

The physical stock-take confirmed that there were 25 units in stock at the year end.

Required

Write up the stock records of Trader Ltd using the transaction basis on the following alternative assumptions:

(a) Issues are made from stock on the FIFO basis.
(b) Issues are made from stock on the LIFO basis.

Solution

(a) **FIFO basis: stock card**

Date	Receipts			Issues			Balance		
	Units	Price	£	Units	Price	£	Units	Price	£
Jan. 1	100	7	700	10	7	70	90	7	630
Jan. 2				20	7	140	70	7	490
Jan. 5				50	7	350	20	7	140
Jan. 7	75	8	600				20	7	140
							75	8	600
Jan. 10				20	7	140	75	8	600
Jan. 12				50	8	400	25	8	200
	175		1,300	150		1,100			

(b) LIFO basis: stock card

Date	Receipts			Issues			Balance		
	Units	Price	£	Units	Price	£	Units	Price	£
Jan. 1	100	7	700	10	7	70	90	7	630
Jan. 2				20	7	140	70	7	490
Jan. 5				50	7	350	20	7	140
Jan. 7	75	8	600				20	7	140
							75	8	600
Jan. 10				20	8	160	20	7	140
							55	8	440
Jan. 12				50	8	400	20	7	140
							5	8	40
	175		1,300	150		1,120			

Stock valuation methods and changing prices

The adoption of the FIFO and LIFO assumptions have the following different effects on the figure for cost of goods sold and the valuation of stock during a period of *rising* prices.

1. *Cost of goods sold* This is higher under LIFO due to the fact that most recent purchases are matched with sales.
2. *Stock* This is valued at a higher figure under FIFO due to the fact that the most recent purchases are assumed to remain in stock.

The effect on the gross profit of Trader Ltd of using the two different methods (Example 8.11) is shown in the following summarized trading accounts:

Summary Trading Accounts, Transaction Basis

	FIFO £	LIFO £
Sales (100 × £9) + (50 × £10)	1,400	1,400
Less: Cost of goods sold	1,100	1,120
Gross profit	300	280

The above example shows that, when prices are rising, reported profit is higher using the FIFO cost-flow assumption. The opposite is the case when prices are falling. It is important that readers should recognize that actual events are unaffected by the choice of valuation method, but the selection usually alters the level of reported profit.

Weighted average cost (AVCO)

A further option is for firms to value cost of goods sold and closing stock at its weighted average cost (AVCO). This is fairly popular with companies and produces results that fall between those achieved by using FIFO or LIFO. The procedure is illustrated in Example 8.12.

Example 8.12

Using the information given in Example 8.11:

(a) Calculate the AVCO value of Trader's stock using (i) the periodic basis and (ii) the transaction basis.
(b) Prepare a summary trading account for Trader Ltd using AVCO on the transaction basis.

Solution

(a) (i) **Periodic basis:**

		Units	Price	£
Purchases:	1 January	100	7.00	700
	7 January	75	8.00	600
		175	7.43*	1,300

Notes
* £1,300/175 = £7.43 per unit.
Stocks are therefore valued at £7.43 × 25 = £186.

(a) (ii) **Transaction basis: stock card**

Date	Receipts			Issues			Balance		
	Units	Price	£	Units	Price	£	Units	Price	£
Jan. 1	100	7	700	10	7.00	70	90	7.00	630
Jan. 2				20	7.00	140	70	7.00	490
Jan. 5				50	7.00	350	20	7.00	140
Jan. 7	75	8	600				95	7.79*	740
Jan. 10				20	7.79	156	75	7.79	584
Jan. 12				50	7.79	389	25	7.79	195
	175		1,300	150		1,105			

Note
* £740/95 (units).

(b) Summary trading account – AVCO (transaction basis)

	£	£
Sales		1,400
Less: Cost of goods sold		1,105
Gross profit		295

Readers should now work Questions 8.6, 8.7 and 8.8 at the end of this chapter.

ACCOUNTING CONCEPTS

Accounting records and statements are based on a number of assumptions, called accounting concepts. The ten considered most important are examined below. The treatment is brief in those cases where the concept has already been discussed in an earlier chapter.

Entity concept

This fixes the boundary for the financial affairs contained in an accounting statement and was examined in Chapter 2. The boundary is often the business, but it may be a smaller or even a larger unit. For instance, a business may be split into a number of departments, each of which is treated as a separate entity for the purpose of preparing accounting statements for management (see Chapter 11). At the other extreme, a number of companies may be regarded as a single entity for accounting purposes. This occurs where a company owns the shares of one or more other companies. The connected companies together form a 'group', and their separate accounts are 'consolidated' for the purpose of reporting to shareholders. This topic is dealt with at a more advanced stage of study.

Money measurement concept

A business asset is reported in the balance sheet only if its value can be measured in money terms with a reasonable degree of precision. This concept was discussed in Chapter 2. A good example of the application of this concept concerns the accounting treatment of goodwill. We saw earlier in this chapter, that goodwill consists of the reputation and business connections built up over a period of time. Most firms enjoy an element of goodwill, but its value continuously fluctuates, and is therefore difficult to quantify with any degree of precision. For this reason the existence of goodwill is usually acknowledged by an entry in the accounts *only* when its value is proved by a market transaction involving its purchase and sale.

Matching concept

The accountant measures profit for a period of time, such as a year, by comparing or 'matching' revenue and expenditure identified with that period. The first step is to identify revenues and the second step is to deduct the expenditures incurred in producing the revenues. This concept was examined in Chapter 4. It should be noted that many of the concepts are closely interrelated. For example, the matching concept is put into effect by applying the realization concept and the accruals concept. These are considered next.

Realization concept

Revenue is assumed to be earned when a sale takes place and a legally enforceable claim arises against the customer. The effect of this rule is that stock usually remains in the books at cost until the sale takes place, at which stage a profit arises or a loss is incurred. This concept was discussed in Chapter 4.

The accruals concept

Costs are matched against revenues when the benefit of the expenditure is received rather than when the cash payment is made. Where the benefit is received *before* the payment is made, the amount owed is treated as a *liability* in the balance sheet. Where the benefit is received *after* the payment is made, the amount paid is treated as an *asset* in the balance sheet, and charged against revenues arising during whichever future accounting period benefits from the payments. This concept was examined in Chapter 4.

Readers should now work Question 8.9 at the end of this chapter.

Historical cost concept

Assets are initially recorded at the price paid to the supplier. In certain circumstances further costs may be added. For example, in the case of a manufacturing concern a proportion of the production costs should be added to the cost of raw materials to arrive at the cost of finished goods (see earlier in this chapter). In the case of fixed assets their recorded cost includes not only the price paid to the supplier but also all incidental costs incurred to make the item ready for use (see earlier in this chapter). A major advantage of this concept is that the accounting records are based on objective facts. A disadvantage of using historical cost is that, during a period of rising prices, the reported figures may significantly understate the asset's true value to the business. It is for this reason that some companies periodically revalue their fixed assets and/or publish supplementary accounts designed to take account of the effects of inflation (see further discussion in Chapter 10).

Going concern concept

This assumes that the business is a permanent venture and will not be wound up in the foreseeable future. Many fixed assets, which cost a great deal, have low resale values because they have been specially designed for a particular business. The going concern concept allows accountants to ignore this low resale value and instead spread the cost of an asset over the accounting periods that benefit from its use. The assumption that the business will continue indefinitely as a going concern is, however, in certain circumstances false and must be dropped. For example, if a company is about to be liquidated, forecasts of the amounts likely to be received by various providers of finance should be based on estimates of what the business assets are expected to realize in the market rather than their historical book value.

Consistency concept

The same valuation methods should be used each year when preparing accounting statements. We have seen that there exist a number of methods for valuing fixed assets and stocks. There are arguments in favour and against most of them and, to some extent, an arbitrary choice must be made. The effect on reported profit is unlikely to be significant, however, provided similar procedures are adopted each year. For example, when prices are rising the FIFO method of matching stock purchased with stock sold produces a higher figure for stock than the LIFO method, but it does not necessarily produce a higher profit figure. Businesses have both opening and closing stock and use of the FIFO approach produces a higher figure for stock at both dates.

Example 8.13

The following information is provided for one of the products traded in by Ridgeway Ltd:

		£
Opening stock,	100 units valued as follows:	
	LIFO basis, £5 per unit × 100	500
	FIFO basis, £8 per unit × 100	800
Purchases during January 19X1, 300 units at £8		2,400
Sales during January 19X1, 300 units at £11		3,300

Required

(a) Valuations of closing stock using (i) LIFO and (ii) FIFO.
(b) Trading accounts for January 19X1 using (i) LIFO and (ii) FIFO.

Solution

(a) **Valuation of closing stock**   Opening stock is 100 units and, as the same number of items are purchased as are sold, closing stock is also 100 units, although these will almost certainly be different items from those owned at the beginning of the month.

(i)   LIFO (this approach assumes that the 300 items sold are the 300 items purchased during January) 100 × £5 = £500.
(ii)   FIFO (this approach assumes that the 300 items sold includes the opening stock of 100 units) 100 × £8 = £800.

(b) Trading Accounts, January 19X1

		LIFO		FIFO	
		£	£	£	£
Sales			3,300		3,000
Less:	Opening stock	500		800	
	Purchases	2,400		2,400	
	Closing stock	(500)		(800)	
	Cost of goods sold		2,400		2,400
Gross profit			900		900

The higher opening and closing valuations, on the FIFO basis, cancel out, and gross profit is unaffected by the valuation method adopted. It should be noted, however, that the balance sheet figure for stocks and, therefore, gross assets and net assets are higher if FIFO is used. It should also be noted that reported profit *does vary* when there are *changes* in the level of stock because, in these circumstances, the opening and closing balances no longer cancel out. However, the difference is unlikely to be large unless the change in the level of stock is substantial, such as occurs when new business operations commence.

The level of reported profit can be significantly inflated or deflated if a company changes from one method to another.

Example 8.14

Assume the same facts as for Example 8.13, except that LIFO is used at the beginning of the year and FIFO at the end.

Required

The trading account for January 19X1.

Solution

Trading Account, January 19X1

		£	£
Sales			3,300
Less:	Opening stock (LIFO)	500	
	Purchases	2,400	
	Closing stock (FIFO)	800	
	Cost of goods sold		2,100
Gross profit			1,200

Gross profit is £1,200 in Example 8.14 as compared with £900 in Example 8.13. Profit is therefore inflated by £300 as the result of switching from one valuation method to another, i.e. the FIFO closing stock figure, of £800, instead of the LIFO closing stock figure of £500. As the result of the change, reported profits are greater than actual profits and wrong conclusions may be reached concerning the performance of Ridgeway Ltd. It is, therefore, important for valuation procedures to be consistently applied so that reported results fairly reflect performance during the year, and valid comparisons can be made with results achieved in previous accounting periods.

While consistency is a *fundamental* accounting concept (see Chapter 10), it does not mean that methods, once adopted, should never be changed. Sound and convincing arguments must be put forward, however, to justify departures from existing practices. The essential test is whether management can show that the new procedures result in a fairer presentation of the financial performance and position of the concern. When a change is made, the impact on comparability between two sets of figures must be noted and, wherever possible, quantified, so that it can be taken into account when measuring performance. For example, if a firm switches from AVCO to FIFO, profit and stock values for the previous year must be recomputed, using FIFO, so that a proper assessment of comparative performance can be made.

It must be emphasized that inconsistent accounting methods can have a marked effect on the information contained in accounting statements. The changes are not always explained as clearly as they should be, and users must scrutinize the accounts vigilantly to ensure that distorted financial information does not cause them to make a wrong decision.

Readers should now work Question 8.10 at the end of this chapter.

Prudence concept

The prudence concept (sometimes called the concept of conservatism) requires the accountant to make full provision for all expected losses and not to anticipate revenues until they are realized. A good example of how this concept affects accounting practice is the basic rule that stock should be valued at the lower of cost and net realizable value (NRV). Where NRV is above cost, the profit likely to arise in the near future is ignored and stock remains in the accounts at the lower figure until the sale occurs, i.e. revenue is not anticipated. On the other hand, where NRV is below cost, stock must be immediately restated at the lower figure so that full provision is made for the foreseeable future loss.

Approval of a prudent approach to profit measurement is based on the potential dangers of an over-optimistic calculation that may be used as the basis for an excessive distribution of funds, to ownership, that deprives the concern of much needed resources. Another possible pitfall is that an attractive presentation of the current position, not justified by the underlying facts, may cause management to expand the level of operations wrongly and, when this happens, heavy losses can result. New projects often involve a substantial commitment of resources, the bulk of which is tied up in fixed assets. The only way the firm is likely to recoup its money is by using the assets to produce and sell goods at a profit. Caution is, therefore, highly desirable when management is considering whether to make an investment, and any accounting statement used to help reach this decision should be prepared on a prudent basis. This may mean that, occasionally, good opportunities are missed, but this will not happen often, and the likely loss from an ill-conceived investment will be many times greater than the profit possibly forgone.

It is important, however, not to take the prudence concept too far. Where there are a number of likely outcomes, it is usually wise to choose the lower figure, but profit should not be deliberately understated. Accounting statements are used as the basis for decision-making, and they should contain realistic not excessively pessimistic financial information. Understatement can be just as misleading as overstatement and, although the potential loss from the misallocation of resources that may result is less, it can be avoided by preparers of accounting reports exercising a reasonable level of caution.

Materiality

Accounting statements should contain only those financial facts that are material, or relevant, to the decision being taken by the recipient of the report. It is, therefore, important for the accountant to be familiar with the user's requirement so that he or she can decide which information should be included and excluded. For example, if an accounting statement is prepared to help management assess which departments are most successful, it is clearly essential for the report to show the profits earned by each of them. This means identifying the revenues and expenditures that relate to each department, but unnecessary detail is omitted – for example, a manager is interested in knowing the individual amounts expended on materials, wages, power, depreciation, etc., but not on Christmas gratuities, the ingredients for morning coffee and paper towels. Trivial items are, therefore, grouped together under the heading 'sundry expenses'. For similar reasons balance sheets contain values for the main categories of assets and liabilities but do not give figures for each item of plant, stock, etc.

Accounting statements prepared for shareholders of limited companies contain even less detail. This is partly because such information is of little interest to them. It is management's job to decide how to allocate resources between various investment opportunities, while the shareholder is primarily interested in assessing whether the overall performance is satisfactory. It is, therefore, considered desirable to keep to a minimum detailed facts that may be difficult to assimilate, and instead concentrate on the broad overall pattern of developments. It must be admitted that the sophisticated institutional investor would welcome far more detail than is sometimes provided in the published accounts, but there is a natural reluctance to publish sensitive material that could be of use to competitors.

There is another aspect of materiality, and this concerns the amount of detail the accountant goes into when measuring profit. A good example is the use of FIFO and LIFO instead of attempting to match individual purchases with sales. Another example is the decision not to distinguish between capital and revenue expenditure where the amount spent on a fixed asset is small. For example, minor items of office equipment such as staplers and punches last for a number of years, but it is not usually considered worth while to capitalize and depreciate them systematically over their expected useful life. Instead they are written off immediately against revenue. A detailed treatment is justified only if the extra costs involved produces a significant improvement in the quality of the information contained in accounting statements. When applying this test, it must be remembered that, because of the need for estimates to be made and judgement to be exercised, the reported profit figure is at best an approximation and is unlikely to be improved by making precise adjustments for trivial items.

QUESTIONS

8.1 (a) How would you distinguish between capital and revenue expenditure and why is it important to make a correct allocation?

(b) State, with reasons, in which of the two categories you would place the following items:

(i)   Replacement of the blade on a cutting machine damaged as the result of using poor-quality raw material inputs.

(ii)   A feeding device costing £1,000 that is fixed to a machine so as to enable a 20 per cent increase in throughput each hour.

(iii)   The cost of transporting, to the factory, a new machine supplied by a Japanese company.

(iv)   Second-hand plant purchased at a cost of £1,500.

(v)   Repairs to the plant mentioned in (iv) above before it is ready for use, £300.

8.2   Simon is a surveyor who purchases old properties in poor condition. He incurs expenditure on improving these properties, which he then resells. His balance sheet at 31 December 19X2 was as follows:

	£		£
Properties on hand (including expenses on purchase)		Capital	79,000
1	30,250		
2	29,350		
Bank balance	19,400		
	79,000		79,000

During 19X3 he bought three more properties:

	Cost	Legal expenses borne by Simon	Cost of improvement
	£	£	£
3	36,250	1,000	260
4	24,000	750	1,000
5	25,000	800	520

and sold the following three properties:

	Sale price £	Legal expenses borne by Simon £
1	34,000	400
3	42,500	500
4	31,250	350

General expenses incurred and paid during 19X3 amounted to £2,500.

Required

(a) Simon's bank account for 19X3.
(b) A profit and loss account for the year 19X3 covering Simon's property deals and a balance sheet at 31 December 19X3.

Notes
1. Cash due from the sale of property 4 was not received until 5 January 19X4.
2. There were no other transactions during the year and all receipts and payments were by cheque.

8.3   On the 1 April 1986 a business purchased a machine costing £112,000. The machine can be used for a total of 20,000 hours over an estimated life of 48 months. At the end of that time the machine is expected to have a trade-in value of £12,000.

The financial year of the business ends on the 31 December each year. It is expected that the machine will be used for:

4,000 hours during the financial year ending 31 December 1986
5,000 hours during the financial year ending 31 December 1987
5,000 hours during the financial year ending 31 December 1988
5,000 hours during the financial year ending 31 December 1989
1,000 hours during the financial year ending 31 December 1990

Required

(a) Calculate the annual depreciation charges on the machine on each of the following bases for each of the financial years ending on the 31 December 1986, 1987, 1988, 1989 and 1990:
  (i)   the straight-line method applied on a month-for-month basis;
  (ii)   the diminishing balance method at 40 per cent per annum applied on a full-year basis; and
  (iii) the units of output method.   (10 marks)
(b) Suppose that during the financial year ended 31 December 1987 the machine was used for only 1,500 hours before being sold for £80,000 on the 30 June.

   Assuming that the business has chosen to apply the straight-line method on a month-for-month basis, show the following accounts *for 1987 only:*

  (i)   the machine account;
  (ii)   the provision for depreciation – machine account; and
  (iii) the assets disposals account.   (10 marks)
                                                              (Total 20 marks)
                                    (*AAT, Basic Accounting, June, 1986*)

8.4   Buy Ltd paid Mr Sale £120,000, cash, to acquire his business, Sale & Co., as a going concern on 1 January 19X1. The assets taken over were considered to be worth the following amounts:

		£
Fixed assets		71,500
Stock		20,000
Debtors		10,000

In addition Buy Ltd assumed responsibility for paying Sale & Co.'s outstanding creditors, which amounted to £5,000. The policy of Buy Ltd is to write off goodwill over a five-year period.

Required

(a) Calculate the goodwill arising on the acquisition of Sale & Co.
(b) Show how goodwill will appear in the balance sheet of Buy Ltd as at 31 December 19X1.

8.5   Give the basic rule for valuing stock. Apply this rule to the facts provided below and calculate the total value of stock to be included in the accounts.

Product	Cost	Net realizable value
	£	£
A	2,400	2,760
B	1,290	740
C	3,680	750
D	2,950	4,760
E	6,280	9,730

8.6.   What do you understand by the terms 'perpetual inventory' and 'periodic stock-take'? In the case of a trader, how is the figure for cost of goods sold obtained under each of these systems?

8.7   Seconds Ltd started trading on 1 January and during that month undertook the following transactions in respect of product Alpha:

Date–Jan.	Purchases units	Cost per unit £	Sales units	Price per unit £
8	100	20	–	–
13	60	25	–	–
14	–	–	125	40
17	75	30	–	–
22	–	–	30	42

Required

Using the periodic basis for matching sales with stock on hand, calculate figures for (a) closing stock; (b) cost of goods sold; (c) gross profit on each of the following bases:

(i)   FIFO,
(ii) LIFO,
(iii) AVCO.

Calculations to the nearest £.

8.8   Stoval Ltd started to trade on 1 January 19X1. Its purchases of trading stock, at cost, during the first three years of business were

	£
19X1	240,000
19X2	252,000
19X3	324,000

The values of stock at 31 December, under different valuation methods, were:

31 December	LIFO cost	FIFO cost	Lower of FIFO cost and net realizable value
19X1	£96,480	£96,000	£88,800
19X2	£87,360	£86,400	£81,600
19X3	£100,320	£105,600	£105,600

Required

(a) Assuming that in any one year prices moved either up or down, but not both in the same year:
   (i) Did prices go up or down in 19X1?
   (ii) Did prices go up or down in 19X3?
(b) Which stock valuation method would show the highest profit for 19X1?
(c) Which stock valuation method applied to opening and closing stock would show the highest profit for 19X3?
(d) Which stock valuation method would show the lowest profit for all three years combined?

8.9   Where accounts are prepared in accordance with the *accruals concept*, cash receipts and payments may precede, coincide with, or follow the period in which revenues and expenses are recognized. Give two examples of each of the following:

(a) A cash receipt that precedes the period in which revenue is recognized.
(b) A cash receipt that coincides with the period in which revenue is recognized.
(c) A cash receipt that follows the period in which revenue is recognized.
(d) A cash payment that precedes the period in which expense is recognized.
(e) A cash payment that coincides with the period in which expense is recognized.
(f) A cash payment that follows the period in which expense is recognized.

8.10   The summarized trading account of Change Ltd for 19X1 contained the following information:

Trading Account for 19X1

		£	£
Sales			100,000
Less:	Opening stock	7,000	
	Purchases	80,000	
	Closing stock	(11,000)	
	Cost of goods sold		76,000
Gross profit			24,000

Opening stock is valued at marginal cost, but the directors have now decided that total cost is more suitable, and this basis was used for the purpose of valuing closing stock. The value of opening stock, on the total cost basis, is found to be £10,000.

Required

(a) Prepare a revised trading account for Change Ltd complying with the consistency concept.
(b) Indicate the effect of the revision on the *net* profit figure reported by Change Ltd for 19X1.

9
Partnerships

INTRODUCTION

Partnerships use the same basic accounting techniques as those described so far in this book in the context of the sole trader, although some modifications are required in their application to suit the different constitution of the partnership. There is no legal requirement for partnerships to prepare annual accounts, but the need to share profits between the partners and for partners to submit tax returns makes their routine production essential if the conduct of the partnership is to proceed smoothly. As with sole traders, there is no requirement for the contents of partnership accounts to be made public even though they may relate to significant economic entities: this contrasts with the disclosure requirements imposed on limited companies described in Chapter 10.

The legal background is provided by the Partnership Act 1890, which defines a partnership as 'the relation which subsists between persons carrying on a business in common with a view of profit'. There is no formal legal procedure necessary to create a partnership; it can be deemed to exist because people are trading in a way that brings them within the definition. It is very important to determine whether a person is a partner as the liability of each partner for all of the firm's debts is unlimited; if the firm cannot pay, then each partner becomes personally liable to the extent of the entire debt. (The Limited Partnership Act 1907 makes special provision for a partnership to have limited partners whose liability is restricted to the value of their capital investment, provided there is at least one general partner who accepts full liability for all of the firm's debts. This provision is not widely used.)

The most common reasons for forming a partnership are to raise the necessary finance to fund planned operations, and to pool together complementary skills, for example, an engineer who is very capable at developing new products may need the services of a salesman or woman to market them.

The number of partners allowed to combine in a partnership is limited to twenty, although some specific exemptions are granted, for example, firms of chartered accountants can have any number of partners. If a firm limited to twenty partners wishes to seek funds from a larger group, then incorporation as a limited company is first necessary (see Chapter 10).

THE PARTNERSHIP AGREEMENT

The owners of a partnership, the partners, also manage it, and each partner can enter into contracts on behalf of the firm that are binding on the partnership as a whole. In these circumstances, the partners must have a great deal of mutual trust, and it is best for the manner in which the partnership is to be conducted to be set out formally in a legally-binding partnership agreement signed by all of the partners. Examples of the matters to be covered by such an agreement are as follows:

1. The purpose for which the partnership is formed.
2. The amount of capital each partner is to contribute.
3. Regulations to be observed when the partnership is created.
4. How profits and losses are to be divided between the partners.
5. Whether separate capital and current accounts are to be maintained.
6. The extent to which partners can make drawings.
7. The frequency with which accounts are to be prepared and whether they are to be subjected to an independent audit.
8. Regulations to be observed when a partner retires or a new partner is admitted, the profit-sharing ratio changes, or the partnership is dissolved.

Where no formal agreement exists, the terms of the partnership may be concluded from past behaviour, for example, if profits have always been divided between two partners in the ratio 2:1, without dissent from either partner, then this is presumed to be the agreed ratio. The Partnership Act 1890 provides a 'safety net' of regulations that apply when there is no agreement, either formal or informal, to the contrary. Among the major of these provisions are the following:

1. All profits and losses are to be shared equally among the partners.
2. No interest on capital or remuneration for conducting the partnership business is payable to any partner.
3. A partner is entitled to 5 per cent per annum interest on any loans to the partnership in excess of his or her agreed capital contribution.
4. Every partner is authorized to take part in the firm's management.
5. All existing partners must agree to the admission of a new partner.

THE CREATION OF A PARTNERSHIP

When a partnership is formed, the contribution of each partner is recorded in its books at its current, agreed value. The capital may consist simply of cash or, where the partner already operates as a sole trader, comprise a collection of assets, and possibly liabilities. As was the case with the sole trader, the value of the capital of each partner is equal to, and can be calculated as, the value of the assets contributed less any liabilities. The entries made in the books to record the assets, liabilities (if any) and capital introduced by a partner, on the formation of a partnership, are:

Debit	Credit	With
Various asset accounts		Assets contributed
	Various liability accounts	Liabilities taken over
	Capital account	Value of assets less liabilities

The merging of two sole traders to create a partnership is shown in Example 9.1.

Example 9.1

Beaver and Burroughes are two sole traders who decide to enter into partnership as from 1 March 1986. Their respective balance sheets as at the close of business on 28 February 1986 were as follows:

BEAVER

	£		£
Capital Account	2,990	Office Furniture	500
Creditors	850	Delivery Van	660
Bank Overdraft	320	Stock	1,440
		Debtors	1,530
		Cash in hand	30
	4,160		4,160

BURROUGHES

	£		£
Capital Account	5,200	Office Furniture	550
Creditors	920	Delivery Van	750
		Stock	1,970
		Debtors	1,730
		Bank	1,120
	6,120		6,120

The partnership acquired *all* the assets and took over *all* the liabilities at the figures shown in the above balance sheets except that:

	Beaver	Burroughes
	£	£
1. Office furniture is to be revalued	400	480
2. Stock is to be revalued	1,300	1,900
3. Goodwill is valued at	–	400
4. Bad debts are to be written off	120	80
5. The bank accounts are to be closed and a new partnership bank account opened.		

Required

(i)   Calculate the opening capital of each of the two partners. (Calculations *must* be shown.)

(ii) Draw up the *opening* Balance Sheet of the partnership.

(LCC, Elementary Book-Keeping, winter, 1986)

Solution

(i)

	Beaver	Burroughes	Total
	£	£	£
Office furniture	400	480	880
Delivery vans	660	750	1,410
Stock	1,300	1,900	3,200
Debtors	1,410	1,650	3,060
Goodwill	–	400	400
Cash	30	–	30
Bank	(320)	1,120	800
Creditors	(850)	(920)	(1,770)
	2,630	5,380	8,010

(ii) Partnership Balance Sheet, 1 March 1986

	£	£
Goodwill		400
Office furniture		880
Delivery vans		1,410
		2,690
Stock	3,200	
Debtors	3,060	
Bank	800	
Cash	30	
	7,090	
Creditors	(1,770)	
		5,320
		8,010

Financed by:
Beaver – Capital account   2,630
Burroughes – Capital account   5,380
                                                                                                            ——
                                                                                                          8,010
                                                                                                            ——

THE DIVISION OF PROFIT

The net profit of a partnership is calculated in the usual way, and is then transferred to the appropriation account where it is divided between the partners in the agreed manner. The agreement may provide for a straightforward allocation in accordance with a specific ratio, such as 3:2; alternatively, precise adjustments may be made to take account of the following factors:

1. The partners may provide different amounts of capital; this involves sacrificing different amounts of interest that could have been earned by, for example, putting the money in a bank deposit account. Compensation for this can be achieved by allowing a deduction to be made in the appropriation account for interest on partner's capital. The rate of interest may be fixed in the agreement or, because rates of interest fluctuate, it could be tied to some external indicator, such as the rate paid on long-term deposit accounts by banks. In whichever way the rate is determined, the greater the amount of capital a partner has invested in the firm, the greater is the interest received.
2. By deciding to join a partnership, each partner forgoes potential earnings as an employee of another firm. The sacrifice of alternative income may not be the same for each partner, for example, one may contribute more valuable skills. This can be recognized by giving each partner a salary related to potential 'outside earnings'. Such salaries are also deducted from profit in the appropriation account.
3. Partners make drawings from the firm that reduce the amount of their investment, and it may be decided to recognize this by charging partners interest on their drawings. This interest is then added to the profit to be shared between the partners.
4. After any interest and salaries have been deducted, there must be agreement on how to divide the residual profit or loss. The ratio in which it is shared may be designed to reflect the partner's seniority, or some other basis, such as equality, may be adopted.

The steps necessary to carry out the division of partnership profit are as follows:

1. Determine the manner in which profit is to be divided.
2. Determine the value of profit or loss to be shared. The value found *takes no account* of any payments to the partners, for example, in the form of salaries, and is transferred to the appropriation account.

3. Add to profit any interest charged on drawings made by the partners.
4. Deduct from profit any interest allowed on capital account balances and any salaries payable to partners.
5. Split the residual profit or loss in the agreed ratio.

Steps 3 to 5 are recorded in the firm's books with the following entries:

Debit	Credit	With
Capital account*	Profit and loss appropriation account	Interest charged on drawings
Profit and loss appropriation account	Capital account*	Interest allowed on capital, salaries and share of profit
Capital account*	Profit and loss appropriation account	Share of losses

Note
* These entries are instead made in the current accounts of partners where such accounts are maintained (see the section on capital and current accounts that follows).

The division of profit in the appropriation account is illustrated in Example 9.2.

Example 9.2

Oak and Tree are in partnership and prepare their accounts on a calendar-year basis. They have agreed that profits are to be shared as follows:

1. Oak is to receive an annual salary of £5,000 and Tree one of £10,000.
2. Interest at 10 per cent per annum is to be paid on each partner's capital account balance as on 1 January.
3. Residual profits and losses are to be shared equally.

On 1 January 19X6 the balance on Oak's capital account was £64,000 and on Tree's it was £30,000.

Required

Prepare the partnership's appropriation account on the alternative assumptions that the profit for 19X6 was:

(a) £30,000,
(b) £20,000.

Solution

(a) **Appropriation Account**

		£		£
Salary:	Oak	5,000	Profit	30,000
	Tree	10,000		
Interest:	Oak	6,400		
	Tree	3,000		
Residue:	Oak	2,800		
	Tree	2,800		
		30,000		30,000

(b) **Appropriation Account**

		£			£
Salary:	Oak	5,000	Profit		20,000
	Tree	10,000	Share of loss:	Oak	2,200
Interest:	Oak	6,400		Tree	2,200
	Tree	3,000			
		24,400			24,400

Note
If there is no agreement to the contrary, the profits in the above example would have been divided between the partners in accordance with the terms of the Partnership Act 1890. Each would have received an equal share, namely, £15,000 in (a) and £10,000 in (b).

Readers should now work Question 9.1, which extends the above example to three partners and includes interest charged on drawings, and Question 9.2, both of which are at the end of this chapter.

CAPITAL AND CURRENT ACCOUNTS

The capital each partner invests in the business can be divided into two elements:

1. The part permanently required to finance the ability of the firm to trade. It is invested in fixed assets and working capital and cannot be withdrawn without reducing the capacity of the business.
2. The part that can be withdrawn by the partners as drawings.

The permanent capital of each partner is entered in a 'capital account'. The partnership agreement usually stipulates the amount of permanent capital invested by each partner, and the balances remain constant until the partners agree to a change. Routine transactions between partners and the firm are entered in a 'current account'. The current account balance fluctuates as it is credited with each partner's share of profits, in the form of interest, salary and share of residue, and is debited with drawings and interest on drawings. To prevent partners withdrawing more than their entitlement, the partnership agreement should state that no current account is allowed to have a debit balance without the consent of the other partners.

Example 9.3

Disk and Drive trade in partnership. The following information relates to 19X7:

	Disk £	Drive £
Current account balance 1 January 19X7	9,130	8,790
Interest allowed on capital	1,000	1,500
Interest charged on drawings	150	390
Salary	5,000	3,000
Share of residual profit	6,250	6,250
Cash drawings	7,160	8,240
Stock drawings	120	80

Required

Prepare the current accounts of Disk and Drive for 19X7. For each entry indicate clearly the location of its corresponding double entry.

Solution

Current Accounts

	Disk £	Drive £		Disk £	Drive £
Appropriation Account:			Balance b/d	9,130	8,790
Interest	150	390	Appropriation Account:		
Drawings:			Interest	1,000	1,500
Cash account	7,160	8,240	Salary	5,000	3,000
Purchases a/c	120	80	Residue	6,250	6,250
Balance c/d	13,950	10,830			
	21,380	19,540		21,380	19,540

It is possible for substantial balances to accumulate in the current accounts where partners consistently withdraw less than their share of the profits. The funds represented by these balances may have been invested in trading assets, and so have taken on the aspect of permanent capital, that is, they are not available for quick withdrawal. This position is shown in Figure 9.1.

			£000
Fixed assets			75
Working capital			25
			—
			100
			—

	Paper	Clip	Total
	£000	£000	£000
Capital accounts	20	20	40
Current accounts	30	30	60
	—	—	—
	50	50	100
	—	—	—

Figure 9.1   Summarized Balance Sheet of Paper and Clip at 31 December 19X9

It is clear that the current account balances could not be withdrawn without reducing the size of the business, since a large proportion of these balances has been invested in fixed assets that would have to be sold to release cash. This is unlikely to happen, and so to bring the balance sheet into line with economic reality, the partners may agree that each of them should transfer, say, £25,000 from current to capital account. The transfer is entered in the books by a debit in each current account and a corresponding credit in each capital account. This increase in capital account balances does not provide the firm with any additional funds, but simply recognizes that the partners have invested funds previously available as drawings in the permanent structure of the undertaking. When *additional* capital funds are required by a partnership, they must be introduced by the partners and credited to their capital accounts.

Readers should now work Question 9.3 at the end of this chapter.

CHANGES IN MEMBERSHIP

The partnership business, unlike a limited company, is not recognized in law as a separate *legal* entity, and so a change in the ownership creates a new business. For accounting purposes, the firm is treated as a continuing entity and the same set of books usually remains in use when a new partner joins or an existing one retires, but entries must be made in the books to give effect to any financial adjustments needed.

Each partner is entitled to their share of the profits, or losses, that have accrued during the period of time for which they have been a partner. Adjustment must be made, when a partner retires or joins, for any increase in value not yet recognized in the accounts, otherwise the retiring partner is not credited with the full amount due and the incoming partner is credited with a share of the assets at below their current value. This is demonstrated in Example 9.4.

Example 9.4

The following is the summarized balance sheet of Lamp and Bulb, who share profits in the ratio 3:2 respectively, at 31 December 19X5:

	£
Net assets	2,000
Financed by:	
Lamp – Capital account	1,000
Bulb – Capital account	1,000
	2,000

The following is agreed:

1. Bulb is to retire on 1 January 19X6.
2. The net assets have a current value of £3,000.
3. Bulb is to be paid the sum due to him in cash immediately.
4. Socket is to be admitted as a partner on 1 January 19X6.
5. Socket and Lamp agree to share future profits and losses equally.
6. Socket agrees to introduce cash equal to the value of Lamp's capital after the assets have been adjusted to current values.
7. Current accounts shall not be maintained.

Required

(a) Calculate the amount due to Bulb on his retirement.
(b) Calculate the amount of capital to be introduced by Socket.
(c) Prepare the opening balance sheet of the Lamp and Socket partnership.
(d) Comment on the consequences of not adjusting the assets to current values.

Solution

(a)

	£	£
Current value of net assets		3,000
Historical cost of net assets		2,000
Increase in value		1,000
Share of increase: Lamp	600	
Bulb	400	
		1,000
Amount due to Bulb:		
Capital		1,000
Revaluation surplus		400
Total due		1,400

(b) Lamp and Socket have agreed to share profits equally and the amount Socket should therefore introduce as capital is the same as the balance on Lamp's capital account:

1,000 (balance) + 600 (revaluation surplus) = 1,600.

(c) **Balance sheet of Lamp and Socket**

	£
Net assets	3,200*
Financed by:	
Lamp – Capital account	1,600
Socket – Capital account	1,600
	3,200

Note
* 2,000 (Original value) + 1,000 (Revaluation) − 1,400 (Paid to Bulb) + 1,600 (Cash from Socket) = £3,200.

(d) Without the revaluation, Bulb would withdraw only the balance on his capital account, i.e. £1,000. He therefore leaves £400 in the business that has accrued under his ownership. Socket would introduce only £1,000, the same as the balance on Lamp's capital account, but would be buying a half share in assets with a current value of £3,000.

We will now examine how these matters are recorded in the books of the partnership. To record the revaluation of assets a revaluation account is used in which the following entries are made:

Debit	*Credit*	*With*
Revaluation account	Asset account	Reduction in asset value
Asset account	Revaluation account	Increase in asset value

The revaluation account contains all the increases and decreases in value, and its balance – the net surplus or deficit – is shared between the partners in the agreed ratio. Each partner's share of the net adjustment is entered in his or her capital account as it is permanent in nature. The revaluation account and capital accounts of Lamp, Bulb and Socket, from Example 9.4, would contain the following information:

Revaluation Account

	£		£
Surplus shared:		Increase in value of	
Lamp – Capital	600	net assets	1,000
Bulb – Capital	400		
	1,000		1,000

Capital Accounts

	Lamp £	Bulb £	Socket £		Lamp £	Bulb £	Socket £
Cash		1,400		Balance b/d	1,000	1,000	
Balance c/d	1,600		1,600	Revaluation	600	400	
				Cash			1,600
	1,600	1,400	1,600		1,600	1,400	1,600

As well as adjusting the values of tangible assets included in the balance sheet, it is also usually necessary to create a balance for goodwill, since the partners are also entitled to share in the value of this intangible asset. The appropriate share of goodwill created during his or her period of ownership is due to a retiring partner, and an incoming partner must expect to pay for a share of existing goodwill.

The partners in the new firm may decide to record the assets taken over at their revalued figures; alternatively they may choose to restate some, or all, of the assets at their pre-revaluation amounts. If the latter course is adopted, the adjustment must be shared between the partners in the new firm in accordance with their agreed profit-sharing ratio. Usually, the revised figures for tangible assets are accepted and goodwill is written off.

Example 9.5

Bill, Ben and Flo are in partnership together and share profits and losses in the ratio of 2:2:1 respectively. The balance sheet of the partnership at 31 December 19X0 was as follows:

	£000	£000
Fixed assets		
Land and buildings		50
Plant and equipment		175
		225

	£000	£000
Brought forward		225
Current assets		
Stock	80	
Debtors	90	
Cash	5	
	175	
Less:		
Trade creditors	110	
		65
		290
Financed by:		
Capital accounts		
Bill	90	
Ben	80	
Flo	70	
		240
Current accounts		
Bill	10	
Ben	25	
Flo	15	
		50
		290

The following information is relevant:

1. Bill decides to retire on 31 December 19X0, while Ben and Flo intend to continue trading, sharing profits and losses equally.
2. To determine the amount due to Bill, the partners agree that the assets should be revalued as follows:

	£000
Land and buildings	165
Plant and equipment	180
Stock	75
Debtors	85
Goodwill	100

3. After the retirement of Bill, the assets are to be left in the books at their revalued amounts, with the exception of goodwill, which is to be written off. All adjustments are to be made through the partner's capital accounts.
4. All sums due to Bill are to be transferred to a loan account.

Required

Prepare the partnership balance sheet for Ben and Flo after all the above adjustments have been put into effect. Show clearly your calculation of the balances on Ben's and Flo's capital accounts and the amount due to Bill.

Solution

Ben and Flo Balance Sheet

	£000	£000
Fixed assets		
Land and buildings		165
Plant and equipment		180
		345
Current assets		
Stock	75	
Debtors	85	
Cash	5	
	165	
Less:		
Trade creditors	110	
		55
		400
Less:		
Loan from Bill		184
		216
Financed by:		
Capital accounts		
Ben	114	
Flo	62	
		176
Current accounts		
Ben	25	
Flo	15	
		40
		216

Workings

Revaluation Account

	£000	£000		£000
Stock		5	Goodwill	100
Debtors		5	Land and buildings	115
Surplus			Plant and equipment	5
Bill (loan a/c)	84			
Ben: Capital account	84			
Flo: Capital account	42			
		210		
		220		220

Capital Accounts

	Ben £000	Flo £000		Ben £000	Flo £000
Goodwill	50	50	Balance b/d	80	70
Balance c/d	114	62	Surplus	84	42
	164	112		164	112

Amount due to Bill

		£000
Balance:	Capital account	90
	Current account	10
	Surplus	84
		184

Note
All sums due to the retired partner are shown as a loan rather than as capital as he is no longer a partner.

Readers should now work Question 9.4 at the end of this chapter.

CHANGE IN PROFIT SHARING RATIO

It is necessary to revalue the assets when there is an alteration in the ratio in which profits are split, so that changes in value up to that time are shared in the ratio that prevailed while they accrued; subsequent changes are shared in the new ratio. Failure to adopt this approach means that all value changes would be shared in the new ratio, even though this did not apply while some of the changes took place. Some assets may have increased in value while others have lost value, and a value should be assigned to goodwill. The necessary adjustments to values are again made through a revaluation account, the balance on which is shared between the partners in the old profit-sharing ratio. If the original values of any assets are to be reinstated, the adjustments are also made through the revaluation account, the balance on which is transferred to the partners' capital accounts in accordance with the new ratio.

Example 9.6

Cut and Hack are in partnership sharing profits and losses equally. The firm's summarized balance sheet at 30 June 19X7 was:

	£
Fixed assets	7,000
Working capital	3,000
	10,000

Financed by:	
Capital accounts	
Cut	5,000
Hack	5,000
	10,000

Hack decides to reduce the amount of time he spends working for the business, and it is agreed that from 1 July 19X7 profits should be shared between Cut and Hack in the ratio 2:1 respectively.

The partners consider that fair current values for the assets on 30 June 19X7 are:

	£
Fixed assets	10,000
Working capital	3,500
Goodwill	5,500

The assets are to be recorded in the books at their original values, after the necessary adjustments consequent upon the change in the profit-sharing ratio have been effected.

Required

(a) Prepare the revaluation account of the partnership to record all the adjustments made to asset values.
(b) Prepare the partners' capital accounts showing clearly the balances after all adjustments have been made.
(c) Prepare the revised balance sheet of Cut and Hack.

Solution

(a) **Revaluation Account**

	£		£
Surplus: Cut	4,500	Fixed assets	3,000
Hack	4,500	Working capital	500
		Goodwill	5,500
	9,000		9,000
		Written off:	
Fixed assets	3,000	Cut	6,000
Working capital	500	Hack	3,000
Goodwill	5,500		
	9,000		9,000

(b) **Capital Accounts**

	Cut £	Hack £		Cut £	Hack £
Revaluation account	6,000	3,000	Opening balance	5,000	5,000
Balance c/d	3,500	6,500	Revaluation account	4,500	4,500
	9,500	9,500		9,500	9,500

(c) **Revised Balance Sheet**

	£
Fixed assets	7,000
Working capital	3,000
	10,000
Financed by:	
Capital accounts	
Cut	3,500
Hack	6,500
	10,000

DISSOLUTION OF PARTNERSHIPS

When a partnership comes to the end of its life, perhaps because the partners decide to sell up and retire, the firm is dissolved. In these circumstances, the assets are sold, the liabilities settled and the partnership ceases to exist. The Partnership Act 1890 requires that the money raised from the sale of assets must be applied in the following order:

1. To settle all the firm's debts, other than those to the partners.
2. To repay any *loans* owed to partners.
3. To settle amounts due to partners on their capital and current accounts.

A realization account is used to record the dissolution of the partnership. The following entries are made in it:

Debit	Credit	With
Realization Account	Sundry Asset Accounts	Book values of assets
Cash Account	Realization Account	Receipts from sale of assets
Realization Account	Cash Account	Expenses of realization
Capital Account	Realization Account	Assets taken over by partners at valuation
Capital Accounts	Realization Account	Share of loss on realization
Realization Account	Capital Accounts	Share of profit on realization
Creditor Accounts	Realization Account	Any gains (e.g. discounts) on settlement

Example 9.7

Tape and Ribbon trade in partnership and share profits and losses equally. The firm's summarized balance sheet at 31 December 19X8 is:

	£		£
Fixed assets	20,000	Capital: Tape	15,000
Current assets	12,500	Ribbon	12,500
			27,500
		Overdraft	1,000
		Sundry creditors	4,000
	32,500		32,500

The partners agree to dissolve the firm. Tape is to take over some of the fixed assets at a valuation of £14,000. The remaining fixed assets are sold for £20,000 and the current assets realize £15,000.

The expenses of realization are £1,000 and a prompt payment discount of £200 is received from the creditors.

Required

(a) The firm's realization account.
(b) The partners' capital accounts.
(c) The firm's cash account.

Solution

(a) **Realization Account**

	£		£
Fixed assets	20,000	Tape (fixed assets)	14,000
Current assets	12,500	Cash (fixed assets)	20,000
Cash (expenses)	1,000	Cash (current assets)	15,000
Tape	7,850	Discount received	200
Ribbon	7,850		
	49,200		49,200

(b) **Capital Accounts**

	Tape £	Ribbon £		Tape £	Ribbon £
Realization a/c	14,000	–	Balance b/d	15,000	12,500
Cash	8,850	20,350	Realization a/c	7,850	7,850
	22,850	20,350		22,850	20,350

(c) **Cash Account**

	£		£
Realization account:		Balance b/d	1,000
Fixed assets	20,000	Realization expenses	1,000
Current assets	15,000	Sundry creditors	3,800
		Tape	8,850
		Ribbon	20,350
	35,000		35,000

Readers should now work Question 9.5 at the end of this chapter.

If, after all the assets have been sold, debts settled and loans repaid, any partner has a net debit balance on his or her combined capital and current accounts, he or she must introduce cash to cover the deficiency so that the other partners can receive the amounts due to them. For example, Red, Green and Blue, after trading in partnership for a number of years, decide to dissolve the business. The balance sheet after all of the assets had been sold and the firm's liabilities settled was as shown in Figure 9.2.

	£
Cash	20,000
Capital accounts:	
Red	15,000
Green	10,000
Blue	(5,000)
	20,000

Figure 9.2   *Effect of debit balance of one partner at dissolution of a partnership*

In these circumstances, Blue must pay £5,000 into the firm's bank account: this raises its balance to £25,000 and eliminates the debit balance on Blue's capital account. Red and Green can then withdraw cash of £15,000 and £10,000 respectively to complete the dissolution.

The rule in Garner v. Murray

If a partner is personally bankrupt and so cannot introduce cash to make good a debit balance on his or her capital account when a partnership is dissolved, then the rule laid down in the case of Garner *v.* Murray must be applied. This requires the deficiency from the realization account to be shared between the remaining partners in the agreed profit-sharing ratio; the irrecoverable debit balance on a partner's capital account is then borne by the solvent partners in the ratio of their capital account balances before the start of the dissolution. The application of this rule is examined in Example 9.8.

Example 9.8

The following is the balance sheet of Pink, Blink and Wink, who share trading profits and losses equally, after all the firm's assets have been sold:

	£
Cash	20,000
Deficiency from realization account	3,000
	23,000

	£
Capital accounts:	
Pink	15,000
Blink	10,000
Wink	(2,000)
	23,000

Wink is personally bankrupt and cannot contribute anything towards the debit balance on his capital account.

Required

Prepare the capital accounts of the partners showing the distribution of the available cash, and explain the basis on which Wink's deficiency has been shared between Pink and Blink.

Solution

Capital Accounts

	Pink £	Blink £	Wink £		Pink £	Blink £	Wink £
Balance b/d	—	—	2,000	Balance b/d	15,000	10,000	—
Share of loss							
on							
realization	1,000	1,000	1,000				
Wink	1,800	1,200		Pink			1,800
Cash	12,200	7,800		Blink			1,200
	15,000	10,000	3,000		15,000	10,000	3,000

The £3,000 debit balance on Wink's account after debiting the loss on realization, is split between Pink and Blink in accordance with the ruling in Garner v. Murray, that is, it is shared in the ratio of the capital account balances of the remaining partners prior to the dissolution. Hence, Pink bears 15,000/25,000 × 3,000 = £1,800, and Blink bears 10,000/25,000 × 3,000 =£1,200. The cash balance of £20,000, which remains, is used to pay off the balances on the capital accounts of Pink and Blink.

QUESTIONS

Questions 9.1 to 9.5 test individual aspects of partnership accounts specifically dealt with in this chapter; questions 9.6 and 9.7 deal with the preparation of a full set of partnership accounts.

9.1   Jack, Jill and Jane trade together in partnership, and they have agreed to share profits and losses on the following basis:

1. Annual salaries of £10,000, £7,500 and £5,000 are to be paid to Jack, Jill and Jane respectively.
2. Interest of 12 per cent is to be allowed on the average balance of each partner's capital account for the year.
3. Interest of 12 per cent is to be charged on drawings.
4. Residual profits and losses are to be shared: Jack and Jill 40 per cent and Jane 20 per cent.

You are given the following additional information:

1. On 1 January 19X2, the balances on the partners' capital accounts were:

	£
Jack	30,000
Jill	20,000
Jane	40,000

On 30 June 19X2, Jill introduced further capital of £5,000.
2. The charges for interest on drawings for 19X2 are:

	£
Jack	600
Jill	450
Jane	400

3. The firm made a profit of £42,000 in 19X2.

Required

Prepare the partnership appropriation account for 19X2.

9.2

Required

(a) Prepare the partnership appropriation account of the Jack, Jill and Jane partnership using the information given in Question 9.1 above and assuming that no partnership agreement exists.
(b) Explain the basis on which you have divided the profit in part (a).

9.3   Ice and Cube are in partnership, sharing profits and losses equally. The balances on their capital and current accounts at 1 January 19X4 are:

	Capital	Current
	£	£
Ice	50,000	30,000
Cube	60,000	20,000

The trading profit for 19X4 was £45,000, and during the year the cash drawings of Ice were £12,500 and of Cube £14,000. In addition, Ice took over one of the firm's cars at its book value of £1,500 to give to his daughter as an eighteenth-birthday present.

The partners review the accounts for 19X4 and decide that, as some of their current account balances have been invested in the expansion of the firm, Ice should transfer £20,000 and Cube £10,000 from current to capital account.

Required

Prepare the partners' current and capital accounts for 19X4.

9.4   Bush and Shrub are in partnership and share profits and losses in the ratio 1:2 respectively. The firm's balance sheet at 31 December 19X4 was:

	£		£
Fixed assets	15,000	Capital: Bush	10,000
Working capital	15,000	Shrub	20,000
	30,000		30,000

The following is agreed:

1. Flower is to join the firm as a partner on 1 January 19X5.
2. After 1 January 19X5 the partners are to share profits and losses equally.
3. Flower is to introduce cash of £14,000 as capital.
4. The assets are to be revalued:

	£
Fixed assets	20,000
Working capital	13,000
Goodwill	9,000

5. The original asset values are to be reinstated after the adjustments resulting from Flower's joining have been made, and goodwill is to be written off.

Required

(a) Prepare the revaluation account of the partnership.
(b) Prepare the partners' capital accounts.
(c) Prepare the partnership balance sheet on 1 January 19X5 after Flower has been admitted and all the consequent adjustments made.

9.5   Jupiter, Mars and Saturn are in partnership sharing profits and losses in the ratio 2:1:1. The balance sheet of the partnership as at 30 June 1984 disclosed the following financial position:

	£	£		£	£	£
				Cost	Dep.	Net
Capital accounts			*Fixed assets*			
Jupiter	55,000		Freehold land			
Mars	32,000		and premises	80,000	—	80,000
Saturn	25,000		Equipment	15,000	6,000	9,000
		112,000	Motor car	5,000	2,000	3,000
Current liabilities						
Creditors	4,100			100,000	8,000	92,000
Bank						
overdraft	6,400		*Current assets*			
		10,500	Stock	24,000		
			Debtors	6,500		
						30,500
		122,500				122,500

On 30 June 1984 it was agreed that the partnership should be dissolved as from that date. Mars will continue in business on his own account; he agrees to take over the equipment, stock and debtors at valuations of £11,000, £26,000 and £6,100 respectively. He also agrees to purchase the freehold land and premises at an agreed valuation of £120,000, and obtains a bank loan over ten years of £90,000, to help finance the purchase. The proceeds are paid into the partnership. It is agreed that any balance owing by Mars at the finalization of the dissolution transactions will be charged to the capital account of Jupiter as the two parties have agreed that the balance owing by Mars and settled by Jupiter, will represent a personal loan to be repaid by Mars, over a four-year period. Saturn agrees to purchase the motor car for £2,900.

Realization expenses amount to £1,500 and, together with amounts owing to creditors, are paid out of the partnership resources. All transactions were completed on 1st July 1984.

Required

(a) The partnership realization account.   (6 marks)
(b) The partnership bank account.   (4 marks)
(c) The capital accounts of the partners.   (7 marks)
(d) The balance sheet of Mars as at 1st July 1984, indicating what
    the balance on the capital account of Mars represents.   (5 marks)
                                                        (Total: 22 marks)

(ICSA, Financial Accounting I, December, 1984)

9.6   Second and Minute started trading as retail grocers in partnership on 1 January 19X4, but did not keep a set of double entry books. The firm's bank account, for 19X4, prepared from the record of cheques issued and cash paid into the bank, was:

	£		£
Capital introduced:		Purchases	160,000
Second	20,000	Wages	17,000
Minute	20,000	Rent and rates	3,500
Sales receipts banked	200,000	Light and heat	1,260
		Delivery van	19,000
		Drawings: Second	18,000
		Minute	16,000
		Balance c/d	5,240
	240,000		240,000

Notes

1. The following payments were made directly from cash sales receipts:

	£
Petrol for van	2,000
Maintenance	1,000
Advertising	900
Purchases	2,500
	6,400

2. The van, purchased on 1 January 19X4, is expected to have a life of five years, at the end of which its scrap value will be £3,000.

3. The partners agree that separate capital and current accounts are to be kept and all profits and losses are to be shared equally.

4. At 31 December 19X4:

	£
Debtors	5,460
Trade creditors	3,800
Prepaid rent	100
Light and heat accrued	140
Stock	9,200

5. During 19X4 both Second and Minute took groceries for personal use at cost price as follows:

	£
Second	1,000
Minute	1,260
	2,260

Required

Prepare the trading and profit and loss account for the year to 31 December 19X4 and the balance sheet at that date.

9.7   The following is the trial balance of Bean and Stalk, who trade in partnership, at 31 March 19X3:

	£	£
Capital account balances at 1 April 19X2:		
Bean		30,000
Stalk		10,000
Current account balances at 1 April 19X2:		
Bean		3,000
Stalk		5,000
Sales		150,000
Stock at 1 April 19X2	30,000	
Wages	14,500	
Rent	5,000	
Expenses	3,000	
Heat and light	1,200	
Debtors/creditors	14,000	11,500
Delivery costs	5,300	
Drawings:		
Bean	7,000	
Stalk	9,000	
Cash	4,500	
Fixed assets	6,000	
Purchases	110,000	
	209,500	209,500

Notes

1. Stock at 31 March 19X3 was valued at £40,000.
2. Depreciation of £1,500 is to be written off the fixed assets for the year to 31 March 19X3.
3. At 31 March 19X3 wages accrued amounted to £500 and rent of £1,000 was prepaid.
4. On 1 February 19X3 the firm ordered and paid for goods costing £700. These were recorded as purchases but were never received as they were lost by the carrier responsible for their delivery. The carrier accepted liability for the loss during March 19X3 and paid full compensation of £700 in April 19X3. No entries had been made in the books in respect of the loss or claim.
5. Bean took goods that had cost the firm £340 for his own use during the year. No entry had been made in the books to record this.
6. The partnership agreement provided that profits and losses should be shared equally between the partners after:
   (a) allowing annual salaries of £2,000 to Bean and £4,000 to Stalk;
   (b) allowing interest of 5 per cent per annum on the balance of each partner's capital account; and
   (c) charging Bean £200 and Stalk £300 interest in drawings.
7. The balances on the capital accounts shall remain unchanged, all adjustments being recorded in the current accounts.

Required

Prepare the trading, profit and loss and appropriation accounts for the Bean and Stalk partnership for the year to 31 March 19X3 and the balance sheet at that date.

10
Company Accounts

FORMATION OF REGISTERED COMPANIES

A limited company is formed by registering under the Companies Act 1985, hence the term 'registered' company. Registration is a fairly simple process, but certain formalities must be complied with. It is possible for the individuals wishing to form a limited company to do the work themselves; alternatively they may choose to employ a specialist company registration agent who charges a fee in the region of £150. The following information must be filed with the Registrar of Companies at, or soon after, the registration date:

1. The names and addresses of the first directors.
2. A statement showing the amount of the company's authorized share capital.
3. The address of the company's registered office.
4. The company's memorandum of association and articles of association.

A company must have at least two shareholders whose names and addresses appear in the memorandum to demonstrate the fact that this requirement has been fulfilled. The memorandum also gives the company's name and the nature of its proposed operations, which are contained in the 'objects' clause(s).

The articles of association set out the internal rules and regulations of the company, which must be observed by both shareholders and management; they deal with such matters as the voting rights of shareholders, the appointment and powers of directors and the borrowing powers of the company. The Companies Act contains a model set of articles that apply to any limited company not filing articles of its own. The specimen articles also apply to the extent that they are not specifically modified or excluded by any articles the company files. The model articles are rarely entirely suitable and articles 'tailor-made' to the company's individual requirements are usually prepared.

Types of company

There are a number of different types of registered company (see Figure 10.1) and the option chosen will depend on the nature and scale of expected business operations. It is first necessary to decide whether the company is to be registered with limited liability or unlimited liability. Usually the main reason for forming a company is to obtain the protection of limited liability for business activities that, by their very nature, are likely to involve a significant element of risk. For this reason unlimited companies are few and far between, and we do not, therefore, need to consider them further.

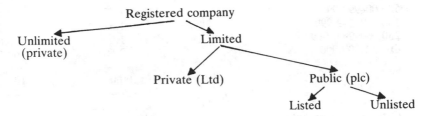

Figure 10.1   Types of registered company

There are two basic categories of limited company: the public company and the private company. The public company must include the designatory letters plc after its name, and must have a minimum issued share capital of £50,000, of which at least one quarter must be collected at the outset. Private companies must use the designatory letters Ltd and are not allowed to make an issue of shares or debentures (see the section on loan capital and debentures in this chapter) to the general public. For both types of company the minimum number of shareholders is two and there is no maximum. Public companies are able to increase the marketability of their shares and debentures by making arrangements for these securities to be listed on the Stock Exchange, but this is a feasible exercise only for very large concerns.

Ownership and control

The powers delegated to the board of directors, in the articles of association, are considerable but they are nevertheless restricted to those needed to manage a business organization on a day-to-day basis. The shareholder theoretically retains overall control in the following respects:

1. Only shareholders are able to authorize a change in the nature of the company's operations, as set out in the memorandum of association.
2. Shareholders control the extent of the company's operations. The level of share capital and borrowing are both stated in the company's constitution and these levels can be raised only with the approval of the shareholders.
3. Shareholders can remove all or any of the directors by passing an appropriate resolution at a general meeting of the company.

These powers are more apparent than real. In a large company there is likely to be a wide dispersal of shares (for example, the shareholding in ASDA–MFI set out in Figure 10.2) and most shareholders regard themselves as passive

Number of shareholders   35,447

Shareholdings range	Shareholders %	Shares %
1–999	30.75	0.47
1,000–9,999	56.23	5.01
10,000–49,999	8.41	5.46
50,000–99,999	1.60	3.44
100,000–249,999	1.51	7.14
250,000–999, 999	1.00	15.88
Over 1,000,000	0.50	62.60
	100.00	100.00

Category of shareholders	Shareholders %	Shares %
Pension funds	0.51	7.45
Insurance companies	1.05	13.44
Investment trusts	0.25	0.54
Banks and nominee companies	16.16	55.79
Other corporate bodies	2.09	6.23
Other shareholders	79.94	16.55
	100.00	100.00

Figure 10.2   Analysis of shareholdings in Asda–MFI at 29 July 1986

recipients of dividends rather than active participants in policy-making. The directors are usually able to exert effective control through their ownership of a significant block of votes (at ASDA–MFI the directors own approximately 11 per cent of the shares), and the fact that many shareholders absent from the annual general meeting (AGM) empower the directors to cast their 'proxy' votes in the manner the directors think fit.

An unusually important issue is required to arouse a sufficient body of shareholders to act, in concert, to outvote the directors. The increased involvement of the institutional investor has made shareholder power a greater reality in recent years. Even then, however, activity is likely to occur behind the scenes resulting in the resignation of a director and the appointment of a capable replacement. In the case of the individual shareholder, dissatisfaction with performance or perhaps policies, for example, investment in South Africa, simply results in shares being sold.

THE ANNUAL REPORT

The form and content of accounts published, for outsiders, is set out in Schedule 4 of the Companies Act 1985. Students are not usually required to prepare accounts in accordance with the detailed legal requirements at an introductory level. However, answers should be presented in a good form and, for this purpose, a specimen layout is given in Figure 10.3, which complies broadly with legal requirements.

Balance Sheet

	£	£
Fixed assets		
Intangible asset: Goodwill		xxx
Tangible assets: Land and buildings	xxx	
Plant and machinery	xxx	
Fixtures and fittings	xxx	xxx
	―	
Investments		xxx
		―
		xxx
		―
Current assets		
Stocks	xxx	
Trade debtors	xxx	
Prepayments	xxx	
Temporary investments	xxx	
Cash at bank	xxx	
	―	
	xxx	
	―	
Less: Current liabilities		
Debenture loans repayable within one year	xxx	
Unsecured loans repayable within one year	xxx	
Bank loans and overdrafts	xxx	
Trade creditors	xxx	
Taxation	xxx	
Dividends payable	xxx	
Accruals	xxx	
	―	
Net current assets (working capital)		xxx
Total assets less current liabilities		xxx
Less: Non-current liabilities		
Debentures	xxx	
Unsecured loans	xxx	
Taxation	xxx	xxx
	―	―
		xxx
		―
Financed by:		
Share capital: Authorized		xxx
		―
Issued		xxx
Share premium account		xxx
Revaluation reserve		xxx
General reserve		xxx
Retained profit		xxx
		―
		xxx
		―

Figure 10.3 Specimen accounts for a limited company

Trading, Profit and Loss and Appropration Account

	£	£
Turnover		xxx
Less: Cost of sales		xxx
Gross profit		xxx
Less: Distribution costs	xxx	
Administration expenses	xxx	xxx
Net profit before tax		xxx
Less: Corporation tax		xxx
Net profit after tax		xxx
Less: Dividends	xxx	
Transfer to reserves	xxx	xxx
Retained profit for the year		xxx
Retained profit at beginning of year		xxx
Retained profit at end of year		xxx

In the case of fixed assets, figures for original cost (or revalued amount) and accumulated depreciation should be provided. The above accounting statements broadly comply with the legal requirements concerning the form of company accounts contained in the Companies Act 1985, Schedule 4, format 1.

Figure 10.3   (cont.)

Copies of the profit and loss account and balance sheet must be sent to every shareholder and debenture holder at least twenty-one days before the AGM. A copy of the accounts approved by the AGM must be filed with the Registrar of Companies, at Companies House, where it is available for inspection by any other interested party. In the case of 'small' and 'medium'-sized companies, as defined by the Act, the accounts filed with the Registrar are abridged versions of the shareholders' accounts. The reason for this concession is to allow what are, in many cases, small, family businesses a measure of confidentiality. A drawback of the information available at Companies House is that accounts need not be filed until seven months (ten months for a private company) after the end of the accounting period to which they relate, and many companies even fail to keep to this generous timetable; hence the material is often hopelessly out of date.

The profit and loss account and balance sheet are normally published in a document called the 'annual report'. For a large company, it is an extensive document; to take an example, the 1986 annual report of ASDA–MFI covers 45 pages. A typical annual report, prepared for a large public company, contains the following range of financial and general information *in addition* to the balance sheet and profit and loss account:

1.   *The chairman's review* This is one area of the annual report not subject to any requirements regarding its content. The chairman is therefore free to

say exactly what he or she wishes, but his or her comments will generally cover the following broad areas:

(a) An assessment of the year's results.
(b) An examination of factors influencing those results, for example, the economic and political climate or the effect of strikes.
(c) A reference to major developments, for example, takeovers or new products.
(d) Capital expenditure plans.
(e) An assessment of future prospects.

The chairman's message usually conveys a fair amount of optimism even if the financial facts published later in the report make depressing reading. A strong point in favour of the chairman's review is that it is readable and easily understood by the lay person. A major drawback is that, with regard to future prospects, it must be based on opinion rather than fact, but it is useful background material when attempting to assess progress by an interpretation of the financial information contained in the accounts.

2. *The directors' report* The content of the directors' report is closely regulated by the Companies Act. It must contain a wide range of information, including the following: details of the principal activities and the changes in those activities during the year; recommended dividends and transfers to reserves, if any; significant changes in fixed assets during the year; substantial differences between the book value and market value of land and buildings; details of political and charitable contributions where they exceed specified levels; certain details regarding the company's employment policies; names of the directors and details of their interests in shares and debentures of the company; and details of any acquisitions, by the company, of its own shares.

3. *The auditors report* We have seen that the directors are legally obliged to prepare accounts that are relied upon by external users to reach a wide range of decisions. The directors usually wish to portray a company's results in the best possible light in order, for example, to persuade the public to buy its shares. It is for this reason that an independent auditor is appointed, by the shareholders, to examine and report on the information contained in the profit and loss account, balance sheet and directors' report. The auditor is not required to report on the chairman's review, but he or she should not sign an unqualified report if the review contained an erroneous factual statement, for example, where the entire loss for the year was blamed on a strike by the workforce, whereas it was actually caused by falling demand. A typical audit report contains the following wording:

> *Report of the Auditors to the Members of Coventry plc*
> We have audited the accounts set out on pages 20 to 40 in accordance with approved auditing standards.
> In our opinion the accounts on pages 20 to 40, prepared under the historical cost

convention, give a true and fair view of the state of affairs of the company at 31 December 19X1 and of the profit and source and application of funds for the year then ended and comply with the Companies Act 1985.

Cardiff 25 March 19X2   Edwards, Mellett & Co.
                                                        Chartered Accountants

The first sentence informs shareholders of the scope of the audit, i.e. that work done complies with the instructions issued by the professional accounting bodies for the guidance of auditors. The second sentence sets out the auditors' findings. You will notice that it does not *certify the accuracy* of the accounts, but instead expresses the opinion that the accounts show a *true and fair view*. The auditor of a limited company must be professionally qualified, however, and would be expected to exercise appropriate skill and judgement in reaching his or her conclusions. If the auditors have any reservations regarding the truth and fairness of the accounts, for example, perhaps they believe that the provision for bad debts is inadequate, they must refer to this fact in their report. Details of the qualification, in these circumstances, normally appears at the beginning of the second sentence.

4. *The statement of source and application of funds* The purpose of this statement is to provide a full record of the financial transactions undertaken during an accounting period. It is, therefore, more broadly based than the profit and loss account, which gives details only of revenues and expenditures during an accounting period. The statement of funds also contains information about capital raised during the year and expenditure on fixed assets. Its function is to provide an insight into the overall financial policy pursued by management and the effect of that policy on the financial structure and stability of the concern. The statement is considered in detail in Chapter 13.

Statements of Standard Accounting Practice (SSAPs)

Accounting practices were the subject of a great deal of criticism in the late 1960s. The main reason for this criticism was increased public awareness of the fact that, by adopting alternative valuation procedures, it was possible to report vastly different profit figures. In 1965, Professor Chambers drew attention to the fact that conventionally acceptable procedures provided scope for 'a million sets of mutually exclusive rules' (*Abacus*, September 1965, p. 15) for profit measurement. The event that brought matters to a head, however, was the GEC bid for AEI in October 1967. In an attempt to resist the takeover bid, the directors of AEI issued a profit forecast of £10 million for 1967. The takeover nevertheless went ahead and, when AEI reported in April 1968, the investing public was amazed to discover that its accounts showed a loss of £4.5 million. Subsequent investigations proved that a major cause of the £14.5 million descrepancy between forecast and actual results was simply the adoption of more conservative valuation procedures by the new management.

The result was a public outcry and a great deal of dissatisfaction was expressed with the degree of latitude allowed to those responsible for preparing financial reports. In the endeavour to restore public confidence, the accounting profession established the Accounting Standards Committee. The job of this committee is to prepare SSAPs designed to achieve the following objectives.

1. To encourage the adoption of best accounting practices.
2. To ensure, as far as possible, that companies adopt similar procedures.
3. To disclose the procedures that have actually been adopted.

SSAP 2, entitled 'Disclosure of Accounting Policies' (issued November 1971), set out the broad framework for financial reporting. In particular, the statement defines and explains the relationship between accounting concepts, acounting bases and accounting policies.

Accounting concepts

SSAP 2 identifies four 'fundamental' concepts (since incorporated in the Companies Act 1985), which form the basis for financial reporting. These are the going concern concept, the accruals concept, the consistency concept and the concept of prudence. No one would dispute the importance of these concepts, though some would argue that other concepts are of at least equal significance. For example, we believe it is difficult to distinguish, in terms of importance, many of the *ten* accounting concepts discussed in Chapter 8 of this book.

Unless otherwise stated, there is a presumption that the four fundamental concepts have been complied with when preparing the published accounts. In certain circumstances, departure from one or more of the concepts is essential. For example, knowledge that the company is in severe financial difficulties and in imminent danger of liquidation requires the going concern concept to be abandoned. The assets are then restated at their likely realizable values, and the shareholders' attention is drawn to this fact.

Accounting bases

These are the range from which valuation procedures may be chosen when preparing the accounts. For a valuation procedure to be acceptable, it must comply with the four fundamental concepts. Acceptable bases for charging depreciation, for example, include straight line, reducing balance, sum of the digits and units of service.

Accounting policies

These are the accounting bases employed by a particular company – for example, it may be decided to depreciate fixed assets on the straight-line basis. The statement requires companies to set out, in the accounts, the accounting policies used to arrive at 'material' balances reported in the accounts. The accounting policies of ASDA–MFI are detailed on pages 32–33 of the 1986 annual report. The list includes the following:

Depreciation
Depreciation is provided to write off the cost or valuation of tangible assets, excluding freehold land, over their estimated useful lives, as follows

Freehold buildings and long leasehold property	50–67 years
Short leasehold property	over period of lease
Plant and equipment	3–20 years
Motor vehicles	4–10 years

Stocks
Stock comprise goods held for re-sale and are valued at the lower of cost and net realisable value.

Other SSAPs deal with the valuation and presentation of individual items in the accounts. For example, SSAP 9, entitled *Stocks and Work in Progress* (issued May 1975), favours the total cost rather than the marginal cost basis for valuing stocks, and FIFO rather than LIFO. It also requires, where applicable, the classification of stocks into each of its main categories, such as work in progress, raw materials and finished goods. SSAP 10 (issued June 1978), by way of contrast, requires companies to publish an additional accounting statement, i.e. the statement of source and application of funds. To date (September 1988) twenty-four SSAPs have been issued. The content of these is examined, in detail, in advanced financial accountancy examinations.

OTHER SOURCES OF INFORMATION

Accounts published by limited companies are an important source, but by no means the only source, of information available for shareholders and other interested parties.

First, there is a whole range of additional information provided by the company itself:

1. A public limited company offering shares to the general public must issue a 'prospectus' containing an accountant's report, which includes the most recent balance sheet and certain specified profit and loss account data for each of the last five years. In addition, the company must provide a forecast of its current year's profits and the planned dividend payment.
2. Companies whose shares are quoted on the London Stock Exchange are required to comply with a range of obligations contained in the *Listing Agreement*. These include the publication, every year, of an interim statement, which is not audited, setting out key profit and loss account and balance sheet data in respect of the first six months of the company's financial year.

3. It is a growing practice for companies to produce house magazines or newsletters for employees. These summarize the company's results in a manner that is easy to assimilate and makes use of pictorial presentations such as bar charts, pie charts and graphs. Although produced principally for employees, it is not unusual for the information to be circulated to shareholders. It is also quite common for such data to be reproduced in the financial press.

4. Shareholders and debenture holders are entitled to attend the AGM where they have the opportunity to ask questions about past performance and the directors' future plans. It is not usual for these meetings to be heavily attended unless the company's affairs are the subject of some controversy, for example, where there is a contested takeover bid. Usually the directors are willing to answer reasonable questions, although they will tend to become evasive if asked for information considered to be particularly sensitive and unsuitable for public disclosure.

5. Shareholders, particularly institutional shareholders, may be able to obtain information about a company's affairs as the result of informal discussions with one or more of a company's directors, perhaps over lunch.

Information about a company's affairs may also be obtained from *external* sources:

1. A limited company is under a legal obligation to file a copy of its accounts with the Registrar of Companies. This information is available for inspection at Companies House in London and in Cardiff. On payment of £1, an applicant is issued with a microfiche that can be taken away. This contains a copy of the company's accounts, a copy of the company's constitution, details of the company's share capital and debentures, details of each mortgage and charge on the assets of the company, a list of the directors and secretary and the address of the registered office.

2. Companies such as Extel publish cards setting out key statistics for each of the last ten years and an analysis of published results.

The remainder of this chapter examines a number of important respects in which a limited company's accounts differs from those prepared for sole traders and partnerships.

SHARE CAPITAL

The memorandum of association contains details of the share capital with which the company is to be initially registered and the division of that share capital into shares of a fixed amount. The figure for the company's registered share capital is described as the *authorized* share capital, and the face value of each share is called the 'nominal' or 'par' value. A company may be registered, for example, with an authorized share capital of £500,000 divided into 500,000 shares of £1 each. There is no fixed rule regarding the nominal value of each share, though £1 is often used.

There are a number of different categories of share capital – the two most common are *preference* shares and *ordinary* or *equity* shares. As the name implies, preference shares are given priority over ordinary shares as regards both payment of the annual dividend and repayment of capital on liquidation:

1. *Dividends* The annual dividend payable on preference shares is fixed at, say, 8 per cent per annum, and the dividend is usually paid if profits are sufficient. If profits are insufficient, the dividend is lost, unless cumulative preference shares have been issued, in which case any arrears must be paid, when trading results improve, before any dividend is paid to the ordinary shareholders. The dividend payable on ordinary shares is entirely at the discretion of the directors; if profits are low and/or the directors wish to retain all profits earned within the company, they may decide to pay no dividend whatsoever.

2. *Capital repayment* On liquidation of the company, business assets are applied, first, to settle outstanding liabilities and, second, to repay the preference shareholders the nominal value of their investment. Any balance remaining is paid out to the ordinary shareholders as they possess the equity interest in the concern. If a company is wound up because of financial difficulties, there is often nothing left over, for shareholders, after repaying creditors the amounts due.

The directors do not necessarily issue the company's entire authorized share capital at the outset. The figure initially registered represents the company's estimated financial requirements over, say, the next ten years. To begin with, however, the scale of activity may be relatively modest and the volume of shares issued should be restricted accordingly. The way in which the shares are issued may differ depending on whether the company is private or public. It is likely that the issued share capital of private companies will be acquired entirely by members of the first board of directors, and perhaps also their families and friends. In the case of a public company, an invitation may be made to the general public to acquire some, if not the whole, of the share capital the directors plan to issue. In the latter case the shares are advertised in the prospectus, the content of which is regulated by company law and, in the case of listed companies, also by the Stock Exchange rules.

Shareholders are not necessarily required to pay immediately the full price of the shares. For example, in the case of a £1 share issued at par, 15p may be payable when the shares are applied for, a further 25p when the shares are issued (called the allotment) and two further instalments, designated calls, of 30p each at some future date. Where shares are offered to the general public, it is extremely unusual for applications to match exactly the number of shares available for issue. If the issue is 50 per cent oversubscribed, one way of dealing with the problem is to issue each subscriber with two-thirds of the shares applied for. If the issue is undersubscribed it is likely to fail unless the company has taken the precaution of arranging for the issue to be underwritten. The function of the underwriter, often a finance house or an insurance company, is to guarantee the success of an issue by undertaking to subscribe for a new issue of shares to the extent it is not taken up by the general public. The transaction is in the nature of a speculation: if the issue is popular the underwriter receives his or her commission and does nothing; if the issue fails to attract the required number of subscriptions the underwriter is obliged to acquire shares for which there is little demand and whose price, initially, is likely to fall.

Example 10.1

Griffin Ltd, a newly-established private company, is registered with a share capital of £1,000,000 divided into 1,000,000 ordinary shares with a nominal value of £1 each. On 1 January 19X1 400,000 shares are issued at par to members of the board of directors and paid for immediately in cash.

Required

Prepare the capital section of Griffin's balance sheet as at 1 January 19X1.

Solution

Extracts from the Balance Sheet of Griffin Ltd as at 1 January 19X1

	£
Share capital:	
Authorized: 1,000,000 ordinary shares of £1 each	1,000,000
Issued: 400,000 ordinary shares of £1 each fully paid	400,000

The location of these items in a full balance sheet can be seen by referring back to Figure 10.2.

SHARE PREMIUM ACCOUNT

The initial issue of shares is normally made at par value and if, a few days later, one of the shareholders decides to sell his or her investment, he or she is likely to obtain a price not materially different from the issue price. This is because the prospects of the company are unlikely to have altered, materially, during the short space of time since the company was formed. As time goes by the position changes and, assuming the company is successful, the demand for its shares is likely to rise. Where this happens, the original shareholders are able to sell their shares at a profit to new investors. It must be recognized, however, that any rise or fall in the market price of the company's shares has no effect on the finances of the company itself, and the shares continue to be reported in the balance sheet at their issue price, which was £1 in the case of Griffin Ltd.

The directors may decide, at some later stage, to make a further issue of shares to help finance an expansion of the company's scale of operations. This additional issue will be made, not at nominal value, but at the best price then obtainable. If the market value of the shares has risen to £1.50, the issue price will be fixed at approximately that figure. An accounting problem arises because of a legal requirement that all share issues, not only the first, must be recorded in the share capital account at their nominal value. This problem is solved by recording any excess of the issue price over nominal value in a share premium account.

Example 10.2

Assume the same facts as in Example 10.1. Also, on 31 December 19X5, Griffin Ltd issues, for cash, a further 200,000 ordinary shares at a price of £1.50 each.

Required

Prepare the capital section of Griffin's balance sheet as at 31 December 19X5, so far as the information permits.

Solution

Extracts from the Balance Sheet of Griffin Ltd at 31 December 19X5

	£
Share capital	
Authorized: 1,000,000 ordinary shares of £1 each	1,000,000
Issued: 600,000 ordinary shares of £1 each fully paid	600,000
Share premium account	100,000

SHARE FORFEITURE

A subscriber to a new issue of shares sometimes pays his or her application money but defaults either when required to pay the amount due on allotment or on one of the later calls. This may happen because he or she is short of money or because he or she feels that the shares are no longer a good buy. Since he or she has contracted to acquire the shares, it is possible for the company to sue for the balance due but, even where the defaulting shareholder is perfectly solvent, this course of action is unlikely to be considered worth while. The directors are more likely to exercise their right, under the company's articles, to consider the shares forfeited. The directors then endeavour to find an investor who is willing to acquire the shares at a price at least equal to the balance outstanding. Any excess received is credited to share premium account.

Example 10.3

Thatchers Ltd is registered with a share capital of £500,000 divided into 1,000,000 ordinary shares with a nominal value of £0.50 each. On 1 January 19X2, 600,000 shares are issued with the agreement that £0.30 is paid immediately and the balance outstanding on 31 March 19X2. The appropriate amounts are received on the dates due, except that Broke, who acquired 500 shares on 1 January, defaults on the payment of the final call. On 1 June the shares are forfeited and reissued to Wealthy for £0.45 each.

Required

Appropriate balance sheet extracts from the capital section of Thatchers Ltd's balance sheet at:

(i)   1 January, after the shares have been issued; and
(ii) 1 June, after Broke's shares have been forfeited and reissued to Wealthy.

Solution

(i) Extracts from the Balance Sheet of Thatchers Ltd at 1 January 19X2

	£
Share capital:	
Authorized: 1,000,000 ordinary shares of £0.50 each	500,000
Issued: 600,000 ordinary shares of £0.50, £0.30 paid	180,000

(ii) Extracts from the Balance Sheet of Thatchers Ltd at 1 June 19X2

	£
Share capital	
Authorized: 1,000,000 ordinary shares of £0.50 each	500,000
Issued: 600,000 ordinary shares of £0.50 each fully paid	300,000
Share premium account	125*

Note
* Collected from: Broke, 500 × £.0.30 — 150
                          Wealthy, 500 × £0.45 — 225
                          Total collected — 375
Less: Nominal value of shares issued, 500 × £0.50 — 250
Surplus to share premium account — 125

Note	£
* Collected from: Broke, 500 × £.0.30	150
Wealthy, 500 × £0.45	225
Total collected	375
Less: Nominal value of shares issued, 500 × £0.50	250
Surplus to share premium account	125

THE RIGHTS ISSUE

A rights issue occurs where a company requires additional capital and the shares are offered to existing shareholders on a pro-rata basis according to their existing holdings. If the share issue described in Example 10.2 was a rights issue, it would mean that the existing shareholders of Griffin Ltd were offered one new share at £1.50 each for every two shares presently held. Public companies are legally required to raise additional share capital by way of a rights issue, unless this course of action is impractical, in which case an invitation to subscribe may be made to the general public. A particular attraction to the company of the rights issue is that it is an inexpensive method of raising funds as the formalities associated with the issue are kept to a minimum, for example, a full prospectus need not be issued. From the shareholders' point of view an advantage of this procedure is that control of the company remains in the same hands.

LOAN CAPITAL AND DEBENTURES

A company's memorandum usually authorizes the directors to raise finance by borrowing money as well as by issuing shares. Such loans may be secured or unsecured. A secured loan normally takes the form of a 'debenture', which may be defined as 'the written acknowledgement of a debt usually made under seal'. The security for the loan may take the form of either a fixed charge or a floating charge on the company's assets. A fixed charge exists where the asset on which the loan is secured is specified in the debenture deed. Ideally the asset should be one likely to appreciate rather than depreciate in value over time, such as land and buildings. As a further protection, the company is prevented from selling the charged asset without the debenture holder's express approval. A floating charge exists where the debenture is secured on particular categories of assets, for example, stocks and debtors, or the assets of the company generally. This form of debenture gives the company greater flexibility, since it is allowed to trade in the assets subject to the floating charge, and their composition may well change on a daily basis.

Debentures are usually issued for a specified period of time, after which they are redeemed. The debenture deed will, however, provide for early repayment in certain circumstances. For example, should the company default on an interest payment, a receiver may be appointed by the debenture holders to take control of the secured assets, sell them and repay the amount owed. The main differences between debentures, unsecured loans and share capital are summarized below:

1. Loans carry interest at a fixed rate payable regardless of profit levels. Dividends, even on preference shares, are payable only if profits are sufficient, and the directors decide to make a distribution approved by the shareholders attending the AGM.
2. Loan interest is an allowable expense in calculating taxable profit; dividends are not an allowable expense.
3. Loan interest is debited to the profit and loss account; dividends are debited to the appropriation account (see later in this chapter).
4. Unsecured loans and debentures are reported in the balance sheet as a non-current liability and deducted from the balance of total assets less

current liabilities (see Figure 10.2). Each year, of course, loans and debentures come closer to their redemption date, and they must be reclassified as a current liability when repayable during the forthcoming accounting period. Share capital is reported as part of the shareholders' equity.

5. Debentures enjoy priority of repayment on liquidation. Unsecured loans rank alongside other unsecured creditors, such as trade creditors. Share capital is repaid, on liquidation, only if resources remain after all liabilities have been satisfied.

6. Loans are almost always redeemable; share capital is redeemable only if a number of conditions are satisfied. In particular, the redemption must be met either out of a fresh issue of shares or out of profits available for distribution. To the extent the redemption is met out of distributable profits, an equivalent amount must be transferred to a non-distributable 'capital redemption reserve' so as to maintain intact the company's permanent capital.

7. A company may at any time purchase its own debentures in the market; these then remain available for re-issue until cancelled. A company may purchase its own shares only if the conditions applicable when there is a redemption of shares are satisfied. Where a company purchases its own shares, they must be cancelled immediately.

THE APPROPRIATION ACCOUNT

Profit is calculated in the trading and profit and loss account; the way in which profit is split between taxation, dividends, transfers to reserves and retention is dealt with in the appropriate account (see Figure 10.3). These allocations are considered, in detail, in the next sections of this chapter.

Corporation tax

Sole traders and partnerships pay income tax on the profits arising from their business activities, whereas the profits of limited companies are subject to corporation tax. The rate of corporation tax differs, depending on the level of profits, and is set out in the budget and, later, incorporated in the annual Finance Act. For example, the Finance Act 1988 fixed the rate of corporation tax on profits arising during the year to 31 March 1989 at 25 per cent on profits up to £100,000 and 35 per cent on profits over £500,000; a sliding scale of rates applies where profits are between £100,000 and £500,000. In the case of a profitable company, corporation tax may well represent the largest single cash outflow during an accounting period, and is therefore of considerable importance.

Corporation tax is levied on taxable profits, and readers must grasp that the figure for taxable profits is rarely the same as the profit figure reported in the company's accounts, which is called accounting profit. The reason for this is that the accountant and the government have different priorities when measuring profit. A good illustration concerns the treatment of capital expenditure. The aim of the accountant is to produce a profit figure that fairly represents the results of the firm for the year. For example, if it is estimated that an item of plant will last ten years, benefit the company equally each year and then be worthless, the accountant would consider it appropriate to make a *straight-line* depreciation charge of 10 per cent for each of those years. A major priority of the government is to ensure equity between taxpayers, and it is for this reason that they replace the depreciation charge, which may vary considerably from one company to another, with fixed rates of capital allowance, which are also laid down in the annual Finance Act. For example, the rate of capital allowance on plant and machinery is presently fixed at 25 per cent per annum on the *reducing balance basis*.

There are many other adjustments that produce less-marked differences between accounting profit and taxable profit. For instance, the cost of entertainment, other than for overseas customers, is disallowed for tax purposes but would be treated as a business cost when accounting profit is computed.

Corporation tax is payable nine months after the end of the accounting period to which it relates. The corporation tax charge is disclosed in the profit and loss appropriation account as a deduction from net profit; in the balance sheet the amount payable appears as a current liability.

Example 10.4

Swan Ltd was incorporated on 1 January 19X1, issued 150,000 ordinary shares of £1 each for cash, and commenced business on the same day. Plant, purchased at a cost of £130,000, was expected to possess a four-year life and be worth £10,000 at the end of that time. The company reported a profit of £90,000 for 19X1, after charging depreciation of £30,000.

Required

(a) A calculation of corporation tax payable for 19X1, so far as the information permits. For this purpose a writing-down allowance of 25 per cent and a corporation tax rate of 25 per cent are to be assumed.
(b) Relevant extracts from the appropriation account of Swan Ltd for 19X1.

Solution

		£
(a)	Accounting profit	90,000
	Add: Depreciation charge disallowed	30,000
		120,000
	Less: Capital allowance (£130,000 × 25%)*	32,500
	Taxable profit	87,500

Corporation tax payable, £87,500 × 25% = £21,875

Note
* The remaining balance (£130,000 − £32,500 = £97,500) is carried forward and claimed against profits in future years.

(b) Profit and Loss Appropriation Account for 19X1

	£
Net profit before tax	90,000
Less: Corporation tax	21,875
Net profit after tax	68,125

Dividends

Investors are willing to finance business activity because they expect that, at some future date, cash returns will exceed their initial investment by an amount sufficient to compensate them for risk and loss of liquidity. The investor in a limited company expects to receive cash returns in two forms, namely, dividends and the proceeds from the eventual sale of the shares. Under British company law it is for management to decide how much the firm can afford to pay as a dividend; the shareholders can only approve the amount proposed or choose to accept a lesser amount. This rule is designed to prevent shareholders from insisting on a level of payout that might undermine the financial position of the concern and prejudice the claims of creditors.

Dividends are expressed in terms of pence per share and appear as a deduction in the appropriation account. Where the directors are fairly confident that results for the year will be satisfactory, it is common practice to pay an interim dividend during the financial year. The final dividend is usually paid some months after the end of the financial year; the amount payable being decided upon when the accounts have been prepared and profit for the year established.

The directors rarely pay out the entire profits in the form of dividends, and shareholders are usually willing to accept a decision to retain resources within the company because, although they forgo immediate income, the expectation is that reinvestment will produce greater future returns. Management usually aims for a reasonable balance between distributions and retentions, although in relatively good years the proportion distributed may be rather lower than in poor years when the bulk of the reported profits may be paid out as dividends to demonstrate management's confidence in the future viability of the concern.

Where the current year's profit is insufficient, dividends can be declared on the basis of undistributed profits brought forward. Where there are accumulated losses brought forward, these must first be made good before a dividend is paid out of the current year's profit.

Example 10.5

Hanbury Ltd has an authorized and issued share capital of £400,000 divided into 800,000 ordinary shares of 50p each. The company made a net profit of £200,000 during 19X1 and, in July of that year, the directors paid an interim dividend of 3p per share. The directors decide to recommend a final dividend of

7p per share, making a total of 10p per share for the year. The retained profit at 1 January 19X1 amounted to £94,000. A provision for corporation tax of £75,000 is to be made on the profits for the year.

Required

The profit and loss appropriation account of Hanbury for 19X1.

Solution

Profit and Loss Appropriation Account of Hanbury Ltd for 19X1

	£	£
Net profit before tax		200,000
Less: Corporation tax		75,000
		125,000
Less: Dividends: Paid	24,000	80,000
Proposed	56,000	
Retained profit for 19X1	——	45,000
Retained profit at 1 January 19X1		94,000
Retained profit at 31 December 1981		139,000

Advance and mainstream corporation tax

The payment of a dividend gives rise to an obligation to make an advance payment of corporation tax to the Inland Revenue. The calculation of the amount of the advance payment depends on the basic rate of income tax; for the fiscal year 1988–9, it is calculated by multiplying the dividend by the fraction 25/75. The payment of a dividend of £75,000 therefore gives rise to the need to pay £75,000 × 25/75 = 25,000 to the Inland Revenue.

Advance corporation tax (ACT) is payable on the quarterly date (31 March, 30 June, 30 September, 31 December) following payment of the related dividend. The amount paid over may be offset against the corporation tax charge debited to the profit and loss account in respect of the accounting period during which the ACT payment is made. Assuming a company makes up its accounts on the calendar-year basis, this means that ACT paid *during* 1987 can be offset against corporation tax levied on profits earned during 1987. The balance of corporation tax then remaining outstanding is called mainstream corporation tax (MCT) and is reported in the balance sheet as a current liability. If a final dividend is proposed, for 1987, it is not paid until 1988 and the related ACT is paid some weeks or months afterwards. ACT paid in respect of the final dividend may, therefore, be offset only against tax levied on the profits for 1988. The effect of the ACT regulations is to speed up the payment of corporation tax, but the total amount paid over to the Inland Revenue remains the same.

As far as the shareholders are concerned, they receive dividends net of income tax at the basic rate. For example, the shareholders receiving £75,000, in cash, are deemed to have received a gross dividend of £100,000 from which tax at the basic rate (of 25 per cent) has been deducted at source. There will be no further liability to income tax unless the shareholder pays higher-rate tax. If, for some reason, a shareholder is not liable to tax at all, for example, because unused personal allowances are available, the tax deducted at source may be reclaimed from the Inland Revenue.

Provisions and reserves

A *provision* is legally defined as any amount written off or retained by way of providing for depreciation, renewals or diminution in the value of assets or retained by way of providing for any known liability of which the amount cannot be determined with substantial accuracy. This definition covers three basic accounting adjustments:

1. The amount written off fixed assets by way of depreciation.
2. The amount written off current assets or investments to reflect the fact that book value exceeds the amount that is ultimately expected to be recoverable. Examples are a provision for bad debts or any provision necessary to reduce stock to net realizable value.
3. The amount set aside to meet a known liability, the amount of which cannot be accurately estimated. This may arise where a company is in breach of contract with an employee, but the amount of damages payable is yet to be decided. A second example is a provision for taxation.

A *reserve* is a transfer made out of profits at the directors' discretion. The reason for retaining profits, as reserves, may be to help finance expansion, to enable dividends to be declared in a future year when profits are low, to earmark funds for the redemption of share capital or debentures (see later in this chapter) or to meet unknown contingencies at the date of the accounts.

The distinction between provisions and reserves is very important because it affects the measurement of profit and the way financial information is presented in the annual accounts. A provision is a cost of carrying on business activity whereas a transfer to reserves is not. Provisions are therefore charged *above the line* (in the profit and loss account) and affect reported profits, whereas transfers to reserves are made *below the line* (in the appropriation account) and leave reported profit unaffected. Clearly it is important for management to identify accurately whether a particular item is in the nature of a provision or a reserve. Equally important, care must be taken when the amount of a provision is estimated, since any under or over provision will directly affect the accuracy of the reported profit figure.

For example, let us assume a company is sued by an employee for unfair dismissal and that the company expects the court to allow its former employee damages amounting to £6,000. A provision for this amount is made when computing the reported profit, of £50,000, for 19X1. If the court subsequently awards damages of £15,000, it is clear that the company's liabilities, at 31 December 19X1, have been understated by £9,000 and that profits, for 19X1, have been overstated by a similar figure. If the directors had succeeded in forecasting accurately the damages payable, a profit of £41,000 would have been reported for 19X1.

In the balance sheet provisions are either:

1. deducted from the value of the asset to which they relate, e.g. depreciation of fixed assets; or
2. included as a current liability, e.g. provision for taxation.

Reserves, on the other hand, remain part of the shareholders' interest and are listed after issued share capital and any balance on share premium account on the face of the balance sheet (see Figure 10.2).

Most of the matters discussed so far in this chapter are contained in Example 10.6.

Example 10.6

Miskin Ltd commenced business on 1 January 19X2 and the following trial balance was extracted as at 31 December 19X2:

	£	£
Share capital		380,000
8% debentures repayable 19X9		100,000
10% unsecured loan repayable 30 June 19X3		20,000
Tangible fixed assets at cost	480,000	
Gross profit		152,000
Trade debtors	61,500	
Trade creditors		37,870
Bank balance	7,400	
Bad debts written off	320	
Administration and selling expenses	63,200	
Interest paid, 30 June 19X2	5,000	
Interim dividend paid	12,000	
Stock in trade at 31 December 19X2	60,450	
	689,870	689,870

The following additional information is provided:

1. The authorized share capital is £500,000 divided into ordinary shares of £1 each. The balance on the share capital account represents the proceeds from issuing 300,000 shares.
2. A provision for doubtful debts is to be made of 2 per cent on outstanding trade debtors.

3. Depreciation is to be charged on fixed assets at the rate of 4 per cent on cost.
4. The directors propose to recommend a final dividend of 5p per share.
5. Corporation tax of £18,000 is to be provided on the profits for 19X2.
6. A transfer of £10,000 is to be made to dividend equalization reserve.

Required

(a) A profit and loss account and an appropriation account for 19X2.
(b) A balance sheet at 31 December 19X2.

Solution

(a) **Profit and Loss Account and Appropriation Account for 19X2**

	£	£
Gross profit		152,000
Less: Administration and selling expenses	63,200	
Bad and doubtful debts, £320 + (2% of £61,500)	1,550	
Interest, £5,000 + £5,000 (1 July–31 Dec. 19X2)	10,000	
Provision for depreciation (4% of £480,000)	19,200	93,950
		58,050
Net profit before tax		58,050
Less: Corporation tax		18,000
		40,050
Net profit after tax		40,050
Less: Dividends: Paid	12,000	
Proposed (5p × 300,000)	15,000	
Transfer to dividend equalization reserve	10,000	37,000
Retained profit for 19X2		3,050

(b) **Balance Sheet at 31 December 1982**

	£	£
Fixed assets		
Tangible assets at cost		480,000
Less: Accumulated depreciation		19,200
		460,800
Current assets		
Stocks	60,450	
Trade debtors (£61,500–£1,230)	60,270	
Bank	7,400	
	128,120	

Balance sheet (cont'd)

	£	£
Balances brought forward	128,120	460,800
Less: Current liabilities		
Unsecured loan repayable 30 June 19X3	20,000	
Trade creditors	37,870	
Taxation due 30 September 19X3	18,000	
Dividend payable	15,000	
Accrual for interest owed	5,000	
	95,870	
Working capital		32,250
Total assets less current liabilities		493,050
Less: Non-current liabilities		
8% debentures repayable 19X9		100,000
		393,050
Financed by:		
Share capital:		
Authorized: 500,000 ordinary shares of £1 each		500,000
Issued: 300,000 ordinary shares of £1 each		300,000
Share premium account (£380,000–£300,000)		80,000
Dividend equalization reserve		10,000
Retained profit		3,050
		393,050

Readers should now work Questions 10.1, 10.2 and 10.3 at the end of this chapter.

REVALUATION RESERVE

Despite determined efforts on the part of successive governments to control inflation, prices have risen almost continuously since 1940. The process has had a significant effect on the usefulness of accounting statements based on the historical cost concept. The major balance sheet items, fixed assets and stocks, are reported at their original cost less, where appropriate, depreciation to comply with this concept. However, fixed assets may have been acquired many years ago when prices were much lower than is the case today; therefore these assets are often reported in the balance sheet at figures far removed from their current value to the concern. This descrepancy has caused many individuals to question the usefulness of the balance sheet as a statement of a company's financial position, and uneasiness increased with the acceleration in the rate of inflation during the 1970s. The revaluation reserve was developed as a means of restoring an acceptable measure of reality to the corporate balance sheet. The adjustment is quite straightforward:

1. The book value of the fixed asset is increased from historical cost less depreciation to the revalued figure.
2. The surplus arising on revaluation is credited to revaluation reserve, which is reported as part of the shareholders' equity in the balance sheet (see Figure 10.2).

The adjustment is entered in the books as follows:

Debit	Credit	With
Revaluation account	Fixed asset at cost account	Historical cost of fixed asset
Provision for depreciation account	Revaluation account	Accumulated depreciation
Fixed asset at revaluation account	Revaluation account	New valuation
Revaluation account	Revaluation reserve	Surplus arising on revaluation

The revaluation reserve is therefore an exception to the general rule that reserves are created as the result of transfers from reported profit.

Example 10.7

The following information is extracted from the balance sheet of Messange plc at 31 December 19X4:

	£000
Freehold land and buildings at cost	2,100
Less: Accumulated depreciation	1,300
	800

The land and buildings were revalued by a firm of chartered surveyors at £5,000,000 on 31 December 19X4. The directors have decided to use the revalued figure for the purpose of the accounts.

Required

(a) The revaluation account of Messange to record the above changes.
(b) Relevant extracts from the balance sheet of Messange plc, at 31 December 19X4.

Solution

(a) **Revaluation Account**

	£000		£000
Fixed asset account	2,100	Accumulated depreciation	1,300
Revaluation reserve	4,200	Fixed asset account	5,000
	6,300		6,300

(b) **Balance Sheet extracts**

	£000
Freehold land and buildings at revalued amount	5,000
Revaluation reserve	4,200

Today some large companies and nationalized industries supplement their historical cost based accounting reports with financial statements adjusted to take account of the effect of changing price levels. This important development in corporate financial reporting procedures is the outcome of the inflation accounting debate that raged between 1970 and 1985. Inflation accounting techniques are examined at a more advanced stage of your financial accounting studies.

REDEMPTION OF DEBENTURES

It is essential that the directors plan a company's finances carefully and, in particular, ensure that a proper balance between short-term, medium-term and long-term funds is achieved. Both share capital and loan capital fall into the category of long-term finance, but share capital may be redeemable and loan capital will invariably be redeemable at some future date. It is management's job to ensure that the long-term capital base is not eroded as a result of the redemption. Indeed, in the case of share capital, the directors are under a strict legal obligation to ensure that this does not happen.

Company law imposes no conditions regarding the redemption of debentures. Debenture holders are treated in law as creditors rather than as providers of permanent capital. Consequently, there exists no requirement that the company should take steps to replace the resources paid out when redemption occurs. However, such obligations may either be imposed by the company's articles of association or be assumed voluntarily by the directors. Debentures may be repayable gradually over a period of years or, at the other extreme, the total amount borrowed may be repayable on a single future date. The effect on the company's finances will be less marked in the former situation, and it is often possible to make the necessary repayments out of funds generated from trading operations. In these circumstances the directors may transfer a sum, equal to the value of debentures redeemed, from profits to a debenture redemption reserve in order to acknowledge the fact that resources have been used in this way.

Example 10.8

The debentures of Arches Ltd are repayable by ten equal annual instalments of £10,000 commencing 31 December 19X1. The relevant balance sheet extracts, immediately before the first repayment are as follows:

Balance Sheet extracts at 31 December 19X1

	£
Issued ordinary share capital	200,000
Profit and loss account balance	50,000
Shareholders equity	250,000
Debentures redeemable by ten equal instalments, 19X1–19Y0	100,000

The company redeems one-tenth of the debentures on 31 December 19X1, at par, and transfers a similar amount from profit to debenture redemption reserve.

Required

Revised extracts from the balance sheet of Arches after the first repayment of debentures has taken place.

Solution

Balance Sheet extracts as at 31 December 19X1

	£
Issued ordinary share capital	200,000
Debenture redemption reserve	10,000
Profit and loss account balance (£50,000 − £10,000)	40,000
Shareholders equity	250,000
Debentures redeemable by nine equal instalments, 19X2–19YO	90,000

Where the debentures are to be repaid on a single date, transfers to the debenture redemption reserve may be made over a number of years in anticipation of this event. Additional action must be taken, of course, to ensure that the necessary amount of cash is available to finance repayment when it falls due. One approach is to invest separately, each year, an amount of cash equal to the figure transferred to the debenture redemption reserve. These investments may be described, in the balance sheet, as 'debenture redemption investment fund', and the balance on this account appears as a separate item amongst the current assets of the company. The investments are sold, when the redemption date approaches, and the debentures redeemed out of the proceeds. The debenture redemption investment fund is seldom employed today.

The balance to the credit of the debenture redemption reserve remains legally available for distribution but, in reality, it forms part of the company's permanent capital. To acknowledge this fact, a further transfer may be made from debenture redemption reserve to a non-distributable capital redemption reserve after the redemption has taken place; a second alternative is to capitalize the credit balance on debenture redemption reserve by making a bonus issue (see the next section).

BONUS (CAPITALIZATION, SCRIP) ISSUE OF SHARES

Figure 10.4 shows a typical balance sheet of a manufacturing company that has traded successfully for a number of years and financed a great deal of its expansion out of retained profits. Over the years Star has generated and retained profits amounting to £575,000 and the whole of this amount is legally available for distribution to the shareholders of the company. An examination

	£	£
Fixed assets		
Plant and machinery at cost		850,000
Less: Accumulated depreciation		360,000
		490,000
Current assets		
Stock and work in progress	426,000	
Trade debtors and prepayments	250,000	
Cash in hand	2,000	
	678,000	
Less: Current liabilities		
Trade creditors and accruals	207,000	
Bank overdraft	136,000	
	343,000	
Working capital		335,000
		825,000
Financed by		
Share capital (£1 ordinary shares)		250,000
Reserves (all distributable)		575,000
		825,000

Figure 10.4   Balance Sheet of Star plc as at 31 December 19X1

of the information contained in the balance sheet in Figure 10.4 clearly shows that, in practice, the company would find it difficult to pay any dividend whatsoever. The company has a cash balance of just £2,000 to meet day-to-day cash outgoings and there is a bank overdraft of £136,000. Clearly the profits retained in the company, although initially in the form of cash, have since been reinvested in business assets. Consequently, although £575,000 remains legally available for distribution, in practice the company is unable to adopt this course of action. It is therefore argued that the equity section of the balance sheet does not fairly represent the financial position of Star.

The directors are able to rectify the position by converting reserves into share capital. The procedure followed is to issue shareholders with additional shares in proportion to their existing holdings, and to make necessary adjustments to the relevant ledger accounts. The process is described as a capitalization of profits and the share issue to existing investors is called a bonus issue or a scrip issue. The adjustment is entered in the books as follows:

Debit	Credit	With
Retained profit	Share	The amount of
(or reserves)	capital	the bonus issue

Assuming the directors of Star make a bonus issue of two shares for every one share presently held, the capital section of the balance sheet is revised as follows:

Balance Sheet extract, Star plc as at 31 December 19X1

Financed by:	£
Share capital (£1 shares)	750,000
Reserves	75,000
	825,000

The term 'bonus issue' is misleading. The implication is that the shareholder has received some additional financial benefit he or she did not previously enjoy. This is not the case. It is true that after the issue has taken place each shareholder holds three times as many shares, but the company receives nothing extra and its profit earning potential remains unchanged. This can be demonstrated by examining the net asset value per share both before and after the bonus issue.

Net asset value per share

Before $\dfrac{£825,000}{250,000} = £3.30$

After $\dfrac{£825,000}{£750,000} = £1.10$

A person who initially owned 100 shares had a total interest in the book value of the company's net assets of $100 \times £3.30 = £330$. After the bonus issue he or she owns 300 shares, but their underlying asset value has fallen to £1.10 each and the total book value of his or her interest remains unchanged at £330 ($300 \times £1.10$). The market price of the share falls in a similar manner to reflect the larger number of shares in circulation.

It has been noted earlier that the source of a bonus issue of shares is not limited to distributable profits; in particular, balances on the share premium account, revaluation reserve, debenture redemption reserve and capital redemption reserve may be applied in this way.

Readers should now attempt Questions 10.4, 10.5 and 10.6 at the end of this chapter.

LIMITATIONS OF COMPANY ACCOUNTS

There is general agreement that shareholders and other external users find company accounts a useful basis for performance assessment and decision-making. At the same time it is accepted that they suffer from a number of important deficiencies. Some criticisms are as follows:

1. The accounts are usually well out of date. If they are prepared on a calendar-year basis, they are unlikely to be available until March or April of the following year. These will be of limited use to, say, a potential creditor as the financial position of a company may have changed dramatically since the accounts were prepared.
2. The information contained in the accounts is based on original cost rather than current value. For example, a freehold property purchased in 1950, for £100,000, might still be reported at this figure despite the fact that it is today worth £5 million. Most people would agree that this is absurd, but the use of £100,000 is fully in accordance with accepted accounting procedures.
3. The balance sheet reports some, but by no means all, the assets belonging to an organization. In broad terms, an asset must possess a fairly readily identifiable cash value for it to be reported in the accounts. Certain assets, although extremely valuable, do not possess this characteristic and are not reported. For example, the favourable trading connections or 'goodwill' of a company, built up over the years, is omitted from the accounts.
4. Annual accounts are past history, whereas the user wants to know what is likely to happen to a company in the future. Last year's accounts may show a good profit and a stable financial position, but trading conditions are subject to constant change, and a series of setbacks may result in heavy losses and a rapid deterioration in the company's financial structure.

Demands for the publication of information about future financial developments, such as cash forecasts and profit forecasts, have been resisted by management and accountants for a number of reasons that include the problem of accurately forecasting future results, the scope which forecasts provide for management to take an over-optimistic view of likely future outcomes, and the difficulties that would arise for the auditor if he or she was required to report on the reliability of forecast data. It is interesting to note, however, that management overcomes its opposition to the publication of forecasts when its company is under threat. For example, the directors often publish profit forecasts as a defensive measure to counter an unwelcome takeover bid. In general, however, information about future developments is restricted to the broad comments made by the chairman in his or her report.

It must therefore be admitted that, although the improvement of financial reporting procedures continues to be the aim of most businessmen and women and accountants, much work remains to be done. The above limitations must therefore be borne in mind in assessing the usefulness of information reported in company accounts.

QUESTIONS

10.1   The following information is provided in respect of the affairs of Newton Ltd, a trading company, for 19X0 and 19X1:

Draft profit and loss account, year to 31 December

	19X0 £000	19X1 £000
Administration expenses	1,620	1,809
Selling costs	520	572
Distribution costs	140	164
Transfer to general reserve	—	500
Depreciation charge	250	300
Proposed dividend	100	200
Balance of profit	300	60
	2,930	3,605

Draft Balance Sheet, 31 December 19X0

	£000	£000
Debit balances:		
Stock	724	771
Debtors	570	524
Plant and machinery at cost	1,840	2,650
Cash at bank	92	305
	3,226	4,250
Credit balances:		
Trade creditors	416	480
Provision for depreciation	520	820
General reserve	—	500
Dividend	100	200
Share capital (£1 shares)	1,600	1,600
Profit and loss account	590	650
	3,226	4,250

Required

(a) Re-draft the above accounts in order to make them more informative. The profit and loss account should show figures for gross profit, net profit and retained profit; the balance sheet should include an appropriate classification of assets and liabilities.

(b) Comment on the view expressed by one of Newton Ltd's directors that the company should not pay the proposed increased dividend because profits have declined.

10.2   The following trial balance was extracted from the accounts of Minto plc at 31 October 1986:

	£	£
Called-up share capital		200,000
Share premium		100,000
12% Debentures		225,000
Fixed assets at cost:		
Freehold premises at cost	435,000	
Machinery and equipment	60,000	
Motor lorries	225,000	
Provisions for depreciation to		
1 November 1985:		
Freehold premises		30,000
Machinery and equipment		24,000
Motor lorries		62,000
Sales		791,600
Discounts allowed	14,200	
Discounts received		9,800
Purchases	458,200	
Debtors and creditors	54,100	31,400
Provision for doubtful debts at		
1 November 1985		3,700
Bad debts	2,900	
Wages and salaries	68,400	
Administrative expenses	32,800	
Research and development expenditure	9,600	
Debenture interest paid	13,500	
Directors' remuneration	40,000	
Retained profits at 1 November 1985		115,200
Stock at 1 November 1985	113,400	
Goodwill at cost	30,000	
Bank balance	35,600	
	1,592,700	1,592,700

Additional information relevant to the year ended 31 October 1986 is as follows:

(i)   Share capital is divided into 200,000 ordinary shares of £1 each and is all issued and fully paid.

(ii)   Stock held at 31 October 1986 is detailed as follows:

	Cost	Net realizable value
Category – small	£36,200	£26,700
Category – large	£47,800	£58,600
Category – magnum	£56,300	£46,800

(iii) The provision for doubtful debts is to be increased to £4,500.

(iv)   Provision is to be made for depreciation as to:
       machinery and equipment at 10 per cent per annum of cost;
       motor lorries at 20 per cent per annum of cost; and
       freehold premises – £6,000.

(v)   Corporation tax on the profits of the year is to be provided for at £33,000.

(vi)   Goodwill is to be amortized at 20 per cent of cost.

(vii) A machinery replacement reserve is to be created of £15,000.

(viii) An ordinary share dividend is proposed at the rate of 10p per share.

(ix)   Wages and motor expenses accruals amount to £1,500 and £900 respectively.

Required

(a) Trading and profit and loss account for the year ended 31 October 1986.
                                                                (15 marks)

(b) The balance sheet as on the above date in vertical format, and with appropriate sub-totals.
                                                                (10 marks)
                                                        (Total: 25 marks)
            (ICSA, Introduction to Accounting, December, 1986)

10.3   (a) Within the field of periodic financial reporting, comment on and distinguish between 'accounting bases' and 'accounting polices' and relate them to the following fundamental accounting concepts:

  (i)   The 'going concern' concept.
  (ii) The 'accruals' concept.
  (iii) The 'consistency' concept.
  (iv) The 'prudence' concept.

                                                                (13 marks)

(b) Explain how the directors of a company attempt to ensure that the annual published financial statements portray a 'true and fair view'.
                                                                (12 marks)
                                                        (Total: 25 marks)
            (ICSA, Financial Accounting I, December, 1984)

10.4   The following trial balance was extracted from the books of Porchester Ltd on 31 March 19X6:

	£	£
Ordinary share capital (£1 shares)		500,000
Retained profit to 1 April 19X5		1,039,000
10% Debentures repayable 19X9		300,000
Freehold land and buildings at cost	400,000	
Plant and machinery at cost	1,300,000	
Provision for depreciation on plant and machinery at 1 April 19X5		512,000
Debtors and prepayments (including trade debtors, £360,000)	370,080	
Stock and work in progress at 31 March 19X6	984,020	
Bank balance	268,000	
Provision for doubtful debts at 31 March 19X6		15,000
Creditors and accrued expenses		351,500
Gross profit for the year		1,020,800
Administration expenses	216,900	
Selling expenses	150,400	
Bad debts written off	8,700	
General repairs and maintenance	25,200	
Debenture interest to 30 September 19X5	15,000	
	3,738,300	3,738,300

Additional information is provided as follows:

1. The company's freehold property was revalued at £900,000 on 1 October 19X5. The directors have decided to use this figure for the purpose of the accounts.
2. The company made a bonus issue of two ordinary shares, fully paid, for each share held on 1 October 19X5. No entry has been made in the books in respect of the issue.
3. The directors propose to pay a dividend of 5 per cent on the nominal value of the ordinary share capital at 31 March 19X6.
4. The company purchased additional plant costing £120,000 on 31 March 19X6. The plant was delivered to the company's premises on that date together with the purchase invoice to be paid within seven days, but no entry has been made in the books in respect of the transaction.
5. Depreciation is to be provided at 25 per cent, reducing balance, on all plant and machinery owned by the company at the year end, except the plant referred to under 4 above. Ignore depreciation of freehold property.
6. Corporation tax of £150,000, due for payment on 1 January 19X7, is to be provided out of the trading profit for the year.
7. The company's authorized share capital is £2,000,000 divided into ordinary shares of £1 each.

Required

The profit and loss account and profit and loss appropriation account of Porchester Ltd for the year ended 31 March 19X6, together with the balance sheet at that date. Particular attention should be given to layout, although the accounts need not necessarily be in a form appropriate for publication.

10.5   What is the purpose of a bonus issue of shares? Using the information prepared in your answer to Question 10.4, consider whether the issue was reasonable in amount.

10.6   The trial balance of Southgate plc at 31 December 19X9 was as follows:

	£	£
Ordinary share capital (shares £1 each)		500,000
Freehold property at cost	500,000	
Furniture and equipment at cost	375,000	
Provision for depreciation of furniture and equipment, 1 January 19X9		59,500
Debtors and prepayments	105,000	
Stock and work in progress at 31 December 19X9	104,200	
Creditors and accruals		85,300
Balance at bank	72,000	
Gross profit on trading		416,500
Rent and rates	30,000	
Office salaries	142,600	
Advertising costs	21,000	
Transport costs	23,600	
Profit and loss account balance, 1 January 19X9		278,500
Taxation due 1 January 19Y0 on 19X8 profits		103,600
Deposit on new equipment	10,000	
Temporary investment	60,000	
	1,443,400	1,443,400

You are given the following additional information:

1. The company has contracted to purchase new equipment at a cost of £50,000. A deposit of £10,000 was paid during December 19X9 and the remainder will be paid during January when delivery is expected.
2. Depreciation is to be provided on furniture and equipment, other than the new equipment referred to under 1, at the rate of 10 per cent on cost.
3. The figure for rent and rates in the above trial balance covers the fifteen months to 31 March 19Y0.
4. During December 19X9 the company used part of the profit and loss account balance at 1 January 19X9 to make a bonus issue of one new share for every five shares already held. The issue was made at par but has not yet been written into the books.

5. During November 19X9 the company's freehold premises were valued at £650,000 by a firm of professional valuers. The company's directors have decided to write the revaluation into the 19X9 accounts and credit the surplus arising to revaluation reserve.
6. Taxation is to be provided at 50 per cent on the company's net profit from trading operations.

Required

(a) The profit and loss account of Southgate for 19X9 and balance sheet at 31 December 19X9. Each accounting statement should be presented in vertical format.
(b) Your comments on the suggestion, from one director, that the company should pay a dividend of 10p per share on the issued share capital in view of the large bank balance and the fact that no dividend was paid for 19X8.

Note
Ignore depreciation of freehold property.

11
Some Specialized Accounting Techniques

INTRODUCTION

The techniques of information collection and analysis described so far have related mainly to trading concerns that operate in a single location and buy and sell goods without further processing; transactions where the amount due is settled in one payment, either immediately or in the near future; and the 'going' concern. There are many occasions when the activities of a business or the information requirements of ownership, management or other interested parties, such as the firm's bankers, do not fit into this framework. This chapter covers the specialised accounting techniques to be used in the following instances:

1. Businesses concerned with manufacturing which buy raw materials and other supplies and spend further sums to process them into finished goods.
2. Businesses that operate a number of distinct departments, require reports on the results achieved by each of them to be provided to management so that their contribution to the overall results is identified and action can be taken to maximize each department's effectiveness, and hence the performance of the entity as a whole.
3. A business that conducts its activities through a number of branches spread over a wide geographical area.
4. Where transactions are entered into on terms that involve the receipt of the total sum due in a number of instalments spread over a fairly long period of time; this occurs especially in the retail trade. Similar terms may be used by companies to purchase their fixed assets.
5. Businesses are themselves sometimes the subjects of purchase and sale or are dissolved.

The system of double entry book-keeping is extremely flexible and can be extended to meet not only the circumstances described above, but also many others that may arise. However, extensions of the system often introduce complications of data accumulation, recording and interpretation, and the cost of these additional impositions should be weighed against the benefits derived from the possession of additional information to decide whether the extra effort is justified. In some instances these extra costs have to be met to comply with legal requirements, such as the collection of value added tax on behalf of the government; the manner in which this may be achieved as part of the routine accounting system is described later in this chapter. Finally, consideration is given to the steps that must be taken to identify losses of stock and cash when the basic records are lost or are considered unreliable.

THE MANUFACTURING ACCOUNT

Where a company manufactures the product in which it trades, it is useful for management to identify separately the cost of production. This is done by preparing a manufacturing account in which all the costs related to production are combined. The total cost of completed items, established in the manufacturing account, is then transferred to the trading account, where it takes the place of purchases and is adjusted for the opening and closing stocks of finished goods, in the usual way, to calculate the cost of goods sold.

The manufacturing account shows how much it has cost to produce the goods sold during a period and so enables management to compare individual elements of cost with either the results of previous periods or predetermined standards. Also, the total cost of production can be compared with the cost of purchasing similar completed products from an outside supplier to give an indication of the efficiency of the manufacturing section. If it is discovered, for example, that finished goods can be purchased elsewhere at a total cost lower than that of internal manufacture, then the cessation of manufacturing should be investigated and the possibility of simply buying the completed product for resale examined.

Management may decide to use the accounting system to identify the manufacturing profit or loss by making the transfer from the manufacturing account to the trading account at the market value for which similar finished goods could be purchased. The manufacturing profit or loss is transferred to the profit and loss account where it is combined with the gross profit on trading.

The technique of making transfers at other than historical cost can be extended. For example, a company may make sub-assemblies for incorporation into a finished product; these may be charged to production at 'outside' prices to allow the performance of the various departments to be assessed. This process may be illustrated by reference to a car manufacturer that produces its own gear boxes – the market price can be used for transfers from the gear-box department to the main car-assembly section to show the profit or loss on internal production. The greater the number of separate departments it is desired to monitor, then the more detailed the analysis of costs has to be.

The preparation of the manufacturing account

When preparing the final accounts of a manufacturing organization, the first step is to examine the data contained in the trial balance to determine which entries relate to manufacturing; these are transferred to the manufacturing account. Typical manufacturing costs are raw materials and depreciation of plant, and these can be identified solely with the production process. However, in some cases it is not possible to relate a cost entirely to one function, for example, a single rent payment may be made for premises that contain a factory, warehouse, transport depot and offices. When this occurs, the total cost recorded in the trial balance must be apportioned, that is, the proportion that relates to the factory is shown in the manufacturing account and the remainder in the profit and loss account. Such apportionments should be made on a rational basis, for example, rent can be divided on the basis of the area occupied by each section. (The usefulness and limitations of apportionments are discussed in the section on departmental accounts later in this chapter.)

The costs entered in the manufacturing account should be classified, for presentation purposes, between prime costs and production overhead costs. Prime costs are the materials and labour used directly in the production process; they vary with the level of production and would not be incurred at all if output fell to zero. Overhead costs are those that do not usually vary with the rate of production, for example, the rent must be paid whether the factory is producing very little or operating at full capacity. (The importance of the behaviour of costs in response to changes in output is discussed in Chapter 14.) The sum of the prime costs and overhead costs is the total factory cost of production.

To determine the cost of raw materials consumed, the value of purchases during a period must be adjusted by the opening and closing stocks by applying the formula:

$$\text{Opening stock of raw materials} + \text{Purchases} - \text{Closing stock of raw materials} = \text{Cost of materials consumed}$$

There may also be stocks of 'work in progress', that is, units of output that are partly completed at the accounting date; closing work in progress is valued and deducted from total factory cost of production to give the cost of completed production. The cost of work in progress is carried forward to the next period, when further costs are incurred to complete the items involved and to make them ready for sale; work in progress appears in the balance sheet as part of the stock included in current assets. The adjustment is made by applying the formula:

$$\text{Opening work in progress} + \text{Total factory cost} - \text{Closing work in progress} = \text{Cost of completed items}$$

Example 11.1

The following balances were among those extracted from the books of Worker, a manufacturing business, on 31 December 19X4:

	Debit £	Credit £
Sales		270,000
Production wages	50,000	
Purchase of raw materials	100,000	
Depreciation of manufacturing equipment in 19X4	10,000	
Production overhead expenses	7,500	
Rent	9,000	
Depreciation of office equipment in 19X4	2,000	
Salaries of sales personnel	16,000	
Delivery costs	12,000	
Advertising costs	6,000	
General administration expenses	22,000	
Stocks at 1 January: Raw materials	15,000	
Work in progress	1,500	
Finished goods	20,000	

Notes

1. Stocks at 31 December were:

	£
Raw materials	12,500
Work in progress	2,500
Finished goods	27,000

2. Two-thirds of the rent charge relates to the factory.

Required

Prepare the manufacturing, trading and profit and loss accounts of Worker for 19X4.

Solution

Manufacturing, Trading and Profit and Loss Account of Worker for the Year to 31 December 19X4

	£	£
Stock of raw materials at 1 January		15,000
Purchases of raw materials		100,000
Less: Stock of raw materials at 31 December		(12,500)
Raw materials consumed		102,500
Production wages		50,000
Prime cost		152,500
Production overhead costs		
Depreciation		10,000
Expenses		7,500
Rent		6,000
Total factory cost		176,000

	£	£
Total factory cost (brought forward)	176,000	
Work in progress at 1 January	1,500	
Less: Work in progress at 31 December	(2,500)	
Cost of completed items transferred to trading account	175,000	
Sales		270,000
Stock of finished goods at 1 January	20,000	
Transferred from production	175,000	
	195,000	
Less: Stock of finished goods at 31 December	(27,000)	
Cost of goods sold		168,000
Gross profit		102,000
Rent	3,000	
Depreciation of office equipment	2,000	
Sales personnels' salaries	16,000	
Delivery costs	12,000	
Advertising	6,000	
General administration	22,000	
		61,000
Net profit		41,000

The identification and elimination of profit on manufacture

The identification of profit on manufacture enables management to judge the efficiency of manufacturing operations, but a problem arises when preparing final accounts for external use. For this purpose, the realization concept (see Chapter 4) allows profit to be recognized *only* when a sale takes place, and this means that unsold stock must be valued at cost. Where transfers of stock have been made within the firm at a value in excess of cost, an adjustment must be made to remove any unrealized profit at the year end. This is done by creating a provision for unrealized profit that is set off against the stock value reported in the balance sheet. As was demonstrated with the provision for doubtful debts (see Chapter 7), once a provision has been created it is only necessary to adjust its value each year with one of the following entries:

	Debit	*Credit*	*With*
either	Profit and loss account	Provision for unrealized profit	An increase in the provision
or	Provision for unrealized profit	Profit and loss account	A decrease in the provision

Example 11.2

Doer Ltd was established on 1 January 19X8. The summarized trading and profit and loss accounts at historical cost for the first year of operations to 31 December 19X8 are:

	£	£
Cost of manufacture: Prime		150,000
Overheads		75,000
Factory cost of completed items		225,000
Sales		375,000
Transfer from manufacturing account	225,000	
Less: Closing stock of finished goods at cost	(50,000)	
Cost of goods sold		175,000
Gross profit		200,000
All other costs		150,000
Net profit		50,000

The company's management wishes to know the profit on manufacturing. It discovers that it could have purchased a similar product at a price 10 per cent greater than its own cost of manufacture. Prices were stable throughout the period, and there was no work in progress at the accounting date.

Required

(a) Prepare the manufacturing, trading and profit and loss accounts of Doer Ltd for the year to 31 December 19X8, making the transfer from the manufacturing account at cost plus 10 per cent.
(b) Show the entry in the balance sheet at 31 December 19X8 for the stock of finished goods.

Note
A provision should be made, in the profit and loss account, for the unrealized profit on unsold stock.

Solution
(a)

	£	£
Costs of manufacture: Prime		150,000
Overhead		75,000
Factory cost of completed items		225,000
Profit on manufacturing		22,500
Transfer to trading account		247,500

	£	£
Sales		375,000
Transfer from manufacturing account	247,500	
Less: Stock at 31 December at		
transfer price (cost + 10%)	(55,000)	
		192,500
Gross profit on trading		182,500
Profit on manufacturing		22,500
		205,000
Less: All other costs	150,000	
Provision for unrealized profit	5,000	
		155,000
Net profit		50,000

(b) **Balance Sheet extract**

	£
Stock of finished goods	55,000
Less: Provision for unrealized profit	5,000
	50,000

Notes
1. The identification of the manufacturing profit results in the following double entry: a debit to the manufacturing account and a credit to the profit and loss account.
2. The revised accounts show that the company makes £22,500 profit by manufacturing its own product, and £182,500 profit from trading.
3. The value of net profit, after providing for an unrealized profit in manufacture, remains unchanged.

Readers should now attempt Question 11.1 at the end of this chapter, which combines the various aspects of the manufacturing account dealt with in this section. Note that the presentation of the profit and loss account is improved if similar items are grouped together under such headings as 'finance costs' and 'selling costs' and their sub-totals calculated.

DEPARTMENTAL ACCOUNTS

Where a business has a number of separate departments, management needs to know which of these are performing well and which poorly so that areas of weakness can be strengthened and successful activities built upon. To achieve this, the costs and revenues of each department must be identified in a way that makes them controllable.

The production of departmental accounting statements relies upon the careful analysis of the flows of expense and revenue at the time of their initial recording in the day books. Where possible, costs should be *allocated*, that is, recorded as belonging directly to a particular department. For example, the wages of an employee who works in a particular department can be allocated directly to that department. However, there are some costs that cannot be allocated, and these have to be *apportioned*. Costs that are apportioned can alternatively be described as 'joint costs' as they give benefit to more than one department, and the benefit itself is not divisible. For example, the cost of overall administration has to be met, but relates to all of the departments of the firm; each department, therefore, has to contribute towards this cost, but does not make its own direct payment in respect of the charge.

It is usual to present departmental accounts in columnar format as this makes comprehension easier and facilitates easy comparison between the separate areas to which the report relates. In columnar presentation, the results of each separate department are entered in a column alongside the results of the others. This technique is illustrated in Example 11.3.

Example 11.3

The following list of balances was extracted from the books of Bucket Ltd in respect of the year to 31 March 19X9:

		£	£
Sales: Department	X	68,000	
	Y	54,000	
	Z	41,000	163,000
Purchases: Department	X	44,880	
	Y	37,060	
	Z	29,060	111,000
Lighting and heating			3,570
Delivery expenses			1,956
Commission paid			3,260
Printing and stationery			750
Salaries and wages			27,000
General expenses			6,900
Opening stock: Department	X		12,410
	Y		9,550
	Z		7,750
Closing stock: Department	X		10,540
	Y		7,350
	Z		8,280

Expenses are to be apportioned between the departments as follows:

1. Delivery expenses in proportion to sales.
2. Commission at 2 per cent of sales.
3. Printing and stationery and wages and salaries in the proportion 6:4:5.
4. Other expenses equally.

Required

A columnar trading and profit and loss account for the year ended 31 March 19X9.

Solution

Departmental trading and profit and loss account for the year to 31 March 19X9

	X £	Y £	Z £	Total £
Sales	68,000	54,000	41,000	163,000
Less:				
Opening stock	12,410	9,550	7,750	29,710
Purchases	44,880	37,060	29,060	111,000
Closing stock	(10,540)	(7,350)	(8,280)	(26,170)
Cost of goods sold	46,750	39,260	28,530	114,540
Gross profit	21,250	14,740	12,470	48,460
Less:				
Delivery expenses	816	648	492	1,956
Commission	1,360	1,080	820	3,260
Printing and stationery	300	200	250	750
Salaries and wages	10,800	7,200	9,000	27,000
Lighting and heating	1,190	1,190	1,190	3,570
General expenses	2,300	2,300	2,300	6,900
Total expenses	16,766	12,618	14,052	43,436
Net profit (loss)	4,484	2,122	(1,582)	5,024

Readers should now work Question 11.2 at the end of this chapter.

BRANCH ACCOUNTS

A company that operates branches has to organize its accounting function so that proper control can be exercised over each branch's activities. The alternative approaches that may be adopted are to keep all of the records at the head office and maintain a single set of books for the whole business, or to allow branches to keep their own separate sets of double entry records. The system adopted in a particular instance is likely to depend, in part, on the degree of autonomy with which branches are allowed to operate; the former approach is more applicable where strict central control is exercised, while the latter suits circumstances where branches are, within limits, allowed to function as autonomous units. This chapter now examines how these alternative accounting methods are operated in practice.

Integrated records at head office

When the branch records are fully integrated with those of the head office, a single set of double entry accounting records is maintained, at head office, which covers the whole organization and so, at the end of each accounting period, a single trial balance is produced. To enable the results of individual branches to be identified, each entry must clearly indicate the branch to which it relates. This method is the same as that used for departmental accounts, described earlier in this chapter, and effectively treats each branch as a department, despite the fact that they are located in different places. To see how this system operates, readers may refer back to Example 11.2 and substitute 'branch' for each occurrence of the word 'department'.

In some instances, goods purchased by head office are entered in its purchases account and then transferred to branches for sale. The transfer to the branch is recorded in the books by the following entry:

Account debited	Account credited	With
Goods to branch	Head office purchases	Costs of goods sent to branch

The balance on the goods sent to branch account is transferred to the branch's trading account at the end of the accounting period and is added to any purchases recorded as specifically relating to the branch.

If the head office provides a wholesale facility for the branches by buying in bulk, it may be desired to identify the profit head office generates from this function. To achieve this, the goods are charged to the branch at a price in excess of cost and the profit element in the transaction is recorded in a 'mark-up' or 'branch stock adjustment' account as follows:

Account debited	Account credited	With
Goods sent to branch		Transfer price of goods (cost plus profit)
	Head office purchases	Cost of goods transferred
	Mark-up	Profit element of transfer price

For *internal* reporting purposes the branch's opening and closing stocks are valued at transfer price, and the profit on the wholesale aspect of the head office operation is given by the balance on the mark-up account. For *external* reporting purposes the stock held by branches must be re-stated at the cost to the business, and so a 'provision for unrealized profit' must be made in the same way as that described earlier in this chapter.

Example 11.4

Organizer operates a head office and two branches, A and B. All purchases of goods for resale are made by the head office and then transferred to the branches at cost plus 25 per cent. The firm's books of account are kept by the head office, and the trial balance at 31 December 19X4 was:

	£000	£000
Goods sent to branches		
Branch A	250	
Branch B	375	
Mark-up account		125
Sales		
Branch A		350
Branch B		450
Capital at 1 January		345
Stock at 1 January at transfer price		
Branch A	50	
Branch B	75	
Provision for unrealized profit at 1 January		
Branch A		10
Branch B		15
Fixed assets	350	
Debtors	60	
Cash	35	
Drawings	45	
General expenses		
Branch A	40	
Branch B	65	
Head office	25	
Creditors		75
	1,370	1,370

The following information is relevant:

1. No stocks were held at the head office at either the beginning or end of the year.
2. At 31 December 19X4 the stocks held at the branches at transfer price were:

Branch A	£55,000
Branch B	£100,000

Required

Prepare, in columnar format, the trading and profit and loss accounts of the branches, and the whole organization, for the year to 31 December 19X4 and the balance sheet as at that date.

Solution (£000)

Trading and Profit and Loss Account for the Year to 31 December 19X4

	Branch A	Branch B	Total
Sales	350	450	800
Less:			
Opening stock	50	75	125
Plus: Goods at transfer prices	250	375	625
Less: Closing stock	(55)	(100)	(155)
Goods sold at transfer price	245	350	595
Gross profit on branch trading	105	100	205
General expenses	40	65	105
Branch profit	65	35	100
Mark-up		125	
Less: Increase in provision for			
unrealized profit		6(W1)	
			119
			219
Head office general expenses			25
Net profit			194

Balance Sheet at 31 December 19X4

	£000	£000
Fixed assets		350
Stock	124 (W2)	
Debtors	60	
Cash	35	
	219	
Creditors	(75)	
		144
		494
Financed by:		
Capital 1 January		345
Profit for 19X4		194
Less: Drawings		(45)
		494

Workings

Stock is transferred at cost plus 25 per cent and so cost is 80 per cent and profit 20 per cent of the transfer price.

	Closing stock at transfer price	W1 Profit = 20%	W2 Cost = 80%
Branch A	55	11	44
Branch B	100	20	80
		31	
Less: Opening provision (10 + 15)		25	
Increase in provision		6	
Closing stock at cost			124

If any transfers of goods take place between branches, an adjustment to reflect this must be made in the accounting records kept at head office:

Account debited	Account credited	With
Goods sent to receiving branch	Goods sent to sending branch	Value of goods transferred

It is possible for the head office to transfer stock to branches at the retail selling price, i.e. the value at which the branch is to sell the goods to its customers. The records relating to the branch are all maintained at selling price, and its profit is identified in the mark-up account after adjusting for unrealized profit. This approach enables the head office to maintain a tight control over branches, as it sets the prices at which sales are to be made, and therefore determines margins, and is able to calculate the theoretical value of closing stock, at selling prices, by using the formula:

$$\begin{matrix} \text{Opening stock} \\ \text{at selling prices} \end{matrix} + \begin{matrix} \text{Goods from head office} \\ \text{at selling prices} \end{matrix} - \text{Sales} = \begin{matrix} \text{Closing stock} \\ \text{at selling prices} \end{matrix}$$

The theoretical closing stock value can then be compared with the results of a physical stock check, valued at selling prices, and any discrepancies investigated.

Separate branch records

The maintenance by a branch of its own complete set of double entry books requires that 'current accounts' are used to enable transactions between the head office and the branch to be recorded. In the head office books there is a 'branch current account' and in the branch's books there is a 'head office current account'. The head office current account in the branch's books can be regarded in the same light as the sole trader's capital account as it represents the amount due to ownership, in this case the head office; conversely, the branch current account in the head office books represents the net investment that has been made in the branch. Example 11.5 shows some specimen entries in current accounts.

Example 11.5

Highlight has a branch that maintains its own set of double entry books. At 1 January 19X5 the balances on the current accounts were:

In the head office books: Branch current account – £50,125 (debit).
In the branch books: Head office current account – £50,125 (credit).

The following transactions took place in January 19X6:

1. The branch sent cash of £2,500 to the head office.
2. The head office sent goods to the branch at cost £7,250.
3. The head office bought for cash a delivery van for the branch at a cost of £10,750.
4. The branch returned to the head office damaged goods that had been transferred to it at a cost of £550.
5. The branch paid wages of £1,000 to its staff in cash.

Required

Show the entry of the above information in the branch current account in the head office books and the head office current account in the branch books and show the closing balances.

Solution

Head office books
Branch Current Account

	£		£
Balance b/d	50,125	1. Cash	2,500
2. Goods to branch	7,250	4. Goods returned	
3. Cash – van	10,750	from branch	550
		Balance c/d	65,075
	68,125		68,125

Branch books
Head Office Current Account

	£		£
1. Cash	2,500	Balance b/d	50,125
4. Goods returned		2. Goods from head	
to head office	550	office	7,250
Balance c/d	65,075	3. Van	10,750
	68,125		68,125

Note
Transaction 5 does not appear in the current accounts as it does not involve a transaction between the head office and the branch. It appears only in the books of the branch: debit wages £1,000 and credit cash £1,000.

The current accounts record all transfers between the head office and the branch and so the balances should be equal, but of opposite value, once all the relevant transactions have been entered in each of them. It is possible for the balances to differ at the accounting date, however, and when this occurs a reconciliation must be carried out to identify the causes of the difference. It may be found, for example, that goods or cash were sent on the final day of the accounting year but were not received until the following day so that at the accounting date they were entered in the sender's book but not the receiver's. After all such items have been identified and adjusted, the balances will agree; trial balances can then be extracted from both sets of books and used as the basis for preparing the final accounts.

Example 11.6

Sundowner has a head office in London and branches in Cardiff and Bristol. Each branch maintains its own set of full double entry books, from which the following trial balances were extracted on 31 December 19X6:

	London Dr. £000	London Cr. £000	Cardiff Dr. £000	Cardiff Cr. £000	Bristol Dr. £000	Bristol Cr. £000
Capital		350				
Sales		200		100		150
Purchases	125		30		70	
Goods sent to branches		25				
Goods from head office			20		5	
Fixed assets at book value	130		70		100	
Stock at 1 January	10		18		22	
Debtors	30		21		28	
Cash at bank	15			3	5	
Creditors		24		26		17
Advertising	52		9		19	
Selling expenses	33		13		23	
Head office administration	17					
Drawings	20					
Head office current account				52		105
Cardiff branch current account	52					
Bristol branch current account	115					
	599	599	181	181	272	272

Notes

1. The Bristol branch sent £10,000 to the head office on 31 December 19X6; it was not entered in the head office books until 2 January 19X7.
2. Depreciation of 10 per cent of the book value is to be written off fixed assets.
3. Stocks at 31 December were:

	£000
London	15
Cardiff	23
Bristol	30

4. All transfers of goods were made at cost.

Required

Prepare, for the head office, the individual branches and the firm as a whole, the trading and profit and loss accounts for the year to 31 December 19X6 and the balance sheets as at that date.

Solution

Trading and Profit and Loss Accounts for the Year to 31 December 19X6

	London £000	Cardiff £000	Bristol £000	Total £000
Sales	200	100	150	450
Opening stock	10	18	22	50
Purchases	125	30	70	225
Goods sent to branches	(25)	20	5	
Closing stock	(15)	(23)	(30)	(68)
Cost of goods sold	95	45	67	207
Gross profit	105	55	83	243
Advertising	52	9	19	80
Selling expenses	33	13	23	69
Depreciation	13	7	10	30
Total costs	98	29	52	179
Branch profit	7	26	31	64
Head office administration				17
Net profit				47

Balance Sheets at 31 December 19X6

	London £000	Cardiff £000	Bristol £000	Total £000
Fixed assets at book value	117	63	90	270
Current assets:				
Stock	15	23	30	68
Debtors	30	21	28	79
Cash	25(W1)	—	5	30
	70	44	63	177
Less: Current liabilities				
Creditors	24	26	17	67
Overdraft	–	3	–	3
	24	29	17	70
Working capital	46	15	46	107
Cardiff branch current account	78(W2)			
Bristol branch current account	136(W3)			
	377	78	136	377
Financed by:				
Capital at 1 January	350			350
Plus: Profit	47	26	31	47
Less: Drawings	(20)			(20)
Head office current account		52	105	
	377	78	136	377

Workings (£000)

W1: 15 (balance) + 10 (cash in transit)
W2: 52(balance) + 26(profit)
W3: 115(balance) − 10(cash in transit) + 31 (profit)

Note
The (intra-company) transfers of goods in the trading accounts cancel out to prevent the overstatement of purchases and sales. Similarly, the current account balances shown in the separate balance sheets cancel to avoid overstatement of assets and liabilities.

It is possible to make transfers of goods at above cost when branches keep their own sets of books in the same way as when all the records are at the head office. The head office identifies and records the profit element in a mark-up account and charges the full transfer price in the branch's current account while the branch enters the full transfer price in its books as the cost of acquiring goods for resale. Any unrealized profit in the stock valuation at the balance sheet date must be eliminated in the usual way when external accounting reports are prepared.

INSTALMENT CREDIT

It is possible for businesses to make both sales and purchases on the basis of instalment credit. This involves the settlement of the total amount due by a number of instalments spread over an agreed period of time. To compensate for the delay in settling the amount outstanding, it is usual to add to the cash price an amount of interest. This chapter now deals with how such transactions can be accounted for in the books of the seller and the buyer.

The seller's books

The application of the realization concept (explained in Chapter 4) means that profit is recognized at the point of sale, and this rule applies whether the sale is on cash or credit terms. There are some circumstances where the strict application of this rule is not, however, believed to portray fairly the underlying economic facts, such as when a sale is made under a hire-purchase or instalment credit agreement whereby the debt is settled by a number of payments spread over a fairly long period of time. It is possible to determine the point of sale for such transactions in strictly legal terms: in the case of hire purchase it is at the time of the last instalment; in the case of instalment credit, the sale is deemed to take place at the outset when the entire debt is created. However, to recognize the whole profit at either the beginning or the end of the entire transaction is generally thought to be misleading. The economic fact is that completion of the sale takes place over a period of time, and this should be recognized when profit is measured.

A rational basis of apportionment is required to spread the expected profit, and a good measure of the degree of completeness is the proportion of the total sales price received during the period for which profit is to be calculated. The application of this approach is shown in Example 11.7.

Example 11.7

A company's accounting date is 31 December. On 1 June 19X1 it made a sale under an instalment credit agreement. The total value of the sale is £480 to be settled by a deposit of £96 and 24 monthly instalments of £16, the first to be made on 30 June 19X1. The cost of the goods sold is £360.

Required

Calculate the profit to be recognized on the sale in 19X1, 19X2 and 19X3 assuming that profit is recognized as cash is received.

Solution

The total gross profit on the sale is £480 − £360 = £120.

	Cash received	Proportion of total cash received	Profit taken
	£		£
19X1 96 + (6 × £16) =	192	40%	40% × 120 = 48
19X2 12 × £16 =	192	40%	40% × 120 = 48
19X3 6 × £16 =	96	20%	20% × 120 = 24
	480		120

The phased recognition of profit on instalment credit transactions can be entered in the books of account in a number of ways. Two of the most common are:

1. to credit the total value of the sale to the trading account in the accounting period during which the sale takes place and create a provision for unrealized profit; and
2. to credit each period's trading account with the cash received during the period and assign a value to stock on the basis of cash not yet collected.

In both cases it is best to operate a separate trading account in which to enter all instalment credit sales so that their results can be separately monitored.

The provision for unrealized profit on instalment credit sales method

With this method, the full value of the sale is entered in the trading account and recorded as a debtor. At the accounting date the value of unrealized profit is calculated and debited to the profit and loss account. The credit balance on the provision account is deducted from the value of instalment sales debtors, which should be disclosed separately in the balance sheet.

Example 11.8

Required

Prepare the trading and profit and loss account for 19X1 based on the information given in Example 11.7, using a provision for unrealized profit, and show the relevant extract from the balance sheet.

Solution

	£
Sales	480
Cost of goods sold	360
	120
Gross profit	120
Provision for unrealized profit (£48 + £24)	72
	48
Profit	48

Balance Sheet extract

	£
Instalment sales debtors	288(W1)
Provision for unrealized profit	72
	206

W1
£480 (Total selling price) − £96 (Deposit) − (£16×6) (19X1 instalments).

Notes
1. In 19X2, £48, and in 19X3 the remaining £24, of the provision are credited to the profit and loss account.
2. There will usually be a number of transactions each year and the provision is adjusted at the year end in the same way as the provision for doubtful debts (see Chapter 7).

The cash receipts method

The cash received as a deposit and the instalments receivable during the accounting period are entered in the trading account, and 'stock out on instalment sales' is carried down as an asset in the balance sheet; no entry for debtors appears in the balance sheet other than for any instalments due but unpaid at the accounting date.

The value of the stock out on instalment sales is found by applying the proportion of sales price still outstanding to the cost of stock sold. The following formula may be used:

$$V = \frac{I}{S} \times C$$

where V = Value of stock out on instalment sales.
    I = Instalments due in future accounting periods.
    S = Total selling price.
    C = Cost of stock sold.

Example 11.9

Required

Prepare the trading and profit and loss accounts for 19X1, 19X2 and 19X3 based on the information given in Example 11.7, using the stock out on instalment sales method.

Solution

To value stock at 31 December:

			19X1	19X2
I	(Instalments due in future accounting periods)	=	288	96
S	(Total selling price)	=	480	480
C	(Cost of goods sold)	=	360	360
$V = \dfrac{I}{S} \times C$		=	216	72

Instalment Sales Trading Accounts

	19X1		19X2		19X3	
	£	£	£	£	£	£
Deposit and instalments receivable		192		192		96
Stock out on instalment credit b/f		—		216		72
Goods sold	360		—		—	
Stock out on instalment credit c/f	(216)		(72)		—	
		144		144		72
Profit		48		48		24

The examples in this section have dealt with only a single sale. Readers should now work Question 11.3, which extends the principle to multiple sales.

The buyer's books

The total amount payable when a company buys a fixed asset on instalment credit terms consists of the cash price of the asset plus interest. To comply with the historical cost concept, the cash price of the asset is recorded in the fixed asset account. The matching concept requires that the interest charge is apportioned between the accounting periods over which the instalments are paid; this concept also requires the cost of the asset to be depreciated in the usual way over its useful life. For a hire-purchase transaction, the following entries are made to record the initial purchase of the fixed asset:

Account debited	Account credited	With
Fixed asset at cost		Cash price of asset
Interest suspense		Total interest payable over the life of the agreement
	Hire-purchase creditor	Total amount payable under the agreement

The deposit paid or trade-in allowance is debited to the hire-purchase creditor account as are the individual instalments as they fall due. At the end of each accounting period the portion of interest that relates to the period is transferred to the profit and loss account, and the balance remaining on the interest suspense account is set against that on the hire-purchase creditor account and the net sum entered in the balance sheet.

Example 11.10

Jacobin Ltd purchased a new delivery van under a hire-purchase agreement on 1 July 19X5. The cash price of the van was £10,000 and Jacobin paid a deposit of £4,000. Hire-purchase interest charges of £1,272 were added to the outstanding balance, the total of which was to be paid off by 24 equal monthly instalments starting on 31 July 19X5.

Jacobin makes up its accounts to the 31 December. It is calculated that the hire-purchase interest charges should be apportioned 19X5 – £424, 19X6 – £652, 19X7 – the remaining balance.

Required

(a) Prepare the hire-purchase creditor and interest suspense accounts as they would appear in the books of Jacobin for the years 19X5, 19X6 and 19X7.
(b) Show the balance sheet extract for the hire-purchase creditor at 31 December 19X5 and 19X6.

Solution

(a) Hire-Purchase Creditor Account

	£		£
19X5		19X5	
Cash deposit	4,000	Delivery van	10,000
Cash 6 instalments	1,818	Interest suspense	1,272
Balance c/d	5,454		
	11,272		11,272
19X6		19X6	
Cash 12 instalments	3,636	Balance b/d	5,454
Balance c/d	1,818		
	5,454		5,454
19X7		19X7	
Cash 6 instalments	1,818	Balance b/d	1,818

Hire-Purchase Interest Suspense Account

	£		£
19X5		19X5	
Hire-purchase creditor	1,272	Profit and loss	424
		Balance c/d	848
	1,272		1,272
19X6		19X6	
Balance b/d	848	Profit and loss	652
		Balance c/d	196
	848		848
19X7		19X7	
Balance b/d	196	Profit and loss	196

Working

Amount of each instalment:

11,272 (HP price of asset) − 4,000 (deposit) =

7,272/24 (instalments) = £303.

(b) **Balance Sheet extracts 31 December**

	19X5	19X6
Hire-purchase creditor	5,454	1,818
Less: Interest not yet due	848	196
	4,606*	1,622

Note
* For the purpose of the published accounts this sum must be split between that part that is a current liability, i.e. due for payment on or before 31 December 19X6, and that payable in more than a year's time.

The method shown above is equally applicable where, instead of hire purchase, an instalment credit agreement is used. In these circumstances, an account titled 'instalment creditor' is used in place of the 'hire-purchase creditor' account.

TRANSFER OF BUSINESS

It is possible for a business to grow by acquiring an existing undertaking. This is known as 'external' expansion and contrasts with 'internal' expansion, which involves the purchase of new trading assets and the creation of additional activity to utilize them. The advantage of external expansion is that management does not have to develop new products or outlets. For example, the owner of a shop may wish to open a branch in another town: internal expansion involves acquiring premises and stock, training staff and attracting customers; external expansion involves the purchase of an existing shop together with its stock, as a going concern, and possibly the retention of the bulk of its staff and customers.

The accounting entries that result from the transfer of a business can be divided into three areas:

1. The record of the assets and liabilities taken over in the books of the purchaser.
2. The record of any transactions carried out by the purchaser on behalf of the vendor of the business.
3. The record of the sale of the business in the vendor's books.

The initial record

The agreement under which an existing business is acquired must contain a clear statement of which assets and liabilities are to be transferred under the deal. This is to avoid any future disputes about, for example, where the responsibility lies for such liabilities as an overdraft or trade creditors created before the takeover, or whether a specific piece of property is included in the price.

The transferred assets should be recorded in the purchaser's books at the agreed price, which is unlikely to be the same as the historical cost at which they are recorded in the vendor's books as they are acquired at current values. A difficulty may arise because a global figure is paid for the acquired business that is not allocated between specific assets taken over. In these circumstances, the price paid must be apportioned between the tangible assets and liabilities acquired, on the basis of their current values, with any excess recorded as goodwill. (See Chapter 8 for a full discussion of goodwill.)

Example 11.11

The balance sheet of Firefly at 31 December 19X4 was:

	£	£		£
Premises		14,000	Capital	20,000
Stock	12,000		Creditors	15,000
Debtors	7,000			
Cash	2,000			
		21,000		
		35,000		35,000

Gloworm agreed to buy the business on 1 January 19X5 for £30,000 cash. The cash balance was not part of the deal and was to be retained by Firefly. The current value of the premises was £20,000; the other assets and liabilities are fairly stated at their balance sheet values.

Required

(a) Calculate the value of goodwill purchased from Gloworm.
(b) Show the journal entry made in Gloworm's books to record the acquisition.

Solution

(a) **Calculation of goodwill**

	£	£
Price paid		30,000
Acquired: Premises	20,000	
Stock	12,000	
Debtors	7,000	
	39,000	
Less: Liabilities assumed	15,000	
Net assets acquired at current value		24,000
Goodwill		6,000

(b) Journal

	Debit £	Credit £
Premises	20,000	
Stock	12,000	
Debtors	7,000	
Creditors		15,000
Goodwill	6,000	
Cash		30,000
	45,000	45,000

Readers should now work Question 11.4 at the end of this chapter.

Transactions on behalf of the vendor

The purchasing company may carry out some transactions on behalf of the vendor, such as collecting debtors or paying creditors that are not taken over. This is a useful way of maintaining continuity with customers and suppliers. All such transactions are entered in a separate account, in the name of the vendor, and a net settlement made as agreed. Care must be exercised not to confuse these transactions with the trading activity that takes place after the acquisition.

Example 11.12

Hotter purchased the business of Colder on 31 December 19X5. It was agreed that the following items should not be included in the acquisition:

	£
Debtors	15,000
Creditors	6,000
Overdraft	1,700

Hotter agreed to collect the sums due from debtors, use this cash to settle the creditors and overdraft, and pay the remaining balance to Colder. By 31 January 19X6, £14,500 had been collected from debtors, the rest being considered bad debts, and Hotter had settled the agreed debts of Colder.

Required

Prepare the account of Colder in the books of Hotter and show the balance due to Colder on 31 January 1986.

Solution

Colder's Account

	£		£
Cash paid to creditors	6,000	Cash collected	
Cash paid – overdraft	1,700	from debtors	14,500
Balance due to Colder	6,800		
	14,500		14,500

Readers should now work Question 11.5 at the end of this chapter.

The vendor's books

When the business of a sole trader is sold, entries must be made in the firm's books to calculate the resulting profit or loss and to record the dissolution of the undertaking. A 'realization account' is opened and the same basic procedure followed as was described for partnerships in Chapter 9. When a limited company is wound up, any surplus or deficit in the realization account is transferred to the profit and loss account. Each ordinary shareholder then receives a share of the cash, which remains after all other liabilities have been paid, on the basis of the proportion of shares owned.

Some modifications to the method of recording dissolution are required when, instead of ceasing to trade, a firm is converted into a limited company. The following discussion and example relate to a partnership, but the same method is used for a sole trader.

The conversion of a partnership into a limited company brings the partnership to an end, and so a realization account is opened that is credited with the value of the shares, debentures, cash and any other form of consideration the limited company has agreed to give in exchange for the net assets it is to acquire. The realization account is then closed by transferring the profit or loss to the partners' capital accounts. The assets of the partnership now consist of the securities and/or any cash, received from the limited company. The securities are shared between the partners on the agreed basis, and any balances remaining on the capital accounts are cleared by the introduction or withdrawal of cash. The process is dealt with in Example 11.13.

Example 11.13

Wing, Beat and Flap trade in partnership and share all profits equally. The firm's balance sheet was as follows:

	£	£		£
Fixed assets		25,000	Capital accounts:	
Current assets	16,000		Wing	9,000
Current liabilities	8,000		Beat	9,000
			Flap	15,000
		8,000		
		33,000		33,000

The partners decide to transfer the business to a limited company and, at the same time, adjust the balance of investment between the partners. To achieve this the partners set up Flyer Ltd and arrange to transfer to it all the assets and liabilities of the partnership in exchange for 27,000 ordinary shares of £1, and debentures worth £15,000. Wing is to receive 50 per cent of the shares and Beat and Flap 25 per cent each; the debentures are to be divided equally between the partners.

Required

Prepare the realization account, the shares in Flyer account, the debentures in Flyer account, and the partners' capital accounts to record the transfer of the business to Flyer Ltd and the dissolution of the partnership.

Solution

Realization Account

	£		£
Fixed assets	25,000	Current liabilities	8,000
Current assets	16,000	Shares in Flyer	27,000
Profit on realization:		Debentures in Flyer	15,000
Wing	3,000		
Beat	3,000		
Flap	3,000		
	50,000		50,000

Shares in Flyer Account

	£		£
Realization account	27,000	Capital account:	
		Wing	13,500
		Beat	6,750
		Flap	6,750
	27,000		27,000

Debentures in Flyer Account

	£		£
Realization account	15,000	Capital account:	
		Wing	5,000
		Beat	5,000
		Flap	5,000
	15,000		15,000

Capital Accounts

	Wing £	Beat £	Flap £		Wing £	Beat £	Flap £
Shares in Flyer	13,500	6,750	6,750	Balance b/d	9,000	9,000	15,000
Debentures in				Profit on			
Flyer	5,000	5,000	5,000	realization	3,000	3,000	3,000
Cash				Cash			
withdrawn		250	6,250	introduced	6,500		
	18,500	12,000	18,000		18,500	12,000	18,000

Readers should now work Question 11.6 at the end of this chapter.

VALUE ADDED TAX (VAT)

Every business that trades in taxable items and has a turnover, including VAT, in excess of £21,300 (1987–88) must register for VAT purposes. The consequence of registration is that VAT at the appropriate rate, at the time of writing the standard rate is 15 per cent, must be added to the selling price of goods and services and charged to the customer. Every three months the VAT collected, known as the output tax, is paid to the government after deducting any VAT the firm has itself paid on its purchases (the input tax). It is usually possible for a trader to reclaim VAT if the amount of input tax paid in any three month period exceeds the amount of output tax collected. This may arise if, for example, a particularly expensive fixed asset is purchased as VAT is charged by the supplier of such items and is immediately recoverable in full!.

The accounting records of a registered trader have to be kept in such a way that all input and output tax is routinely identified so that the correct settlement can be made. This objective is achieved by identifying and recording separately the VAT element of any transactions in a separate column of the books of prime entry. The total from the VAT analysis column of the sales day book is credited to a VAT account in the main ledger: the total from the VAT analysis column of the purchases day book is debited to the VAT account. The VAT account is balanced every three months to find the amount due to HM Customs and Excise. The trading results of the enterprise are therefore reported net of

VAT, and any balance on the VAT account at the balance sheet date is shown as a current asset or a current liability. For example, if a company sells on credit an item for £230 of which £30 is VAT, the following entries are made in the books:

1. Debit the customer's account with £230. This is the full amount that has to be collected in respect of the sale.
2. Credit sales account £200. The company retains this amount after paying over the tax.
3. Credit VAT account with £30. This is the sum owed to the tax authorities as a result of the transaction and is a current liability until it is paid.

It is clear from the above that VAT is accounted for on the accruals basis at the time of purchase or sale, and not when the related cash is payable. A possible result is that, if a customer takes a long period of credit, VAT has to be paid before the cash for the sale has been received. This is partially offset if a correspondingly long credit period is taken from suppliers.

Example 11.14

The following are summaries of the totals on the sales and purchases day books and petty cash books of Collector Ltd at the end of its three-monthly VAT accounting period:

Sales day book

Total	VAT	Sales
£	£	£
109,250	14,250	95,000

Purchases day book

Total	VAT	Materials	Cleaning	Advertising
£	£	£	£	£
65,550	8,550	37,500	5,000	14,500

Petty cash book

Total	VAT	Stationery	Sundries	Motor expenses
£	£	£	£	£
345	45	150	100	50

Required

Prepare the VAT account to record the above items, showing the balance due.

Solution

VAT Account

	£		£
Purchases day book	8,550	Sales day book	14,250
Petty cash book	45		
Balance due	5,655		
	14,250		14,250

Some items, such as food, are not subject to VAT and carry a *zero rate*. A business that sells zero rated items still has to maintain a VAT account so that input tax can be entered and reclaimed. Other items, such as the provision of health care, are *exempt* from VAT, which means that no tax is charged on their sale, but none of the related tax paid on inputs can be reclaimed; firms that trade only in exempt items do not need to register for VAT or keep a VAT account.

LOSSES OF STOCK AND CASH

The accounts of businesses only reflect those economic events the initial data collecting process has been designed to record. Some activity remains unrecorded, such as losses of stock or cash. Stock may be lost through theft or accident, such as fire, and cash may be lost if, for example, the employee responsible for handling it steals some before recording the amount received. It is possible, where such losses are known or suspected, to calculate their value by using the techniques of incomplete records described in Chapter 4. This ability relies on the fact that the accounting process uses known relationships between the elements it reports, and if all the elements are known, except one, then the unknown value can be determined. For example, if all of the balances in a balance sheet are known with the exception of capital, the missing figure can be found as the amount needed to balance the balance sheet (see Chapter 3 where this technique is used).

Stock losses

The value of stock lost is calculated by constructing the trading account from the date at which reliable data was last available to the time of the suspected loss. A theoretical value for closing stock is estimated as the balancing figure in the account and is compared with the actual value found by a physical stock check; the difference between these two figures is the amount of the loss. The figures in the trading account are determined as follows:

1. *Sales* Sales are known where a business maintains a system of double entry

ledger accounts; alternatively, it may be necessary to convert cash received into the value of sales by adjusting for such matters as opening and closing debtors and discounts given to customers.

2. *Purchases* The value of purchases is known where a business maintains a system of double entry ledger accounts; alternatively, it may be necessary to convert cash paid into purchases by adjusting it for opening and closing creditors and discounts received.

3. *Opening stock* This is taken from the closing balance sheet of the previous period, the date of which must be the starting point from which sales and purchases are measured.

4. *Gross profit* The difference between the selling price and the cost of goods sold is the 'gross profit' or 'margin' and can be assumed with some accuracy for a particular trade. The appropriate margin, expressed as a percentage, for the trade concerned is assumed to apply to the business under consideration. Care must be taken to ascertain whether the percentage relates to the value of sales or to the cost of goods sold. For example, if sales are £100 and the cost of goods sold £80, then the margin is £20; this is 20 per cent of the value of sales, or 25 per cent of the cost of goods sold.

The value of stock lost may now be calculated as follows:

1. Calculate the expected gross profit by applying the assumed mark-up to the value of sales.
2. Calculate the cost of goods sold by deducting the expected gross profit (found in 1) from sales.
3. Calculate the theoretical closing stock by using the formula:

$$\text{Closing stock} \quad = \quad \text{Opening stock} \quad + \quad \text{Purchases} \quad - \quad \begin{array}{c} \text{Cost of goods sold} \\ \text{(found in 2)} \end{array}$$

4. Calculate the value of stock lost by deducting the value of any stock that remains from the theoretical value of stock (found in 3).

Example 11.15

During the night of 14 March 19X2 a fire occurred in the premises of Smoke and Company, which destroyed a large quantity of stock and all the stock records. The following information was found from the accounting records:

	£
Stock at 31 December 19X1 as shown in the balance sheet	15,865
Sales 1 January to 14 March 19X2	78,640
Purchases 1 January to 14 March 19X2	57,103
Value of stock not destroyed as counted on the morning of 15 March 19X2	2,856

The company makes a gross profit of 25 per cent calculated on selling prices.

Required

Calculate the value of stock lost in the fire.

Solution

Step
1   Expected profit = 25% × 78,640 = 19,660.
2   Cost of goods sold = 78,640 − 19,660 = 58,980.
3   Theoretical closing stock = 15,865 + 57,103 − 58,980 = 13,988.
4   Stock lost = 13,988 − 2,856 = £11,132.

Note
It is possible to reconstruct directly the theoretical closing stock from the trading account:

	£	£
Sales		78,640
Opening stock	15,865	
Purchases	57,103	
Closing stock	(13,988)‡	
Cost of goods sold		58,980†
Gross profit		19,660*

Notes
* Calculated as 25 per cent of sales.
† Found as first balancing figure.
‡ Found as second balancing figure.

Readers should now work Question 11.7 at the end of this chapter, which tests the calculation of the value of lost stock with adjustments for debtors and creditors.

Cash losses

Businesses must establish adequate control over their cash as it is a mobile asset that is difficult to trace and easily exchanged. Receipts from cash sales are potentially vulnerable because control is only established once the sale has been recorded; prior to that point theft would not be highlighted by, for example, the failure of the amount of money taken from the till to agree with the till roll recording receipts. The value of suspected losses can be calculated as follows:

1. Calculate the cost of goods sold applying the formula:

Opening stock + Purchases − Closing stock = Cost of goods sold.

2. Calculate the theoretical value of sales by applying the expected mark-up to the cost of goods sold (found in 1).
3. Deduct recorded sales from theoretical sales (found in 2) to calculate the shortfall in recorded sales, and hence cash.

Example 11.16

The manager of a shop suspects that takings are being stolen. He ascertains the following for the month of July 19X9:

	£
Stock at 1 July	15,762
Purchases during July	68,570
Stock at 31 July	17,056
Recorded sales	80,840

All goods are sold at a price to yield a gross profit of 20 per cent on selling price.

Required

Calculate the value of any cash discrepancy.

Solution

Step
1 The cost of goods sold is £15,762 + £68,570 − £17,056 = £67,276.
2 Of the selling price, 20 per cent is gross profit, and so the cost of goods sold is 80 per cent of the selling price. The theoretical value of sales is therefore:

$$£67,276 \times 100/80 = £84,095$$
(i.e. goods are sold at cost plus 25%).

3 The value of takings stolen is: £84,095 − £80,840 = £3,255.

Note
The usefulness of this technique is reliant on the accuracy of the assumed gross margin.

QUESTIONS

11.1

Note
This question tests the principles dealt with at pp 242–7 of this chapter.

The following is the trial balance of Midwich, a manufacturer, at 31 March 19X6:

	£	£
Capital		50,000
Sales		208,000
Loan		30,000
Raw materials: Purchases	40,000	
Stock at 1 April 19X5	12,000	
Production wages	30,000	
Production equipment: At cost	70,000	
Provision for depreciation at 1 April 19X5		14,000
Rent	6,400	
Light, heat and power	12,000	
Production overhead expenses	17,500	
Administration expenses	7,500	
Administration salaries	15,000	
Work in progress at 1 April 19X5	2,000	
Finished goods stock at 1 April 19X5	11,500	
Provision for unrealized profit at 1 April 19X5		1,500
Hire of office equipment	7,000	
Postage and telephone	5,350	
Loan interest	3,000	
Bank charges	1,250	
Overdraft		10,000
Hire of delivery vans	2,000	
Van driver's wages	7,000	
Petrol and other van expenses	1,000	
Debtors	20,000	
Creditors		5,000
Drawings	48,000	
	318,500	318,500

Notes

1. The production equipment has a life of 10 years and a zero scrap value.
2. Stocks at 31 March 19X6 were:

	£	
Raw materials	14,000	(at cost)
Work in progress	7,000	(at cost)
Finished goods	13,800	(at transfer price)

3. Of the rent and light, and heat and power, 75 per cent relates to the factory.
4. Transfers are made from the manufacturing account at cost plus 15 per cent.

Required

The manufacturing, trading and profit and loss account of Midwich for the year to 31 March 19X6 and the balance sheet at that date.

11.2   Calc Ltd has a head office and three branches. The company's results for 19X6 were:

		£000	£000
Sales:	Branch 1	250	
	Branch 2	300	
	Branch 3	175	
			725
Cost of goods sold:	Branch 1	125	
	Branch 2	160	
	Branch 3	67	
			352
Gross profit			373
Running costs:	Branch 1	60	
	Branch 2	85	
	Branch 3	47	
			192
			181
Head office costs			90
Profit			91

Required

Re-draft the accounts to show the results achieved by each branch.

11.3   Lingwood commenced business as a hire-purchase trader on 1 January 19X5, with a cash capital of £10,000. He decided to sell vacuum cleaners (VC) and electric polishers (EP) and his terms were that payment should be made in eight equal instalments, the first payable on the date of sale, and the remainder at quarterly intervals thereafter.

The following information is extracted from Lingwood's books at the end of 19X5:

	Numbers purchased	Numbers sold	Cost per unit	Cash selling price per unit	Total selling price per unit
			£	£	£
VCs	300	250	96	144	168
EPs	250	200	144	216	252

Bank Account for 19X5

	£			£
Opening balance	10,000	Purchases		
Receipts in respect of sales:		Vcs–250 at £96	24,000	
VCs–250 at £84	21,000	EPs–250 at £144	36,000	
EPs–200 at £63	12,600	Expenses	1,980	
	———	Drawings	3,500	
	43,600	Bank interest	1,086	
Overdraft at 31 Dec. X5	22,966			
	———		———	
	66,566		66,566	

All instalments due from customers were received on due date. On 31 December 19X5, Lingwood still owed his suppliers for 50 VCs; creditors for expenses were £460.

Note
Credit for profit on sales is only to be taken in respect of instalments received.

Required

The hire-purchase trading and profit and loss account of Lingwood for 19X5 and his balance sheet at 31 December.

11.4 The following are the balance sheets of Sharpner and Pencil at 31 December 19X7.

	Sharpner		*Pencil*	
	£	£	£	£
Fixed assets				
Land and buildings		32,100		10,000
Motor vans		20,000		3,000
		———		———
		52,100		13,000
Current assets				
Stock	10,700		6,000	
Debtors	7,600		3,000	
Cash	5,200		700	
	———		———	
	23,500		9,700	
Current liabilities				
Trade creditors	7,000		3,200	
	———		———	
Working capital		16,500		6,500
		———		———
		68,600		19,500
		———		———
Financed by:				
Capital		68,600		19,500
		———		———

On 1 January 19X8 Sharpner purchased all of the assets, except cash, and liabilities of Pencil for £29,000 cash. The current values of Pencil's assets were:

	£
Land and buildings	15,000
Motor van	2,700
Stock	5,800

To finance the acquisition, Sharpner took out a loan of £25,000 repayable in ten years' time.

Required

Prepare the balance sheet of Sharpner on 1 January 19X8 after the acquisition of Pencil's business has been completed.

11.5 The balance sheet of the business owned by I. Sellup at 31 December 19X2 was as follows:

	£		£
Fixed assets			
Freehold land and		Capital	28,694
buildings	22,100	Trade creditors	7,462
Motor vans	1,975	Bank overdraft	1,893
	24,075		
Current assets			
Stock	8,992		
Debtors	4,982		
	13,974		
	38,049		38,049

Mr Buyit agrees to purchase Sellup's business on 1 January 19X3 for £40,000 cash. He sells some investments and opens a business bank account with a deposit of £50,000 and immediately pays from it the sum due to Sellup. Buyit did not take over the debtors or liabilities, and accepted no responsibility for Sellup's bank overdraft. He did agree to collect the debts and to account to Sellup for the amount collected. Land and buildings, the van and stocks were taken over and were recorded in the books of Buyit at the values reported above.

The following balances were extracted from Buyit's books, maintained strictly in accordance with double entry principles, as at 31 December 19X3:

	£
Sales revenue	92,968
Cost of sales	71,034
Expenses	13,168
Collected from Sellup's debtors	2,740
Paid to Sellup	2,610

	£
Debtors	6,949
Creditors for supplies	4,972
Stock in trade	15,594
Creditors for expenses	192

Depreciation on the van is to be charged at 20 per cent per annum on the takeover price.

Required

(a) A summary of Buyit's bank account for 19X3.
(b) The trading and profit and loss account of Buyit's business for 19X3 and a balance sheet at 31 December 19X3.

11.6   The following is the balance sheet of Purlin at 30 June 19X5:

Fixed assets	£		£	£
		Capital		50,000
Premises	27,000	Trade creditors	10,000	
Equipment	5,000	Overdraft	3,000	
Motor car	2,000			13,000
	34,000			
Stock and debtors	29,000			
	63,000			63,000

Lintel Ltd acquired the business of Purlin on 1 July 19X5 for £50,000, with the exceptions of the equipment, motor car and ovedraft. Purlin sold the equipment separately for £4,000 cash and took the car over at book value for his own use.

Required

Prepare the realization account, equipment account, cash account and capital account to record the dissolution of the firm as they appear in the books of Purlin.

11.7   The premises of Advance & Co. suffered a fire during the night of 18 February 19X4, which destroyed a quantity of stock together with the stock records. The stock was insured against fire and the company wishes to submit a claim. The following information is available:

(a) The company's accounting date is 31 December, and the balance sheet at that date in 19X3 showed stock in trade of £66,000, debtors of £54,000 and creditors for purchases of £42,000.

(b) During the period 1 January to 18 February 19X4, the following transactions took place:

	£
Cash collected from debtors	97,000
Discounts allowed	1,000
Cash paid to creditors	68,000
Discounts received	400
Cash sales	36,000
Stock drawings by owner at cost	600

(c) The company's ledger shows that on 18 February 19X4 debtors owed £57,000 and creditors were owed £39,000.
(d) A stock-take, carried out immediately after the fire, showed the value of undamaged stock to be £18,000.
(e) The company makes a gross profit of 25 per cent on the selling price of its goods.

Required

A calculation of the cost of stock lost in the fire.

12
Interpretation of Accounts: Ratio Analysis

THE NEED FOR PROFIT AND CASH

It is widely accepted that the maximization of profit is a major business objective, and it is part of management's job to devise an effective means of achieving this aim. Management must, however, recognize that there exists an effective constraint on the rate of expansion, and this limitation is the quantity of cash available at any point in time. If management pursues a policy of expansion without first taking steps to ensure that sufficient cash is available for this purpose, the consequence will be, at the very least, financial embarrassment and, at worst, bankruptcy or liquidation.

It is, therefore, important for management to plan carefully future business developments, and this planning process should concentrate attention on two separate, but related, areas:

1. profitability; and
2. financial stability.

Each area is of equal importance, and any tendency to emphasize one aspect to the exclusion of the other is likely to produce unfavourable repercussions. For instance, pre-occupation with financial stability is likely to discourage innovation. Constant changes in consumer demand are facts of business life, and the failure of management to anticipate, or at least respond to, these changes will result in a decline in the demand for the company's products to a level where the business is no longer viable. On the other hand, investment in a project that promises high profits in the near future, without first attempting to assess whether the company can afford the project, is equally ill-advised. Recognition of the importance of financial stability should not cause management to ignore the need for profit, but it will cause management to follow a policy of *long-run* rather than *short-run* profit maximization.

A proper assessment of business performance must therefore focus attention on the adequacy of both profit and cash. The way in which ratio analysis is used to achieve such an assessment is examined in this chapter.

PRINCIPLES OF RATIO ANALYSIS

Accounting ratios are calculated by expressing one figure as a ratio or percentage of another with the objective of disclosing significant relationships and trends that are not immediately evident from the examination of individual balances appearing in the accounts. The ratio that results from a comparison of two figures only possesses real significance, however, if an identifiable economic relationship exists between the numerator and the denominator. For example, one would expect there to be a positive relationship between net profit and the level of sales. Assuming that each item sold produces a profit, one would expect a higher sales figure to produce more profit. So the knowledge that profit is £5 million is not particularly illuminating. What is of greater interest is net profit expressed as a percentage of sales (see later in this chapter).

The significance of an accounting ratio is enhanced by comparison with some yardstick of corporate performance. There are three options available, namely comparison with:

1. results achieved during a previous accounting period by the same company (trend analysis);
2. results achieved by other companies (inter-firm comparisons); and
3. predetermined standards or budgets.

The advantage of making comparisons is that it enables users to classify a company's performance as good, average or poor in certain key areas. However, the user must realize that there are certain attractions and limitations attached to each of the three bases for comparison listed above.

1. Last year's results are readily available, in the case of a limited company, because there is a legal requirement for them to publish accounts giving corresponding figures for the previous accounting period. In the case of sole traders and partnerships, the ability to obtain access to the relevant data will depend on the particular circumstances of each case. For example, a banker can insist on the provision of relevant accounting information as a precondition for granting a loan. A limitation of trend analysis is that it provides little useful guidance about whether a business is doing as well as it should. For example, a comparison may show that there is an improvement in the net profit percentage, but last year's results may have been disastrous.
2. Problems with inter-firm comparisons include the difficulty of finding a company engaged in a similar range of business activities, while differences in accounting policies might detract from the significance of any findings. It is, however, important to discover how a company is performing in relation to its competitors since this throws a great deal of light on the efficiency of management and the long-term prospects of the concern.
3. A comparison of actual results with predetermined budgets or standards should, in theory, be the best test of whether the work force has achieved a

reasonable level of efficiency. There is, however, the difficulty and cost of establishing realistic standards. Also, it is of little consolation to discover that work is being carried out efficiently if, due to the existence of a declining market, profits are falling. In practice, management rarely publishes budgeted future results, or standards, and so external users of accounting reports usually have to confine their attention to trend analysis and inter-firm comparisons.

CLASSIFICATION OF ACCOUNTING RATIOS

A meaningful accounting ratio is calculated by comparing two financial balances between which there exists some identifiable economic relationship, such as profit and sales. The most important accounting ratio is the return on capital employed examined next in this chapter, while ratios designed to analyse profit margins, solvency, asset utilization and gearing are dealt with later. Finally, the relationship between the various financial ratios is examined.

Accounting ratios are used to build up a corporate profile of the company under investigation. The ratios rarely point unanimously in the same direction; profits, for example, may have declined during the same accounting period that solvency has improved. This emphasizes the importance of not attaching too much attention to individual accounting ratios, and a balanced assessment of the company's progress requires a careful examination to be made of the relative significance of the ratios that are calculated.

RETURN ON CAPITAL EMPLOYED (ROCE)

The amount of profit earned by a business is important but, to assess the relative performance of a number of businesses, or even the performance of the same business over a number of years, it is necessary to examine the figure for profit in relation to the amount of money invested (capital employed) in the business. The return on capital employed is calculated as follows:

$$\text{Return on capital employed} = \frac{\text{Net profit*}}{\text{Capital employed}} \times 100$$

Note
* It is generally acceptable to use either net profit *before* or net profit *after* tax for the purpose of this calculation. Whichever approach is adopted it should be consistently applied. When tax complications are introduced later in this chapter, the pre-tax version is used.

Example 12.1

The following information is provided for 19X1:

	Company A £	Company B £
Net profit	100,000	150,000
Capital employed	500,000	1,500,000

Required

Calculate the return on capital employed for each company.

Solution

$$\text{Company A} = \frac{£100,000}{£500,000} \times 100 = 20\%$$

$$\text{Company B} = \frac{£150,000}{£1,500,000} \times 100 = 10\%$$

Company A has reported a net profit of £100,000 whereas company B has reported a net profit of £150,000, i.e. company B has generated 50 per cent more profit than company A but, to achieve this, three times as much has been invested. When profit is related to the amount invested we find that company A has earned a return of 20 per cent compared with 10 per cent by company B, i.e. on every £1 invested in company A, a return of 20p is earned whereas, on every £1 invested in company B, a return of 10p is earned. It is therefore clear that, contrary to the initial impression conveyed by the figures provided in the question, company A is by far the better business proposition for, say, the prospective investor.

Calculation of capital employed

Capital employed is the amount of money invested in the business. The two most common methods of calculating capital employed are as follows:

1. *Owners' (proprietors') capital employed* This is the amount invested by the owner or owners. It is the balance on the sole trader's capital account; the aggregate of the balances on the partners' capital and current accounts or, in the case of a limited company, the ordinary shareholders' capital plus share premium account, retained profits and any balances on reserve accounts. Using the asset-based approach, owners' capital employed is calculated by taking total assets and deducting non-ownership liabilities.
2. *Total capital employed* This is found by adding together all sources of finance, i.e. capital, non-current liabilities and current liabilities. Using the asset-based approach, total capital employed is calculated by combining the balances for each category of asset belonging to the business.

Example 12.2

The following balances were extracted from the books of Compass Ltd at 31 December 19X2:

	£
Fixed assets	130,000
Ordinary share capital	100,000
Share premium account	20,000
10% Loan repayable 19X8	50,000
Trade creditors	25,000
Current assets	105,000
Revaluation reserve	12,000
Proposed dividend	10,000
Retained profit	18,000

Required

(a) The balance sheet of Compass Ltd at 31 December 19X2, presented in horizontal format.
(b) The figures for:
   (i)   owners' capital employed; and
   (ii) total capital employed.

Solution

(a) **Balance Sheet of Compass Ltd at 31 December 19X2**

	£		£
Fixed assets	130,000	Ordinary share capital	100,000
Current assets	105,000	Share premium account	20,000
		Revaluation reserve	12,000
		Retained profit	18,000
			150,000
		10% Loan repayable 19X8	50,000
			200,000
		Current liabilities	
		Trade creditors	25,000
		Proposed dividend	10,000
	235,000		235,000

(b) (i) Owners' capital employed, £150,000.
    (ii) Total capital employed, £235,000.

Matching profit with capital employed

The profit figure used for the purpose of calculating ROCE will differ depending on the version of capital employed under consideration:

1. *Owners' capital employed* Use net profit before tax reported in the accounts.
2. *Total capital employed* Use net profit before tax and before deducting interest charges, including interest on any bank overdraft.

The different purposes of these calculations are as follows: the former measures the return earned for ordinary shareholders; the latter directs attention to the efficiency with which management utilizes the total resources at its disposal.

Example 12.3

Assume the same facts as for Example 12.2. In addition, the summarized profit and loss account of Compass Ltd for 19X2 is as follows:

Profit and Loss Account of Compass Ltd for 19X2

	£	£
Gross profit		100,000
Less: Administrative costs	54,000	
Selling and distribution costs	17,000	
Interest on long-term loan	5,000	76,000
Net profit before tax		24,000
Less: Taxation		8,000
		16,000
Less: Dividends		10,000
Retained profit for 19X2		6,000
Retained profit at 1 January 19X2		12,000
Retained profit at 31 December 19X2		18,000

Required

Calculations of the return on:

(a) owners' capital employed; and
(b) total capital employed.

Solution

(a) Owners' capital employed:

$$\text{Return} = \frac{24,000}{150,000} \times 100 = 16\%$$

(b) Total capital employed:

$$\text{Return} = \frac{29,000^*}{235,000} \times 100 = 12.3\%$$

Note
* £24,000 (net profit) + £5,000 (all interest charges).

The directors of Compass have managed to achieve a return of 12.3 per cent on the total resources at their disposal. The return earned on the owners' capital employed is significantly higher, at 16 per cent. There are two reasons for this:

1. Compass benefits from 'free' finance amounting to £35,000, consisting of the dividend not yet due (£10,000) and trade credit (£25,000). It is for this reason that businessmen or women usually take the maximum amount of finance offered in the form of credit by suppliers.
2. The directors have raised a long-term loan at a favourable rate of interest, i.e. the £50,000 loan repayable in 19X8 attracts interest at the rate of 10 per cent per annum and, because the return earned on total capital employed is higher (12.3 per cent), the surplus accrues to the ordinary shareholders who are, as a result, better off. The division of total capital between shares and loans – technically referred to as gearing – is discussed further later in this chapter.

The rates of return, calculated in this section, are based on capital employed at the *year end*. Profit arises throughout the twelve-month period, however, and a more precise calculation is made by using *average* capital employed during the year. Because the information needed to calculate average capital employed is rarely provided, and because absolute accuracy is not a priority, it is perfectly acceptable to use the year-end figure, which usually produces a close approximation.

PROFIT RATIOS

The purposes of profit ratios are to help assess the adequacy of profits earned, to discover whether margins are increasing or declining, and to help choose between alternative courses of action. A proper appreciation of the significance of the gross profit margin and the net profit percentage is dependent upon a thorough understanding of the different ways in which business costs, both fixed and variable, respond to changes in the levels of production and sales (see Chapter 14).

Gross profit margin (ratio)

The gross profit margin is calculated, as a percentage, using the formula:

$$\text{Gross profit margin} = \frac{\text{Gross profit}}{\text{Sales}} \times 100.$$

In the case of a trader, where cost of goods sold is a variable cost, the ratio is expected to remain *constant* when the level of sales rises or falls.

Example 12.4

The sales, cost of goods sold and gross profit of Printer Ltd for 19X4 and 19X5 were:

	19X4	19X5
	£	£
Sales	162,000	196,000
Cost of goods sold	121,500	147,000
Gross profit	40,500	49,000

Required

Calculate the gross profit margin for each year.

Solution

Gross profit margin:

$$19X4: \quad \frac{40,500}{162,000} \times 100 = 25\%$$

$$19X5: \quad \frac{49,000}{196,000} \times 100 = 25\%$$

The constant gross profit margin results from the fact that for each additional unit sold, an extra unit is purchased, and prices, both for buying and selling, are unchanged. In practice, the margin does not always remain stable for reasons that include the following:

1. *A reduction in the unit cost of goods sold* Increased purchases, for example, may enable bulk purchase discounts to be obtained.
2. *Under- or over-valuation of stocks* If stocks are undervalued, for example, cost of goods sold is inflated and profit understated. An incorrect valuation may be the result of an error during stock-take or it may be due to fraud, for example, a businessman or women might intentionally undervalue his or her stocks so as to reduce the amount of tax payable. The closing stock of one period is the opening stock of the next, of course, and so the effect of errors cancels out unless repeated.
3. *Price variations* The directors may decide to cut the selling price in an attempt to increase sales. This reduces the gross profit margin but, provided sufficient extra units are sold, gross profit may still increase.

The gross profit margin of manufacturing businesses varies with changes in the level of activity even where prices are stable and stocks correctly valued. This is because manufacturing expenses include some *fixed* costs and, as production increases, the fixed costs are spread over a greater number of units with the result that the total cost per unit falls.

Example 12.5

Yale Ltd incurs annual fixed manufacturing costs of £75,000 and a variable manufacturing cost per unit of £5. Each unit sells for £10. In 19X1 20,000 units were produced and sold and 25,000 in 19X2. There were no opening or closing stocks in either year.

Required

(a) Calculate the average fixed manufacturing cost per unit.
(b) Calculate the company's total gross profit and gross profit margin for each year.
(c) Comment briefly on the results prepared in answer to parts (a) and (b).

Solution

(a)

	19X1	*19X2*
Average fixed manufacturing cost per unit	$\dfrac{£75,000}{£20,000} = £3.75$	$\dfrac{£75,000}{£25,000} = £3$

(b)

	19X1:		19X2:	
	£	£	£	£
Sales		200,000		250,000
Less: Variable costs	100,000		125,000	
Fixed costs	75,000		75,000	
		175,000		200,000
Gross profit		25,000		50,000

Gross profit margin:

$$19X1: \quad \frac{£25,000}{£200,000} \times 100 = 12.5\%$$

$$19X2: \quad \frac{£50,000}{£250,000} \times 100 = 20\%.$$

(c) An increase in sales of 25 per cent has resulted in an increase in gross profit of 100 per cent and in the gross profit margin of 60 per cent. This is because the average fixed cost per unit has fallen from £3.75 to £3.00.

Net profit percentage (ratio)

The net profit percentage expresses net profit as a percentage of sales. It is calculated as follows:

$$\text{Net profit percentage} = \frac{\text{Net profit}}{\text{Sales}} \times 100$$

The expenses debited to the profit and loss account are both fixed and variable with respect to sales. For example, interest paid on debentures is a fixed expense, provided that no further loans are taken out, while delivery costs are likely to respond to changes in the level of sales. The net profit percentage of traders *and* manufacturers can be expected to increase or decrease in line with the level of sales.

Example 12.6

Crackle is a trader who buys and sells goods. His trading results for 19X6 and 19X7 were:

Summarized trading results

	19X6 £	19X7 £
Sales	80,000	100,000
Cost of goods sold	60,000	75,000
Gross profit	20,000	25,000
Expenses	10,000	12,000
Net profit	10,000	13,000

There were no opening or closing stocks in either year. The cost of goods Crackle sells rose by 10 per cent on 1 January 19X7.

Required

(a) Calculate Crackle's gross profit margin and net profit percentage for 19X6 and 19X7.

(b) Comment on the changes in the percentages calculated in part (a).

Solution

(a)

	19X6	19X7
Gross profit margin	$\dfrac{20,000}{80,000} \times 100 = 25\%$	$\dfrac{25,000}{100,000} \times 100 = 25\%$
Net profit percentage	$\dfrac{10,000}{80,000} \times 100 = 12.5\%$	$\dfrac{13,000}{100,000} \times 100 = 13\%$

(b) The gross profit margin has remained constant at 25 per cent, and so we can conclude that Crackle has been able to pass on the 10 per cent increase in costs to his customers. The growth in the value of sales is due not only to the price rise, but also to an increase in the volume of sales. If sales had simply risen in line with the price rise, they would have amounted to only £80,000 + (80,000 × 10%) = £88,000.

The value of sales has increased by 25 per cent, while expenses have increased by only 20 per cent (some of them must be fixed costs). As a result, the net profit percentage has increased from 12.5 to 13 per cent.

To examine the relative impact of changes in level of activity on the cost structure, it is useful to express all costs as a percentage of sales. This is demonstrated in Example 12.7, which also shows that changes in the gross profit margin have a 'knock-on' effect on the net profit percentage.

Example 12.7

Stamp Ltd, a trading company, did not increase its selling prices between 19X6 and 19X7, but the cost of the goods it sells rose 1.25 per cent on 1 January 19X7. Its trading and profit and loss accounts for 19X6 and 19X7 were:

Summarized Trading and Profit and Loss Accounts

	19X6 £	19X7 £
Sales	50,000	60,000
Cost of goods sold	40,000	48,600
Gross profit	10,000	11,400
Rent	1,200	1,200
Other expenses	2,000	2,400
	3,200	3,600
Net profit	6,800	7,800

Required

(a) Prepare statements for 19X6 and 19X7 in which each of the cost categories, the net profit and the gross profit are expressed as percentages of sales.
(b) Comment on the results shown in the statement prepared in part (a).

Solution

(a)

	19X6 %	19X7 %
Sales	100.0	100.0
Cost of goods sold	80.0	81.0
Gross profit	20.0	19.0
Rent	2.4	2.0
Other expenses	4.0	4.0
	6.4	6.0
Net profit	13.6	13.0

(b) The gross profit has risen, but the gross profit margin has fallen by 1 per cent as a result of the rise in the cost of the goods it sells (1.25 per cent of cost is equivalent to 1 per cent of sales price where the gross margin is 20 per cent).

Turning to the profit and loss account, rent is a fixed cost, and its impact has fallen from 2.4 to 2 per cent. Other expenses continue to account for 4 per cent of sales. The net results is a fall in total profit and loss account costs from 6.4 to 6 per cent.

The overall impact is a fall in the net profit percentage by 0.6 per cent, although the amount of net profit has risen. If the gross profit margin could have been maintained by passing on the price rise to customers, the net profit percentage would also have risen.

Readers should now work Question 12.1 at the end of this chapter.

Earnings per share and the price/earnings ratio

SSAP 3 requires quoted companies to state their earnings per share (EPS) in the accounts, and shareholders use this figure as one basis for assessing the performance of their investment. The EPS is calculated as follows:

$$\text{EPS} = \frac{\text{Earnings}}{\text{Equity shares}}$$

where

1. earnings is defined as profit, in pence, after deducting taxation and any preference dividends (this is the amount available for the equity shareholders); and
2. equity shares are the number of ordinary shares in issue and a ranking for dividend.

Example 12.8

Walnut has an issued share capital of £1 million, divided into ordinary shares of 25p each, and 500,000 £1 preference shares carrying a dividend of 7 per cent. The following information is provided in respect of 19X0 and 19X1:

Profit and Loss Account extracts

	19X0 £	19X1 £
Profit before taxation	700,000	900,000
Less: Taxation	165,000	200,000
Profit after taxation	535,000	700,000
Dividends: Ordinary shares	(100,000)	(150,000)
Preference shares	(35,000)	(35,000)
Retained profit	400,000	515,000

Required

A calculation of the earnings per share for 19X0 and 19X1.

Solution

$$EPS = 19X0 \quad \frac{50000000p}{4000000} = 12.5p$$

$$EPS = 19X1 \quad \frac{66500000p}{4000000} = 16.6p$$

The earnings per share is also used as the basis for calculating the price/earnings ratio, which is widely used by financial analysts as a means of assessing the performance of an individual company and comparing it with the performance and prospects of other companies in the same industry. The price/earnings ratio is calculated as follows:

$$P/E \ ratio = \frac{Market \ price \ of \ share}{Most \ recent \ EPS}$$

We can, therefore, see that the ratio is calculated by expressing the current market price of the share as a multiple of *past* earnings per share. The figure for market price is taken from the daily list issued by the London Stock Exchange and the earnings per share can be obtained from the company's most recent accounts. A number of daily newspapers give an up-to-date calculation of the P/E ratio of quoted companies. A high P/E ratio indicates that the market believes the company has good prospects whereas a low P/E ratio suggests that the experts think that the next results published for the company are likely to show a deterioration. It follows from this that companies favoured by the stock market will have higher P/E ratios.

SOLVENCY RATIOS

Working capital ratio

A business must be able to meet its debts as they fall due if it is to maintain its credit worthiness and continue as a going concern. For this desirable state of affairs to exist, a business must have an adequate balance of working capital (i.e. current assets − current liabilities). A secure financial position is illustrated in Example 12.9.

Example 12.9

The following balances were extracted from the books of Campion Ltd as at 31 December 19X1:

	£
Share capital	100,000
Reserves	75,000
Taxation due at 30 September 19X2	10,000
Trade creditors	15,000
Balance of cash at bank	5,000
Fixed assets at cost less depreciation	150,000
Stock	22,000
Trade debtors	23,000

Required

A calculation of Campion's working capital balance at 31 December 19X1.

Solution

Calculation of working capital:

		£	£
Current assets:	Stock		22,000
	Trade debtors		23,000
	Bank balance		5,000
			50,000
Less: Current liabilities:	Trade creditors	15,000	
	Taxation payable	10,000	25,000
Working capital			25,000

The above calculation shows that Campion is able to pay its current liabilities out of resources made available by the conversion of current assets into cash and, in addition, it shows that £25,000 will remain after the necessary payments have been made. The fact that business activity is continuous means that additional purchases will be made during January 19X2 and more sales will also occur. Consequently, the £25,000 surplus will never actually arise in a single lump sum. Nevertheless, the working capital calculation provides a useful indication of the company's ability to meet its short-term debts as they fall due for payment, i.e. it focuses attention on the solvency position of the firm.

The significance that can be attached to the balance for working capital, taken in isolation, is limited. A figure of £25,000 suggests financial stability in the case of a small business, such as Campion, but probably not in a much larger enterprise. In another company, the deduction of current liabilities amounting to, say, £975,000 from current assets of £1,000,000 would also show a working capital balance of £25,000 but, in view of the much larger scale of short-term commitments, it would probably be regarded as a totally inadequate financial 'cushion'. It is for this reason that users of accounting statements pay more attention to the working capital (or current) *ratio*, which examines the proportional relationship between current assets and current liabilities. It is calculated as follows:

$$\text{Working capital ratio} = \frac{\text{Current assets}}{\text{Current liabilities}} : 1$$

The working capital ratio of Campion is:

$$\text{Working capital ratio} = \frac{£50,000}{£25,000} : 1$$

$$= 2:1$$

The purpose of the working capital ratio is to help assess the solvency position of a business, and a question naturally asked by students and business-men and women is, 'What is an acceptable ratio?' Unfortunately it is not possible to give a definite answer because much depends on the nature of the trade in which the company is engaged. It may be assumed, for the purpose of illustration, that Campion is a trading company that purchases and sells goods on credit, and also that the company receives from suppliers the same period of credit it allows to customers. Thirty days is the normal credit period, although the exact duration is unimportant because, provided a company allows custo-mers, on average, the same period of credit as is granted by its suppliers, the amount of money due from customers will be received in time for the creditors to be paid as their debts fall due. Because Campion sells goods on credit none of the money presently tied up in stock will be converted into cash in time to pay the existing current liabilities as they mature. It is true that some stock will be sold in the next few days, but it will be a further thirty days, at least, before the cash is collected from the customer. It will be even longer before the remaining stock is converted into cash. The conclusion that arises from this analysis is that the working capital ratio must be sufficiently high to accommodate the inclusion of stock amongst the current assets. If stock comprises no more than 50 per cent of total current assets, as is the case at Campion, an adequate ratio of current assets to current liabilities is in the region of 2:1.

In practice a ratio of 2:1 is conventionally regarded as the acceptable 'norm'. It cannot be emphasized too strongly, however, that this is a broad generaliza-tion that should be treated with great caution. For example, companies in certain sectors of the economy turn stock into cash very quickly and, for them, a ratio of well below 2:1 is quite acceptable (ASDA–MFI's liquidity ratio for 1986 was 0.7:1). This state of affairs usually exists in the retail trade where sales are made mainly for cash. In circumstances where resources are tied up in stock for a much longer time period, as happens in the construction industry, a working capital ratio of perhaps 4:1 may be regarded as essential.

Readers should now work Question 12.2 at the end of the chapter.

Liquidity ratio

The purpose of the liquidity ratio is similar to the working capital ratio, in that it is designed to assess the ability of a business to meet its debts as they fall due. The calculation is as follows:

$$\text{Liquidity ratio} = \frac{\text{Liquid assets}}{\text{Current liabilities}} : 1$$

It is a more rigorous test of solvency than the working capital ratio, because it omits current assets that are unlikely to be converted into cash in time to meet liabilities falling due in the near future. The ratio is for this reason sometimes described as the 'acid test' of solvency. Non-liquid current assets that must be left out of the calculation include stock (unless sales are made on the cash basis, as in the case of a food supermarket, in which case stock is a liquid asset) and any trade debts not receivable in the near future because customers have been allowed an extended period of credit.

The liquidity ratio of Campion (Example 12.9) is as follows:

$$\text{Liquidity ratio} = \frac{£23,000 + £5,000}{£25,000} : 1$$

$$= 1.1 : 1$$

This calculation shows that Campion Ltd has sufficient liquid assets to cover its current liabilities. A ratio of 1:1 is generally considered desirable in practice and, on the whole, this is a fair test. However, readers should be aware of the fact that the conventional method of calculation can understate the short-term financial position of the firm because, although current assets are carefully examined and less-liquid items excluded, the same distinction is not made in the case of current liabilities. Normally all current liabilities are included despite the fact that some of the amounts outstanding, particularly taxation, may not be payable for a number of months. In Campion's case, for example, current liabilities include taxation that is not due for payment until 30 September 19X2, nine months after the balance sheet date. Readers should therefore be aware of the fact that the conventional method of calculating the liquidity ratio, which includes all current liabilities, is consistent with the accounting concept of 'prudence' but may, in certain circumstances, be a little over-cautious.

Readers should now work Question 12.3 at the end of the chapter.

ASSET TURNOVER RATIOS

The ratios calculated in this section are designed to answer the following question: 'Is management making full enough use of the resources placed at its disposal by shareholders and creditors?'

Rate of stock turnover

This ratio measures the speed with which a company turns over its stock. The calculation is made as follows:

$$\text{Rate of stock turnover} = \frac{\text{Cost of goods sold}}{\text{Average stock level}}$$

Example 12.10

The accounts of Treadmill Ltd show figures for cost of goods sold and average stock levels of £150,000 and £25,000 respectively.

Required

Calculate the rate of stock turnover of Treadmill.

Solution

$$\text{Rate of stock turnover} = \frac{150,000}{25,000} = 6 \text{ times a year}$$

Two queries often raised by students concerning the calculation of the above formula are as follows: 'Why use cost of sales rather than sales?' 'Why use average stock levels rather than closing stock?' The reason, in both cases, is to ensure that both the numerator and denominator are computed on a comparable basis.

Stocks, which make up the denominator, are valued at cost for accounting purposes, and the numerator must be computed on a similar basis. The sales figure can be used to produce a ratio that enables users to make helpful inter-period comparisons, when cost of sales figures are not available, but there is a risk that wrong conclusions will be drawn when there are changes in the gross profit margin from one accounting period to another.

Turning to the reason for using *average* stock levels, the numerator measures the cost of goods dispatched to customers *during* an accounting period, and the denominator should therefore represent the average investment in stocks during the same period. The average is usually based on opening and closing stock figures but, because stock levels fluctuate a great deal, a more precise calculation would make use of stock levels at various dates during the year, perhaps at the end of each month.

The term 'ratio' is used loosely, in accountancy, to cover all the calculations that measure the relationship between two financial totals. We have already seen, for example, that net profit is conventionally expressed as a percentage of sales rather than as an actual ratio. In the case of the stock turnover ratio, many analysts prefer to present it in terms of the number of days (weeks or months) that elapse between the date that goods are delivered by suppliers and dispatched to customers, i.e. the stock holding period. This can be done by dividing the result of the calculation presented in Example 12.10 into 365 (52 or 12), or by modifying the formula so as to achieve the desired result in a single step.

Rate of stock turnover, in days

$$= \frac{\text{Average stock}}{\text{Cost of goods sold}} \times 365$$

$$= \frac{25,000}{150,000} \times 365 = 61 \text{ days}$$

Companies strive to keep the stock holding period as low as possible in order to minimize associated business costs. If Treadmill held its stock for an average of four months, rather than 61 days, its investment in stocks would double to approximately £50,000. Extra finance would then have to be raised, handling costs would increase, and the potential loss from stock damage and obsolescence would be much greater. Although management's aim is to keep stocks to a minimum, it must nevertheless ensure that there are sufficient raw materials available to meet production requirement (in the case of a manufacturer) and enough finished goods available to meet consumer demand. It is, therefore, managements's job to maintain a balance between these conflicting priorities.

Example 12.11

The following information is provided in respect of the affairs of Hutchinson, which makes up its accounts on the calendar year basis:

	19X5 £	19X6 £
Sales	500,000	600,000
Purchases	350,000	400,000
Cost of goods sold	330,000	360,000
Stock at 31 December	60,000	100,000
Debtors at 31 December	102,000	98,000
Creditors at 31 December	25,000	40,000
Total assets at 31 December	185,000	300,000

Stock and debtors at 1 January 19X5 amounted to £70,000 and £98,000 respectively.

Required

(a) Calculations of the rate of stock turnover expressed (i) as a ratio and (ii) in days, for each of the years 19X5 and 19X6.
(b) Comment briefly on your results.

Solution

(a) (i) *Ratio*

$$19X5: \quad \frac{330,000}{\frac{1}{2}(70,000 + 60,000)} \quad : 1 \quad = 5:1$$

$$19X6: \quad \frac{360,000}{\frac{1}{2}(60,000 + 100,000)} \quad : 1 \quad = 4.5:1$$

(ii) *Days*

$$19X5: \quad \frac{\frac{1}{2}(70,000 + 60,000)}{330,000} \quad \times 365 \quad = 72 \text{ days}$$

$$19X6: \quad \frac{\frac{1}{2}(60,000 + 100,000)}{360,000} \quad \times 365 \quad = 81 \text{ days}$$

(b) In 19X6 Hutchinson achieved a 20 per cent increase in sales from £500,000 to £600,000. In these circumstances, a proportionate increase in the volume of stock held might be expected. However, a disproportionate increase in stock levels, from £60,000 to £100,000, has occurred. This has been caused by a growth in the average stockholding period from 72 days to 81 days, i.e. it has taken the company, on average, 9 days longer to turnover stock in 19X6 compared with the previous year.

Rate of collection of debtors

The period of credit allowed to customers is an important business decision. Too little credit makes it difficult to achieve a satisfactory level of sales, whereas too much credit deprives a company of essential liquid resources. The 'normal' credit period varies between industries but, in practice, it is quite usual for customers to take from six to eight weeks to pay their bills. The rate of collection of debtors is calculated, in days, as follows:

$$\text{Rate of collection of debtors} = \frac{\text{Average trade debtors}}{\text{Credit sales}} \times 365$$

Note that the denominator is confined to credit sales, since only these give rise to debts outstanding. Where the split between cash and credit sales is not given, the total sales figure may be used to calculate a ratio that gives useful comparative information provided there is no significant change in the proportion of total sales made for cash.

The debt collection ratio measures the effectiveness of a company's system of credit control. When an order is received, the credit controller (usually the owner in the case of a small business but a specialist function in the case of a large corporation) must assess the credit worthiness of the potential customer. This may involve taking up references, from say a bank, speaking to colleagues in the trade and perhaps examining a recent copy of the company's accounts. If it is decided to supply the goods requested, it is important that they should be invoiced immediately following dispatch. Any time lag inevitably increases the credit period and the volume of resources tied up in debts outstanding.

At the end of the credit period, often 30 days, a check should be made to ensure that cash has been received. Indeed, a list of debtor balances, classified by the length of time outstanding, should be prepared as a matter of systematic routine. If the credit period is exceeded, the customer's attention should be drawn to this fact by sending either a statement or a letter requesting immediate payment. The debt should subsequently be kept under continuous scrutiny and no further goods supplied until payment is made. Failure to respond to the second request for payment should result in determined attempts to recover the balance outstanding by such devices as persistent telephone calls or a solicitor's letter threatening legal action. Whether legal action will in fact be taken depends on the amount outstanding, the likelihood of recovery (has the customer the money?) and the costs involved.

Example 12.12

Using the information given in Example 12.11, calculate the rate of collection of debtors, in days, for each of the years 19X5 and 19X6 and comment briefly on your results.

Solution

Rate of collection of debtors:

$$19X5: \quad \frac{\frac{1}{2}(98,000+102,000)}{500,000} \times 365 = 73 \text{ days}$$

$$19X6: \quad \frac{\frac{1}{2}(102,000+98,000)}{600,000} \times 365 = 61 \text{ days}$$

The company has reduced the average period taken to collect debts from 73 days to 61 days. As a result, the average debtor balance outstanding has remained at £100,000, despite a significant increase in sales. Possible explanations are a strong demand for the company's product, enabling credit periods to be cut, or improved efficiency in the credit control department.

Rate of payment of creditors

This ratio measures the average period of time taken by companies to pay their bills. As a general rule, companies extract the maximum credit period from suppliers since, in the absence of discounts for prompt payment, it represents a free source of finance. At the same time, undue delays should be avoided as these will have a harmful long-run effect on the company's credit standing. The result of the calculation must be interpreted with particular care since not all suppliers grant similar credit terms but, provided there are no significant changes in the 'mix' of trade creditors, the average payments period should remain stable. The rate of payment of creditors is calculated, in days, as follows:

$$\text{Rate of payment of suppliers} = \frac{\text{Average trade creditors}}{\text{Credit purchases}} \times 365$$

A change in the rate of payment of suppliers' invoices may well reflect an improvement or decline in a company's liquidity. For instance, if a company is short of cash it is likely that creditors will be made to wait longer for the payment of amounts due to them. This may be an acceptable short-term strategy, particularly where suppliers are familiarized with their customer's 'temporary' predicament and are willing to accept an extension of credit terms. Management should, however, take prompt steps to arrange for additional finance; otherwise supplies of goods will eventually be curtailed.

Example 12.13

Using the information given in Example 12.11 calculate the rate of payment of creditors, in days, for each of the years 19X5 and 19X6 and comment briefly on your results.

Solution

Hutchinson's figure for trade creditors at 1 January 19X5 is not provided. It is, therefore, impossible to calculate the ratio by using the *average* creditors figure for that year. We could make the calculation, based on averages, for 19X6 but, without a comparative figure for 19X5, this would be of little interpretive value. The best course is to make calculations, for each year, using the closing figures, instead of average figures, for trade creditors. This measures the approximate number of days' purchases represented by the closing balances of trade creditors. The result of the calculation is open to criticism since purchases are unlikely to have occurred at a uniform rate throughout the year. It must be remembered, however, that too much weight ought not to be attached to an individual ratio that should be used only to help build up an overall business profile.

Rate of payment of creditors:

$$19X5: \quad \frac{25,000}{350,000} \times 365 = 26 \text{ days}$$

$$19X6: \quad \frac{40,000}{400,000} \times 365 = 36.5 \text{ days}$$

Trade creditors have increased disproportionately between the end of 19X5 and 19X6; at the latter date the volume of creditors outstanding represents 10½ days additional purchases. One possible explanation is that the company is now making full use of credit periods allowed by suppliers. Alternatively, the company may simply be short of cash. As usual, ratios merely measure change and investigation is needed to discover what actions have caused these changes to occur.

The cash operating cycle

The period of time that elapses between the payment for goods supplied and the receipt of cash from customers in respect of their sale is called 'the cash operating cycle'. During this time period the goods acquired must be financed by the company. The shorter the length of time between the initial outlay and the ultimate collection of cash, the smaller the value of working capital to be financed. The length of the cycle is calculated as follows:

$$\text{Stockholding period} + \text{Debt collection period} - \frac{\text{Credit from}}{\text{suppliers}}$$

Using the figures calculated above, the cash operating cycle of Hutchinson is as follows:

	19X5	19X6
	Days	Days
Stockholding period	72.0	81.0
Debt collection period	73.0	61.0
	145.0	142.0
Credit from suppliers	(26.0)	(36.5)
Cash operating cycle	119.0	105.5

Total asset turnover

It is management's job to make the fullest use of available resources; only if this objective is achieved are profits likely to be maximized. The stock turnover and debt collection ratios are designed to measure management's ability to control the level of investment in certain selected areas, whereas 'total asset turnover' has the broader aim of assessing the extent to which management utilizes all available resources. It is computed as follows:

$$\text{Total asset turnover} = \frac{\text{Sales}}{\text{Average total assets}} \quad :1$$

A high ratio indicates that management is using the assets effectively to generate sales; most probably the company is working at, or near, full capacity. Possible reasons for a decline in the ratio include the following:

1. A fall in either the stock turnover or debt collection ratios which have a 'knock-on' effect on the total asset turnover ratio.
2. Temporary inconveniences such as a strike or a fire, which destroys essential equipment.
3. The collapse in demand for a product line, unless steps are promptly taken to dispose of the equipment or transfer it to an alternative use.
4. The acquisition of fixed assets. A new company needs to make arrangements for accommodation and for the installation of any necessary plant and equipment. These facilities are unlikely to be used to their full capacity immediately but, as business builds up, the level of utilization increases. The point is eventually reached where existing fixed assets are used to their full capacity, and further expansion of business activity involves the acquisition of additional plant. It normally takes some time before demand increases sufficiently to absorb the extra capacity and, meanwhile, fixed asset turnover declines.

Example 12.14

Using the information given in Example 12.11, calculate the total asset turnover for each of the years 19X5 and 19X6 and comment briefly on your results.

Solution

Total asset turnover:

$$19X5: \quad \frac{500,000}{185,000} \quad :1 = 2.7:1$$

$$19X6: \quad \frac{600,000}{300,000} \quad :1 = 2:1$$

The ratio may be expressed either in the above form or as an amount of sales per £1 invested in assets, i.e. sales were £2.70 per £1 invested in 19X5 and £2 per £1 invested in 19X6. It is therefore apparent that a significant reduction in asset utilization has occurred.

A limitation of the asset turnover ratio is that it gives a high result for companies using older assets. This is partly the effect of inflation, but also because company accounts show fixed assets at net book value, which declines each year.

RELATIONSHIP BETWEEN ACCOUNTING RATIOS

Analyses of corporate performance made by students, and even by trained accountants, are often unsatisfactory; a common weakness is the failure to explore the *relationship* between the various ratios that have been calculated. The essence of the relationship is contained in the following formula:

Primary ratio		Secondary ratios	
		Margin ×	*Utilization*
Return on total capital employed	=	Net profit percentage	× Total asset turnover

A principal managerial objective is to maximize the return on total capital employed, sometimes referred to as the 'primary ratio'. It can accomplish this objective in the following ways: it can increase the net profit percentage and/or it can achieve a higher rate of asset utilization. It may well happen that greater asset utilization, for instance more sales, can only be achieved by lowering prices, and management has to judge whether the larger volume of activity will be sufficient to justify the lower gross and net margins that result from implementing a policy of price reductions.

Example 12.15

Double and Quick are suppliers of computer software. Double rents premises and advertises his products in popular magazines. He supplies goods by mail order and insists on the receipt of cash before the software is dispatched. Quick owns a shop in the centre of town and advertises heavily on local radio and television, as well as in trade journals. Goods are supplied over the counter for cash or on a credit basis. The following information is provided in respect of 19X9 for each of these businesses:

	Double £	Quick £
Net profit	120,000	200,000
Sales	600,000	800,000
Average total capital employed	400,000	1,000,000

Required

Calculate the primary and secondary ratios for Double and Quick and comment on the results.

Solution

Applying the formula:

Return on capital employed = Net profit percentage × Total asset turnover

Double: $$\left(\frac{120,000 \times 100}{400,000}\right) = \left(\frac{120,000 \times 100}{600,000}\right) \times \left(\frac{600,000}{400,000}\right)$$

$$30\% \qquad = \quad 20\% \qquad \times \quad 1.5$$

Quick: $$\left(\frac{200,000 \times 100}{1,000,000}\right) = \left(\frac{200,000 \times 100}{800,000}\right) \times \left(\frac{800,000}{1,000,000}\right),$$

$$20\% \qquad = \quad 25\% \qquad \times \quad 0.8$$

The above calculations show that Double achieves the greater asset utilization (£1.50 of sales per £1 invested as compared with the £0.80 achieved by Quick) but his net profit percentage is lower (20 per cent compared with Quick's 25 per cent). Overall, Double's policy of maintaining a retail outlet in the centre of town seems to be more successful, i.e. the greater asset utilization more than compensates for the lower margins, and he achieves a rate of return on gross assets of 30 per cent.

The above analysis may be extended by producing a 'pyramid' of accounting ratios in the form demonstrated in Figure 12.1. The pyramid can be used to tackle questions in a structured manner. It is not, of course, necessary to reproduce the ratios in pyramid format, though readers may decide that such a presentation is helpful. The first step is to calculate the primary ratio, i.e. the return on gross assets. Ideally, it will be possible to calculate comparative figures for a previous accounting period or another company in the same industry. The secondary ratios can then be calculated to discover profit margins and the extent of asset utilization. The discovery that the net profit percentage is stable would suggest that further investigation of profit margins is probably unnecessary. A significant variation in asset utilization, however, points to the need to calculate ratios further down the pyramid to discover the reasons for observed changes.

Readers should now attempt Questions 12.4 and 12.5 at the end of this chapter.

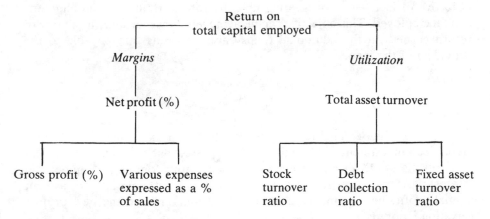

Figure 12.1   Pyramid of accounting ratios

GEARING (OR LEVERAGE)

The return earned for shareholders is dependent on management's achievements in three key areas:

1. Profit margins.
2. Utilization of assets.
3. Gearing.

The previous section demonstrates the fact that the rate of return on gross assets is a function of profit margins and asset utilization, but it takes no account of the company's capital structure. The effect of gearing on the return earned for the equity shareholders is now examined.

Capital is derived from two sources: shares and loans. Quite often only shares are issued when a company is formed, but loans are usually raised at some later date. There are numerous reasons for issuing loan capital. For instance, the owners might want to increase their investment but minimize the risk involved, and this can be done by making a secured loan. Alternatively, management might require additional finance that the shareholders are unwilling to supply, and so a loan is raised instead. In either case, the effect is to introduce an element of gearing or leverage into the capital structure of the company. There are numerous ways of measuring gearing, but the debt/equity ratio is perhaps most commonly used. It is calculated as follows:

$$\text{Debt/equity ratio} = \frac{\text{Total financial debt*}}{\text{Shareholders' equity}} \times 100$$

Note
* Includes preference shares, loans from directors and bank overdrafts.

The use of debt capital is likely to affect the amount of profit accruing to the ordinary shareholders, and expansion is often financed in this manner with the objective of increasing, or 'gearing up', the rate of return on shareholders' capital employed. This objective can be achieved, however, only if the rate of return earned on the additional funds raised exceeds that payable to the providers of the loan.

Example 12.16

The directors of Beulah Ltd are planning to undertake a new project that involves an investment of £10 million in fixed assets and working capital. The directors plan to finance the whole investment with a long-term loan bearing interest at 15 per cent per annum. The company's accountant forecasts an annual profit, before finance charges, of £2 million from the new project (taxation ignored).

Required

Calculate the financial benefit accruing to the equity shareholders from undertaking the project. Comment on the implications of your calculation.

Solution

	£m
Additional profit contributed by new project	2.0
Less: Interest charge, 15% of £10 million	1.5
Surplus	0.5

The existing shareholders are expected to be better off to the tune of £0.5 million, each year, as the result of undertaking the new project. This is because the new venture yields a return of 20 per cent whereas the loan creditors have contracted for interest at the lower rate of 15 per cent. Profit may, of course, not come up to expectations, and if it is less than £1.5 million the introduction of gearing will be detrimental to the ordinary shareholders. For example, if the new project generates profits before interest charges of £0.8 million, interest of £1.5 million must still be paid and the shortfall of £0.7 million (£1.5 million–£0.8 million) must be borne by the ordinary shareholders.

The shareholders of a highly-geared company reap enormous benefits when there are increases in earnings before interest and tax. The interest payable on loan finance remains unchanged and a growing surplus accrues to a relatively small group of equity shareholders. The converse is also true, and a highly-geared company is likely to find itself in severe financial difficulties if it suffers a succession of trading losses. It is not possible to specify an optimal level of gearing for companies but, as a general rule, gearing should be low in those industries where demand is volatile and profits are subject to fluctuation.

Readers should now attempt Question 12.6 at the end of this chapter.

LIMITATIONS OF ACCOUNTING RATIOS

The various calculations illustrated in this chapter suffer from a number of limitations that should be borne in mind by anyone attempting to interpret their significance. The main limitations are as follows:

1. Accounting ratios can be used to assess whether performance is satisfactory, by means of inter-firm comparison, and also whether results have improved, worsened or remained stable, by comparing this year's results with those achieved last year. The ratios do not, however, provide explanations for observed changes, and further enquiry is needed for this purpose. The external use s' ability to obtain further information is usually extremely limited, for example, the shareholder may ask questions at the annual

general meeting. It is only management that has direct access to the information needed to provide the right answer.

2. A deterioration in an accounting ratio cannot necessarily be interpreted as poor management. For example, a decline in the rate of stock turnover might appear undesirable, but further investigation might reveal the accumulation of scarce raw materials that enable the plant to continue working when competitors are forced to suspend production.

3. Too much significance should not be attached to individual ratios, for example, a rate of return on total capital employed of 30 per cent might indicate that all is well, but this conclusion would be unjustified if further analysis revealed a liquidity ratio of 0.4:1.

4. Company financial statements are usually based on historical cost and, therefore, accounting ratios based on these figures would be expected to improve, irrespective of efficiency, during a period of rising prices, for example, total asset turnover of £3 per £1 invested might be computed from historical cost accounts, whereas a figure of £1.80 per £1 invested might be obtained if assets were restated at their current worth.

5. Differences in accounting policies may detract from the value of inter-firm comparisons, for example, the valuation of stock on the AVCO basis rather than the FIFO basis would probably produce a much lower working capital ratio.

6. Financial statements and accounting ratios can be distorted as the result of 'one-off' large transactions such as cash raised from issuing a debenture and awaiting investment, or a profit on the sale of a fixed asset. Analysts should similarly be on their guard for evidence of 'window-dressing', perhaps designed to conceal a deteriorating financial position.

7. Particular care must be taken when interpreting accounting ratios calculated for seasonal businesses. Where sales are high at a particular time during the year, for example, at Christmas, stock might be expected to increase and cash to decline in the months leading up to the busy period. In these circumstances, deteriorations in both the liquidity ratio and the rate of stock turnover are not necessarily causes for concern.

8. Consideration must be given to variations in commercial trading patterns when assessing the significance of accounting ratios computed for particular companies. For example, a retail chain of supermarkets would be expected to have a much lower liquidity ratio and a much higher rate of stock turnover than a constructional engineering firm. In this context, accepted 'norms' such as a working capital ratio of 2:1 must be used with care.

QUESTIONS

12.1 The summarized trading and profit and loss account of Rubber Ltd for 19X1 and its summarized balance sheet at 31 December 19X1 are as follows:

Trading and Profit and Loss account for 19X1

	£		£
Cost of sales (variable)	126,000	Sales	180,000
Gross profit	54,000		
	180,000		180,000
Expenses (fixed)	39,000	Gross profit	54,000
Net profit	15,000		
	54,000		54,000

Note
A dividend of £10,000 is proposed for 19X1.

Balance Sheet as at 31 December 19X1

	£		£	£
Fixed assets	113,000	Share capital		100,000
Current assets	70,000	Retained profit		50,000
				150,000
		Current liabilities		
		General	23,000	
		Dividend	10,000	33,000
	183,000			183,000

The company could expand production to a sales level of £255,000 with no increase in fixed expenses and the cost of sales would remain the same percentage of sales as for 19X1.

Required

(a) Calculate the gross profit percentage, net profit as a percentage of sales and the return on capital employed for 19X1.
(b) A calculation of the level of sales that would have been necessary to increase the return on capital employed by 2 per cent.

Note
For the purpose of the answer, capital employed is to be interpreted as issued capital plus retained profit on 31 December.

12.2 The balance sheets of Galston Ltd as at 31 December 19X5 and 19X6 are as follows:

	19X5		19X6	
	£	£	£	£
Fixed assets at cost		303,000		367,500
Less: Accumulated depreciation		124,500		157,500
		178,500		210,000
Current assets				
Stock	37,500		75,000	
Debtors	34,500		43,500	
Bank	18,000		1,500	
	90,000		120,000	
		268,500		330,000
Share capital		150,000		150,000
Retained profit at 31 Dec. 19X5		73,500		73,500
Profit for 19X6		—		51,000
		223,500		274,500
Current liabilities		45,000		55,500
		268,500		330,000

The figure of current liabilities as at 31 December 19X5 includes a proposed dividend of £7,500 for the year to that date. No decision has been taken yet about the dividend to be paid for 19X6, and nothing is included in the 19X6 balance sheet for such a dividend.

The directors are considering the dividend that should be paid for 19X6 in the light of the excellent results for that year.

Required

(a) Calculations of Galston's working capital and working capital ratio as at 31 December 19X5 and 31 December 19X6.
(b) A calculation of the maximum dividend that should be declared for 19X6 if the working capital ratio at 31 December 19X6 is to be the same as at 31 December 19X5.
(c) A brief discussion of the financial policy pursued by the directors of Galston Ltd in 19X6.

12.3   The following information has been extracted from the accounts of Lock Ltd, a wholesale trading company:

Balances at 31 December

	19X1 £000	19X2 £000
Fixed assets	500	550
Trade debtors	125	150
Cash at bank	25	—
Proposed dividend	20	60
Overdraft	—	20
Trade creditors	80	100
Stocks	150	200

Results for the year to 31 December

	19X1 £000	19X2 £000
Sales	2,000	3,000
Cost of sales	1,000	1,450
Overhead costs	800	1,300

Required

(a) A statement showing the return on capital employed, the working capital ratio and the liquidity ratio. Your answer should be presented in the following form:

	19X1	19X2
Return on capital employed	——	——
Working capital	——	——
Working capital ratio	——	——
Liquidity ratio	——	——

(b) A brief discussion of the implications of the information calculated above.

Note
For the purpose of your calculations, capital employed is defined as shareholders' equity.

12.4 The summarized accounts of Brunel, a trader, for the years 1983 and 1984 are as follows:

Trading and Profit and Loss Account

	1983		1984	
	£	£	£	£
Sales		240,000		300,000
Less: Opening stock	24,000		25,000	
Purchases	191,000		265,000	
Closing stock	(25,000)		(60,000)	
Cost of sales		190,000		230,000
Gross profit		50,000		70,000
Less: Running expenses		28,000		30,000
Net profit		22,000		40,000

Balance Sheet at 31 December

	1983	1984
	£	£
Capital and liabilities		
Capital	99,500	100,500
Net profit	22,000	40,000
Drawings	(21,000)	(26,000)
	100,500	114,500
Trade creditors	25,500	37,000
Bank overdraft	—	11,000
	126,000	162,500
Assets		
Fixed assets at cost less depreciation	75,000	73,500
Stock	25,000	60,000
Trade debtors	21,000	29,000
Bank balance	5,000	—
	126,000	162,500

At 31 December 1982, trade debtors and trade creditors amounted to
£19,000 and £23,500 respectively. All sales and purchases are on credit.

Required

(a) Calculate the following ratios for 1983 and for 1984:

    (i)   The rate of stock turnover.
    (ii) The rate of debtors turnover.
    (iii) The rate of creditors turnover.

(iv) The working capital ratio.

(v) The percentage return on capital employed. (20 marks)

(b) Examine the progress and position of Brunel's business based on your calculations under (a). You should indicate whether each ratio has improved or declined over the two years. (10 marks)

Note

Calculations to *one* decimal place.

(RSA, Accounting, Stage II, May, 1985)

12.5 The following information is obtained in connection with the affairs of two companies, manufacturing specialized metal products, in respect of the year ended 31 December 19X5:

	Metalmax Ltd *£000*	*Precision Products Ltd* *£000*
Sales	800	950
Administration expenses	30	30
Selling expenses (including promotional costs)	45	60
Plant and machinery at cost	360	360
Depreciation to 31 December 19X4	110	110
Current assets	240	400
Trade creditors	120	320
Share capital (£1 ordinary shares)	200	200

It is also established that both companies incur variable costs of sales, excluding depreciation, of 80 per cent on sales. Depreciation should be charged at 15 per cent on the cost of machinery. Reserves may be treated as the balancing figure in the balance sheets.

Required

(a) Summary trading and profit and loss accounts for the year ended 31 December 19X5 and balance sheets at that date for each company in vertical format to facilitate comparison.

(b) A comparison of the profitability of the two companies during 19X5 and of their respective financial positions at the end of the year. Relevant accounting ratios should be used to support the discussion.

Notes

1. Within the current asset totals are included balances in respect of stocks and work-in-progress as follows:

Metalmax Ltd	£120,000
Precision Products Ltd	£200,000

2. Ignore taxation.

12.6 The following information is provided relating to the affairs of two companies engaged in similar trading activities:

	Hot Ltd £	Cold Ltd £
Ordinary share capital	800,000	500,000
15% Debentures	200,000	500,000

Each company earned a trading profit before finance charges of £110,000 in year 1 and £190,000 in year 2. Corporation tax is charged at 50 per cent on the trading profits after finance charges have been deducted. The company pays out as dividends its entire post-tax profits, i.e. there are no reserves.

Required

(a) Summary profit and loss accounts, dealing with the results of each of the two companies' activities during years 1 and 2, so far as the information given above permits.
(b) Calculations of profits before tax expressed as percentages of ordinary share capital for each company in respect of both years 1 and 2.
(c) A discussion of the returns earned for shareholders over the two-year period.

13
Interpretation of Accounts: the Statement of Source and Application of Funds

INTRODUCTION

For very many years companies have been legally obliged to publish, annually, both a balance sheet and a profit and loss account. During the 1960s, a number of companies voluntarily adopted the practice of supplementing these two documents with a third financial statement, called the 'statement of sources and applications of funds' often abbreviated to 'statement of funds'. This development reflected management's recognition of an important gap in the information made available to external users of accounting reports.

The balance sheet sets out the financial state of a business at a particular point in time, whereas the profit and loss account reports some, but not all, transactions undertaken during an accounting period – i.e. it includes only those transactions that directly give rise to revenues and expenditures. Other transactions, such as issues of shares and debentures, and the purchase of a fixed asset, are not reported in the profit and loss account since they are *capital* as opposed to *revenue* transactions. The view developed that capital transactions, which often involve significant amounts of money, were of interest to investors and should also be reported to them. The statement of funds, which was devised to provide this information, may be defined as follows: *the statement of funds sets out, in an orderly manner, the sources of finance that have been raised and generated by a business during the year and the ways in which those funds have been applied.* SSAP 10, issued in 1975, made the publication of a statement of funds (described there as the statement of source and application of funds) standard accounting practice for all companies with turnover or gross income of £25,000 or above.

The various sources of finance available to businesses, and the ways in which they are employed, are examined in the next three sections. The construction of the statement is then examined.

SOURCES OF FUNDS

It is management's job to ensure that there is a satisfactory balance between long-, medium- and short-term finance. The main sources of finance and the periods for which they are available are listed below:

1. *Owners capital* This is the amount invested by the owner(s) in the business and is long-term finance.
2. *Debentures and loans* In the case of debentures, the advance is normally made on a long-term basis, for between ten and forty years. The duration for which loans are made depends on the terms of the agreement between the borrower and the lender.
3. *Hire purchase and extended credit* These are useful ways for a company to spread the heavy cost of a new fixed asset. The finance is either short term, where the instalments are all payable within one year, or a mixture of short and medium term where payments extend over two or three years.
4. *Trade credit from suppliers* This is short-term finance, although new creditors usually replace those currently paid thus ensuring a more or less permanent source of finance in this form.
5. *Taxation and dividends payable* These are liabilities but, until the payment is made, the cash may be used by the company. They are therefore short-term finance.
6. *Bank overdraft* This is, in theory, a short-term source of finance, but, in practice, this form of finance is employed on a long-term basis by many businesses.
7. *Sale of fixed assets* The cash inflow from the sale of fixed assets is available for management to invest on a long-term basis.
8. *Funds generated from operations* This normally consists of profit plus depreciation and is examined further in the next section.

NON-CASH EXPENSES: DEPRECIATION

During the course of trading activity a company generates revenue, principally in the form of sales receipts, and incurs expenditure comprising a wide range of different outlays, some of which result in an outflow of funds in the current accounting period and others which do not. Most outlays fall into the first category, for example, expenditure on purchases of materials, wages, salaries and rent. There are, however, a small number of items, the most important of which is depreciation, that are charged against profit but do not result in a current outflow of funds.

The purpose of the depreciation charge is to reflect the fact that sales revenue has benefited, during the period under review, from the use of fixed assets acquired in a previous accounting period. The effect of making the charge is to earmark an equivalent amount of cash for retention within the business, which may be used, in due course, to help finance replacement of the asset when it is worn out.

Because depreciation is charged in the profit and loss account, but does not result in a current outflow of funds, it must be added back to reported profit in order to identify total funds generated from operations, i.e.:

Funds generated from operations = Profit + Depreciation.

Students often find it difficult to grasp the fact that the depreciation charge is *represented* by an equivalent *inflow* of cash. The link is demonstrated in Example 13.1.

Example 13.1

The balance sheet of Pencil Ltd, which purchases and sells goods for cash, is as follows at 31 December 19X1:

Balance Sheet at 31 December 19X1

	£	£		£
Fixed assets at cost		1,800	Share capital	1,000
Less: Depreciation		540	Retained profit	360
		1,260		1,360
Current assets			10% Loan repayable	
Stock	400		19X7	500
Cash	200	600		
		1,860		1,860

During 19X2 cash sales and cash purchases amounted respectively to £4,000 and £2,500. The stock level remained unchanged during the year and £600 was *paid out* for wages and other operating expenses. In addition, loan interest was paid on 31 December 19X2, and depreciation of £240 was charged on fixed assets.

Required

(a) The cash account for 19X2.
(b) The trading and profit and loss account for 19X2.
(c) The balance sheet at 31 December 19X2.
(d) A calculation of funds generated from operations during 19X2, i.e. profit + depreciation.

Solution

(a) **Cash Account for 19X2**

	£		£
Opening balance	200	Purchases	2,500
Sales	4,000	Wages, etc.	600
		Interest	50
		Closing balance	1,050
	4,200		4,200

(b) **Trading and Profit and Loss Account for 19X2**

	£		£
Opening stock	400	Sales	4,000
Purchases	2,500		
Less: Closing stock	(400)		
Cost of goods sold	2,500		
Gross profit	1,500		
	4,000		4,000
Wages, etc.	600	Gross profit	1,500
Interest	50		
Depreciation	240		
	890		
Net profit	610		
	1,500		1,500

(c) **Balance Sheet at 31 December 19X2**

	£	£		£
Fixed assets at cost		1,800	Share capital	1,000
Less: Depreciation		780	Retained profit (360+610)	970
		1,020		1,970
Current assets			10% Loan repayable	
Stock	400		19X7	500
Cash	1,050	1,450		
		2,470		2,470

(d) Funds generated from operations:

	£
Profit	610
Add: Depreciation	240
Funds from operations	850

The cash balance has increased from £200 to £1,050 and the cash account shows, in detail, how this increase of £850 has been brought about. The profit and loss account shows a profit figure of £610, and this is less than the increase in the cash balance because a 'non-cash' item of expenditure, i.e. depreciation, £240, has been debited to the profit and loss account. It is, therefore, necessary to add back depreciation to reported profit in order to reconcile the opening cash balance with the closing cash balance:

	£	£
Opening cash balance		200
Add: Profit	610	
Depreciation	240	
Funds generated from operations		850
Closing cash balance		1,050

In practice, it is rare for the change in the cash balance to be entirely due to funds generated from operations. There are numerous other transactions that cause it to change, for example, new plant is purchased or additional shares issued.

A note of warning

A common misconception is that the depreciation charge *produces* an inflow of cash, and that the amount of cash available can be increased by raising the charge. This is wrong. Cash is generated from trading transactions, and the depreciation charge is simply a 'book entry' that earmarks a proportion of funds generated from operations for retention within the business. If the depreciation charge, in Example 13.1, is increased from £240 to £400, profit falls from £610 to £450 and funds generated from operations remain unchanged at £850 (depreciation £400 + profit £450). An effect of raising the charge is, however, to earmark a *larger* quantity of funds for retention within the business in the current year; later in the asset's life, charges and retentions will be correspondingly lower because the balance that remains to be written off at 31 December 19X2 is reduced by £240.

Example 13.2

Assume the same facts as appear in the solution to Example 13.1.

Required

Calculate the closing cash balance of Pencil, on 1 January 19X3, in each of the following circumstances:

(a) The entire profit of £610 is paid out as dividends on 1 January 19X3.

(b) The depreciation charge is amended to £400 and the entire profit of £450 is paid out as dividends on 1 January 19X3.

Note
No other transactions occur on 1 January 19X3.

Solution

	(a)	(b)
	£	£
Cash balance at 31 December 19X2	1,050	1,050
Less: Dividends	610	450
Cash balance at 1 January 19X3	440	600

Note
The increase in the depreciation charge, under (b), reduces the maximum dividend payable by £160 and, as a result, the remaining cash balance is £160 higher at £600.

APPLICATIONS OF FUNDS

The sources of funds, described in the previous section, may be applied in the following ways:

1. *Repayment of loan capital.*
2. *Redemption or purchase of share capital.*
3. *Purchase of fixed assets* This is a long-term investment.
4. *Payment of tax and dividends* These payments are claims against profit earned during the year.
5. *Investment in stock* This is a short-term investment in the sense that the stock is sold after a relatively short interval. Further purchases must be made, however, to replace items sold, and resources are permanently tied up in this areas. The level of investment in stock increases when there is an expansion of business activity.
6. *Credit allowed to customers* This, again, ties up resources on a short-term basis, but debts collected are usually replaced by further credit sales.

The main sources and applications of funds, discussed above, are summarized in Figure 13.1.

STATEMENT CONSTRUCTION

The statement of funds was defined earlier in this chapter as a statement that sets out the sources of finance that have been raised and generated by a business during the year and the way in which those funds have been applied. Since the balance sheet shows the accumulated sources of finance and investment in business assets up to a particular point in time, most of the information required to prepare a statement of funds can be obtained by subtracting the balances appearing in the opening balance sheet from those appearing in the closing balance sheet.

	Sources	Applications
Capital and loans raised	X	
Capital and loans repaid		X
Increase in current asset balances (e.g. stock, debtors, bank)		X
Decrease in current asset balances	X	
Increase in current liability balances (e.g. creditors and overdrafts)	X	
Decrease in current liability balances		X
Funds generated from operations (positive)	X	
(negative)		X
Taxation and dividend payments		X

Figure 13.1   Checklist of sources and applications of funds

Illustration 13.1

The following information is provided for Ruler Ltd:

Balance Sheets 31 December

	19X3		19X4		Differences (19X4—X3) Source	Application
	£000	£000	£000	£000	£000	£000
Fixed assets						
Machinery at cost		320		470		150
Less: Accumulated depreciation		150		192	42	
		170		278		
Current assets						
Stock	86		107			21
Trade debtors	53		75			22
Bank	12		64			52
	151		246			

	19X3 £000	19X3 £000	19X4 £000	19X4 £000	Differences (19X4—X3) Source £000	Application £000
Balance brought forward	151	170	246	278	42	245
Less: Current liabilities						
Trade creditors	46		61		15	
Working capital		105		185		
		275		463		
Financed by:						
Share capital		200		220	20	
Retained profit		75		103	28	
		275		323		
12% Loan repayable 19X9		—		140	140	
		275		463	245	245

The worksheet in Illustration 13.1 shows sources of funds, totalling £245,000, and the ways in which those funds have been applied. The statement of source and application of funds (Illustration 13.2) re-arranges these items in two groups.

1. Sources and applications of funds that *cause* working capital to increase or decrease. (Sources are further analysed into (i) funds generated from operations, and (ii) funds from other sources.)
2. Changes in the various items that make up working capital, i.e. stocks, trade debtors, cash and trade creditors.

Illustration 13.2

Statement of Source and Application of Funds for 19X4

Source of funds	£000	£000
Profit		28
Add: Item not involving an outflow of funds		
Depreciation		42
Funds generated from operations		70
Funds from other sources:		
Share issue	20	
Loan	140	160
		230
Application of funds		
Purchase of machinery		150
Increase in working capital		80

	£000	£000
Changes in working capital items		
Increases in working capital (applications)		
Increase in stock	21	
Increase in trade debtors	22	
Increase in bank	52	
Decrease in working capital (sources)		
Increase in trade creditors	(15)	80

The statement in Illustration 13.2 shows that Ruler raised and generated long-term finance amounting to £230,000 during 19X4; funds from operations contributed £70,000 and other sources £160,000. Of the total amount made available, £150,000 was invested long term, in new machinery, and the surplus, of £80,000, increased working capital from £105,000 to £185,000 (see balance sheet figures for working capital in Illustration 13.1). The second part of the statement gives details of changes in the various items that make up the balance of working capital. Current assets have increased, in total, by £95,000 (£21,000 + £22,000 + £52,000). This has been partly financed by additional credit from suppliers, £15,000, with the remaining £80,000 provided from longer-term sources.

Readers should now work Question 13.1 at the end of the chapter.

SOME COMPLICATIONS

In Illustration 13.1 it was possible to obtain the figures needed to construct a statement of funds simply by calculating and analysing the differences between the balances reported in two consecutive balance sheets. In practice the procedure is usually a little more complicated, and account must be taken of the matters discussed below.

Identification of gross changes

A comparison of the information in two balances sheets given figures for 'net' sources and applications of working capital. The informative value of the statement is improved by reporting instead 'gross' changes. To build up these figures it is necessary to take account of data contained in the profit and loss account and in the notes to the accounts. The balances most commonly requiring amendment are those for profit and expenditure on fixed assets.

Profit

Assume that we are also told that the directors of Ruler paid an interim dividend of £15,000 during July 19X4. We can build up the profit figure as follows:

	£000
Retained profit for 19X4	28
Add: Interim dividend	15
Total profit from operations for 19X4	43

In the statement of funds, profit of £43,000 should be shown as a source of funds and the dividend paid, of £15,000, as an application of funds.

Fixed assets

Quite often a company purchases *and* sells fixed assets during the year. In these circumstances the worksheet shows only the 'net' change and it is necessary to prepare a fixed asset schedule that shows gross changes during the year. The preparation of the schedule is based on the following known relationships:

Cost of fixed assets: Opening balance + Additions − Cost of assets sold
= Closing balance

Accumulated depreciation: Opening balance + Charge for the year −
Accumulated depreciation
on asset sold   = Closing balance

Example 13.3

The following information is extracted from the balance sheet of Staple Ltd at 31 December:

Fixed assets	*19X0*	*19X1*
Motor vehicles at cost	£40,000	£57,500
Less: Accumulated depreciation	22,700	31,600
	17,300	25,900

On 1 July 19X1, Staple sold a motor vehicle for £750. The machine had cost £6,000 some years ago, and accumulated depreciation at 31 December 19X0 was £4,900. The company's policy is to charge a full year's depreciation in the year of purchase and none in the year a vehicle is sold.

Required

(a) Calculations of additions during the year and depreciation charged.
(b) Calculate the profit or loss on disposal of vehicles.
(c) Show the information to be included in the statement of funds relating to motor vehicles.

Solution

(a)

	Cost £	Dep. £
Opening balance	40,000	22,700
Add: Purchases/depreciation charge for year	23,500*	13,800*
Less: Sales	(6,000)	(4,900)
Closing balance	57,500	31,600

Note
* These are the balancing figures.

(b)

	£
Book value (cost £6,000 − depreciation £4,900)	1,100
Less: Sales proceeds	750
Loss on sale	350

(c)

		£
Source:	Depreciation charged	13,800
	Loss on sale of vehicle	350*
	Sales proceeds	750
Application:	Purchase of motor vehicles	23,500

Note
* The loss on disposal, of £350, is debited to the profit and loss account to make up for the fact that insufficient depreciation has been charged. Like depreciation, the loss on sale is a non-cash expense and must be added back to profit to produce the figure for funds generated from operations. Any profit on sale, credited to the profit and loss account, must likewise be deducted from profit, as the entire sales proceeds appear in the statement under the heading 'funds from other sources'.

Readers should now work Questions 13.2 and 13.3 at the end of the chapter.

Taxation and dividends

When preparing accounts for publication, there are two exceptions to the general rule that the statement of funds sets out sources and applications of *working capital*. SSAP 10 requires companies to account for dividends on the cash basis rather than the accruals basis, i.e. dividends paid during the current year are shown as an application of funds, instead of showing dividends paid and proposed for the current year as an application of funds, with the difference between the previous and the current year's proposed dividend accounted for as a change in working capital. In addition, it is accepted practice to show taxation on the cash basis in the statement of funds. There is no obvious reason why dividends and taxation should have been singled out for a different treatment, but the use of the cash basis to account for these items has produced the accusation, in some quarters, that the statement of funds is a hybrid document that mixes together working capital and cash definitions of funds.

FINANCIAL POLICY

The purposes of the statement of funds are to provide some insights into the financial policy pursued by management during the year, and to show the effect of that policy on the financial position of the company. The interpretation of information contained in the statement is discussed in the following sections.

Over-capitalization

A company sometimes finds itself with cash in excess of operating requirements. This may occur because initial financial requirements were overestimated and too much capital was raised at the outset. A second possible reason is a sharp contraction in the level of business operations, for example, the closure of a segment of a business or the sale of a valuable freehold property. It is essential that excess funds should not be allowed to lie idle – otherwise a decline in the return on capital employed will be the inevitable result. The usual solution is for management to make plans for the investment of these resources. Where this is not possible, cash should be returned to the shareholders in the form of a reduction of capital. Stringent legal formalities must be complied with, when undertaking such a scheme, to ensure that the position of the creditors is not jeopardized.

Financing long-term investment

It is management's job to ensure that sources and applications of funds are properly matched, i.e. short-term finance should only be committed for a short period of time while long-term investment must be paid for out of long-term finance. For example, the purchase of a fixed asset should be paid for by raising a long-term loan, or by issuing shares, or by retaining profits permanently within the business. The reason for this is that a company is likely to suffer acute financial embarrassment if it attempts to finance the purchase of factory premises, for example, using a short-term source of finance such as a bank overdraft. The new acquisition is expected to generate sufficient revenue to cover its cost and produce an adequate balance of profit, but this process will probably take a number of years and short-term finance will have to be repaid long before it is complete.

Over-trading

Over-trading is a condition that arises when a company attempts to do too much too quickly and, as a result, fails to maintain a satisfactory balance between profit maximization and financial stability. Over-trading usually occurs when a company rapidly expands its scale of business activities but fails, first, to make available sufficient long-term finance for this purpose. Where a company has over-traded some, or all, of the following features will be apparent from an examination of consecutive balance sheets:

1. A sharp increase in expenditure on fixed assets.
2. A decrease in the balance of cash, and perhaps the emergence of a bank overdraft.
3. The structure of the current assets becomes less liquid, probably because the proportion of current assets 'tied up' in stock increases dramatically.
4. A sharp increase in creditors caused by the company's inability to pay debts as they fall due.
5. The working capital and liquidity ratios decline to an inadequate level.

The actual *causes* of over-trading are clearly demonstrated in the statement of funds which shows how much long-term finance has been made available during the year, the extent to which it covers long-term applications, and the effect of developments on the working capital of the business.

Example 13.4

Madoc is confused and worried and has come to you for advice. He tells you that, although he made a bigger profit in 19X7 than in 19X6, and has also made fewer drawings, he does not seem to be any better off and is finding it difficult to pay his creditors.

The balance sheets of Madoc's business at the end of 19X6 and 19X7 are shown below:

Balance Sheets at 31 December

	19X6 £	19X7 £		19X6 £	19X7 £
Machines at cost	10,000	20,500	Opening capital	12,000	11,000
Less: Depreciation	3,000	5,500	Add: Net profit	5,000	7,000
			Less: Drawings	(6,000)	(4,000)
	7,000	15,000			
Stock	1,700	4,900	Closing capital	11,000	14,000
Debtors	1,800	3,700	Creditors	3,000	10,000
Bank	3,500	400			
	14,000	24,000		14,000	24,000

Required

Explain to Madoc what has happened, and support your explanation with an appropriate numerical statement. Briefly advise Madoc on future policy. (Readers should first prepare a 'worksheet', although this can be omitted with practice, as is done in this case.)

Solution

Statement of Funds for 19X7

	£	£
Source of funds		
Net profit		7,000
Add: Depreciation		2,500
Funds generated from operations		9,500
Application of funds		
Drawings	4,000	
Purchase of fixed assets	10,500	14,500
Reduction in working capital		(5,000)
Changes in working capital items		
Increases in working capital:		
Increase in stocks	3,200	
Increase in debtors	1,900	
Decreases in working capital:		
Increase in creditors	(7,000)	
Decrease in bank balance	(3,100)	(5,000)

The cause of Madoc's confusion is that he mistakenly believes that profit produces an equivalent increase in the bank balance. This may happen in certain circumstances, but only if no additional investment takes place. The above statement of funds shows that Madoc has invested heavily in additional fixed assets, and there have also been substantial increases in stocks and debtors. In total, these outlays significantly exceed funds generated from operations; the result is that the bank balance has fallen dramatically and the amount owed to creditors has more than trebled.

Madoc is in a very difficult financial position, as a result of *over-trading*, and it is important that he undertakes no further investment at this stage. He should also keep drawings to a minimum and use future profits to reduce his firm's reliance on short-term credit.

Cash flow statement The kind of confusion experienced by Madoc, in Example 13.4, often gives rise to the following question: 'How can the firm possibly have earned a profit when there is less cash in the bank than there was a year ago?' A cash flow statement, which is simply a rearrangement of the information given in the solution to Example 13.4, provides a more succinct answer.

Cash Flow Statement for 19X7

	£	£
Opening cash balance		3,500
Source of cash		
Net profit	7,000	
Add: Depreciation	2,500	
Funds generated from operations	9,500	
Increase in creditors	7,000	16,500
		20,000

	£	£
Balance brought forward		20,000
Application of cash		
Drawings	4,000	
Purchase of fixed assets	10,500	
Increase in stocks	3,200	
Increase in debtors	1,900	19,600
Closing cash balance		400

The differences between the cash flow statement and the funds flow statement may be summarized as follows:

1. The cash flow statement begins with the opening cash position and ends with the closing cash position; the funds flow statement includes the *change* in the cash position as a single item which is given no particular priority.
2. The cash flow statement lists, together, both the source of funds and any decreases in working capital, e.g. more trade credit, which help to improve the cash balance.
3. The cash flow statement lists, together, both the application of funds and any increases in working capital, e.g. a greater investment in stock, which reduces the cash balance.

Readers should now work Question 13.4 at the end of this chapter.

Retrieving financial stability

The management of a company that has over-traded must take prompt steps to correct the financial imbalance, otherwise it is quite possible that the company will fail. There are a number of possible courses of action open to management. These include the following:

1. *Reduce the level of business investment* Money is tied up in both fixed assets and current assets, and management should look carefully at the feasibility of releasing cash resources by reducing the amount invested in each of these areas. It is also possible that there is a building or a piece of land that can be sold without any unfavourable repercussions for the company's operating capability. Ratio analysis may be used to examine stock levels and debtor levels to discover whether these are unduly inflated. The company's stock ordering, processing and distribution policies will come under scrutiny as will the effectiveness of the company's system of credit control. The possibility of reducing the investment in debtors, by offering discounts for prompt payment, may also be examined. It must, of course, be borne in mind that discounts, although helpful in improving cash flow, reduce sales proceeds and therefore profit. The employment of the services of a debt factor and the sale and lease back of freehold property are other options that

need to be investigated if there is a substantial liquidity problem that cannot be solved by more conventional means.

2. *Raise additional finance* The total finance to be raised depends on the period over which the cash shortage is expected to persist. Temporary cash difficulties may be overcome by arranging a bank overdraft facility or a short-term loan. Severe over-trading is likely to be corrected, however, only by raising long-term finance in the form of share capital or debentures. Access to either of these sources of long-term finance depends on the particular circumstances of the company under review. If loan finance is presently at a low level and the company has adequate security in the form of tangible assets, the issue of a debenture may well be appropriate. A share issue is, however, more likely to be the answer to the company's financial problems for the following reasons.

The fact that the company is in financial difficulties obviously places a question mark against the competence of the management team. They have not been successful in anticipating the present cash-flow problems, and a potential lender might be doubtful whether management is able to do better in the future. It is the shareholders who will be at greatest financial risk if the company goes into liquidation. They are the last source of finance to be repaid and, in a forced sale, assets are likely to realize significantly less than their book values, often leaving little or nothing over for the providers of equity finance. On the other hand, if the company recovers, the share-holders have most to gain in the form of profits distributed to them in dividends or re-invested on their behalf. At a time of financial difficulty, it will therefore be necessary for the shareholders to confirm their confidence in the future of the company and subscribe to a rights issue.

3. *Funds generated from operations* The third possibility is for the company to recover on the basis of internally generated funds. The component elements of internal funds flow are usually net profit before tax plus depreciation. Tax must, of course, be paid out of this balance, but management is able to exercise a fair amount of discretion concerning the disposition of what remains. Usually, of course, a dividend is paid and investments are made in fixed assets, stocks and debtors. At a time of severe cash shortage, it is important that such outlays are kept to a minimum so that funds generated from operations may instead be used to improve the financial stability of the concern. Indeed, it may be necessary to abandon the payment of a dividend and, if possible, delay the replacement of old plant until the financial position improves. In the case of a profitable company, funds generated from operations and retained within the business can quickly restore an element of financial stability.

4. *A combination of remedies* A number of possible schemes have been considered to help the recovery of a company that has over-traded. It is unlikely that any individual course of action will be the complete solution to the problem. Steps may be taken to economize on working capital and raise, say, a two-year loan to 'tide the company over' until sufficient finance has

been generated internally to complete the recovery. Quite obviously, the appropriate remedy will depend entirely on the particular circumstances of the company in difficulty.

The kind of problems discussed in this section are often avoidable. Financial imbalance is usually the result of management's failure to plan future financial developments. Forward planning and the use of forecast accounts to help management decide how to allocate resources is discussed in Chapter 14.

LINKING TOGETHER FUNDS FLOW ANALYSIS AND RATIO ANALYSIS

Accounting ratios can be used to assess the performance of a company during an accounting period. Comparisons with earlier years and the performance of other businesses provide useful yardsticks for assessing whether or not an improvement has occurred and for gauging whether or not results are as good as they could be. The statement of funds complements these calculations by helping to explain how improvements in a company's financial position have been brought about or why a deterioration has occurred. Example 13.5 illustrates how the two forms of financial analysis may be employed, alongside one another, to gain an understanding of the financial performance and position of a business enterprise. In addition, it shows how the annual accounts, although relating to a *past* time period, may be used as a basis for estimating likely future prospects.

Example 13.5

Expansion Ltd is a private company that has carried on copper-mining activities for a number of years. At the beginning of 19X2 the company purchased a small established tin mine at a cost of £350,000; production commenced at once. Tin extracted from the new mine in 19X2 amounted to 600 tonnes. This is expected to increase to 900 tonnes by 19X8 and then decline gradually. Finance for the new mine was partly provided by a two-year loan of £300,000 repayable by equal monthly instalments.

The summarized balance sheets for 19X1 and 19X2 are as follows:

Assets	19X1		19X2	
Fixed assets	£	£	£	£
Mines at cost	465,000		815,000	
Less: Depreciation	150,000	315,000	190,000	625,000
Plant and equipment at cost	213,250		263,250	
Less: Depreciation	56,200	157,050	75,200	188,050
		472,050		813,050

	19X1		19X2	
	£	£	£	£
Balances b/f		472,050		813,050
Current assets				
Stocks of tin and copper	143,100		169,000	
Debtors	86,250		118,250	
Cash at bank	44,100	273,450	1,800	289,050
		745,500		1,102,100
Capital and liabilities				
Share capital		500,000		500,000
Profit and loss account		182,500		314,000
		682,500		814,000
Current liabilities				
Trade creditors and				
accrued expenses		63,000		138,100
Short-term loan		—		150,000
		745,500		1,102,100

The net profit earned during 19X2 was £181,500 (19X1 £103,000) of which £50,000 (19X1 £25,000) was paid out in dividends. Turnover increased from £1,060,000 in 19X1 to £1,500,000 in 19X2.

Required

Examine the financial policies pursued by the directors of Expansion Ltd during 19X2 and comment on proposals to develop further by acquiring an additional site in the early months of 19X3. You should use a statement of funds and relevant accounting ratios to support your analysis.

Solution: examination of solvency

Statement of Funds for 19X2

Source of funds	£	£
Profit		181,500
Add: Depreciation: Mine		40,000
Plant		19,000
		240,500
Funds from operations		
Application of funds		
Purchases: Mine	350,000	
Plant	50,000	
Dividend	50,000	450,000
Decrease in working capital		(209,500)
Changes in working capital items		
Decreases in working capital		
Bank	(42,300)	
Trade creditors	(75,100)	
Short-term loan	(150,000)	

	£	£
Balance brought forward	(267,400)	
Increases in working capital		
Stocks	25,900	
Debtors	32,000	(209,500)

Ratios

	19X1	19X2
Working capital ratio	4.3:1	1:1
Liquidity ratio	2.1:1	0.4:1

The company had surplus funds at the end of 19X1 and so decided to expand. It financed the remainder of the expansion with a two-year loan to be repaid out of funds generated from operations. The financial position at the end of 19X2 is weak due to the failure to raise sufficient long-term finance to meet the cost of the investment programme.

Examination of profitability

Ratios

	19X1	19X2
	%	%
Net profit percentage	9.7	12.1
Return on total capital employed	13.8	16.5
Return on owners' equity	15.1	22.3

A significant improvement in profitability has occurred, which might be expected to continue with further increases in output from the new mine. The company has paid a good dividend.

Conclusions and prospects

Expansion has been funded out of short-term finance and the financial position at the end of 19X2 is weak. This is risky and an element of over-trading has undoubtedly occurred. The project is profitable, however, and it seems that the company will recover on the basis of funds generated from operations that, in 19X2, amounted to £240,500. Further expansion appears undesirable at present; there should be a delay of a year to 18 months. If this is not possible, the company should raise medium- or long-term finance to cover the cost of the additional site.

Readers should now work Question 13.5 at the end of the chapter.

QUESTIONS

13.1 The balance sheets of Southall Ltd at 31 December 19X1 and 31 December 19X2 are as follows:

	19X1		19X2	
	£	£	£	£
Fixed assets				
Plant at cost	52,000		70,000	
Less: Depreciation	16,500	35,500	22,700	47,300
Transport at cost	10,000		10,000	
Less: Depreciation	3,600	6,400	4,800	5,200
		41,900		52,500
Current assets				
Stock	10,200		12,600	
Debtors	8,300		13,700	
Bank	4,900		—	
	23,400		26,300	
Less: Current liabilities:				
Trade creditors	5,100		5,800	
Bank overdraft	—		1,300	
	5,100		7,100	
Working capital		18,300		19,200
		60,200		71,700
Financed by:				
Share capital		50,000		54,000
Profit and loss account		10,200		17,700
		60,200		71,700

Required

A statement of funds for 19X2.

13.2 (a) 'Funds statements as generally prepared may be regarded as a hybrid, using elements of the cash and working capital concepts of funds.' Discuss this statement and indicate the functions of the source and application of funds statement in financial reporting.

(10 marks)

(b) The following summarized balance sheets of Sticker Ltd for the two years to 31 August 1984 and 31 August 1985 are made available for your further analysis:

Balance Sheets at 31 August

	1984 £	1985 £		1984 £	1985 £
Called-up share capital	60,000	75,000	Fixed assets (tangible) at cost	116,100	153,000
General reserve	16,500	21,000	Less: Depreciation	41,100	50,250
Retained profits	6,750	11,700			
Debentures	10,500	7,500		75,000	102,750
Current liabilities			*Current assets*		
Taxation	8,550	9,750	Stock	28,500	31,500
Creditors	9,450	10,800	Debtors	12,000	9,450
Proposed dividends	6,750	9,000	Bank	3,000	1,050
	118,500	144,750		118,500	144,750

Note
No fixed assets were sold in the year ending 31 August 1985.

Required

A source and application of funds statement for the year ended 31 August 1985, showing within the statement (i) the source of funds, (ii) the application of funds and (iii) the movements in working capital.

(15 marks)

(Total: 25 marks)

(ICSA, Financial Accounting I, December, 1985)

13.3   The following balances relate to the affairs of Tufton Ltd as at 31 March 19X0 and 31 March 19X1:

	19X0 £	19X1 £
Share capital	500,000	600,000
Retained profit	395,800	427,100
10% Debentures	200,000	300,000
Creditors	179,800	207,500
Proposed dividend	50,000	60,000
Bank overdraft	—	36,900
	1,325,600	1,631,500
Plant at cost	658,300	796,900
Less: Depreciation	263,500	371,600
	394,800	425,300
Freehold property at cost	300,000	350,000
Stock	327,100	608,300
Debtors	265,700	247,900
Cash at bank	38,000	—
	1,325,600	1,631,500

You are given the following information:

(i) During the year to March 19X1, plant with a written-down value of £202,500 was sold for £169,500. This plant had originally cost £390,000.
(ii) A bonus issue of one ordinary share for every five held was made out of retained profit on 1 June 19X0.

Required

A statement of source and application of funds for the year to 31 March 19X1. You should prepare a worksheet and show the build-up of your figures for profit, purchases of plant and equipment and depreciation charged.

13.4   The following information is provided for Sharpener Ltd:

Balance Sheets 31 December

	19X4		19X5	
Fixed assets	£	£	£	£
Cost		650,000		680,000
Less: Accumulated depreciation		176,500		203,700
		473,500		476,300
Current assets				
Stock	126,400		127,500	
Trade debtors	97,700		95,000	
Bank balance	23,600		—	
	247,700		222,500	
Less: Current liabilities				
Trade creditors	72,900		87,100	
Proposed dividend	44,000		44,000	
Bank overdraft	—		37,900	
	116,900		169,000	
Working capital		130,800		53,500
		604,300		529,800
Share capital		400,000		400,000
Retained profit		104,300		109,800
		504,300		509,800
6% Debentures repayable 19X9		100,000		20,000
		604,300		529,800

During 19X5 the directors offered to repay the debentures, and this invitation was accepted by the majority of the debenture holders.

Required

(a) A cash flow statement for 19X5.
(b) A brief explanation for the decline in the bank balance based on the information contained in the statement.

13.5   The following information relates to the affairs of General Engineering plc:

Balance Sheets at 31 December

	19X7		19X8	
	£000	£000	£000	£000
Plant at cost less depreciation		2,600		2,760
Property at cost less depreciation		800		700
Investments at cost		300		250
		3,700		3,710
Current assets				
Stock and work-in-progress	900		2,120	
Debtors	660		700	
Short-term loans and deposits at bank	290		620	
	1,850		3,440	
Current liabilities				
Creditors	520		720	
Proposed final dividend	400		400	
	920		1,120	
Working capital		930		2,320
		4,630		6,030
Financed by:				
Issued share capital		2,000		2,500
Share premium account		—		200
Retained profit		2,630		3,030
		4,630		5,730
Long-term loan (12%)		—		300
		4,630		6,030

Extracts from the Profit and Loss Account for 19X8

	£000
Trading profit for the year after charging all costs, including depreciation of plant, £250,000, and depreciation of property, £100,000	700
Interest and dividends received, less interest paid	20
Net profit from ordinary activities	720
Add: Profit from the sale of an investment	80
	800
Less: Proposed dividend	400
Retained profit for the year	400
Retained profit at 1 January 19X8	2,630
Retained profit at 31 December 19X8	3,030

During 19X8 investments that had cost £50,000 some years earlier were sold for £130,000.

Required

(a) A statement of funds for the year to 31 December 19X8.
(b) A discussion of the change in the financial position of General Engineering between the end of 19X7 and the end of 19X8. You are not required to examine the profitability of the firm, but should use the working capital and liquidity ratios to help assess financial developments.

Note
Ignore taxation.

14
Decision-Making

INTRODUCTION

The accounting process has many aspects and, so far, this book's emphasis has been on recording, reporting and analysing the financial consequences of past economic activity. The essence of this approach is that it is a post-fact exercise and concentrates on events that have already taken place. An important application of accounting techniques is to provide a basis on which management decisions of the following type can be taken:

1. Whether existing activity should be expanded or reduced.
2. Whether a new product should be introduced.
3. How existing production techniques could be improved.
4. Whether new products should be manufactured or purchased ready-made.
5. The manufacturing techniques to be used for new products.

All possible business decisions must be examined in the light of their expected impact on profit, and management must be satisfied, before resources are committed, that any proposed activity, or change in existing activity, will add to overall profit. Financial forecasts are therefore needed so that the likely outcomes of alternative courses of action can be analysed and the most profitable ones adopted.

This chapter introduces the study and interpretation of cost behaviour that must be understood as the basis for preparing forecasts; it reviews some of the analytical techniques available to assist management when it makes investment decisions; and it examines the impact of anticipated activity on cash flow, and funds flow, profit and the balance sheet.

COST BEHAVIOUR

The manner in which production or trading activity is organized sets the capacity of the undertaking and influences its costs. For example, the acquisition of a particular machine sets the maximum output that can be achieved before an additional machine must be bought; similarly, the size of premises used by a shop determines their cost and the maximum number of product lines that can be displayed and stored; above a certain level, further space is needed. The capacity of the business sets the upper level of activity and the output of a firm is the extent to which the available capacity is utilized – the lowest level is zero, and the greatest is the largest amount permitted by available capacity. Management must decide what the likely output will be and arrange capacity accordingly, bearing in mind the costs of servicing the capacity and that growth may take place. In the long run it may prove cheaper to acquire at the start of a project the additional capacity likely to be needed so as to take advantage of the economies of scale that can result from the use of capital intensive techniques.

It is necessary for management to understand how costs behave, or are likely to behave, so that they can be controlled, and the most appropriate mix of inputs, with their related costs, selected. This section examines a number of ways in which costs can be analysed to enable management to gain this understanding.

Fixed and variable costs

Business costs may be classified according to how they behave in response to changes in output:

Fixed costs These remain constant over a range of output and include such
   items as rent and depreciation. For example, the rent for premises or a
   straight-line depreciation charge related to a machine are constant irrespective of whether these assets are being used at full capacity or well below.
   However, if an output in excess of the existing full capacity is contemplated,
   then an additional set of fixed costs must be incurred to provide additional
   capacity.
Variable costs These vary in direct proportion to output, and include the costs
   of raw material and manufacturing wages. For example, if no production
   takes place, then no raw materials have to be purchased while, at full
   capacity, the total cost of materials is the number of units produced times the
   material cost per unit.

Forecast output is unlikely to be achieved exactly in practice, and calculations of the profit expected at different levels of output are helpful in making a
decision about whether a new project should be undertaken. This is shown in
Example 14.1.

Example 14.1

The management of Glass Ltd is considering the possibility of manufacturing a new product that will sell at £15 per unit. Existing capacity is fully utilized, and so a new factory would have to be rented and plant, with a life of ten years, purchased. The expected costs are:

	£
Annual factory rent	10,000.00
Purchase price of plant	75,000.00
Raw material cost per unit	2.10
Labour cost per unit	1.50
Other variable costs	1.00
Fixed costs (excluding rent and depreciation)	6,500.00

Note
The company depreciates plant on the straight-line basis assuming a zero residual value.

Required

Forecast the profit that will be made from sales of the new product at the alternative annual rates of:

(a) 2,500 units,
(b) 5,000 units.

Solution

Profit forecasts at different sales levels

	(a) £	(a) £	(a) £	(b) £	(b) £	(b) £
Sales			37,500			75,000
Fixed costs						
Rent	10,000			10,000		
Depreciation	7,500			7,500		
Other	6,500			6,500		
		24,000			24,000	
Variable costs						
Raw materials	5,250			10,500		
Labour	3,750			7,500		
Other	2,500			5,000		
		11,500			23,000	
			35,500			47,000
Profit			2,000			28,000

Output has doubled, but profit has increased fourteen times. This result is examined later in the chapter.

Another use of forecasts, of the type prepared in Example 14.1, is to help decide the method of production; the choice often lies between 'capital intensive' and 'labour intensive' techniques. Capital intensive production uses automatic machines, such as the 'robots' seen on car production-lines, and requires a large investment in plant with a consequent high level of fixed costs. Variable costs are lower as each additional unit produced requires only a small labour input. Additional potential benefits from capital intensive methods are that raw materials are used more efficiently, and therefore cost less per unit, and there is a lower rejection rate at the stage of inspecting the finished product. Labour intensive methods use relatively little plant and have low fixed costs, but high variable costs per unit as each additional item produced requires a large input of labour.

Example 14.2

The directors of Hasard Ltd are sure that 10,000 units a year of a newly-developed product can be sold at £90 each. They are undecided about how to produce it. The alternatives are:

	Method 1 £	Method 2 £
Investment in plant with a ten-year life	125,000	750,000
Fixed costs (excluding depreciation)	185,000	200,000
Variable cost per unit		
Raw materials	35	30
Labour	20	5
Other	6	2

Note

The company calculates depreciation on the straight-line basis assuming a zero scrap value.

Required

Prepare financial statements to show the likely profit from each of the two methods at the expected level of sales.

Solution

Forecast trading results

	£	*Method 1* £	£	£	*Method 2* £	£
Sales			900,000			900,000
Fixed costs						
Depreciation	12,500			75,000		
Other	185,000			200,000		
		197,500			275,000	
Variable costs						
Raw materials	350,000			300,000		
Labour	200,000			50,000		
Other	60,000			20,000		
		610,000			370,000	
			807,500			645,000
Profit			92,500			255,000

Readers should now work Question 14.1 at the end of this chapter.

Some costs are neither completely fixed nor fully variable – they are termed 'semi-variable'. Although semi-variable costs respond to volume changes, they do not change in direct proportion to them. It is possible for semi-variable costs to remain constant over a relatively small range of activity, and each successive set of costs may differ in price from its predecessor. For example, an increase in manufacturing output creates additional work in the accounts department. The initial load may be carried by an accountant who alone performs all the necessary activities. When his or her capacity is exceeded, a book-keeper may be added to the staff, and then a clerk. Each additional employee, hired to increase the capacity of the accounts department in response to an increase in manufacturing output, adds relatively less to costs as an accountant is paid more than a book-keeper, who in turn earns more than a clerk. This type of response to changes in output occurs in the case of general expenses in Question 14.2 at the end of this chapter, which should now be worked.

Direct and indirect costs

Direct costs are those that can be traced in full to an individual costing unit. Indirect costs are those that relate only partially to a particular costing unit and must be apportioned to it. Care has to be taken when interpreting results based on apportioned (joint) costs as they have to be met in full irrespective of whether activity in a particular department continues or is discontinued. An initial examination of results may produce the conclusion that a department or branch is making a loss and so should be closed, but it must be remembered that its share of apportioned costs will then have to be met by the remaining cost centres.

Example 14.3

The business of Bits & Co. is divided into three departments of equal size: A, B and C. The departmental results for 19X7 were (£000):

Departmental trading results

	Department A	B	C	Total
Sales	50	120	180	350
Cost of goods sold	25	60	90	175
Gross profit	25	60	90	175
Departmental wages	10	20	30	60
	15	40	60	115
Rent (shared equally)	20	20	20	60
Profit (loss)	(5)	20	40	55

Mr Bits is considering closing department A because it is making a loss. He says it is better to leave the floor space empty than to use it to lose money.

Required

Prepare a statement to show Mr Bits the effect on total profit if department A is closed.

Solution (£000)

Revised departmental trading results

	Department		Total
	B	*C*	*Total*
Sales	120	180	300
Cost of goods sold	60	90	150
Gross profit	60	90	150
Departmental wages	20	30	50
	40	60	100
Share of rent*	30	30	60
Profit (loss)	10	30	40

Note
*Rent and rates shared equally between the remaining departments.

Department A should be kept open as it meets 75 per cent of its share of apportioned costs. Total profit is reduced by £15,000 if it is closed. The revised departmental trading results show that the plan of Mr Bits to close department A is based on his failure to appreciate the difference between direct and indirect costs.

It is sometimes argued that, because the accounting information that results can lead to wrong decisions, the apportionment of indirect costs should not be made. If indirect costs are not apportioned, the departmental trading results of Bits & Co. would be presented as follows (£000):

	Department			Total
	A	*B*	*C*	*Total*
Sales	50	120	180	350
Cost of goods sold	25	50	100	175
Gross profit	25	50	100	175
Departmental wages	10	20	30	60
Departmental surplus	15	30	70	115
Rent				60
Profit				55

The above presentation highlights the fact that all departments are making a positive *contribution* to general overhead costs that are not controllable at the departmental level.

The nature of a cost, that is whether it is direct or indirect, has to be decided in accordance with the costing unit under examination. For example, if the costing unit is a manufacturing department, then the depreciation of machines located in it and the salary of the departmental supervisor are direct costs. However, if the costing unit is a single item of output, then the depreciation and supervisor's salary are indirect costs as they also relate to the rest of the output. Raw materials and manufacturing wages are examples of direct costs where the costing unit is a single item of output.

Contribution costing

A useful technique to apply when examining the way in which fixed and variable costs respond to changes in the level of activity, is to calculate the 'contribution' each unit sold makes towards fixed costs. Analysis based on this approach assumes that the revenue from each unit is applied first to meet its related variable costs, and any surplus, the contribution, is then set against total fixed costs. Once the fixed costs have been completely recovered, the contribution of each additional unit sold adds to profit. The contribution of each unit is calculated by the formula:

$$\text{Contribution} = \frac{\text{Selling price}}{\text{per unit}} - \frac{\text{Variable cost}}{\text{per unit.}}$$

Example 14.4

Product Z incurs the following variable costs per unit:

	£
Materials	5.00
Wages	4.50
Expenses	1.25

Required

Calculate the contribution of product Z if its selling price per unit is:

(a) £12,
(b) £15.

Solution

The total variable cost is:

	£
Materials	5.00
Wages	4.50
Expenses	1.25
Total	10.75

(a) Contribution = £12 − £10.75 = £1.25.
(b) Contribution = £15 − £10.75 = £4.25.

The technique of contribution costing is used in break-even analysis and margin of safety and target profit calculations, which are dealt with later in this chapter.

Break-even analysis

A forecast of sales should be prepared as part of the appraisal of whether a particular project should be undertaken. The volume of anticipated sales sets the capacity that has to be provided and also determines the total value of variable costs. Forecasts cannot be wholly accurate, and so it is usual to examine results based on a number of alternative outcomes. A particularly useful piece of information to know is the volume of sales needed to achieve break even, which occurs where total costs equal total revenues and neither a profit nor loss is made. Looked at another way, a company breaks even when the contribution from sales is exactly equal to fixed costs. The break-even point is calculated with the formula:

$$\text{Break-even point, measured in units sold} = \frac{\text{Fixed costs}}{\text{Contribution}}$$

The break-even point in terms of the value of sales can be calculated by multiplying the number of units by the selling price per unit.

The importance of the break-even point is that below it a loss is suffered, and above it a profit is earned. It is, therefore, very important that management selects projects that are likely to achieve at least enough sales to break even.

Example 14.5

The directors of Cumberland Ltd are considering an investment project that has a maximum output of 50,000 units and is expected to involve the following costs and revenues:

	£
Annual fixed costs	100,000
Selling price per unit	10
Variable cost per unit	6

Required

(a) Calculate the sales in terms of both units and value that have to be made for the project to break even.
(b) Calculate the profit or loss that would occur if sales are:

  (i) 1,000 units greater than those needed to break even; and
  (ii) 1,000 less than those needed to break even.

Solution

(a) Contribution $\qquad\qquad = £10 - £6 = £4$

Break-even point (in units) $\quad = \dfrac{£100,000}{£4} = 25,000 \text{ units}$

or Break-even point (in value) $= 25,000 \text{ (units)} \times £10 \text{ (selling price per unit)}$
$\qquad\qquad\qquad\qquad\qquad\quad = £250,000$

(b)

	(i) 1,000 less	*(ii) 1,000 more*
Sales in units	39,000	41,000
	£	£
Contribution (unit sales × 4)	96,000	104,000
Fixed costs	100,000	100,000
Profit (loss)	(4,000)	4,000

Note
An alternative way to calculate the effect of changes in the level of sales on profit is to calculate the increase, or decrease, in the contribution. In this case, the starting profit is zero, and the contribution from sales of 1,000 units = 1,000 × £4 = £4,000. Therefore, an increase in sales of 1,000 units gives a profit of £4,000, and a decrease of 1,000 units gives a loss of £4,000.

The certainty with which sales can be forecast may influence the choice of production method and also affect decisions about which products to trade in. Where there is great uncertainty, production methods and products with low break-even points may be chosen to minimize the risk of losses. However, the choice of a method or product with a low break-even point may restrict the total profits that can be earned if high sales are achieved.

Example 14.6
The directors of Trestle Ltd are considering the following alternative methods of manufacturing a new product:

	Method 1	Method 2
	£	£
Plant with a life of ten years	50,000	150,000.00
Other annual fixed costs	3,000	3,000.00
Variable cost per unit	7	6.50
Selling price per unit	8	8.00

The plant is expected to have a zero scrap value at the end of its life, and the company uses the straight-line method of depreciation.

Method 2 has a lower variable cost because it uses less labour and has lower wastage rates for raw materials.

Required

(a) Calculate the break-even point for each method of production.
(b) Calculate the profit or loss for each method that results from sales levels of 10,000 units, 20,000 units and 30,000 units.
(c) What is the greatest loss that might be suffered under each method?
(d) Advise management on which method should be adopted.

Solution

	Method 1 £		Method 2 £	
(a)				
Fixed costs				
Depreciation	5,000		15,000	
Other	3,000		3,000	
	8,000		18,000	
Contribution	£8−£7 = £1		£8−£6.50 = £1.50	
Break-even point	8,000		18,000	
	——— = 8,000		——— = 12,000	
	1 units		1.50 units	
(b)				
10,000 units				
Contribution	10,000		15,000	
Fixed costs	8,000		18,000	
Profit (loss)	2,000		(3,000)	
20,000 units				
Contribution	20,000		30,000	
Fixed costs	8,000		18,000	
Profit	12,000		12,000	
30,000 units				
Contribution	30,000		45,000	
Fixed costs	8,000		18,000	
Profit	22,000		27,000	

(c) The greatest loss occurs when there is no contribution (i.e. zero output), and is equal to the fixed costs. Therefore, the maximum loss of method 1 is £8,000 and of method 2 is £18,000.
(d) Once method 2 breaks even, £1.50 is added to profit by every additional unit sold, while method 1 adds only £1. However, method 1 breaks even at

a lower level of sales. Both methods make the same profit at sales of 20,000 units.

The decision about which method to select therefore rests on expected sales. If 20,000 is the maximum level of expected sales, then method 1 is better; if sales are expected easily to exceed that level, then method 2 is better.
Readers should now work Question 14.3 and at the end of this chapter.

It is sometimes useful, for example, when preparing a report for considera-tion at a meeting, to present the results of break-even analysis in the form of a graph. Figure 14.1 shows how this is done using the information given in Example 14.5. All of the relationships expressed in the graph are represented by straight lines, and so each of them can be plotted by calculating two points. This is done by considering the costs and revenues that arise at levels of output of zero and full capacity which, in Example 14.5, was 50,000 units:

	Zero output	*Full capacity*
Revenue	0 × £10 = £0	50,000 × £10 = £500,000
Fixed cost	£100,000	£100,000
Variable cost*	0 × £6 = £0	50,000 × £6 = £300,000
Total cost	£0 + £100,000	£300,000 + £100,000
(Variable plus fixed costs)	= £100,000	= £400,000

Note
* It is possible to omit this line without reducing the usefulness of the chart, especially to save excessive contents when the results of two alternatives are being plotted on the same graph.

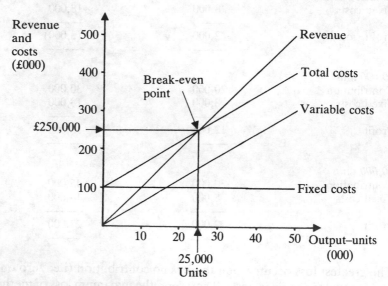

Figure 14.1   A break-even graph

The break-even point can be found in terms of either units or value and is where the total cost line crosses the revenue line. At levels of sales below this point a loss is made, and above it a profit. The extent of the divergence between the revenue and total cost lines above the break-even point indicates the rate of growth in profit as sales increase.

The graph should not be extended beyond the stated full capacity as, after this point, an additional set of fixed costs has to be incurred, and no information is given on the resulting cost structure, or how demand in this region would be met.

Question 14.4 at the end of this chapter should now be worked.

Profit-volume graph

The relationship between the volume of activity and profit can also be expressed in a profit-volume graph which shows the profit (or loss) arising at various levels of output. When output is zero, a loss equal to the fixed costs is suffered; each additional unit sold reduces the loss by an amount equal to its contribution until the break-even point is reached. Thereafter, each extra unit's contribution adds to profit until maximum output is achieved. Figure 14.2 shows the profit-volume graph using the information given in Example 14.5. The relationship between profit and volume is a straight line, and so can be plotted using figures for profit or loss at zero and maximum levels of activity. In the case of Figure 14.2 these two figures are:

1. At zero output a loss of £100,000, the fixed costs, results.
2. At full capacity the profit is:

$$(50,000(\text{output}) \times £4(\text{contribution per unit})) - £100,000 (\text{fixed costs}) = £100,000.$$

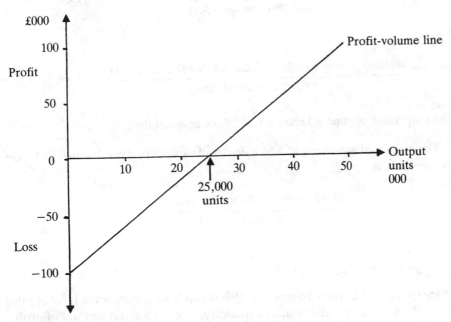

Figure 14.2 A profit-volume graph

The break-even point is found where the profit-volume line crosses zero, indicating that neither a profit nor loss is made at that point.

The margin of safety

The margin of safety gives an indication of how vulnerable a company is to changes in the volume of sales. It shows, as a percentage, how far sales can fall from their expected level before the break-even point is reached – a fall to below this point results in a loss. The margin of safety is calculated, using data on either value or units, by the formula:

$$\frac{\text{Expected sales} - \text{Sales at break-even point}}{\text{Expected sales}}$$

Example 14.7

Using the information in Example 14.5, calculate, using both values and quantities, the margin of safety of the project under consideration by Cumberland if the expected annual sales are 40,000 units.

Solution

Quantity:

$$\frac{40,000 \text{ (Expected sales)} - 25,000 \text{ (Break-even point)}}{40,000 \text{ (Expected sales)}} = 37.5\%$$

Value:

$$\frac{400,000 \text{ (Expected sales)} - 250,000 \text{(break-even point)}}{400,000 \text{ (Expected sales)}} = 37.5\%$$

Note
The same result is obtained using either values or quantities.

The margin of safety can also be calculated using actual results, in which case the formula is:

$$\frac{\text{Actual sales} - \text{Actual break-even point}}{\text{Actual sales}}$$

Target profit calculation

Once the contribution is known, it is also possible to calculate the level of sales needed, in terms of either value or quantity, to earn a given amount of profit. First, sales have to be sufficient to earn a total contribution equal to fixed costs, and then sufficient additional sales must be made to give the required profit. The formula to calculate the sales, in units, for a particular profit is:

$$\text{Sales in units} = \frac{\text{Fixed costs} + \text{Required profit}}{\text{Contribution}}$$

The value of sales can then be calculated by multiplying the number of units by the selling price per unit.

Example 14.8

The directors of Carp Ltd are considering the manufacture of a new product that sells at £16 per unit. Its manufacture would involve annual fixed costs of £147,500 and a variable cost per unit of £9.50. The directors are only willing to undertake the project if a profit of £80,000 can be made.

Required

Calculate the sales required, in terms of both quantity and value, to produce the desired profit.

Solution

	£
Selling price per unit	16.00
Variable cost per unit	9.50
Contribution per unit	6.50

$$\text{Required sales} = \frac{£147,500 + £80,000}{£6.50}$$

$$= 35,000 \text{ units}$$
$$or\ 35,000 \times £16 = £560,000$$

Readers should now work Question 14.5 at the end of this chapter.

INVESTMENT APPRAISAL

Management must decide how to invest the resources at its disposal, and usually the funds available are not sufficient to carry out all the possible projects that have been put forward, even if they all appear profitable. Some decisions still remain even after an initial decision of which projects to pursue has been taken, for example, once it has been decided to acquire a piece of machinery the options remain of whether to buy it or lease it. Therefore, a selection process has to be carried out to choose those projects to be undertaken, and to decide how the plans are to be put into operation. A number of techniques have been developed to help management make such decisions, and some of the more common ones are described in the following sections.

Payback

The payback method of investment appraisal is based on the time taken by a project to generate the amount of cash that has been invested in it. The decision of which projects to undertake depends on the speed with which the available projects recover their initial investment:

1. If there is no limit on the funds available, all projects that recover their investment within a set period of time are chosen.
2. If funds are limited, those projects that recover their investment the quickest are selected.

Example 14.9

The management of Applause Ltd is considering the following proposed investment projects. All of the fixed assets are expected to have a life of five years at the end of which their value will be zero:

	A £	Project B £	C £
Initial investment in fixed assets	25,000	50,000	60,000
Inwards cash flow:			
Year 1	10,000	30,000	10,000
Year 2	10,000	20,000	20,000
Year 3	10,000	15,000	20,000
Year 4	10,000	5,000	40,000
Year 5	10,000	5,000	60,000

Assume that the cash flows arise evenly throughout the year.

Required

(a) Calculate the payback period of each project.
(b) State which projects would be chosen if all projects that payback in three or less years are selected.
(c) State which projects would be chosen if only £70,000 is available for investment, i.e. only one of the projects can be undertaken.

Solution

(a) Project A pays back the initial investment of £25,000 in 2.5 years, i.e. £10,000 + £10,000 + (£10,000 × 0.5). Project B pays back £50,000 in 2 years, i.e. £30,000 + £20,000. Project C pays back £60,000 in 3.25 years, i.e. £10,000 + £20,000 + £20,000 + (£40,000 × 0.25).

(b) Projects A and B would be chosen as they both payback in three or less years. Project C is rejected as it takes more than three years to earn a sum equal to its initial investment.

(c) Only one of the projects can be chosen as the combination of any two of them involves an outlay in excess of the £70,000 available. Project B recovers the sum invested most quickly, and so it would be selected.

The selection of investment projects on the basis of their payback periods has been criticized because it ignores cash received after the payback period and so it may exclude a very profitable project if the bulk of its returns are not expected until near the end of its life, for example, project C in Example 14.9. A counter to this argument is that companies do not like to take risks and are exposed to less risk if projects are chosen that recover their cash outlay most quickly. A further advantage of payback is that it focuses on earlier rather than later forecasts, which become less reliable the further they are projected into the future.

Return on capital employed (ROCE)

The calculation of the ROCE was explained in Chapter 12 and can be used to choose between alternative investment projects:

1. If there is no limit on the funds available, all projects that have a ROCE in excess of a stated minimum are chosen.
2. If funds are limited, those projects that have the higher ROCE are selected.

It is usual to base the calculation of the forecast ROCE on the average investment as, over the life of the project, the value of the fixed assets decreases from their cost price at the start of the project to their scrap value at the end. The average investment is found by the formula:

(Cost of fixed assets − scrap value) ÷ 2.

Example 14.10

The management of the Applause Ltd in Example 14.9 decide to use the expected ROCE of the projects under consideration as the basis on which to make their investment decision.

Required

(a) Calculate the ROCE of each project.
(b) State which projects would be selected if all those with a ROCE of 25 per cent or more are to be undertaken.
(c) State which project would be carried out if only one can be selected.

Solution

(a)

		Project	
	A £	B £	C £
Annual Profit (loss)*			
Year 1	5,000	20,000	(2,000)
Year 2	5,000	10,000	8,000
Year 3	5,000	5,000	8,000
Year 4	5,000	(5,000)	28,000
Year 5	5,000	(5,000)	48,000
	25,000	25,000	90,000
Average annual profit	5,000	5,000	18,000
Average capital invested	12,500	25,000	30,000
Expected ROCE	5,000/12,500 = 40%	5,000/25,000 = 20%	18,000/30,000 = 60%

Note
* Calculated by deducting a straight-line depreciation charge from the forecast cash flows of each project. The depreciation charges are: project A £5,000 (£25,000/5); project B £10,000 (£50,000/5); and project C £12,000 (£60,000/5).

(b) Projects A and C are selected as they give a return on capital employed of 25 per cent or more.

(c) Project C is chosen as it has the highest ROCE.

Example 14.10 produces a different selection of projects compared with payback. Because all the returns over the life of the project are included, project C becomes the most desirable whereas project B is excluded. However, it can be argued that the returns in the more distant future should not be given the same weight as the more imminent ones, as they carry greater uncertainty and, even if they transpire as predicted, they are less valuable as it has been necessary to wait longer for them.

Net present value (NPV)

The NPV method of investment appraisal brings into consideration all the cash flows over the life of a project, but gives decreasing weight to them the further into the future they are expected to arise. The weights applied are based on the *time value of money*, a concept that holds that sums of money received in the future are worth less than the same sum received today. The link between the present and future values is determined by the rate of interest, also known as the discount rate, faced by the entity making the calculation. For example, if a firm's discount rate is 10 per cent per annum, then £100 receivable in two year's time is worth only £82.65 today as £82.65 invested at a compound annual interest rate of 10 per cent will accumulate as follows:

	£
Invested today	82.65
Year 1 interest	8.26
Value at the end of year 1	90.91
Year 2 interest	9.09
Value at the end of year 2	100.00

Based on this calculation, it can be stated that the present value of £100 in two year's time at a 10 per cent discount rate is £82.65. Note the operation of compound interest whereby the interest earned is added to the sum invested at the end of each year, and so itself earns interest from then on.

To avoid the need to make complicated calculations, tables of discount factors are available that show, for different discount rates, the present value of £1 received at various times in the future. Such a table of discount factors is shown in Table 14.1. This table is used to find the present value of future sums

	Discount Factor		
Discount rate	10%	15%	20%
Year			
0	1.000	1.000	1.000
1	0.909	0.870	0.833
2	0.826	0.756	0.694
3	0.751	0.658	0.579
4	0.683	0.572	0.482
5	0.621	0.497	0.402

Table 14.1   A discount table showing the present value of £1

of money by multiplying the sums by the appropriate discount factor. For example:

1. The present value of £10,000 receivable in 4 year's time by a firm with a cost of capital of 15 per cent is £10,000 × 0.572 = £5,720.
2. The present value of £15,000 receivable in 3 year's time by a firm with a cost of capital of 10 per cent is £15,000 × 0.751 = £11,265.

The steps to carry out an investment appraisal using NPV are as follows:

1. Calculate the cash flows of the project. The cash outflow of the initial investment takes place immediately and is given a weight of 1. The other

cash flows are assumed to take place at the end of the year in which they occur.

2. Determine the discount rate. This is the rate of interest paid to borrow funds to carry out the project – it is also known as the firm's cost of capital.
3. Use a discount factor table to find the factors appropriate to the timing of the cash flows (from step 1) and the discount rate (from step 2).
4. Calculate the present values of the cash flows from step 1 by applying the factors found in step 3.
5. The present values, positive and negative, from step 4 are summed to find the NPV.
6. If there is no limit on the funds available, all projects with a positive NPV are chosen. If funds are limited and the initial investments are the same, the project with highest positive NPV is selected. Where the initial investments are not equal, the project with the highest profitability index in excess of 1 is selected. The profitability index is calculated by the formula:

$$\text{Profitability index} = \frac{\text{Present value of cash inflows}}{\text{Initial investment}}$$

Example 14.11

The directors of Applause Ltd determine that the company's cost of capital is 15 per cent.

Required

Using the information on cash flows in Example 14.9, but assuming that the annual cash inflow from project A is £5,000:

(a) calculate the NPV of each project;
(b) calculate the profitability index of each project;
(c) state which projects would be accepted if unlimited funds are available; and
(d) state which project would be accepted if limited funds are available and only one can be undertaken.

Solution

(a) (See p. 361.)

Solution to Example 14.11(a)

	Discount factor	Project A		Project B		Project C	
		Cash flow £	Present value £	Cash flow £	Present value £	Cash flow £	Present value £
Investment	1.000	−25,000	−25,000	−50,000	−50,000	−60,000	−60,000
Year 1	0.870	5,000	4,350	30,000	26,000	10,000	8,700
2	0.756	5,000	3,780	20,000	15,120	20,000	15,120
3	0.658	5,000	3,290	15,000	9,870	20,000	13,160
4	0.572	5,000	2,860	5,000	2,860	40,000	22,880
5	0.497	5,000	2,485	5,000	2,485	60,000	29,820
NPV			(8,235)		6,435		29,680

(b) **Profitability index**

Project A	Project B	Project C
16,765/25,000	56,435/50,000	89,680/60,000
= .67	= 1.13	= 1.49

(c) If funds are unlimited, projects B and C are chosen as they both have positive NPVs.
(d) If only one project can be undertaken, project C is chosen as it has the highest profitability index, i.e. it gives the greatest NPV per £ invested.

As is the case with all techniques of investment appraisal, it must be remembered that NPV analysis is only a guide for management and relies on forecasts of the future that must be subject to uncertainty. Management also has to contend with the fact that different techniques can give different advice, and so judgement must be exercised when making a final selection.

Readers should now work Question 14.6 at the end of this chapter.

FORECAST RESULTS

Management is often faced with a number of alternative courses of action, especially when it is considering the long-term development of the company. It is of great assistance to management to prepare forecasts that predict the likely outcome of alternatives so that choices are based on the best possible information available.

Forecasts cannot be completely accurate, as many of the factors that influence actual results, such as the cost of raw materials and the actual demand for the product, are outside the control of management. However, this does not invalidate the exercise of preparing forecasts since the alternative is to make decisions without evaluating the outcome of management's expectations. To prepare forecasts, management must answer such vital questions as, 'How many units do you expect to sell?' 'What will be the selling price per unit?' 'How much labour, at what cost, will it take to produce each unit?' Forecasts bring together the answers to all these questions in accounting statements, and show the expected impact of alternatives on key financial magnitudes such as cash, profit and working capital. Cash forecasts are considered in the next section of this chapter, the forecast trading and profit and loss account and balance sheet are then dealt with, and finally how to prepare a forecast statement of funds.

Cash forecasts

Management must ensure that the company can afford any new project that is under consideration, that is, the company will not run out of cash if a particular plan is followed. Additional external finance, such as a bank overdraft, can be sought if the company's own cash resources are insufficient, but lenders will only be willing to provide funds that are likely to be repaid. The impact of plans on the cash resources of a company can be predicted using a cash forecast, and this is also of great interest to any person or organization, such as a bank, which is approached for funds. If cash forecasts are not prepared, a company may suddenly find itself short of cash or holding unproductive surplus funds in its bank account. A cash forecast enables a company to foresee a deficit, for which appropriate funding can be sought, or a surplus for which uses can be prepared in advance.

The preparation of a monthly cash forecast involves the identification of the cash flows expected to take place in each month and the calculation of the forecast cash position at the end of each month. The following techniques are used to predict cash transactions:

1. *Sales* Cash sales are entered in the forecast as receipts for the month in which they take place. The time lag has to be taken into account for credit sales, for example, cash from March sales may be received in April.
2. *Purchases* Cash purchases are entered in the month in which they take place. The time lag has to be taken into account for credit purchases, for example, cash for October purchases may be paid in November.
3. *Regular items* Regular payments are entered in the appropriate month, possibly with adjustment for a lag between the date when the expense is incurred and when it is paid.
4. *Irregular items* Irregular items, such as the purchase of fixed assets or the payment of tax, are also entered according to their incidence.

Example 14.12

Hamel runs a shop that makes all of its sales for cash. Forecasts for the first half of 19X6 are:

Sales	January to March – £25,000 per month. April to June – £30,000 per month.
Purchases	A gross margin of 20 per cent on selling prices is made. Every item sold is immediately replaced. Suppliers are paid in the month following delivery.
Payments	Wages and other expenses, £4,000 per month. Drawings, £1,000 per month. Delivery van cost £7,000; received on 1 January and paid for in February.
Opening balances	Owed to suppliers £16,000. Cash £1,000.

Ignore interest on any overdraft that may arise.

Required

(a) Calculate the value of monthly purchases.
(b) Prepare a cash forecast for Hamel for the first six months of 19X6 that shows the cash balance at the end of each month.
(c) Comment on the position shown by the forecast.

Solution

(a)

	Sales	*Purchases (sales − 20%)*
	£000	*£000*
January	25	20
February	25	20
March	25	20
April	30	24
May	30	24
June	30	24

(b)

	Jan. £	*Feb.* £	*March* £	*April* £	*May* £	*June* £	*Total* £
Cash in							
Sales	25,000	25,000	25,000	30,000	30,000	30,000	165,000
Cash out							
Purchases	16,000	20,000	20,000	20,000	24,000	24,000	124,000
Wages and other expenses	4,000	4,000	4,000	4,000	4,000	4,000	24,000
Drawings	1,000	1,000	1,000	1,000	1,000	1,000	6,000
Delivery van		7,000					7,000
	21,000	32,000	25,000	25,000	29,000	29,000	161,000
Opening balance	1,000	5,000	(2,000)	(2,000)	3,000	4,000	1,000
+Cash in	25,000	25,000	25,000	30,000	30,000	30,000	165,000
−Cash out	21,000	32,000	25,000	25,000	29,000	29,000	161,000
Closing balance	5,000	(2,000)	(2,000)	3,000	4,000	5,000	5,000

(c) The purchase of the van creates a cash deficit in February and March, but this is made good from trading cash inflows by April. The bank should be approached for a temporary loan – an overdraft would be best. By the end of June the business is accumulating a cash surplus that will continue to increase if trade stays at the same level. Thought should be given to how any permanently spare cash is to be used.

Note the columnar layout of the solution to part (b) of the example. The use of this presentation is recommended because:

1. it saves time as the descriptions of cash flows do not have to be repeated for each month;
2. errors are less likely to occur as any inconsistent entries are more easily identified; and
3. it aids comparison throughout the period covered by the forecast of the individual elements of cash flow.

Readers should now work Question 14.7 at the end of this chapter.

Forecast trading and profit and loss account and balance sheet

The preparation of a trading and profit and loss account and balance sheet from the cash account, and opening and closing values for assets and liabilities, was explained in Chapter 4 in the context of past results. Once the cash forecast has been prepared, the same techniques may be applied to prepare a forecast trading and profit and loss account and balance sheet.

Example 14.13

The balance sheet of Hamel at 31 December 19X5 was:

	£	£
Fixed assets		
Premises		10,000
Current assets		
Stock	18,500	
Cash	1,000	
	19,500	
Current liabilities		
Trade creditors	16,000	
		3,500
		13,500
Capital		13,500

Hamel expects to undertake the transactions given in Example 14.12 during the first six months of 19X6. You may assume that the monthly cash forecast has been prepared, which gives a summary of cash transactions in the 'total' column.

The van is expected to have a life of five years and a zero scrap value at the end of that time. Hamel uses the straight-line method to calculate depreciation.

Required

Prepare Hamel's forecast trading and profit and loss account for the six months to 30 June 19X6 and a balance sheet at that date.

Solution

Forecast Trading and Profit and Loss Account

	£	£
Sales		165,000
Less: Cost of goods sold (W1)		132,000
Gross profit		33,000
Wages	24,000	
Depreciation $(0.5 \times 7,000/5)$	700	
		24,700
Net profit		8,300

Balance Sheet

	£	£
Fixed assets		
Premises		10,000
Van	7,000	
Less: Depreciation	700	
		6,300
		16,300
Current assets		
Stock	18,500	
Cash	5,000	
	23,500	
Current liabilities		
Trade creditors (June purchases)	24,000	
		(500)
		15,800

Capital	£
Opening balance	13,500
Plus: Profit	8,300
	21,800
Less: Drawings	(6,000)
	15,800

Working 1

Purchases = Payments − Opening creditors + Closing creditors.
Purchases = 124,000 − 16,000 + 24,000 (June purchases) = 132,000.

The level of stock has remained unchanged, and so purchases and cost of goods sold have the same value.

Readers should now work Question 14.8 at the end of this chapter.

Forecast statement of funds

The preparation of the statement of funds from historical data was dealt with in Chapter 13. The same principles can be applied to prepare a statement of funds from forecast data such as that in Example 14.13 (question and solution).

Example 14.14

Required

Prepare the forecast statement of funds of Hamel for the six months to 30 June 19X6 using the information given in Example 14.13 (question and solution).

Solution

Statement of Funds for the Six Months to 30 June 19X6

	£	£
Sources of funds		
Profit		8,300
Add: Depreciation		700
Funds generated from operations		9,000
Application of funds		
Purchase of van	7,000	
Drawings	6,000	
		13,000
		(4,000)
Increase (decrease) in working capital		
Increase in creditors	(8,000)	
Increase in cash	4,000	
		(4,000)

QUESTIONS

14.1   Rock Ltd manufactures a single product that passes through two separate processes, designated X and Y, in two separate factories; all products must pass through both processes before they are ready for sale.

Rock's summary revenue account for 19X5 is as follows:

	£
Process X	
Raw materials	20,000
Wages	30,000
Depreciation	12,000
Rent	8,000
Transfer to process Y	70,000
Process Y	
Raw materials	10,000
Wages	40,000
Depreciation	12,000
Rent	8,000
Cost of production	140,000
General expenses	36,000
Net profit	24,000
Sales (100,000 units)	200,000

There are no stocks of any type at the beginning or at the end of the year.

There is a heavy demand for the product. Production costs and selling price are to be maintained at the same level as in 19X5.

Consideration is being given to three proposals for increasing production as follows:

(i) The expansion of manufacturing capacity at both factories. The cost of rent and the depreciation charge will in both cases be double that for 19X5. Materials consumed and wage rates would continue for both factories at the same unit cost as for 19X5.

(ii) The purchase of the additional process X components from an outside source at a price of 80p per unit. Expansion of manufacturing capacity at factory Y on the same terms and the same cost as for proposal (i).

(iii) The purchase of the additional finished goods from an outside source at 180p per unit and their sale at 200p per unit. No additional capacity would be required.

General expenses will increase in all cases at the rate of £2,000 per additional 25,000 units sold.

Required

Prepare a financial statement for management that shows the forecast *additional* profit under each of the three proposals if outputs and sales increase by (a) 25,000 units and (b) 50,000 units.

14.2   Glen Eagles is the proprietor of a small but long-established manufacturing business that has consistently made an annual profit of £20,000. The financial results of the business have shown little change in recent years, and the financial position has been very stable, supported by the fact that annual drawings have generally been lower than the profit. The expectation is that there will be little change over the next few years and that the level of profit will be maintained.

Eagles has recently been invited by Troon Ltd to increase his production to meet an export demand in a market where the prospects of development and increased sales are very substantial. Additional plant with a life of ten years, and a zero residual value at the end of that period, will be needed for such an expansion. Machines that will produce 46,000 items per annum are available at a cost of £36,000 each.

The selling price per item is £1, and the variable costs of manufacture for the export market will be 55p per item. Additional general expenses will amount to £10,000 for the first £46,000 increase in sales, but will fall to £4,000 for each £46,000 block of additional sales above the first £46,000.

Eagles has no private resources. The existing liquid resources of the business would cover any additional working capital required, and also provide £10,000 towards the capital cost of the new project. A bank is willing to lend up to £100,000 to Eagles at an interest rate of 15 per cent per annum.

An alternative proposal is made to Eagles. Troon Ltd offers him £120,000 in cash for his entire business and is prepared to retain his services as a manager on a ten-year contract at a salary of £14,000 per annum plus an additional £3,000 per annum for each £46,000 increase in turnover.

Eagles can expect to invest the proceeds of the sale of his business to earn interest of 10 per cent per annum.

Required

(a) Statements reporting on the profit likely to be received from overseas sales at the rate of £46,000, £92,000 and £138,000 per annum respectively.
(b) Prepare a report to Eagles that shows the results of the alternative course of action open to him.

14.3 During 19X4 Feather Ltd, which has a maximum possible output of 100,000 units, sold 60,000 units of a product and made a net profit of £20,000. The contribution per unit was £2, and the selling price was £5 per unit.

A competitor entered the market in November 19X4, and is selling a very similar product to Feather's at £4.60 per unit. The management of Feather decides that it must introduce automation to meet this challenge and decides upon the following plan for 19X5:

(a) Reduce the selling price per unit to £4.50. This should increase sales to 90,000.
(b) Introduce new machinery with the result that annual fixed costs increase by £80,000.
(c) The new machinery will decrease variable costs by £1 per unit.

Required

(a) Prepare the summary profit and loss account for 19X4, showing sales, variable costs, fixed costs and profit.
(b) Calculate the break-even level of sales for 19X4 in terms of units and £s.
(c) Prepare the forecast profit and loss account for 19X5, showing sales, variable costs, fixed costs and profit.
(d) Calculate the break-even level of sales for 19X5 in terms of both units and £s.

14.4 Use the information in Question 14.3 to prepare a break-even chart that shows the results of both 19X4 and 19X5.

14.5 The summarized profit and loss account of Latchmere Ltd for 19X6 is as follows:

	£		£
Raw materials	50,000	Sales (100,000 units	
Wages	100,000	at £2 each)	200,000
Depreciation	10,000		
Gross profit	40,000		
	200,000		200,000
General expenses	20,000	Gross profit	40,000
Net profit	20,000		
	40,000		40,000

The company's plant has now reached its maximum level of production and the directors are considering proposals for expansion.

Two plans have been suggested:

1. The purchase of additional plant of the same type and capacity as that in use at present, and which will operate at exactly the same raw materials and wages costs per unit as the existing plant, in the expectation of doubling the level of sales. It is thought that a market exists at the current selling price of £2 per unit. The plant will cost £100,000.
2. The purchase of additional plant, at a cost of £200,000, capable of manufacturing a similar product with the same raw material content as the current product, but for which the wages cost will be reduced to 15 per cent of the expected selling price of £2 per unit.

Under both plans, *additional* general expenses amounting to £5,000 will be incurred for any increase in turnover up to £100,000 (total sales £300,000) and a further £10,000 will be incurred for any increase in turnover above £100,000 and up to £200,000 (total sales £400,000). The cost of production and the selling price per unit of the first £200,000 of sales will be the same as for 19X6, and the profit on those sales will be unchanged.

For both plans, the life of the new plant will be ten years at the end of which it will have a zero scrap value. The purchase will be financed by a fixed term ten-year loan at 10 per cent per annum.

Required

(a) Prepare a trading and profit and loss account of Latchmere Ltd for 19X7 assuming that plan 1 is implemented and that the expected sales increase of £200,000 is achieved.
(b) Calculate the minimum increase in sales needed under plan 2 to ensure that the net profit after charging interest is equal to the profit it is calculated will be produced under plan 1.
(c) Calculate the sales necessary in 19X7 under plan 2 that give the company as a whole the same net profit, after interest, as was earned in 19X6, that is, £20,000.

14.6   The directors of Axmede Ltd have decided that it has £100,000 available for investment in fixed assets and is considering the following two alternative projects, both of which are expected to have a life of four years at the end of which the plant will have a zero scrap value:

	Project Zero £000	Project Nemo £000
Initial investment in fixed assets	80	90
Cash inflows		
Year 1	50	30
2	40	30
3	30	40
4	20	60
	140	160

The company's cost of capital is 20 per cent.

Required

(a) Calculate the payback period of each project.
(b) Calculate the return on capital employed of each project.
(c) Calculate the net present value of each project.
(d) Calculate the profitability index of each project.
(e) Advise management as to which project it should undertake.

14.7   Grant commences business on 1 January 19X6 and introduces £20,000 cash as capital. He also borrows £8,000 from his brother at 10 per cent per annum interest, payable half yearly in June and December. He makes the following estimates about the first six months of 19X6:

Fixed assets	£20,000 purchased for cash in January.
Sales	£12,000 per month. Two months' credit to be given to customers.
Purchases	£16,000 in January and £8,000 per month thereafter. Suppliers will allow one month's credit.
Expenses	£800 per month average, excluding interest, payable in the month in which they are incurred.
Drawings	£200 per month.

Required

Prepare a cash forecast for the business of Grant for the first six months of 19X6 that shows the cash balance at the end of each month.

14.8

Required

Use the information in Question 14.7 to prepare Grant's forecast trading and profit and loss account for the six months to 30 June 19X6 and his balance sheet at that date.

The fixed assets are to be depreciated at the rate of 20 per cent per annum on cost, and Grant calculates selling prices of goods by adding 50 per cent to their cost price.

Grant expects that the interest on the forecast overdraft will cost £300 and be paid in July.

14.9

Required

Use the information in Question and Solution 14.8 to prepare Grant's statement of funds for the six months to 30 June 19X6.

15
Computers and Accountancy

INTRODUCTION

A common theme running through this book is that accountancy involves the identification of data that is then recorded and processed so that reports can be produced. These functions are ideally suited to computerization, which is, today, within the price range of almost every organization. In practice, the computer does nothing it would be impossible to achieve with a manual system, but computerized accounting systems are much quicker, less labour intensive and allow a wide variety of analyses to be performed very speedily.

Computerization is not essential for every business – many small units are adequately served by manual accounting systems and the benefits to be derived from a computer would be outweighed by the costs.

A computer system has two distinct parts: the hardware and the software. The hardware is what most people identify as 'the computer' and consists of such items as the keyboard, printer and processing unit, while the software are the programs that give instructions to the computer to make it carry out the required functions. There is on the market a great range of hardware, which varies in such respects as price, size and speed of operation, and also a great variety of software, which can usually be used on a number of different types of computer. As a result, this chapter does not attempt to describe any specific hardware/software combination, but instead aims to introduce three aspects of computerization that are particularly relevant to accountants – these are computerized accounting systems, spreadsheets and data bases.

One important point to bear in mind is that the computer is merely a tool to be used by the accountant and so its use does not remove the need for a knowledge of accountancy. In some ways a more rigorous knowledge of procedures is needed in the computer environment as the computer is totally logical and will carry out any instructions that are allowed by its program, even if the result is nonsense. Therefore, the accountant has to have a thorough understanding of what should happen to be able to spot any deviations. 'GIGO' is a well-known acronym that stands for 'garbage in – garbage out' and tells us that if the computer is given absurd input data it will still use it as a basis for its calculations and reports. For example, an employee's rate of pay may be wrongly entered as £1,000 per hour instead of £10; unless the computer program includes checks to reject such a figure, the employee may be paid on the basis of the wrong amount when the hours worked in a week are input.

COMPUTERIZED ACCOUNTING SYSTEMS

A firm's overall accounting system consists of a number of subsystems, for example, a wages system to calculate the amounts due to each employee and allocate them to expense headings, such as production departments, and a purchases system to record creditors and analyse the purchases made between various types of goods and services. Figure 15.1 shows how a firm's accounting system consists of a number of separate, but inter-linked, subsystems.

Computer programs are readily available for each subsystem, indicated by an asterisk in Figure 15.1 and, provided they are from an integrated package of programs, the appropriate links will have been established as part of the program. A fact has to be input only once for all the related aspects to be updated, for example, the fact that a sale has been made, when recorded in the sales system, could also update the stock records and form part of the total sales value automatically posted to the nominal ledger. The sales program may also produce the sales invoice and the stock program may check the resulting stock level to see if more of the item needs to be ordered.

The basic requirements of the subsystems are fairly standard, and so little adaptation by the user is needed. For example, the principles of calculating wages and the related tax deductions or running a debtors ledger are generally uniform between businesses. However, before a system is acquired, the user must determine the basis on which the analysis is to be carried out, and this, in turn, is largely determined by the content of the reports it is desired to produce. Therefore, before a computerized system is put into operation, careful thought must be given to the accounting system as a whole to ensure that the program is capable of performing the necessary analysis and that the first stages of raw data input will eventually lead to the desired output.

Once the desired analysis has been determined, a system of coding must be developed to enable the computer to accumulate data in the appropriate accounts in the nominal ledger. Because each business is likely to have its own

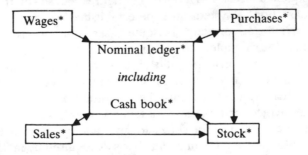

Figure 15.1 Some subsystems in an accounting system. The arrows indicate the direction of information flows

organization and analysis requirement, and to give flexibility, accounting programs usually leave the setting of codes to the user. The compilation of a list of codes is a straightforward task, and Figure 15.2 shows the steps used to produce some specimen codes in the context of an organization with a number of branches that are subdivided into departments.

Step 1: Allocate codes to branches, departments and type of transaction. For example:

Code	Meaning
01	Branch 1
02	Branch 2
08	Department 8
09	Department 9
441	Sales
442	Wages

Step 2: Combine the codes from Step 1 to produce detailed codes that can be applied to every transaction the business undertakes:

	Branch	Department	Transaction type
First code	01	08	441
Second code	01	09	441
Third code	02	08	441
Fourth code	01	08	442

Figure 15.2   Specimen transaction codes

Once a code number has been allocated to each branch, department and transaction type in step 1, it is possible, by combining these codes, to develop a code number for each individual transaction as shown in step 2. Thus, as 441 is the code for a sale in Figure 15.2, then the first code number refers to a sale by department 8 of branch 1 and the second code to a sale by department 9 of the same branch; the third code indicates a sale made by department 8 of branch 2. Transaction type 442 relates to wages, and so the fourth code is the payment to an employee in department 8 of branch 1.

As subsequent analysis and reporting of figures is based on the initial coding of each transaction, a system must be established to ensure that the initial coding is carried out correctly. In some cases transactions might be coded automatically, for example, the code for each employee may be held by the computer and wage payments allocated accordingly. If this is done, the employee must be re-coded when transferred to another department. In other cases, individual transactions must be examined and coded manually, for example, an invoice for repairs to a branch's premises.

It is possible to add extra codes to give additional analysis, which the computer could carry out on an *ad hoc* basis as required by management – for example, data on sales may be analysed by salesperson, location of customer or value of sale. Such exercises emphasize the need to decide and record in advance the necessary basic data; if this is not done, each analysis would involve the laborious procedure of returning to the prime documents to re-code them.

The next stage in computerizing the accounts system is to open a nominal ledger account for each valid code. Such an account would be opened for each code produced under step 2 in Figure 15.2 but, although it could be derived, one would not be needed, for example, for sales by the accounts department that only provides a service for the rest of the organization. The computer can then post every transaction with the appropriate code to an account, and copies of each account can be printed out to show the individual transactions that have been combined to give the closing balance. The usual cross-referencing is done automatically so that each entry can be traced to its source.

The computer is also able to construct and print out the books of prime entry (that is, the day books, cash book and journal) in the form of a list of all the transactions that have been entered in a particular batch. Security is achieved by numbering all such lists consecutively and producing them as an automatic part of the operation; they can then be filed and checked for completeness. Additional security is given if access to parts of the system, such as the cash book and journal, is granted with the use of passwords known only to authorized personnel.

Finally, the trial balance is periodically prepared, usually monthly, and converted into a profit and loss account and balance sheet. This process can be handled by the computer and the reports can be prepared on a number of bases, such as monthly, cumulatively, in comparison with budgets or the same period of the previous year. The production of reports highlights the speed and flexibility of a computerized accounting system as a single set of input data can be manipulated and presented in a number of different ways with great ease.

SPREADSHEETS

A spreadsheet is a computer program that provides the user with a grid consisting of cells, as shown in Figure 15.3. The columns are usually identified by letters and the rows by numbers. The size of the grid depends on the capacity of the computer being used, but a fairly simple personal computer can support one which is 255 cells' square. Each individual cell is identified by its letter and number: A1 is in the top left hand corner with B1 to its right and A2 below it.

The user moves around the grid by means of the cursor movement keys and can enter in any cell either:

1. a label, such as 'SALES'; or
2. a number; or
3. a formula linking it with any other cell.

Labels and numbers appear in the appropriate cell on the face of the spreadsheet as they are entered, but a formula entered in a cell is displayed in

	A	B	C	D	E	etc.
1						
2						
3						
4						
etc.						

Figure 15.3   A blank spreadsheet

the top or bottom margin when the cursor is on the cell that contains it. The cell itself shows the figure that results from applying the formula it contains.

Example 15.1

A company makes sales of 250 and has a cost of sales of 200.

Required

Prepare a spreadsheet to calculate gross profit and gross profit as a percentage of sales.

Solution

	A	B	C	D	E	etc.
1	SALES		250			
2	COST OF SALES		200			
3	GROSS PROFIT		50			
4	GROSS PROFIT (%)		20			

Cells A1 to A4 have had labels put in them (if a label is too long for a cell, it runs over into the next column, which is column B in the above example) and cells C1 and C2 the numbers given in the example. The value in cell C3 is found by entering the formula C1–C2, and the formula for C4 is C3/C1*100. The formulae are retained in the computer's memory, and the figures they produce shown in the spreadsheet. (The following are used in formulae to perform the function stated: + add; − minus; / divide; and * multiply.)

Example 15.1 does not involve any difficult calculations, but the power of the spreadsheet can be demonstrated by considering the effect of changing cell C2 to 220 with C1 unchanged at 250: the recalculation of C3 as 30 and C4 as 12 per cent (30/250*100) is done automatically. Therefore if, for example, a complex forecast is prepared on a spreadsheet, calculations, which if done manually would be extremely time consuming and repetitive, are performed with no effort other than changing a variable. The spreadsheet can be used to answer quickly any number of 'What if . . .?' questions and a print-out obtained of any desired results. A great number of different programs are readily available, some of which have additional features such as automatic preparation of graphs.

The best way to learn how to use a spreadsheet is to work with one, but there are some general features given below that assist with their preparation together with two examples of how they can be applied to problems already covered elsewhere in this book.

Spreadsheet preparation

The spreadsheet contains two separate elements:

1. *Facts* These are known quantities or relationships (that between sales and cost of sales in the above example) which can be set by the user and changed if desired to see the effect on the outcome.
2. *Solution* This is the outcome derived by the spreadsheet from a given set of facts (the gross profit and gross profit percentage in the above example).

Before a spreadsheet is prepared, careful thought must be undertaken to:

1. define the problem it is desired to solve;
2. isolate the facts relevant to the problem; and
3. decide how to combine and present the facts to produce a solution.

A thorough knowledge of accountancy is needed for this process as, for example, a model based on the balance sheet cannot be produced without appreciating what a balance sheet is and the relationship between the elements it contains.

During preparation, sufficient detail should be included in the spreadsheet to explain what it is for and its contents so that its future use is not dependent on the memory of the preparer. Also, some thought should be given to flexibility, and features likely to be of later use, but not relevant to the current problem, built in at an early stage. This is illustrated in Example 15.2, which is based on the information given in Question 2.5; the capacity to record 'office equipment' is included when dealing with the facts from part (a), even though it is not relevant until part (b) is attempted.

Example 15.2

Required

Prepare a spreadsheet that will produce the answer to Question 2.5, showing the formulae in the cells in which they must be entered.

Solution

```
             A       B          C            D           E          F
1    PROGRAMME TO FIND CAPITAL AS A BALANCING FIGURE
2    FACTS:    CASH                     1750
3              STOCK                    5250
4              OWED BY CUSTOMERS        3340
5              OWED TO SUPPLIERS        2890
6              BUSINESS PREMISES        9000
7              LOAN FROM WEAKLY         3000
8              OFFICE EQUIPMENT            0
9
10   SOLUTION: BALANCE SHEET
11   PREMISES          +D6            CAPITAL          +F16–F12–F13
12   OFFICE EQUIP.     +D8            LOAN FROM WEAKLY +D7
13   STOCK             +D3            OWED TO SUPPLIERS +D5
14   OWED BY CUSTMRS   +D4
15   CASH              +D2
16   TOTAL ASSETS*     @SUM(C11..C15) TOTAL LIABILITIES +C16
```

Note

* To remove the need to enter a complete list of the individual cells to be summed when totalling a row or column, programs usually contain a quick method, such as that shown here, to achieve this result.

If this is entered into a spreadsheet on a computer, the solution appears as follows:

```
             A          B           C         D           E          F
10   SOLUTION: BALANCE SHEET
11   PREMISES                    9000 CAPITAL                   13450
12   OFFICE EQUIP.                  0 LOAN FROM WEAKLY           3000
13   STOCK                       5250 OWED TO SUPPLIERS          2890
14   OWED BY CUSTMRS             3340
15   CASH                        1750
16   TOTAL ASSETS              19340 TOTAL LIABILITIES          19340
```

The solution puts into balance sheet format all of the known assets and liabilities. The values of the assets are then totalled in cell F16 and, as the total value of assets in the balance sheet must be the same as the total liabilities, the computer then enters this amount in cell C16 to record the value of total liabilities. The value of capital is found in cell C11 by deducting non-ownership liabilities from total liabilities.

Once the spreadsheet has been prepared in this manner, any of the facts can be changed and a revised value of capital calculated. All of the changes to the facts that result from part (b) of Question 2.5 can be entered individually in the 'facts' section, and revised balance sheets would be prepared automatically after each one. For example, the first transaction in part (b) of the question adds £500 to office equipment and £500 to creditors, and their entry in the 'facts' section would result in the following changes:

```
            A         B         C         D         E         F
  1   PROGRAMME TO FIND CAPITAL AS A BALANCING FIGURE
  2   FACTS:    CASH                   1750
  3             STOCK                  5250
  4             OWED BY CUSTOMERS      3340
  5             OWED TO SUPPLIERS      2890
  6             BUSINESS PREMISES      9000
  7             LOAN FROM WEAKLY       3000
  8             OFFICE EQUIPMENT        500
  9
 10   SOLUTION: BALANCE SHEET
 11   PREMISES              9000 CAPITAL               13950
 12   OFFICE EQUIP.          500 LOAN FROM WEAKLY       3000
 13   STOCK                 5250 OWED TO SUPPLIERS      2890
 14   OWED BY CUSTMRS       3340
 15   CASH                  1750
 16   TOTAL ASSETS         19840 TOTAL LIABILITIES     19840
```

Note that, in this format, all profits and drawings are adjusted on the value of capital – a spreadsheet could be devised to show opening capital, profit, drawings and closing capital as separate entries. The further changes caused by the remaining transactions given in part (b) of the question can be found in that question's solution and used to check their answers by any reader who has entered the above spreadsheet on a computer.

Using the spreadsheet

The fact that a spreadsheet has been used to perform the programmed calculations and a neat print-out of the results obtained does not necessarily mean that the solution produced is correct. If the program has not been entered correctly or, owing to a design fault, it is incapable of performing the task required of it, the answer obtained will be wrong. It is, therefore, important to test the program before accepting that it is finalized, which is done by entering test data for which the correct answer is known. The solution produced by the spreadsheet can then be checked with the predetermined one. Care must be taken to ensure that the test verifies all aspects of the program, after which further, unsolved, data can be entered.

At the end of the computing session the spreadsheet can be saved, usually on disc, so that it can, if required, be recalled and used at a later date. Over time a series of spreadsheets may be developed and saved, and it is useful if a catalogue is prepared that gives details of each one and is updated for any subsequent changes. In this way a library of useful programs can be built up, the contents of which can be found without relying on the preparer's memory.

	A	B	C	D	E	F	G (NOTES)	H
1	Grant cash budget							
2	FACTS:	PAYMENTS		TIMING				
3		Fixed assets		January		20000		
4		Purchases		per month		8000	one month's credit	
5		Stock		January		8000	one month's credit	
6		Expenses		per month		800	current month	
7		Drawings		per month		200	current month	
8		RECEIPTS						
9		Sales		per month		12000	two month's credit	
10		Capital		January		20000		
11		Loan		January		8000		
12		Loan interest %		per annum		10	Pay June & Dec.	

13 SOLUTION - CASH BUDGET 6 MONTHS TO 30 JUNE 19X6

	JAN	FEB	MARCH	APRIL	MAY	JUNE	TOTAL
14							
15 PAYMENTS							
16 Fixed assets	+F3						@SUM(C16..H16)
17 Purchases		+F4+F5	+F4	+F4	+F4	+F4	@SUM(C17..H17)
18 Expenses	+F6	+F6	+F6	+F6	+F6	+F6	@SUM(C18..H18)
19 Drawings	+F7	+F7	+F7	+F7	+F7	+F7	@SUM(C19..H19)
20 Interest						+F11/2#F12/100	@SUM(C20..H20)
21 Total payments	@SUM(C16..C20)	@SUM(D16..D20)	@SUM(E16..E20)	@SUM(F16..F20)	@SUM(G16..G20)	@SUM(H16..H20)	@SUM(I16..I20)
22 RECEIPTS							
23 Capital	+F10						@SUM(C23..H23)
24 Loan	+F11						@SUM(C24..H24)
25 Sales	+F9	+F9	+F9	+F9	+F9	+F9	@SUM(C25..H25)
26 Total receipts	@SUM(C23..C25)	@SUM(D23..D25)	@SUM(E23..E25)	@SUM(F23..F25)	@SUM(G23..G25)	@SUM(H23..H25)	@SUM(I23..I25)
27							
28 Opening balance		+C31	+D31	+E31	+F31	+G31	
29 +Receipts	+C26	+D26	+E26	+F26	+G26	+H26	+I26
30 -Payments	+C21	+D21	+E21	+F21	+G21	+H21	+I21
31 Closing balance	+C28+C29-C30	+D28+D29-D30	+E28+E29-E30	+F28+F29-F30	+G28+G29-G30	+H28+H29-H30	+I28+I29-I30

Figure 15.4 Solution to Example 15.3

A further example

The spreadsheet's ability to compute easily and quickly new solutions in response to changes in the underlying facts makes it ideal for preparing forecasts. As forecasts deal with the future, the facts on which they are based are subject to varying degrees of uncertainty; the spreadsheet model enables the accountant to examine the effect on key variables, such as net profit and cash, of a wide range of different assumptions about such matters as the expected level of sales. This enables management to identify those elements of the plan whose outcome is crucial to its overall success or failure. Example 15.3, which is based on Question 14.7, deals with the preparation of a spreadsheet (with the formulae shown in the cells to which they relate) to predict the cash balance at the end of each of the first six months of a company's life.

Example 15.3

Required

Prepare a spreadsheet, based on the information given in Question 14.7, to predict Grant's monthly cash balance, showing the formulae in the cells in which they would be entered.

The spreadsheet in Figure 15.4, in accordance with previous suggestions, gathers together the facts in the top section with, in this case, the addition of notes that would be useful if it is consulted some time after its initial preparation. The solution combines the facts in summaries, the totals from which are then used to calculate the monthly balances.

Some features introduced in this model that deserve further explanation are as follows:

1. The formula in cell H20, +F11/2*F12/100, calculates half a year's interest on the loan; F11 is the amount of the loan divided by two as only six months is involved. This is then multiplied by F12/100, which converts the percentage given in cell F12 into a decimal. The use of this formula allows easy variation in the amount and cost of the loan.
2. The value of payments in row 30 remains positive as it is given a negative value by the formula in row 31.
3. Where similar formulae are used repeatedly, for example those for total payments in row 21, spreadsheet programs enable a single entry to be replicated to other cells where it is to be used. This greatly speeds up the preparation of spreadsheets that use the same formula a number of times.

When this spreadsheet is entered into a computer, the solution as shown in Figure 15.5 results. Any of the facts can be changed to generate a new result and, in more complex models, sales could be adjusted via a variable formula to derive the cost of sales. A forecast trading and profit and loss account and balance sheet could also be produced. Example 15.4 shows how two of these aspects, a change in the forecast level of sales and the creation of a link between sales and cost of sales, could be applied to the data given for Grant in Example 15.3.

Example 15.4

Examine, using the spreadsheet prepared in Example 15.3, the effect on Grant's cash position if sales are expected to be £15,000 per month and all purchases are to be sold to give a gross profit of 30 per cent. Each month sufficient purchases are to be made to replace stock sold. All other details remain unchanged, including the acquisition of an initial stock of £8,000.

Solution

To change the level of sales, the value in cell F9 is revised to 15,000 and to link the cost of goods sold to sales, a formula is entered in cell F4: +F9*.7; the note is revised accordingly (see Figure 15.6).

DATABASES

A database program enables the user to store information in an ordered way so that it can be easily retrieved. The database itself can be imagined as a set of cards, each of which comprises a record and contains fields in which pieces of data are entered. This is illustrated in Figure 15.7, which contains details about names and addresses.

The format of each record and the fields it contains are set by the user and, once data has been entered, the computer is able to (1) put the information into order and (2) sort through it to select specified records.

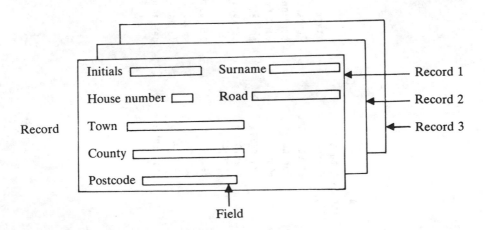

Figure 15.7   A database

	A	B	C	D	E	F	G	H	I
1	Grant cash budget								
2	FACTS:	PAYMENTS		TIMING			NOTES		
3		Fixed assets		January		20000			
4		Purchases		per month		8000	one month's credit		
5		Stock		January		8000	one month's credit		
6		Expenses		per month		800	current month		
7		Drawings		per month		200	current month		
8		RECEIPTS							
9		Sales		per month		12000	two month's credit		
10		Capital		January		20000			
11		Loan		January		8000			
12		Loan interest %		per annum		10	Pay June & Dec.		

13 SOLUTION - CASH BUDGET 6 MONTHS TO 30 JUNE 19X6

	JAN	FEB	MARCH	APRIL	MAY	JUNE	TOTAL
14							
15 PAYMENTS							
16 Fixed assets	20000						20000
17 Purchases		16000	8000	8000	8000	8000	48000
18 Expenses	800	800	800	800	800	800	4800
19 Drawings	200	200	200	200	200	200	1200
20 Interest						400	400
21 Total payments	21000	17000	9000	9000	9000	9400	74400
22 RECEIPTS							
23 Capital	20000						20000
24 Loan	8000						8000
25 Sales			12000	12000	12000	12000	48000
26 Total receipts	28000	0	12000	12000	12000	12000	76000
27							
28 Opening balance		7000	-10000	-7000	-4000	-1000	
29 +Receipts	28000	0	12000	12000	12000	12000	76000
30 -Payments	21000	17000	9000	9000	9000	9400	74400
31 Closing balance	7000	-10000	-7000	-4000	-1000	1600	1600

Figure 15.5   Grant's cash budget in spreadsheet form

```
        A        B          C              D       E    F      G       H        I
1  Grant cash budget
2  FACTS:  PAYMENTS        TIMING                      NOTES
3          Fixed assets    January        20000
4          Purchases       monthly sales x .7  10500  one month's credit
5          Stock           January         8000  one month's credit
6          Expenses        per month        800  current month
7          Drawings        per month        200  current month
8          RECEIPTS
9          Sales           per month      15000  two month's credit
10         Capital         January        20000
11         Loan            January         8000
12         Loan interest % per annum         10  Pay June & Dec.
```

SOLUTION - CASH BUDGET 6 MONTHS TO 30 JUNE 1976

		JAN	FEB	MARCH	APRIL	MAY	JUNE	TOTAL
13								
14								
15	PAYMENTS							
16	Fixed assets	20000						20000
17	Purchases		18500	10500	10500	10500	10500	60500
18	Expenses	800	800	800	800	800	800	4800
19	Drawings	200	200	200	200	200	200	1200
20	Interest						400	400
21	Total payments	21000	19500	11500	11500	11500	11900	86900
22	RECEIPTS							
23	Capital	20000						20000
24	Loan	8000						8000
25	Sales			15000	15000	15000	15000	60000
26	Total receipts	28000	0	15000	15000	15000	15000	88000
27								
28	Opening balance		7000	-12500	-9000	-5500	-2000	0
29	+Receipts	28000	0	15000	15000	15000	15000	88000
30	-Payments	21000	19500	11500	11500	11500	11900	86900
31	Closing balance	7000	-12500	-9000	-5500	-2000	1100	1100

Figure 15.6 Solution to Example 15.4 (cont.)

1. *Ordering records* The records can be sorted into order based on the contents of any field. For example, the products sold by a company could be sorted into alphabetical order by name; ascending price; or by price within alphabetical order. In fact, the number of different ways in which the information can be sorted is almost limitless.
2. *Selection* The program can select records that comply with given criteria. For example, an estate agent could use a data base to record all the available properties on the firm's books. When a client has specified the area in which he or she wishes to live and the range of prices he or she can afford, the computer can select and report all the houses that come into this category.

CONCLUSION

The relatively low cost of computers and their suitability for use in the accountancy function makes it most unlikely that a person who becomes significantly involved in the field of accounting will not come into contact with them. This should not be seen as a discouragement because to use computers it is not necessary to be able to program them, an aspect often seen as daunting. Earlier sections of this chapter considered ready-made programs the accountant can use, and it is possible to obtain versions of them for desk-top, and even home, computers. These can be used to enable the principles involved to be grasped and, once these have been understood, the skills acquired can be put to use on larger applications.

There is no substitute for the 'hands-on' experience of actually using the programs on a computer, and the mastering of the techniques not only provides a stimulating intellectual exercise but also consolidates the underlying accountancy techniques. Any reader with access to a computer and the appropriate programs may now wish to attempt to apply them to questions given elsewhere in this book.

Appendix
Solutions to Questions

Question 2.1   Business transactions: 2, 3, 4. Personal transaction: 1. Part business/part personal transaction: 5.

Question 2.2

(a) **Balance Sheet of John's business, 1 April 19X2**

	£		£
Cash at bank	4,000	Capital	4,000

(b) **Balance Sheet of John's business, 2 April 19X2**

	£		£
Cash at bank	4,600	Capital	4,000
		Loan from John's father	600
	4,600		4,600

(c) **Balance Sheet of John's business, 4 April 19X2**

	£		£
Cash at bank	4,600	Capital	4,000
Cash in hand	150	Loan from John's father	600
		Loan from Peter	150
	4,750		4,750

Question 2.3

(a) **Balance Sheet of Roger's business, 1 September 19X3**

	£		£
Cash at bank	1,200	Capital	1,200

(b) **Balance Sheet of Roger's business, 2 September 19X3**

	£		£
Machine	750	Capital	1,200
Bank (£1,200 + £1,000)	2,200	Endridge Local Authority	1,000
		Creditors	750
	2,950		2,950

(c) **Balance Sheet of Roger's business, 3 September 19X3**

	£		£
Machines (£750 + £1,820)	2,570	Capital	1,200
Stock	420	Endridge Local Authority	1,000
		Creditors	750
		Bank overdraft	
		(£2,200−£1,820−£420)	40
	2,990		2,990

(d) **Balance Sheet of Roger's business, 4 September 19X3**

	£		£
Machines	2,570	Capital	1,200
Stock (£420 +£215)	635	Endridge Local Authority	1,000
		Creditors (£750 + £215)	965
		Bank overdraft	40
	3,205		3,205

Question 2.4

(a) **Balance Sheet of Jeff's business, 2 October 19X5**

	£		£
Machine	2,200	Capital	5,300
Stock (£2,870−£360)	2,510	Add: Profit (£80+£75)	155
Debtors (£800 + £315)	1,115		5,455
Bank (£120 + £200)	320	Trade creditors	690
	6,145		6,145

(b) **Balance Sheet of Jeff's business, 3 October 19X5**

	£		£
Machinery	2,200	Capital	5,455
		Trade creditors	
Stock (£2,510 + £190)	2,700	(£690 + £190)	880
Debtors (£1,115 − £150)	965		
Bank (£320 + £150)	470		
	6,335		6,335

(c) **Balance Sheet of Jeff's business, 4 October 19X5**

	£		£
Machines (£2,200 + £600)	2,800	Capital	5,455
		Trade creditors	
Stock	2,700	(£880 − £75)	805
Debtors	965	Bank overdraft	
		(£470 − £75 − £600)	205
	6,465		6,465

Question 2.5

(a) **Balance Sheet of Daley at 31 December 19X1**

	£		£
Business premises	9,000	Capital (balancing figure)	13,450
Stock	5,250	Loan from Weakly	3,000
Trade debtors	3,340	Trade creditors	2,890
Cash	1,750		
	19,340		19,340

(b) **Balance Sheet of Daley at:**

Sources of finance	1 Jan. £	2 Jan. £	3 Jan. £	4 Jan. £	5 Jan. £	6 Jan. £	7 Jan. £
Capital	13,450	13,450	13,450	13,450	13,450	13,450	13,450
Add: Profit					180	180	180
Less: Drawings							(100)
					13,630	13,630	13,530
Loan from Weakly	3,000	3,000	3,000	3,000	3,000	2,000	2,000
Trade creditors	3,390	3,390	2,720	2,980	2,980	2,980	2,980
	19,840	19,840	19,170	19,430	19,610	18,610	18,510
Assets							
Business premises	9,000	9,000	9,000	9,000	9,000	9,000	9,000
Typewriter	500	500	500	500	500	500	500
Stocks	5,250	5,250	5,250	5,510	5,160	5,160	5,060
Trade debtors	3,340	3,150	3,150	3,150	3,150	3,150	3,150
Cash	1,750	1,940	1,270	1,270	1,800	800	800
	19,840	19,840	19,170	19,430	19,610	18,610	18,510

Question 2.6

Balance Sheet at 31 December 19X1

Sources of finance	A £	B £	C £	D £	E £	F £
Capital at 1 January 19X1	2,500	2,000	3,000	4,000	3,800	7,400
Add: Profit	1,000	3,200	1,400	5,700	2,300	7,000
Less: Drawings	(800)	(3,000)	(1,000)	(4,900)	(2,500)	(4,500)
	2,700	2,200	3,400	4,800	3,600	9,900
Current liabilities	750	400	600	1,300	1,700	2,100
	3,450	2,600	4,000	6,100	5,300	12,000
Assets	£	£	£	£	£	£
Fixed assets	1,800	1,750	2,800	4,200	3,700	8,500
Current assets	1,650	850	1,200	1,900	1,600	3,500
	3,450	2,600	4,000	6,100	5,300	12,000

Question 2.7

1. *Accountancy* This is a system for recording and reporting business transactions, in financial terms, to interested parties who use this information as the basis for decision-making and performance assessment.

2. *Entity concept* It is assumed, for accounting purposes, that the business entity has an existence separate and distinct from owners, managers and other individuals with whom it comes into contact during the course of its trading activities.

    The assumption requires business transactions to be separated from personal transactions and accounting statements to concentrate upon the financial position of the firm and its relationship with outsiders.

3. *Balance sheet* This is a financial statement that shows, on the one hand, the sources from which a business has raised finance and, on the other, the ways in which those monetary resources are employed. The balance sheet sets out the financial position at a particular moment in time and has been colourfully described as an instantaneous financial photograph of a business.

4. *Realization concept* This assumes that profit is earned or realized when the sale takes place. The justification for this treatment is that a sale results in the replacement of stock by either cash or a legally enforceable debt due from the customer.

5. *Trade credit* This is the period of time that elapses between the dates goods are supplied and paid for.

6. *Trading cycle, credit transactions* This is a series of transactions that begins with the delivery of stock from suppliers. The stock is then sold and delivered to customers resulting in a profit being realized or a loss incurred. Next, cash is collected from customers and the cycle is completed by paying suppliers the amount due.

7. $C + L = A$ This formula expresses the balance sheet relationship between sources of finance and assets where

$$C = \text{Capital invested by the owners, including retained profits.}$$
$$L = \text{Liabilities.}$$
$$A = \text{Assets.}$$

    The balance sheet must always balance because all assets appearing on the right-hand side of the balance sheet must be financed, and the various sources employed appear on the left.

8. *Owner's capital* This is the amount of the initial investment in the concern, to which is added any further injections of capital plus profit earned, and from which is deducted drawings made by the owner for personal use.

9. *Money measurement concept* Assets are reported in the balance sheet only if the benefit they provide can be measured or quantified, in money terms, with a reasonable degree of precision.

10. *Fixed assets* These are purchased and retained to help carry on the business. Fixed assets are not sold in the normal course of business and their disposal will usually occur only when they are worn out, e.g. machinery.

11. *Current assets* These are assets that are held for resale or conversion into cash, e.g. stock-in-trade and trade debtors.

12. *Current liabilities* These are debts payable within twelve months of the balance sheet date, e.g. trade creditors and a bank overdraft.

13. *Gross assets* These are the total assets belonging to a business entity and therefore include both fixed assets and current assets.

Question 2.8   Current liabilities: 4 and 9. Current assets: 2 and 7. Fixed assets: 1 and 3. Items not indicated:

5. *Capital investment* This is reported in the capital section, i.e. the first item on the sources of finance side of the balance sheet.

6. *Pearl knecklace and gold wristwatch* These are the personal belongings of Mrs Greasy and must be excluded from the balance sheet.

8. *Loan* This is a non-current liability and is reported between the capital and current liability sections of the balance sheet.
10. *Shop* This must be excluded from the balance sheet since it belongs to the property company.

Question 2.9

Balance Sheet of C. Forest at 31 December 19X3

	£	£		£	£
Fixed assets			Opening capital		52,380
Leasehold premises	25,000		Add: Profit		12,600
Plant and machinery	26,500		Less: Drawings		(10,950)
		51,500			54,030
			Loan repayable 19X9		9,000
Current assets			*Current liabilities*		
Stock-in-trade	14,200		Loan repayable 19X4	2,500	
Trade debtors	14,100		Trade creditors	10,600	
Cash-in-hand	270	28,570	Bank overdraft	3,940	17,040
		80,070			80,070

Question 3.1

(a) Gross assets, £6,700. Net assets, £6,500 (gross assets £6,700 − liabilities £200). Working capital, £4,500 (current assets £4,700 − current liabilities £200).

(b)

Trans.	Profit	Net assets	Gross assets	Working capital
1	NIL	NIL	NIL	NIL
2	NIL	Increase, £500	Increase, £500	Increase, £500
3	Decrease, £100	Decrease, £100	Decrease, £100	Decrease, £100
4	NIL	Decrease, £50	Decrease, £50	Decrease, £50
5	NIL	NIL	Increase, £150	NIL
6	NIL	NIL	NIL	Decrease, £700

Question 3.2

(a) Calculation of capital by deducting liabilities from assets:

Statement of assets, liabilities and capital at 30 June 19X4

	£	£
Assets		
Fixed assets		9,850
Stocks		4,270
Debtors		1,450
Cash at bank		570
Cash in hand		30
		16,170

	£	£
Balance b/f		16,170
Less: Liabilities		
Loan	3,000	
Trade creditors	1,890	4,890
Capital		11,280

(b) Calculation of profit on the basis of the increase in capital:

	£
Closing capital	11,280
Less: Opening capital	10,330
Profit	950

(c) **Balance Sheet at 30 June 19X4**

	£	£
Fixed assets		9,850
Current assets		
Stocks	4,270	
Debtors	1,450	
Cash at bank	570	
Cash in hand	30	
	6,320	
Less: Current liabilities		
Trade creditors	1,890	
Working capital		4,430
		14,280
Financed by:		
Opening capital		10,330
Add: Net profit		950
Closing capital		11,280
Loan		3,000
		14,280

Question 3.3

(a) Calculation of capital

Statement of assets, liabilities and capital at 31 December

	19X3		19X4	
	£	£	£	£
Gross assets				
Fixed assets		9,000		12,144W1
Stocks		2,650		3,710
Trade debtors		5,200		5,600
Bank balance		—		50
		16,850		21,504
Less: Liabilities				
Trade creditors	1,710		1,210	
Bank overdraft	360	2,070	—	1,210
Capital		14,780		20,294

	£
Calculation of profit	
Closing capital	20,294
Less: Opening capital	14,780
Increase in capital	5,514
Add: Drawings	8,100W2
Less: Capital introduced	(600)
Profit	13,014

Workings

W1 £9,000 + £3,144 = £12,144
W2 (£150 × 52) + £300 = £8,100

(b) Balance Sheet at 31 December 19X4

	£	£		£	£
Fixed assets		12,144	Opening capital		14,780
			Add: Net profit		13,014
			Additional capital		
			investment		600
					28,394
Current assets					
Stocks	3,710		Less: Drawings–cash	7,800	
Trade debtors	5,600		stock	300	8,100
Bank balance	50	9,360			20,294
			Current liabilities		
			Trade creditors		1,210
		21,504			21,504

Question 3.4

A   The company has purchased stocks, on credit, for £27,000.

B   The company has purchase land and buildings, costing £35,000, and financed the purchase by raising a loan of an equal amount.

C   The company has sold stock, costing £20,000, on credit for £30,000. The net effect is a profit of £10,000 that has increased capital from £730,000 to £740,000.

D   A trade debt due to the firm, of £13,000, has been paid in cash.

E   £2,000 due from a trade debtor has been written off as a bad debt, causing capital to fall from £740,000 to £738,000.

F   Cash at bank has fallen by £8,000. Based on the information provided, it appears that £3,000 has been paid to expense creditors and the owner has withdrawn £5,000.

G   Equipment, with a book value of £30,000, has been sold for £21,000. The loss arising on sale, of £9,000, has caused the balance of capital to fall from £733,000 to £724,000.

H   The owner has withdrawn from the business stocks with a book value of £1,000.

I   Possible explanations for this transaction are as follows:
   (i) the owner has withdrawn £6,000 in cash; or
   (ii) cash of £6,000 has been stolen causing the value of the owner's investment to fall from £723,000 to £717,000.

Question 4.1

(a)

Balance Sheet at 31 December 19X4

	£	£		£
Fixed assets			Capital (A−L)	3,190
Furniture and fittings at			*Current liabilities*	
cost less depreciation		400	Trade creditors	1,630
Current assets				
Stock	2,040			
Debtors	1,900			
Bank	480	4,420		
		4,820		4,820

(b) **Trading and Profit and Loss Account of Stoll for 19X5**

	£	£	
Sales		32,004	W2
Less: Purchases	25,100 W1		
Add: Opening stock	2,040		
Less: Closing stock	(1,848)		
Cost of goods sold		25,292	
Gross profit		6,712	
Less: General expenses	2,524		
Rent	300		
Depreciation	40	2,864	
Net profit		3,848	

Workings

Convert cash flows to flows of goods.

		£
W1 Purchases:	Payments to suppliers	24,800
	Less: Opening creditors	(1,630)
	Add: Closing creditors	1,930
		25,100
W2 Sales:	Received from debtors	31,560
	Less: Opening debtors	(1,900)
	Add: Closing debtors	2,344
		32,004

Balance Sheet of Stoll at 31 December 19X5

	£	£
Fixed assets		
Furniture at cost less depreciation		360
Current assets		
Stock	1,848	
Debtors	2,344	
Bank	816	
	5,008	
Less: Current liabilities		
Trade creditors	1,930	
Working capital		3,078
		3,438
Financed by:		
Opening capital		3,190
Add: Net profit		3,848
Less: Drawings		(3,600)
		3,438

Question 4.2

Trading and Profit and Loss Account for 19X1

	£	£
Sales		40,440 W1
Less: Purchases	21,140 W2	
Add: Opening stock	3,750	
Less: Closing stock	(4,600)	
Cost of goods sold		20,290
Gross profit		20,150
Add: Bank interest received		50
		20,200
Less: General expenses	7,490 W3	
Depreciation	2,800	
Loan interest (£2,000 × 15%)	300	10,590
Net profit		9,610

Balance Sheet at 31 December 19X1

	£	£	
Fixed assets			
Motor vehicles at cost		14,000	W4
Less: Accumulated depreciation		4,800	W5
		9,200	
Current assets			
Stock	4,600		
Debtors	1,840		
Bank deposit account (£650+£50)	700		
Prepaid expenses	520		
	7,660		
Less: Current liabilities			
Creditors	1,140		
Loan interest	300		
Accruals	310		
Bank overdraft	4,630	W6	
	6,380		
Working capital		1,280	
		10,480	
Financed by:			
Opening capital		8,720	
Add: Capital injection–legacy		2,650	
Net profit		9,610	
Less: Drawings		(12,500)	
		8,480	
Loan at 15%		2,000	
		10,480	

Workings

W1 Sales	£	W4 Vehicles	£
Proceeds from: Credit sales	7,560	Balance at 1 January	10,000
Cash sales	32,100	Add: Purchases	4,000
	39,660		14,000
Less: Opening debtors	(1,060)		
Add: Closing debtors	1,840		
		W5 *Vehicles: Accum. dep.*	
	40,440	Balance at 1 January	2,000
		Add: Charge for year	2,800*
			4,800

W2 Purchases			
Payments to suppliers	20,850		
Less: Opening creditors	(850)	W6 Bank overdraft	
Add: Closing creditors	1,140	Opening balance	2,030
		Add: Payments	44,910
	21,140	Less: Receipts	(42,310)
			4,630

W3 *General expenses*	
Payments	7,560
Add: Opening prepayments	400
Less: Opening accruals	(260)
Less: Closing prepayments	(520)
Add: Closing accruals	310
	7,490

Note
*£14,000 (cost of vehicles owned at year end) $\times$ 20% = £2,800.

Question 4.3

(a) **Balance Sheet of Stondon at 31 December 19X3**

	£	£		£	£
Fixed assets			Capital (A−L)		9,947
Furniture and			*Current liabilities*		
fittings		800	Trade creditors	3,586	
Motor van at cost			Bank overdraft	782	4,368
less depreciation		2,500			
		3,300			
Current assets					
Stock	6,891				
Trade debtors	4,124	11,015			
		14,315			14,315

(b)

	£
Capital at 31 December 19X3	9,947
Less: Capital at 31 December 19X2	7,940
Increase in capital	2,007
Add: Drawings	12,840
	14,847
Less: Capital introduced	4,200
Net profit for 19X3	10,647

(c) **Trading and Profit and Loss account for 19X3**

	£	£
Sales (25,067 × 4)		100,268 (4)
Less: Purchases (by difference)	76,708 (8)	
Add: Opening stock	5,384 (7)	
Less: Closing stock	(6,891) (6)	
Cost of goods sold		75,201 (5)
Gross profit		25,067 (3)
Less: Running expenses		14,420 (2)
Net profit		10,647 (1)

Note

The numbers in brackets indicate the order in which the trading and profit and loss account is reconstructed.

Question 4.4

(a) **Bar Trading Account for 19X8**

	£			£
Opening stock	8,200		Sales	107,600
Add: Purchases	81,248	W2		
Less: Closing stock	(11,936)			
Costs of goods sold	77,512			
Gross profit	30,088			
	107,600			107,600

(b) **Income and Expenditure Account for 19X8**

	£			£
Rent	2,800		Bar profit	30,088
Rates	2,000		Subscriptions	12,400
General expenses	5,448	W3	Interest	4,160
Depreciation	3,040	W4		
Salaries	16,840			
Surplus	16,520			
	46,648			46,648

(c) **Balance Sheet at 31 December 19X8**

	£	£		£	£	
Fixed assets			Accumulated fund		96,840	W1
Furniture		30,400	Add: Surplus		16,520	
Less: Depreciation		3,040				
					113,360	
		27,360				
			Current liabilities			
Current assets			Creditors: Supplies	4,568		
Investments	75,200		Expenses	248		
Stocks	11,936					
Bank	3,680				4,816	
		90,816				
		118,176			118,176	

Workings

W1 **Balance Sheet at 1 January 19X8**

	£		£
Furniture	30,400	Accumulated fund (A − L)	96,840
Investments	49,200	Creditors: Supplies	4,080
Stocks	8,200	Expenses	160
Bank	13,280		
	101,080		101,080

W2 Purchases

	£
Payments for purchases	80,760
Less: Opening creditors	(4,080)
Add: Closing creditors	4,568
	81,248

W3 General expenses

	£
Payments for general expenses	5,360
Less: Opening creditors	(160)
Add: Closing creditors	248
	5,448

W4 Depreciation
£30,400 × 10% = £3,040.

Question 4.5

(a) **Bar Trading Account and General Income and Expenditure Account for 19X1**

	£			£
Opening stock	4,400		Sales	69,660
Purchases	48,980 W4			
Closing stock	(5,280)			
	————			
Cost of goods sold	48,100			
Wages	7,800			
	————			
	55,900			
Bar profit	13,760			
	————			————
	69,660			69,660
	————			————
General expenses	17,440 W5		Bar profit	13,760
Rates	1,100		Tennis surplus	6,080 W2
Depreciation of furniture	500		Rugby surplus	180 W3
	————			
	19,040			
Surplus	980			
	————			————
	20,020			20,020
	————			————

(b) **Balance Sheet at 31 December 19X1**

	£	£		£
Fixed assets			Accumulated fund at 1 Jan.	68,680 W1
Clubhouse at cost		38,000	Add: Surplus	980
				————
Tennis courts at cost				69,660
less depreciation		35,200	Subscriptions in advance	10,800
Furniture and equip-			*Current liabilities*	
ment at book			Creditors: Bar purchases	4,300
value		4,500	General expenses	640
		————		
		77,700		
Current assets				
Bar stocks	5,280			
Bank balance	2,420	7,700		
	————	————		————
		85,400		85,400
		————		————

Workings

W1 Accumulated fund	£	W3 Rugby section		£
Assets		Subscriptions		1,300
Clubhouse	38,000	Collections		180
Tennis courts	24,000			———
Furniture and equipment	5,000			1,480
Bar stocks	4,400	Less: Kit	£900	
Bank balance	1,500	Rental	£400	1,300
	———			———
	72,900	Surplus		180
Less: Liabilities				———
Creditors £3,720 + £500	4,220	W4 Bar purchases		
	———	Payments		48,400
	68,680	Less: Opening creditors		(3,720)
	———	Add: Closing creditors		4,300
W2 Tennis section				———
Tournament fees	240			48,980
10-year subscriptions	1,200*			———
Other subscriptions	6,400	W5 General expenses		
Court fees	5,700	Payments		17,300
	———	Less: Opening creditors		(500)
	13,540	Add: Closing creditors		640
				———
Less: Repairs £2,520				17,440
Prizes 140				———
Depreciation 4,800†	7,460			
	———			
Surplus	6,080			

Notes

* One-tenth of the 10-year tennis membership subscriptions is credited to the income and expenditure account; the remainder is reported in the balance sheet as subscriptions received in advance. The ten-year subscription might alternatively have been credited, in full, direct to the accumulated fund.

† (£40,000 × 10%) + (£16,000 × 10% × 0.5).

Question 5.1

Cash Account

January		£	January		£
1	Capital introduced	5,000	2	Van	4,000
1–31	Cash sales	2,250	3	Rent	100
1–31	Debtors	450	1–31	Creditors	2,500
			15	Drawings	110
			30	Insurance	120
			31	Balance c/d	870
		7,700			7,700
February					
1	Balance b/d	870			

Question 5.2

	£	£
Balance per bank statement		1,960
Less: Outstanding cheques		104
Correct cash book balance		1,856
Balance per cash book		1,801 W1
Plus: Bank interest	76	
Receipt from debtor	89	
		165
Less: Standing order		(110)
Correct cash book balance		1,856

Workings

W1 – to find the cash book balance:

	£	£
Balance per statement		1,960
Less: Interest not entered in cash book	76	
Debtor receipt not in cash book	89	
Outstanding cheques (21+44+39)	104	
		(269)
Plus: Standing order payment		110
Balance per cash book		1,801

Question 5.3

Double column cash book

	Cash £	Bank £		Cash £	Bank £
Capital		10,000	Premises		8,000
Loan	5,000		Equipment		2,750
Cash		750	Van	4,000	
Sales	5,500		Bank	750	
Cash		4,250	Purchases	1,000	3,000
			Wages	100	
			Drawings	150	
			Rates		250
			Bank	4,250	
			Balance c/d	250	1,000
	10,500	15,000		10,500	15,000
Balance b/d	250	1,000			

Question 5.4

Analysed cash book

Day	Detail	Total £	Sales £	Sundry £
1	Sales	1,790	1,790	
2	Sales	2,190	2,190	
3	Sales	1,250	1,250	
	Sale of fixed asset	1,000		1,000
4	Sales	3,720	3,720	
5	Sales	1,540	1,540	
6	Sales	2,710	2,710	
		14,200	13,200	1,000
6	Balance b/d	1,070		

Day	Detail	Total £	Purchases £	Wages £	Sundry £
1	Balance b/d	6,510			
1	Purchases	2,250	2,250		
2	Wages	380		380	
4	Interest	400			400
5	Purchases	3,140	3,140		
6	Wages	450		450	
6	Balance c/d	1,070			
		14,200	5,390	830	400

Note
To agree the cross-cast of the payment columns, the opening and closing balances have to be subtracted from the total column as they do not have a corresponding entry in the analysis columns.

Question 5.5

Petty cash account

£	1985 Oct.		Total £	Wages £	Postage £	Stationery £	Purchase Ledger £
1985 Oct. 1 Balance b/d 3.75	4	Wages	11.60	11.60			
1 Bank 46.25	5	Postage	3.94		3.94		
	8	Stationery	4.09			4.09	
	11	Postage	2.00		2.00		
	18	Wages	12.93	12.93			
	21	F. Smith – creditor	3.42				3.42
	24	Stationery	4.66			4.66	
	28	Postage	3.80		3.80		
			46.44	24.53	9.74	8.75	3.42
	31	Balance c/d	3.56				
50.00			50.00				
Nov. 1 Balance b/d 3.56							
1 Bank 46.44							

Question 5.6

Sales day book

Day	Detail	Total £	Typewriters £	Stationery £	Repairs £
1	Gum Ltd	375	300	75	
	Glue Ltd	100			100
2	Stick Ltd	70		70	
3	Fast Ltd	450	450		
	Stick Ltd	50			50
		1,045	750	145	150

Question 6.1

	Debit £	Credit £
Capital		8,500
Current liabilities		4,600
Plant and machinery	4,500	
Stock	2,700	
Debtors	5,200	
Cash	700	
	13,100	13,100

Question 6.2

Sales day book (SDB)

Customer	£
Vision	7,000
Sister	4,000
Batty	2,700
Flat	200
Broke	300
	14,200

Purchases day book (PDB)

Supplier	Total £	Goods for resale £	Motor expenses £	Office expenses £
Tele	3,000	3,000		
Trany	2,000	2,000		
Valve	2,400	2,400		
Garage	100		100	
Paper	50			50
	7,550	7,400	100	50

Returns inwards day book (RIDB)

Customer	£
Vision	300
Batty	200
	500

Returns outwards day book (RODB)

Supplier	£
Trany	100
Valve	150
	250

Cash book (CB) receipts (debit)

Detail	Discount £	Cash £	Debtors £	Sundry £
Balance b/d		700		
Vision	50	6,350	6,350	
Sister	40	3,500	3,500	
Batty	25	2,600	2,600	
Scrap		100		100
	115	13,250	12,450	100

Cash book (CB) payments (credit)

Detail	Discount £	Cash £	Creditors £	Wages £	Motor expenses £	Sundry £
Tele	55	2,950	2,950			
Trany	35	1,950	1,950			
Valve	20	2,200	2,200			
Plantmax		1,000				1,000
Wages		1,500		1,500		
Accom.		600				600
Supplies		250				250
Garage		300			300	
	110	10,750	7,100	1,500	300	1,850
Balance c/d		2,500				
		13,250				

Question 6.3

Capital

	£			£
		Journal		8,500

Purchase Ledger Control Account

		£			£
January	RODB	250	January	Journal	4,600
	CB Discounts	110		PDB	7,550
	CB Cash	7,100			
	Balance c/d	4,690			
		12,150			12,150

Plant and Machinery

		£			£
January	Journal	4,500	January	Balance c/d	5,500
	CB	1,000			
		5,500			5,500

Stock

		£			£
January	Journal	2,700			

Sales Ledger Control Account

		£			£
January	Journal	5,200	January	RIDB	500
	SDB	14,200		CB Discounts	115
				CB Cash	12,450
				Balance c/d	6,335
		19,400			19,400

Sales

		£			£
January	RIDB	500	January	SDB	14,200
	Balance c/d	13,700			
		14,200			14,200

Purchases

		£			£
January	PDB	7,400	January	RODB	250
				Balance c/d	7,150
		7,400			7,400

Motor Expenses

		£			£
January	PDB	100	January	Balance c/d	400
	CB	300			
		400			400

Office Expenses

		£			£
January	PDB	50	January	Balance c/d	300
	CB	250			
		300			300

Discounts Allowed

		£			£
January	CB	115			

Discount Received

		£			£
			January	CB	110

Sale of Fixed Assets

		£			£
January	CB	100			

Wages

		£			£
January	CB	1,500			

Rent

		£			£
January	CB	600			

Question 6.4

Sales ledger

Vision

		£			£
January	Balance b/d	2,500	January	RIDB	300
	SDB	7,000		CB Discounts	50
				CB Cash	6,350
				Balance c/d	2,800
		9,500			9,500

Sister

		£			£
January	Balance b/d	1,500	January	CB Discounts	40
	SDB	4,000		CB Cash	3,500
				Balance c/d	1,960
		5,500			5,500

Batty

January	Balance b/d	£ 1,200	January	RIDB	£ 200
	SDB	2,700		CB Discounts	25
				CB Cash	2,600
				Balance c/d	1,075
		3,900			3,900

Flat

January	SDB	£ 200			£

Broke

January	SDB	£ 300			£

Purchases ledger

Tele

January	CB Discounts	£ 55	January	Balance b/d	£ 2,300
	CB Cash	2,950		PDB	3,000
	Balance c/d	2,295			
		5,300			5,300

Trany

January	RODB	£ 100	January	Balance b/d	£ 1,000
	CB Discount	35		PDB	2,000
	CB Cash	1,950			
	Balance c/d	915			
		3,000			3,000

Valve

January	RODB	£ 150	January	Balance c/d	£ 1,300
	CB Discount	20		PDB	2,400
	CB Cash	2,200			
	Balance c/d	1,330			
		3,700			3,700

Garage

	£				£
		January	PDB		100

Paper

	£				£
		January	PDB		50

Question 6.5

Sales ledger

	£
Vision	2,800
Sister	1,960
Batty	1,075
Flat	200
Broke	300
As per control account	6,335

Purchase ledger

	£
Tele	2,295
Trany	915
Valve	1,330
Garage	100
Paper	50
As per control account	4,690

Question 6.6

	Debit £	Credit £
Cash	2,500	
Capital		8,500
Creditors		4,690
Plant and machinery	5,500	
Stock	2,700	
Debtors	6,335	
Sales		13,700
Purchases	7,150	
Motor expenses	400	
Office expenses	300	
Discounts allowed	115	
Discounts received		110
Wages	1,500	
Rent	600	
Sale of fixed asset		100
	27,100	27,100

Question 6.7 (a)

(i) Real accounts represent assets, or items of property other than claims against external persons. Balances on real accounts are, in normal circumstances, assets, for example, when motor vehicles, furniture or plant and machinery are purchased, real accounts under those headings are debited.

(ii) Personal accounts are those which show the relationship of the business with other persons or firms. A debit balance on a personal account is an asset and represents the right to receive money in the future. A credit balance is a liability.

(iii) Nominal accounts are used to record items of income and expense. Debit balances are expenses and credit balances are income.

(b)

(i) Fixed asset at cost £10,000 – real account.
(ii) Wages £700 – nominal account.
(iii) Discounts received £1,400 – nominal account.
(iv) Balance due from Double Ltd £1,500 – personal account.

Question 6.8   The accountant uses the trial balance:

(a) To check the accuracy of the entries in the ledger, but note that some of the errors are not revealed.

(b) As the basis for preparing the trading and profit and loss accounts and balance sheet.

Question 6.9

Sales Ledger Control Account

19X4		£	19X4		£
1 October	Balance b/d	102,300	1 October	Balance b/d	340
	Sales	630,800		Cash	498,660
				Returns	2,700
				Discounts	11,790
				purchase ledger	
				Contras	5,200
				Bad debts	3,950
19X5			19X5		
30 September	Balance c/d	510	30 September	Balance c/d	210,970
		733,610			733,610

Note
Items 4, 6 and 8 do not belong in the sales ledger control account.

Question 6.10

(i) **Error Co. Ltd – Journal**

	Dr. £	Cr. £
(a) Suspense account	1,000	
Creditors control account		1,000
Sum due to Zed omitted from control account		
(b) Debtors control account	2,400	
Sales account		2,400
Correction of undercast sales day book		
(c) Discounts allowed account	4,890	
Suspense account		4,890
Discounts for June not posted to nominal ledger		
(d) Purchases account	24,100	
Accruals		24,100
Invoice for goods in stock not invoiced at 30 June 19X2		
(e) Sales account	1,920	
Debtors control account		1,920
Correction of wrong posting		

(ii) **Effect on profit for year**

	£
Decreases in profit:	
Discounts allowed (c)	4,890
Purchases omitted (d)	24,100
Cash posted to sales account in error (e)	1,920
	30,910
Increase in profit:	
Undercast sales day book (b)	2,400
Reduction in profit	28,510

(iii) **Calculation of suspense account balance**

Suspense Account

	£		£
Creditors control account (a)	1,000	Discounts allowed (c)	4,890
Original balance*	3,890		
	4,890		4,890

Note
* Balancing figure.

Question 7.1   (a)

Item	Location	Comment
Sales	Trading account	Revenue
Returns inwards	Trading account	Reduces the value of sales
Stock 1 January	Trading account	Charged against sales
Returns outwards	Trading account	Reduces purchases
Purchases	Trading account	Expense
Capital	Balance sheet	Liability to ownership
Cash at bank	Balance sheet	Asset
Debtors	Balance sheet	Asset
Creditors	Balance sheet	Liability
Premises	Balance sheet	Asset
Wages	Profit and loss account	Expense
Discounts received	Profit and loss account	Sundry revenue
Rent and rates	Profit and loss account	Expense
Delivery costs	Profit and loss account	Expense
Cash withdrawn	Balance sheet	Reduces capital
Heat and light	Profit and loss account	Expense
Sundry expenses	Profit and loss account	Expense

(b) **Trading and Profit and Loss Account for the Year to 31 December 19X4**

	£	£
Sales		130,000
Less: Returns inwards		250
		129,750
Opening stock	15,000	
Purchases	80,000	
Less: Returns outwards	(150)	
Closing stock	(17,750)	
Cost of goods sold		77,100
Gross profit		52,650
Discounts received		300
		52,950
Wages	17,300	
Rent and rates	3,000	
Delivery	2,750	
Heat and light	3,500	
Sundry expenses	2,750	
		29,300
Net profit		23,650

Balance Sheet at 31 December 19X4

	£	£		£
Premises		8,000	Capital, 1 January	27,600
Stock	17,750		Profit for year	23,650
Debtors	15,400			
Cash	3,100			51,250
			Drawings	(12,000)
		36,250	Capital, 31 December	39,250
			Creditors	5,000
		44,250		44,250

Question 7.2 (a)

Fixed Assets at Cost

		£		£
1 Jan. X1	Asset A	5,000	31 Dec. X1 Balance c/d	7,500
	Asset B	2,500		
		7,500		7,500
1 Jan. X2	Balance b/d	7,500	1 Jan. X3 Disposal of asset B	2,500
1 Feb. X3	Asset C	7,000	Balance c/d	12,000
		14,500		14,500

Accumulated Depreciation

	£		£
31 Dec. X2 Balance c/d	3,000	31 Dec. X1 Profit and loss	1,500
		31 Dec. X2 Profit and loss	1,500
	3,000		3,000
1 Jan. X3 Disposal of Asset B	1,000	1 Jan. X3 Balance b/d	3,000
31 Dec. X3 Balance c/d	4,400	31 Dec. X3 Profit and loss	2,400
	5,400		5,400

Disposal of Fixed Assets

	£		£
1 Jan. X3 Fixed assets	2,500	1 Jan. X3 Depreciation	1,000
		Proceeds	900
		Profit and loss	600
	2,500		2,500

(b) Balance sheet extracts

	31 Dec. X1 £	31 Dec. X2 £	31 Dec. X3 £
Fixed assets at cost	7,500	7,500	12,000
Less: Accumulated depreciation	1,500	3,000	4,400
Written-down value	6,000	4,500	7,600

Question 7.3

Trading and Profit and Loss Account for the Year to 30 June 19X7

	£	£
Sales		108,920
Opening stock	9,470	
Purchases	72,190	
Closing stock	(9,960)	
Cost of goods sold		71,700
Gross profit		37,220
Depreciation	3,000	
Rent	1,000	
Wages	14,330	
Other costs	4,590	
		22,920
Net profit		14,300

Balance Sheet at 30 June 19X7

	£	£
Fixed assets		
At cost		35,000
Less: Accumulated depreciation		
(12,500 + 3,000)		15,500
		19,500
Current assets		
Stock	9,960	
Debtors	7,350	
Cash	1,710	
	19,020	
Current liabilities		
Creditors	6,220	
		12,800
		32,300
Capital		
At 1 July 19X6		30,350
Profit		14,300
		44,650
Drawings		(12,350)
		32,300

Question 7.4

(a) Motor Vehicles at Cost Account

	£		£
Balance per trial balance	127,000	Van scrapped (1)	2,000
Disposals – Trade in(2)	1,500	Disposal – Car (2)	5,000
Disposal of van (4)	2,500	Disposal – Car (3)	4,000
		Disposal – Van (4)	10,000
		Balance c/d	110,000
	131,000		131,000

Motor Vehicles Depreciation Account

	£		£
Van scrapped (1)	2,000	Balance per trial balance	76,000
Disposal – Car (2)	3,000	Profit and loss	
Disposal – Car (3) (W1)	2,750	Account – Charge for	
Disposal – Van (4) (W2)	6,750	19X3	25,000
Balance c/d	86,500		
	101,000		101,000

Disposal of Motor Vehicles Account

	£		£
Car at cost (2)	5,000	Balance per trial balance	1,600
Car at cost (3)	4,000	Trade in allowance (2)	1,500
Van at cost (4)	10,000	Depreciation (2)	3,000
		Depreciation (3) (W1)	2,750
		Proceeds on sale of van (4)	2,500
		Depreciation (4)(W2)	6,750
		Loss on disposal of vehicles transferred to profit and loss account	900
	19,000		19,000

Workings
W1. Disposal of car
Using the formula:
Written down value = Cost − Accumulated depreciation
then 1,250   = 4,000 − Accumulated depreciation
∴ Accumulated depreciation = £2,750

W2. Disposal of delivery van
Using the formula:
Proceeds − (Cost − Accumulated depreciation) = Profit (loss) on disposal
then 2,500 − (10,000 − Accumulated depreciation) = (750)
∴ Accumulated depreciation = £6,750

(b) **Balance Sheet extract at 31 December 19X3**

	£
Motor vehicles at cost ·	110,000
Less: Accumulated depreciation	86,500
	23,500

Note
The number in brackets after some of the entries in the accounts refers to the number of the note given in the question on which the entry is based.

Question 7.5

Insurance Account

19X8		£	19X8		£
1 January	Balance b/d	450	31 December	Balance c/d	510
June	Cash	1,020		Profit and loss	
				account	960
		1,470			1,470

Rates Account

19X8		£	19X8		£
1 January	Balance b/d	290	31 December	Balance c/d	390
March	Cash	780		Profit and loss	
September	Cash	780		account	1,460
		1,850			1,850

Gas Account

19X8		£	19X8		£
March	Cash	850	1 January	Balance b/d	600
June	Cash	840	31 December	Profit and loss	
September	Cash	610		account	3,340
December	Cash	960			
31 December	Balance c/d	680			
		3,940			3,940

Electricity Account

19X8		£	19X8		£
February	Cash	900	1 January	Balance b/d	300
May	Cash	820	31 December	Profit and loss	
August	Cash	690		account	3,050
November	Cash	550			
31 December	Balance c/d	390			
		3,350			3,350

Question 7.6 (a)

Sales Ledger Control Account

	£		£
Balance b/d	156,937	B. Clyde – bad debt	560
		M. Poppins – bad debt	227
		Balance c/d	156,150
	156,937		156,937

Bad Debts Account

	£		£
Balance b/d	750	Profit and loss account	1,537
Sales ledger control account	560		
Sales ledger control account	227		
	1,537		1,537

Doubtful Debts Account

	£		£
Provision for doubtful debts accounts	1,648	Profit and loss account	1,648

Provision for Doubtful Debts Account

	£		£
Balance c/d	4,248	Balance b/d	2,600
		Doubtful debts account*	
		S. Wars	340
		M. Express	78
		M. Ash	80
		Increase in provision	1,150
	4,248		4,248

Note
* Total value £1,648.

(b) **Balance sheet – extract**

	£
Debtors	156,150
Less: Provision for doubtful debts	4,248
	151,902

Question 7.7

Trading and Profit and Loss Account for the Year to 31 December 19X6

	£	£
Sales		234,481
Stock 1 January	32,193	
Purchases	164,770	
	196,963	
Less: Goods taken as drawings	(1,250)	
Stock 31 December	(34,671)	
Cost of goods sold		161,042
Gross profit		73,439
Profit on sale of van		500
		73,939
Rent and rates (3,000 − 300)	2,700	
General expenses	7,263	
Wages (26, 649 + 271)	26,920	
Bad debts (693 + 104)	797	
Depreciation	7,000	44,680
Net profit		29,259

Balance Sheet at 31 December 19X6

	£	£	£
Fixed assets			
Freehold land and buildings			114,000
Motor vans at cost (37,500 − 2,500 + 1,500)		36,500	
Less: Depreciation (15,450 + 7,000 − 1,500)		20,950	
			15,550
			129,550
Current assets			
Stock		34,671	
Debtors	20,911		
Less: Provision for doubtful debts (876 + 104)	980		
		19,931	
Prepaid rent and rates		300	
Cash		32,728	
		87,630	
Less: Current liabilities			
Creditors	13,006		
Accrued wages	271		
		13,277	
Working capital			74,353
			203,903
Capital			
At 1 January			193,894
Profit for 19X6			29,259
			223,153
Less: Drawings: Cash		18,000	
Stock		1,250	
			19,250
			203,903

Question 7.8

(a) **S. Top – Journal**

	Debit £	Credit £
1. Plant and machinery	2,750	
Repairs to machinery		2,750
Transfer of purchase of lathe wrongly recorded		
2. Repairs	350	
Manufacturing wages		350
Transfers of repair costs wrongly recorded		
3. Bad debts	1,290	
Debtors		1,290
Irrecoverable debt due from J. Jones written off		
4. Drawings	200	
Rates		200
Transfer of rates on S. Top's private house		
5. Purchases	1,500	
Creditors		1,500
Goods received but not recorded at year end		
6. Provision for depreciation	1,000	
Machinery		1,000
Fully-depreciated machine scrapped during year		
7. Drawings	150	
Purchases		150
Goods taken for S. Top's personal use		
8. Delivery	125	
Purchases		125
Transfer of delivery cost wrongly recorded		

(b) **Statement of effect of adjustments on profit**

	Decrease profit £	Increase profit £
1. Expense capitalized		2,750
3. Increase in bad debts	1,290	
4. Expense charged to owner		200
5. Increase in purchases	1,500	
7. Purchases charged to owner		150
	——	——
	2,790	3,100
		2,790
		——
Net increase in profit		310
		——

Question 8.1 (a) There are two main tests:

(i) Expenditure that enhances the ability of the firm to earn profits is capital, whereas expenditure designed merely to maintain the existing level of operation is revenue.

(ii) Capital expenditure is incurred on the purchase of assets that are expected to possess a useful life that extends over a number of accounting periods; moreover, it is not intended to sell these assets in the normal course of business. Revenue expenditure is incurred in acquiring goods and services that are consumed in a short space of time. A correct allocation is important, because otherwise profit and asset values are wrongly reported. For example, the misallocation of capital to revenue causes both profit and gross assets to be understated.

(b) (i) *Revenue* This is a normal repair to make good wear and tear.
(ii) *Capital* Hourly capacity is increased.
(iii) *Capital* This is part of the cost of acquiring the new asset.
(iv) *Capital* This increases the firm's productive capacity.
(v) *Capital* This expenditure is needed to make the plant ready for use.

Question 8.2

(a) **Bank Account for 19X3**

	£		£
Bank balance 1 Jan. 19X3	19,400	General expenses	2,500
Receipts	76,500	Cost of properties	85,250
		Legal expenses on	
		purchases	2,550
		Legal expenses on sales	1,250
		Improvements	1,780
		Closing balance	2,570
	95,900		95,900

(b) **Profit and Loss Account for 19X3***

	£	£
Sales		107,750
Less: Cost of properties sold:		
No. 1	30,250	
3 36,250 + 1,000 + 260	37,510	
4 24,000 + 750 + 1,000	25,750	
	93,510	
Selling expenses	1,250	
General expenses	2,500	
Net profit		97,260
		10,490

Balance Sheet at 31 December 19X3

	£		£
Properties at hand:		Opening capital	79,000
2	29,350	Profit	10,490
5 25,000 + 800 +			
520	26,320		
	55,670		
Bank balance	2,570		
Debtors	31,250		
	89,490		89,490

* An alternative presentation:	£	£
Sales		107,750
Opening stock	59,600	
Purchases (including legal expenses, on		
purchase and improvements)	89,580	
Closing stock	(55,670)	93,510
Gross profit		14,240
Less: Legal expenses on sales	1,250	
General expenses	2,500	3,750
Net profit		10,490

Question 8.3 (a)

	(i) Straight line	(ii) Diminishing Balance	(iii) Units of output
	£	£	£
1986	18,750	44,800	20,000
1987	25,000	26,880	25,000
1988	25,000	16,128	25,000
1989	25,000	9,677	25,000
1990	6,250	—	5,000
	100,000	97,485	100,000

Workings
Straight line: (£112,000−£12,000)/4 = £25,000 per annum (full year). Diminishing balance: 40 per cent charge applied to net book value. Units of output: (£112,000−£12,000)/20,000 (hours) = £5 per hour.

(b) **Machine Account**

	£		£
Opening balance	112,000	Asset disposal account	112,000

Provision for Depreciation Account

	£		£
Asset disposal account	31,250	Opening balance	18,750
		Depreciation account	12,500
	31,250		31,250

Asset Disposal Account

	£		£
Machine account	112,000	Provision for depreciation account	31,250
		Cash	80,000
		Profit and loss account	750
	112,000		112,000

Question 8.4

		£	£
(a) Goodwill			
Price paid			120,000
Less: Net assets acquired			
Fixed assets		71,500	
Stocks		20,000	
Debtors		10,000	
		101,500	96,500
Deduct trade creditors		5,000	
			23,500
(b) Goodwill at cost			23,500
Less: Amount written off (£23,500 ÷ 5)			4,700
			18,800

Question 8.5   The fundamental rule is that stock should be valued at the *lower* of cost and net realizable value, taking each item or groups of similar items separately.
    Valuation of stock calculated as follows:

Product	Cost	NRV	Lower of cost and NRV
A	2,400	2,760	2,400
B	1,290	740	740
C	3,680	750	750
D	2,950	4,760	2,950
E	6,280	9,730	6,280
Value of stock			13,120

Question 8.6   *Perpetual inventory* Stock records are written up on a regular basis to record receipts and issues of stock and the quantity on hand after each transaction. Sometimes the records are also maintained in terms of values and, where this is done, values for total issues (cost of goods sold) and closing stock are readily available under this system. Where values are not recorded, the cost of goods sold is obtained as the balancing item (see below).
    Periodic stock-take Stocks are physically counted and valued at the end of each accounting period. The figure for cost of goods sold is the balancing item obtained by applying the formula:

Opening stock + Purchases − Closing stock = Cost of goods sold.

Question 8.7   (a) Units of stock on hand: 235 − 155 = 80 (*workings*).
    Valuation of stock   £

(i)   FIFO: 75 units at £30   2,250
            5 units at £25   125
            ──   ────
            80   2,375
            ──   ────

(ii)   LIFO: 80 units at £20   1,600

(iii) AVCO: 80 units at £24.47 (£5,750 ÷ 23)   1,958

(b) Calculation of cost of goods sold (balancing item):

	FIFO £	LIFO £	AVCO £
Opening stock	0	0	0
Add: Purchases (*workings*)	5,750	5,750	5,750
Less: Closing stock	2,375	1,600	1,958
Cost of goods sold	3,375	4,150	3,792

(c) Calculation of gross profit:

	FIFO £	LIFO £	AVCO £
Sales (*workings*)	6,260	6,260	6,260
Less: Cost of goods sold	3,375	4,150	3,792
Gross profit	2,885	2,110	2,468

Workings

Purchases	Units	Price	£
January: 8	100	20	2,000
13	60	25	1,500
17	75	30	2,250
	235		5,750

Sales			
January: 14	125	40	5,000
22	30	42	1,260
	155		6,260

Question 8.8 (a) (i) *Down* LIFO uses older prices than FIFO and gives a higher value for the same volume of goods. Also net realizable value at 31 December 19X1 is lower than the FIFO value calculated on the basis of purchases immediately prior to the year end.

(ii) *Up* FIFO values stock at the most recent purchase price, and this is higher than the LIFO value.

(b) *LIFO* It gives the highest value for closing stock and hence the lowest value for cost of goods sold.

(c) *Lower of FIFO and net realizable value* Cost of goods sold is calculated by applying the formula;

$$\text{Opening stock} + \text{Purchases} - \text{Closing stock.}$$

Cost of goods sold will be lowest, and hence profit highest, when closing stock is greater than opening stock, and the difference between them is maximized.

(d) *LIFO* This method gives the lowest stock value at 31 December 19X3, and hence the highest cost of goods sold figure for the three-year period.

Answers (b) to (d) may alternatively be based on the following calculations:

	19X1 £	19X2 £	19X3 £	Totals £
LIFO				
Opening stock	—	96,480	87,360	—
Purchases	240,000	252,000	324,000	816,000
Closing stock	(96,480)	(87,360)	(100,320)	(100,320)
Cost of goods sold	143,520	261,120	311,040	715,680
FIFO				
Opening stock	—	96,000	86,400	—
Purchases	240,000	252,000	324,000	816,000
Closing stock	(96,000)	(86,400)	(105,600)	(105,600)
Cost of goods sold	144,000	261,600	304,800	710,400
Lower of FIFO and net realizable value				
Opening stock	—	88,800	81,600	—
Purchases	240,000	252,000	324,000	816,000
Closing stock	(88,800)	(81,600)	(105,600)	(105,600)
Cost of goods sold	151,200	259,200	300,000	710,400

Question 8.9 Examples are as follows:

(a) Insurance premiums received before the period covered by the insurance; rents received before the rental period.
(b) Cash sales of goods; sale of goods on credit where the cash is collected in the same accounting period.
(c) Collection of customers' accounts in the period following the sale; receipt of interest after the period to which it relates.
(d) Prepayment of insurance premiums or subscription fees.
(e) Payments for office salaries and telephone charges in the period in which they are used (debit entry is to an expense account).
(f) Payment of suppliers' accounts outstanding at the year end; payment for rent accrued at the year end.

Question 8.10   (a) Trading Account for 19X1

	£	£
Sales		100,000
Less: Opening stock	10,000	
Purchases	80,000	
Closing stock	(11,000)	
Cost of goods sold		79,000
Gross profit		21,000

(b) The effect of the revision is to reduce gross profit and, therefore, net profit by £3,000.

Question 9.1

Appropriation Account

	£	£		£	£
Salaries: Jack	10,000		Profit		42,000
Jill	7,500		Interest on drawings:		
Jane	5,000		Jack	600	
		22,500	Jill	450	
			Jane	400	
Interest on capital:					
Jack	3,600				1,450
Jill (W1)	2,700				
Jane	4,800				
		11,100			
Residue: Jack	3,940				
Jill	3,940				
Jane	1,970				
		9,850			
		43,450			43,450

Workings

W1. 12% × 20,000 (opening capital) + 12% × 5,000 × .5 (Capital introduced half way through the year) = 2,700.

Question 9.2   (a)

Appropration Account

	£		£
Share of profit:		Profit	42,000
Jack	14,000		
Jill	14,000		
Jane	14,000		
	42,000		42,000

(b) In the absence of an agreement to the contrary, the provisions of the Partnership Act 1890 apply. The profit is divided equally between the partners and there are no charges for salaries or interest.

Question 9.3

Current Accounts

	Ice £	Cube £		Ice £	Cube £
			Balance b/d	30,000	20,000
Drawings:			Share of profit	22,500	22,500
Cash	12,500	14,000			
Car disposal a/c	1,500				
Transfer to					
capital account	20,000	10,000			
Balance c/d	18,500	18,500			
	52,500	42,500		52,500	42,500

Capital Accounts

	Ice £	Cube £		Ice £	Cube £
Balance c/d	70,000	70,000	Balance b/d	50,000	60,000
			Transfer from		
			current account	20,000	10,000
	70,000	70,000		70,000	70,000

Question 9.4   (a) **Revaluation Account**

	£		£
Working capital	2,000	Fixed assets	5,000
Bush	4,000	Goodwill	9,000
Shrub	8,000		
	14,000		14,000
Fixed assets	5,000	Working capital	2,000
Goodwill	9,000	Bush	4,000
		Shrub	4,000
		Flower	4,000
	14,000		14,000

(b) Capital Accounts

	Bush £	Shrub £	Flower £		Bush £	Shrub £	Flower £
Revaluation account	4,000	4,000	4,000	Balance b/d	10,000	20,000	—
Balance c/d	10,000	24,000	10,000	Cash	—	—	14,000
				Revaluation account	4,000	8,000	—
	14,000	28,000	14,000		14,000	28,000	14,000

(c) Balance Sheet at 1 January 19X5

	£		£
Capital:			
Bush	10,000	Fixed assets	15,000
Shrub	24,000	Working capital	29,000*
Flower	10,000		
	44,000		44,000

Note
* Includes the cash received from Flower.

Question 9.5 (a) Realization Account

	£		£
Freehold land & property	80,000	Mars capital account:	
Equipment	9,000	Property	120,000
Motor car	3,000	Equipment	11,000
Stock	24,000	Stock	26,000
Debtors	6,500	Debtors	6,100
Cash – expenses	1,500	Total assets acquired	163,100
Profit on realization		Saturn capital account:	
Jupiter	21,000	Car	2,900
Mars	10,500		
Saturn	10,500		
	166,000		166,000

(b) Bank Account

	£		£
Mars capital account	90,000	Balance b/d	6,400
		Realization expenses	1,500
		Creditors	4,100
		Capital accounts:	
		Saturn	32,600
		Mars	45,400
	90,000		90,000

(c) Capital Account

	Jupiter £	Mars £	Saturn £		Jupiter £	Mars £	Saturn £
Realization account		163,100	2,900	Balance b/d	55,000	32,000	25,000
				Realization account	21,000	10,500	10,500
Mars	30,600			Jupiter		30,600	
Cash	45,400		32,600	Cash		90,000	
	76,000	163,100	35,500		76,000	163,100	35,500

(d) Balance Sheet at 1 July 1984

	£	£
Fixed assets		
Freehold land and premises		120,000
Equipment		11,000
		131,000
Current assets		
Stock	26,000	
Debtors	6,100	
		32,100
		163,100
Less:		
Loan from Jupiter	30,600	
Bank loan	90,000	
		120,600
		42,500
Financed by:		
Capital account – Mars		42,500

The above balance sheet shows that the balance on the capital account of Mars represents his personal investment in the business; a substantial part of the firm's assets are financed by funds from outside sources.

Question 9.6

Trading and Profit and Loss Account Year to 31 December 19X4

	£	£
Sales (200,000 + 6,400 + 5,460)		211,860
Purchases: 160,000 (bank)		
2,500 (cash)		
3,800 (creditors)		
−2,260 (drawings)		
	164,040	
Less: Closing stock	9,200	
Cost of goods sold		154,840
Gross profit		57,020
Less:		
Rent and rates (3,500 − 100)	3,400	
Light and heat (1,260 + 140)	1,400	
Depreciation (19,000 − 3,000)/5	3,200	
Wages	17,000	
Petrol	2,000	
Maintenance	1,000	
Advertising	900	
		28,900
Net profit		28,120
Appropriation:		
Minute	14,060	
Second	14,060	
		28,120

Balance Sheet at 31 December 19X4

	£	£	£
Van: Cost			19,000
Depreciation			3,200
			15,800
Current Assets:			
Stock		9,200	
Debtors		5,460	
Prepaid rent		100	
Cash		5,240	
		20,000	
Current liabilities:			
Trade creditors	3,800		
Accrued light and heat	140		
		3,940	
Working capital			16,060
			31,860

	Second	*Minute*	
Capital accounts	20,000	20,000	40,000
Current accounts:			
Profit	14,060	14,060	
Drawings: Cash	(18,000)	(16,000)	
Stock	(1,000)	(1,260)	
	(4,940)	(3,200)	(8,140)
			31,860

Question 9.7

Trading and Profit and Loss Account for the Year to 31 March 19X3

	£	£
Sales		150,000
Opening stock	30,000	
Purchases	110,000	
Goods lost	(700)	
Stock drawings	(340)	
Closing stock	(40,000)	
Cost of goods sold		98,960
Gross profit		51,040
Depreciation	1,500	
Wages (14,500 + 500)	15,000	
Rent (5,000 − 1,000)	4,000	
Expenses	3,000	
Heat and light	1,200	
Delivery	5,300	
		30,000
Net trading profit		21,040
Appropriation:		
Interest on drawings:		
Bean		200
Stalk		300
		21,540
Salaries		
Bean	2,000	
Stalk	4,000	
		6,000
		15,540
Interest:		
Bean	1,500	
Stalk	500	
		2,000
		13,540
Residue:		
Bean	6,770	
Stalk	6,770	
		13,540

Balance Sheet at 31 March 19X3

	£	£	£
Fixed assets			6,000
Less: Depreciation			1,500
			4,500
Current assets:			
Stock		40,000	
Debtors		14,000	
Debtor for goods lost		700	
Prepaid rent		1,000	
Cash		4,500	
		60,200	
Current liabilities:			
Creditors	11,500		
Accrued wages	500		
		12,000	
Working capital			48,200
			52,700

	Bean	*Stalk*	
Capital	30,000	10,000	40,000
Current accounts:			
Balance 1 April 19X2	3,000	5,000	
Interest on drawings	(200)	(300)	
Drawings: Cash	(7,000)	(9,000)	
Stock	(340)	—	
Interest on capital	1,500	500	
Salaries	2,000	4,000	
Share of residue	6,770	6,770	
	5,730	6,970	12,700
			52,700

Question 10.1 (a) Profit and Loss Account

	19X0 £000	19X1 £000
Gross profit	2,930	3,605
Less: Administration expenses	1,620	1,809
Selling costs	520	572
Distribution costs	140	164
Depreciation costs	250	300
	2,530	2,845
Net profit	400	760
Less: Proposed dividend	100	200
Transfer to general reserve	—	500
	100	700
Retained profit for the year	300	60
Add: Retained profit at 1 January	290	590
Retained profit at 31 December	590	650

Balance Sheet at 31 December

	19X0 £000	19X0 £000	19X1 £000	19X1 £000
Plant and machinery at cost		1,840		2,650
Less: Depreciation		520		820
		1,320		1,830
Current assets:				
Stock	724		771	
Debtors	570		524	
Bank	92		305	
	1,386		1,600	
Current liabilities:				
Creditors	416		480	
Dividend	100		200	
	516		680	
Working capital		870		920
		2,190		2,750
Financed by:				
Share capital		1,600		1,600
General reserve		—		500
Profit and loss account		590		650
		2,190		2,750

(b) The revised accounts show that the *retained* profit is much lower in 19X1, but the *net* profit earned is almost twice as high as in 19X0. The draft accounts do not distinguish between *charges* against profit and *appropriations* of profit, and the revised accounts show that the lower retained profit is principally due to the large transfer to general reserve that was not made in the previous year. The fact that profits have substantially increased fully justifies the directors' decision to increase the dividend to £200,000. A further point that should be considered is whether there is sufficient cash available to finance the proposed distribution. However, there is £305,000 in the bank account and this suggests that the company will have no difficulty in meeting the dividend payment when it falls due.

Question 10.2 (a) **Trading and Profit and Loss Account, Year to 31 October 1986**

	£		£
Sales			791,600
Less: Opening stock	113,400		
Purchases	458,200		
Closing stock	(121,300)	W1	
Cost of goods sold			450,300
Gross profit			341,300
Less: Discounts allowed less received	4,400	W2	
Bad and doubtful debts	3,700	W3	
Wages and salaries	69,900	W4	
Administrative expenses	33,700	W5	
Research and development expenditure	9,600		
Directors' remuneration	40,000		
Depreciation	57,000	W6	
Goodwill amortized	6,000		
Debenture interest	27,000		251,300
Net profit			90,000
Less: Corporation tax			33,000
			57,000
Retained profit at 1 November 1985			115,200
			172,200
Less: Ordinary dividends	20,000		
Transfer to machinery replacement reserve	15,000		35,000
Retained profit at 31 October 1986			137,200

(b) Balance Sheet at 31 October 1986

Fixed assets	£	£	£
Tangible	Cost	Depreciation	
Freehold premises	435,000	36,000	399,000
Machinery and equipment	60,000	30,000	30,000
Motor lorries	225,000	107,000	118,000
			547,000
Intangible: Goodwill			24,000

Current assets			
Stock		121,300	
Debtors		49,600 W7	
Bank		35,600	
		206,500	

Less: Creditors due within one year			
Creditors		31,400	
Corporation tax		33,000	
Dividends		20,000	
Accruals		15,900 W8	
		100,300	

Net current assets			106,200
Total assets less current liabilities			677,200
Less: Creditors due in more than one year			
12% Debentures			225,000
			452,200

Financed by:			
Called up share capital			200,000
Share premium account			100,000
Machinery replacement reserve			15,000
Retained profit			137,200
			452,200

W1   26,700 (NRV) + 47,800 (Cost) + 46,800 (NRV) = 121,300.
W2   14,200 − 9,800 = 4,400.
W3   2,900 (Bad debts) + 800 (Increase in doubtful debt provision) =   3,700.
W4   68,400 + 1,500 (Accruals) = 69,900.
W5   32,800 + 900 (Accruals) = 33,700.
W6   6,000 (Machinery and equipment) + 45,000 (Lorries) + 6,000 (Premises) = 57,000.
W7   54,100 − 4,500 (Provision for doubtful debts) = 49,600.
W8   1,500 + 900 + 13,500 = 15,900.

Question 10.3

(a) Accounting bases is the term used, in SSAP 2, to describe the various methods that have been developed for valuing assets and liabilities. For example, the alternative bases available to account for the decline in value of fixed assets include reducing balance basis, straight-line and the units of service method.

Accounting policies is the term used to describe the particular accounting bases adopted by a company for the purpose of valuing assets and liabilities when preparing the accounts. The policies adopted must be described by the company in its report. The accounting policies used by a company must be consistent with the following four fundamental accounting concepts:

   (i) The going concern concept, which assumes that the company will continue in business for the foreseeable future. The main significance of this assumption is that the liquidation values of fixed assets can be ignored and it is instead assumed that the company will remain in business long enough to enable the resources tied up in fixed assets to be fully recovered.

   (ii) The accruals concept requires revenues and expenses to be reported in the periodic profit and loss account as they are earned and incurred rather than when the amounts of cash are received and paid.

   (iii) The consistency concept requires the company to employ the same accounting policy for valuing a particular asset in each consecutive accounting period. The purpose of this is to enable comparisons to be made.

   (iv) The concept of prudence stipulates that a company should not take credit for profits before they are earned but should make provision for all foreseeable losses.

An accounting policy such as the reducing balance basis conforms to each of the four fundamental concepts. It spreads the cost of the fixed asset, over a number of accounting periods, on the assumption that the company will continue indefinitely as a going concern. It allocates the cost of the fixed asset less residual value between accounting procedures based on benefits received. This achieves compliance with both the accruals concept and the consistency concept. Compliance with the prudence concept is also assured because, by the time the asset is written off, all foreseeable losses are provided for.

(b) Compliance with the requirements of SSAP 2 goes a long way towards ensuring that the published accounts show a true and fair view. There are, however, other matters that require attention in the case of a limited company. It is necessary for the directors to take steps to ensure that there is compliance with the Companies Act 1985 and the many other SSAPs issued by the accounting profession. In the case of quoted companies, there are further stock exchange rules that have to be satisfied, for example, the obligation to publish interim accounting statements. These regulations are useful because they ensure an adequate level of disclosure, comparability between accounting periods and comparability between one company and another.

It is, of course, important for the directors to ensure that their company's accounts portray a true and fair view, because a reputation for openness and frankness is likely to make it easier to raise the finance needed to carry on business operations. At the same time, it is necessary to guard against the possibility of the directors manipulating the accounts in order to make the company appear a more attractive proposition than is justified by the underlying commercial performance. It is for this reason that the Companies Act makes provision for appointment of independent auditors to report whether the accounts prepared and presented to the shareholders and filed with the Registrar of Companies portray a true and fair view.

Question 10.4

Profit and Loss Account Year ended 31 March 19X6

	£	£
Gross profit		1,020,800
Less: Administration expenses	216,900	
Selling expenses	150,400	
Bad debts written off	8,700	
General repairs and maintenance	25,200	
Debenture interest	30,000	
Depreciation, 25% of £1,300,000−£512,000	197,000	628,200
Net profit before tax		392,600
Corporation tax		150,000
Net profit after tax		242,600
Less: Proposed dividend		75,000
Retained profit for the year		167,600
Retained profit at 1 April 19X5	1,039,000	
Less: Bonus issue	1,000,000 W1	39,000
Retained profit at 31 March 19X6		206,600

Balance Sheet as at 31 March 19X6

	£	£	£
Fixed assets			
Freehold land and buildings at valuation			900,000
Plant and machinery at cost		1,420,000 W2	
Accumulated depreciation to April 19X5	512,000		
Charge for current year	197,000	709,000	711,000
			1,611,000
Current assets			
Stock and work in progress		984,020	
Debtors and prepayments	370,080		
Less: Provision for doubtful debts	15,000	355,080	
Bank balance		268,000	
		1,607,100	
Less: Current liabilities			
Creditors and accrued expenses		471,500 W2	
Debenture interest outstanding		15,000	
Proposed dividend		75,000	
Corporation tax due 1 Jan. 19X7		150,000	
		711,500	
Net current assets			895,600
Total assets less current liabilities			2,506,600
Less: 10% Debentures repayable 19X9			300,000
			2,206,600
Financed by:			
Ordinary share capital: Authorized			2,000,000
Issued (£1 shares)			1,500,000
Revaluation reserve			500,000
Retained profit			206,600
			2,206,600

Workings

W1 The directors could alternatively choose to make part of the bonus issue from revaluation reserve.

W2 Includes £120,000 for plant delivered on 31 March 19X6.

Question 10.5   The purpose of the bonus issue is to give formal acknowledgement to the fact that profits, retained by the directors in previous years, have been permanently invested in business assets and no longer remain available for distribution. At 31 March 19X6 the company has cash available of £268,000, of which £75,000 is required to finance the proposed dividend, and £120,000 is needed to pay for the plant recently purchased. This leaves a modest balance to meet operating expenses. It is therefore clear that the company has no surplus cash resources, and it was therefore perfectly reasonable to capitalize the bulk of the retained profits. It is possible to argue that a smaller bonus issue might have been made some years earlier, but certain formalities are involved and it is not a process management will wish to undertake on a regular basis.

Question 10.6   (a)

Profit and Loss Account, Year ended 31 December 19X9

	£	£
Gross profit on trading		416,500
Less: Rent and rates (£30,000−£6,000)	24,000	
Office salaries	142,600	
Advertising costs	21,000	
Transport costs	23,600	
Depreciation	37,500	248,700
Net profit before tax		167,800
Taxation		83,900
Net profit after tax		83,900
Retained profit at beginning of year	278,500	
Less: Bonus issue	100,000	178,500
Retained profit at end of year		262,400

Balance Sheet at 31 December 19X9

	£	£
Freehold property at valuation		650,000
Furniture and equipment at cost	375,000	
Less: Accumulated depreciation £59,500 + £37,500	97,000	278,000
		928,000

Current assets		
Stock and work-in-progress	104,200	
Debtors and prepayments £105,000 + £6,000	111,000	
Deposit	10,000	
Temporary investment	60,000	
Balance at bank	72,000	
	357,200	

Current liabilities		
Creditors and accruals	85,300	
Taxation due 1 Jan. 19Y0	103,600	
1 Jan. 19Y1	83,900	
	272,800	

Working capital		84,400
		1,012,400

Financed by:		
Ordinary share capital £500,000 + £100,000		600,000
Revaluation reserve		150,000
Profit and loss account		262,400
		1,012,400

(b) A dividend of 10p per share on the revised share capital of £600,000 would involve a payment of £60,000. There is no doubt that the bank balance at 31 December 19X9 appears sufficient to support this payment, and the after tax profits for the year are £83,900. Consideration must, however, be given to the company's future commitments. During January 19Y0, a tax payment of £103,6000 must be made as well as £40,000 for the new equipment when delivery takes place. This would suggest that bank overdraft facilities will be required during January even if no dividend is paid, although the position would be partially alleviated by the sale of the temporary investment. Funds generated from trading operations during 19X9 amounted to £205,300 (profit £167,800 and depreciation £37,500), and this should soon make good any cash shortage if the results are repeated during 19Y0. Nevertheless a dividend payment of £60,000 is probably unwise at this stage.

Question 11.1

Manufacturing, trading and profit and loss account for the year to 31 March 19X6

	£	£	£
Raw materials: Opening stock		12,000	
Purchases		40,000	
		52,000	
Closing stock		(14,000)	
Consumed		38,000	
Production wages		30,000	
		68,000	
Depreciation		7,000	
Rent		4,800	
Light, heat and power		9,000	
Overheads		17,500	
		106,300	
Work in progress at 1 April X5		2,000	
		108,300	
at 31 March X6		(7,000)	
Manufacturing cost of goods completed		101,300	
Manufacturing profit (15% of total cost)		15,195	
Transfer to trading account		116,495	
Sales			208,000
Finished goods: Stock at 1 April X5		11,500	
Transfers		116,495	
		127,995	
Stock at 31 March X6		(13,800)	
			114,195
Gross profit on trading			93,805
Manufacturing profit			15,195
Carried forward			109,000

	£	£	£
Brought forward			109,000
Administration expenses:			
Rent	1,600		
Light, heat and power	3,000		
Expenses	7,500		
Salaries	15,000		
Hire of equipment	7,000		
Postage and telephone	5,350		
		39,450	
Finance costs:			
Bank charges	1,250		
Loan interest	3,000		
		4,250	
Delivery costs:			
Van hire	2,000		
Wages	7,000		
Petrol, etc.	1,000		
		10,000	
Adjustment for unrealized profit (W1)		300	
			54,000
Net profit			55,000

Balance Sheet at 31 March 19X6

	£	£	£
Fixed assets at cost			70,000
Less: Accumulated depreciation			21,000
			49,000
Current assets			
Stocks: Raw materials		14,000	
Work in progress		7,000	
Finished goods (W1)		12,000	
		33,000	
Debtors		20,000	
		53,000	
Current liabilities			
Overdraft	10,000		
Creditors	5,000		
	15,000		
Working capital			38,000
			87,000
Financed by:			
Capital at 1 April 19X5			50,000
Profit for year			55,000
			105,000
Less: Drawings			48,000
Capital at 31 March 19X6			57,000
Loan			30,000
			87,000

W1: The transfer price of stock is 115 per cent of its cost. To convert it to cost, it must be multiplied by 100/115, i.e.:

$$£13,800 \times 100/115 = £12,000.$$

The unrealized profit in closing stock is £13,800 − £12,000 = £1,800.
The required adjustment to the provision is £1,800−£1,500 (opening balance) = £300.

Question 11.2 (£000)

	Branch			Total
	1	*2*	*3*	
Sales	250	300	175	725
Cost of goods sold	125	160	67	352
Gross profit	125	140	108	373
Branch expenses	60	85	47	192
Branch surplus	65	55	61	181
Head office expenses				90
Profit				91

Question 11.3

Hire Purchase Trading and Profit and Loss Account for 19X5

	£	£
Cash received		33,600
Cost of sales:		
VCs (250 × 96)	24,000	
EPs (200 × 144)	28,800	
	52,800	
Less: Stock held by HP debtors (W1)	33,600	
		19,200
		14,400
Gross profit		
Expenses (1,980 + 460)	2,440	
Bank interest	1,086	
		3,526
Net profit		10,874

Balance Sheet 31 December 19X5

	£			£
Stock with H.P. debtors	33,600 (W1)	Capital at start		10,000
Stocks held		Add profit		10,874
VCs	4,800			
EPs	7,200 12,000			20,874
		Less drawings		3,500
				17,374
		Current liabilities	£	
		VCs	4,800	
		Expenses	460	
		Bank overdraft	22,966 28,226	
	45,600			45,600

Workings

W1   Stock with H.P. debtors

	Vacuum Cleaners	*Electric Polishers*
C = Cost of goods sold =	24,000	28,800
S = Total selling price =	$250 \times 168 = 42,000$	$200 \times 252 = 50,400$
Cash collected	21,000	12,600
I = Instalments due in future accounting periods	21,000	37,800

V = Stock out on HP =

$$\frac{I}{S} \times C = \qquad \frac{21,000}{42,000} \times 24,000 = \underline{12,000} \quad \frac{37,800}{50,400} \times 28,800 = \underline{21,600}$$

	Total
Vacuum cleaners	12,000
Electric polishers	21,600
	£33,600

Question 11.4

Balance Sheet of Sharpner at 1 January 19X8

	£	£
Fixed assets		
Land and buildings (32,100 + 15,000)		47,100
Motor vans (20,000 + 2,700)		22,700
Goodwill (W1)		5,700
		75,500
Current assets		
Stock (10,700 + 5,800)	16,500	
Debtors (7,600 + 3,000)	10,600	
Cash (W2)	1,200	
	28,300	
Current liabilities		
Trade creditors (7,000 + 3,200)	10,200	
Working capital		18,100
		93,600
Financed by:		
Capital		68,600
Loan		25,000
		93,600

Workings

W1. *Goodwill*	£	£
Paid		29,000
Acquired: Land and buildings	15,000	
Motor van	2,700	
Stock	5,800	
Debtors	3,000	
	26,500	
Creditors	3,200	
		23,300
		5,700

W2 Cash

	£
Opening balance	5,200
Loan raised	25,000
Paid to Pencil	(29,000)
	1,200

Question 11.5 (a) Bank Account

	£		£
Capital	50,000	Purchases (W2)	72,664
Sales (W1)	86,019	Expenses (W3)	12,976
Sellup's debtors	2,740	Purchase of business	40,000
		Paid to Sellup	2,610
		Closing balance	10,509
	138,759		138,759

(b) Trading and Profit and Loss Account 19X3

	£	£
Sales		92,968
Cost of sales		71,034
Gross profit		21,934
Expenses	13,168	
Depreciation	395	
		13,563
Net profit		8,371

Balance Sheet at 31 December 19X3

	£	£	£
Fixed assets			
Freehold land and buildings			22,100
Motor vans		1,975	
Less Depreciation		395	
			1,580
Goodwill (W4)			6,933
			30,613
Current assets			
Stock		15,594	
Debtors		6,949	
Bank		10,509	
		33,052	
Current liabilities			
Purchases	4,972		
Expenses	192		
Sellup (2,740−2,610)	130		
		5,294	
Working capital			27,758
			58,371
Financed by:			
Capital			
Balance at 1 January			50,000
Profit			8,371
			58,371

Workings

W1 Cash from sales

	£
Sales	92,968
Less Closing debtors	6,949
	86,019

W2 Cash to suppliers

	£
Cost of sales	71,034
Plus Closing stock	15,594
Less Opening stock	(8,992)
Purchases	77,636
Less Closing creditors	4,972
	72,664

W3 Cash for expenses

	£
Cost of expenses	13,168
Less Closing creditor	192
	12,976

W4 Goodwill

	£	£
Purchase price		40,000
Assets taken over:		
Freehold land	22,100	
Motor van	1,975	
Stock	8,992	
		33,067
		6,933

Question 11.6

Realization Account

	£		£
Premises	27,000	Creditors	10,000
Stock and debtors	29,000	Purchaser	50,000
Loss on equipment	1,000		
Profit transferred to capital account	3,000		
	60,000		60,000

Equipment Account

	£		£
Balance b/d	5,000	Cash	4,000
		Loss transferred to realization account	1,000
	5,000		5,000

Cash Account

	£		£
Purchaser	50,000	Balance b/d	3,000
Equipment	4,000	Purlin – Capital	51,000
	54,000		54,000

Capital Account

	£		£
Motor car	2,000	Balance b/d	50,000
Cash	51,000	Profit on realization	3,000
	53,000		53,000

Question 11.7

	£
Sales (W1)	137,000
Gross profit (25% × 137,000)	34,250
Cost of goods sold	102,750
Opening stock	66,000
Purchases (W2)	64,800
Closing stock (balancing figure)	(28,050)
	102,750
Theoretical closing stock	28,050
Undamaged stock	18,000
Stock lost	10,050

Workings

W1 Sales	£	W2 Purchases for resale	£
Cash from debtors	97,000	Cash paid	68,000
Discounts allowed	1,000	Discounts received	400
Closing debtors	57,000	Closing creditors	39,000
Opening debtors	(54,000)	Opening creditors	(42,000)
Cash sales	36,000	Drawings	(600)
	137,000		64,800

Question 12.1

(a) Gross profit margin

$$\frac{54,000}{180,000} \times 100 = 30\%$$

Net profit as a % of sales

$$\frac{15,000}{180,000} \times 100 = 8.3\%$$

Return on capital employed

$$\frac{15,000}{150,000} \times 100 = 10\%$$

(b) An increase in the ROCE to 12.5 per cent would require additional profit of £150,000 × 2.5% = £3,750. The gross profit margin is 30 per cent and an additional turnover of £3,750 × (100 ÷ 30) = £12,500 would produce the required increase in net profit.

Question 12.2

(a) 31 December	19X5 £	19X6 £
Current assets	90,000	120,000
Less: Current liabilities	45,000	55,500
Working capital	45,000	64,500
Working capital ratio	2:1	2.16:1

(b) 31 December 19X6:	£
Current assets per balance sheet	120,000
Current liabilities, assuming a working capital ratio of 2:1	60,000
Current liabilities per balance sheet	55,000
Maximum permissible dividend	4,500

(c)   The directors have made an additional net investment of £31,500 in fixed assets, but this is amply covered by the retained profits of £46,500 (£51,000 − dividend of £4,500) and the working capital ratio has been maintained at 2:1. The financial policy pursued by the directors appears a little less sound when we look at the cash position. The heavy investment in stock has been at the expense of cash; debtors have also increased, but at a rate that is not unreasonable in relation to the other changes.

Question 12.3

	19X1			19X2		
Return on capital employed	$\frac{200}{700}$	× 100	28.6%	$\frac{250}{720}$	× 100	34.7%
Working capital			200			170
Working capital ratio	$\frac{300}{100}$	: 1	3:1	$\frac{350}{180}$	: 1	1.9:1
Liquidity ratio	$\frac{125+25}{100}$	: 1	1.5:1	$\frac{150}{180}$	:1	0.8:1

Workings

Balance Sheet, 31 December

	19X1 £000	19X1 £000	19X2 £000	19X2 £000
Fixed assets		500		550
Current assets: Stock	150		200	
Trade debtors	125		150	
Cash at bank	25		—	
	300		350	
Less: Current liabilities: Trade creditors	80		100	
Proposed dividend	20		60	
Overdraft	—		20	
	100		180	
Working capital		200		170
Shareholders' equity (capital employed)		700		720

Profit and Loss Account

	19X1 £000	19X1 £000	19X2 £000	19X2 £000
Sales		2,000		3,000
Less: Cost of sales	1,000		1,450	
Overhead costs	800	1,800	1,300	2,750
Net profit		200		250

(b) Lock Ltd earned a high rate of return on the shareholders' investment during 19X1, which has been improved on during 19X2. The balance sheet, at 31 December 19X1, shows a strong financial position with the working capital and liquidity ratios each at a high level for a wholesale trading company. There has been a significant decline in the solvency position during the year. The ratios suggest that the company will find it difficult to meet its debts as they fall due for payment. The proposal to pay a final dividend three times last year's level may need to be reconsidered.

Question 12.4   (a)

		1983	1984
(i)	Rate of stock turnover	7.8 times (47 days)	5.4 times (68 days)
(ii)	Rate of debtors turnover	12.0 times (30 days)	12.0 times (30 days)
(iii)	Rate of creditors turnover	7.8 times (47 days)	8.5 times (43 days)
(iv)	Working capital ratio	2:1	1.85:1
(v)	Percentage return on capital employed	21.9%	34.9%

(b) The rate of stock turnover has slowed down significantly during the year; goods now remain in stock for three weeks longer than was previously the case. The company's debt collection procedures appear efficient, and the average period for which bills remain outstanding has remained fairly stable at 30 days. There has been a modest decline in the working capital ratio from 2:1 (the accepted norm) to 1.85:1. This is not a cause for concern, particularly in view of the fact that there are no indications of cash-flow problems. Indeed, the company is now managing to pay its creditors more quickly than in the previous year.

The percentage return on capital employed has risen significantly from 21.9 to 34.9 per cent. This will be welcomed by the shareholders. The signs are that the significant expansion, during 1984, has been entirely successful. A note of caution may be sounded concerning the slow down in the rate of stock turnover, which may lead to liquidity probems if it is not arrested.

Question 12.5 (a)

Trading and Profit and Loss Accounts for 19X5

	Metalmax		Precision Products	
	£000	£000	£000	£000
Sales		800		950
Less: Variable cost of sales	640		760	
Depreciation	54		54	
Cost of sales		694		814
Gross profit		106		136
Less: Administration expenses	30		30	
Selling expenses	45	75	60	90
Net profit		31		46

Balance Sheets at 31 December 19X5

	Metalmax		Precision Products	
	£000	£000	£000	£000
Plant and machinery at cost		360		360
Less: Depreciation		164		164
	120	196	200	196
Current assets:	120		200	
Stocks and work in progress	—		—	
Other current assets	240		400	
	120		320	
Less: Current liabilities				
Working capital	—		—	
		120		80
		316		276
Share capital		200		200
Reserves		116		76
		316		276

(b)

Accounting ratios	Metalmax	Precision Products
Gross profit margin	13.3%	14.3%
Net profit percentage	3.9%	4.8%
Return on total capital employed	7.1%	7.7%
Return on owners' equity	9.8%	16.7%
Working capital ratio	2:1	1.25:1
Liquidity ratio	1:1	0.6:1

Metalmix is the more solvent whereas Precision Products is the more profitable.

Variable cost of sales is 80 per cent in the case of both companies. Precision Products produces the higher gross profit margin because, on the basis of an identical investment in fixed assets, it produces a significantly higher level of sales. The selling expenses of Precision Products are much higher, perhaps due to the fact that they advertise their products more heavily and distribute them more widely. However, the company retains its advantage and achieves the higher net profit margin. The rates of return on both versions of capital employed are higher at Precision Products. The difference is substantial in the case of return on owners' equity. This is because a large proportion of Precision Products' current assets are funded out of the 'free' finance provided by trade creditors. The consequence of this, however, is that Precision Products' solvency position, at the end of 19X5, is extremely weak. Metalmax, with a working capital ratio and liquidity ratio in line with conventional 'norms', is in a sound financial condition.

Question 12.6 (a)

	Hot Ltd		Cold Ltd	
	Year 1	Year 2	Year 1	Year 2
	£	£	£	£
Profit before finance charges	110,000	190,000	110,000	190,000
Loan interest	30,000	30,000	75,000	75,000
Profit before tax	80,000	160,000	35,000	115,000
Corporation tax	40,000	80,000	17,500	57,500
Profit after tax	40,000	80,000	17,500	57,500
Dividends	40,000	80,000	17,500	57,500

(b)　Return on ordinary
　　shareholders' capital　　　10%　　　20%　　　7%　　　23%

(c)　Changes in the relative performance of the companies over the two-year period are explicable in terms of the financial effects of gearing. Cold Ltd is relatively high-geared and a disproportionately large slice of the company's earnings is required to finance debt capital when profits are low. In year 1 the pre-tax return on long-term capital is 11 per cent (£110,000/£1,000,000 × 100) but the interest rate payable on loans is 15 per cent producing a pre-tax return of only 7 per cent for the shareholders of Cold Ltd. This may be contrasted with Hot Ltd where the claims of the debenture holders are far less and so the ordinary shareholders get more, in this case 10 per cent. The position alters as profits rise. Additional profits of £80,000 represent a return of 10 per cent on the investment made by the shareholders of Hot Ltd but 16 per cent on the shareholders of Cold Ltd's investment. Therefore, the return to the ordinary shareholders of Hot Ltd increases at only a slightly faster rate than profits before finance charges, whereas the return earned for the shareholders of Cold Ltd increases three times more quickly.

Question 13.1

Worksheet

	19X1		19X2		Differences	
					Sources	Appli-cations
	£	£	£	£	£	£
Fixed assets:						
Plant at cost	52,000		70,000			18,000
Less: Depreciation	16,500	35,500	22,700	47,300	6,200	
Transport at cost	10,000		10,000			
Less: Depreciation	3,600	6,400	4,800	5,200	1,200	
		41,900		52,500		
Current assets:						
Stocks	10,200		12,600			2,400
Debtors	8,300		13,700			5,400
Bank	4,900		—		4,900	
	23,400		26,300			
Less: Current liabilities						
Trade creditors	5,100		5,800		700	
Bank overdraft	—		1,300		1,300	
	5,100		7,100			
Working capital		18,300		19,200		
		60,200		71,700		
Financed by:						
Share capital		50,000		54,000	4,000	
Profit and loss account		10,200		17,700	7,500	
		60,200		71,700	25,800	25,800

Statement of Funds for 19X2

Sources of funds	£	£
Profit		7,500
Add: Depreciation		7,400
		———
Funds generated from operations		14,900
Funds from other sources:		
Share capital		4,000
		———
		18,900
Applications of funds		
Purchase of plant		18,000
		———
Increase in working capital		900
Changes in working capital items		
Decrease in working capital		
Bank	(6,200)	
Trade creditors	(700)	
Increase in working capital		
Stocks	2,400	
Debtors	5,400	900
	———	———

Question 13.2 (a) The statement of funds contains full details of resources that came available to the firm during an accounting period and the way in which those funds have been employed. The presentation of data is analysed to distinguish long-term from short-term movements of funds. The first part of the statement lists transactions that *effect* the level of working capital whereas the second part of the statement *analyses* the change in working capital between the end of one accounting period and another. The purpose of the statement of funds is to answer the following kinds of question: 'What happened to the proceeds arising from the share issue?' 'How did the company manage to expand in the same year that it suffered an operating loss?' 'What sources were used to finance the acquisition of a new business?'

It is quite right to describe the statement of funds as 'hybrid'. The calculation of the bulk of the items is based on the working capital conception of funds, i.e. transactions that cause, or represent, changes in working capital are included. The exceptions are taxation and dividends, which are reported on the cash basis to comply with SSAP 10 and generally accepted accounting practice.

(b) Statement of Source and Application of Funds year to 31 August 1985

	£	£	
Source of funds			
Profit before tax		28,200	W1
Add: Depreciation		9,150	W2
		———	
Funds generated from operations		37,350	
Funds from other sources:			
Share issue		15,000	
		———	
		52,350	
Application of funds			
Purchase of fixed assets	36,900		
Repayment of debentures	3,000		
Taxation paid	8,550		
Dividends paid	6,750	55,200	
	———	———	
		(2,850)	
Increase (decrease) in working capital items			
Increase in stock	3,000		
Decrease in debtors	(2,550)		
Increase in creditors	(1,350)		
Decrease in bank	(1,950)	(2,850)	
	———	———	

W1 4,950 (Increase in retained profits) + 4,500 (Increase in general reserve) + 9,000 (Proposed dividends) + 9,750 (Taxation).
W2 50,250 (Accumulated depreciation at 31.8.85) − 41,100 (Accumulated depreciation at 31.8.84.

Question 13.3

Worksheet

	Balance Sheet 31 March		Differences	
	19X3 £	*19X4* £	*Sources* £	*Appli- cations* £
Share capital	500,000	600,000	100,000	
Retained profit	395,800	427,100	31,300	
10% Debentures	200,000	300,000	100,000	
Creditors	179,800	207,500	27,700	
Proposed dividend	50,000	60,000	10,000	
Bank overdraft	—	36,900	36,900	
	1,325,600	1,631,500		
Plant at cost	658,300	796,900		138,600
Less: Depreciation	263,500	371,600	108,100	
	394,800	425,300		
Freehold property	300,000	350,000		50,000
Stock	327,100	608,300		281,200
Debtors	265,700	247,900	17,800	
Cash at bank	38,000	—	38,000	
	1,325,600	1,631,500	469,800	469,800

Statement of Source and Application of Funds

	£	£
Sources of funds		
Net profit		191,300 W1
Add: Depreciation	295,600	
Loss on sale of plant and equipment	33,000 W2	328,600
Funds generated from operations		519,900
Funds from other sources		
Debentures issued	100,000	
Sale of plant and equipment	169,500	269,500
		789,400
Applications of funds		
Freehold property	50,000	
Plant and equipment	528,600 W1	
Dividend proposed	60,000	638,600
Increase in working capital		150,800
Changes in working capital items		
Decrease in working capital		
Creditors	(27,700)	
Dividend	(10,000)	
Bank	(74,900)	
Debtors	(17,800)	
Increase in working capital		
Stock	281,200	150,800

Workings

W1

	Plant £	Depreciation £	Profit £
Net increase (worksheet)	138,600	108,100	31,300
Add: Sale of plant	390,000	187,500*	
Proposed dividend			60,000
Bonus issue			100,000†
Gross changes	528,600	295,600	191,300

* Accumulated depreciation £187,500 = Cost, £390,000 − Book value, £202,500.
† The bonus issue is a book entry and does not result in a flow of funds. It must therefore be added back to profit so that funds generated from operations is stated correctly and so that the increase in share capital does *not* appear as a source of funds.
W2 Loss on sale, £33,000 = £202,500 (Book value of plant sold) − £169,500 (Sales proceeds).

To comply with SSAP 10, entitled the Statement of Source and Application of Funds, dividends and tax must be accounted for on the *cash* basis rather than the *accruals* basis, i.e. the amount shown as an application would be the amount paid *during* the year rather than the amount paid and provided for the year. Use of the cash basis to account for dividends, in the above example, results in the payment of £50,000 reported as an application and the increase in the dividend provision omitted from the list of changes in working capital items. A disadvantage of this procedure is that the actual change in working capital does not appear in the statement of funds.

Question 13.4

(a) **Cash flow statement for 19X5**

	£	£
Opening bank balance		23,600
Source of cash		
Profit (£5,500 + £44,000)	49,500	
Add: Depreciation	27,200	
	———	
Funds generated from operations	76,700	
Increase in trade creditors	14,200	
Decrease in trade debtors	2,700	93,600
	———	———
		117,200
Application of cash		
Purchase of fixed assets	30,000	
Dividends	44,000	
Debentures repaid	80,000	
Increase in stock	1,100	155,100
	———	———
Closing bank overdraft		(37,900)

(b) The company plans to pay out nearly all of its profits in the form of dividends, while the funds retained in the business by way of the depreciation charge have been used to purchase fixed assets. There are no other long-term sources of finance and the debentures have been repaid by increasing the amount of credit taken from suppliers and running down the bank balance. The result is a large bank overdraft and, probably, severe liquidity problems.

Question 13.5

(a) **Statement of Funds for 19X8**

Sources of funds	£000	£000
Net profit from ordinary activities		720
Add: Depreciation		350
Funds generated from operations		1,070
Funds from other sources		
Share issue (500+200)	700	
Long-term loan	300	
Sale of investment	130	1,130
		2,200
Applications of funds		
Purchase of plant	410	
Dividends paid	400	810
Increase in working capital		1,390
Changes in working capital items		
Decrease in working capital		
Increase in creditors	(200)	
Increase in working capital		
Increase in stocks	1,220	
Increase in debtors	40	
Increase in short-term loans and deposits at bank	330	1,390

(b)

	19X7	*19X8*
Accounting ratios		
Working capital	2:1	3.1:1
Liquidity	1:1	1.2:1

The financial position at the end of 19X7 appears satisfactory when judged on the basis of relevant accounting ratios. The liquidity ratio is 1:1 and the working capital ratio is 2:1, both of which are about right for an engineering firm. At the end of 19X1, the working capital appears to be too high and the company is verging on excess liquidity.

The statement of funds shows that the company both raised and generated long-term funds significantly in excess of present business requirements. Funds generated from operations more than cover the dividend and plant acquisition, yet the company has issued shares, raised a loan and benefited from the sale of investments. A great deal of the surplus finance is tied up in stocks; a non-income producing asset. The company's system of stock control should be examined to check whether it is being operated efficiently.

The effect of financial developments during 19X8 is a very strong financial position at the end of the year, but there is some doubt whether available resources are being effectively employed. Perhaps additional resources have been raised to finance *future* expansion, but there is no indication that this is the case.

Question 14.1

Rock Ltd – forecast results for additional sales

Proposal	(i)		(ii)		(iii)	
Additional sales (in units)	25,000	50,000	25,000	50,000	25,000	50,000
Process X						
Materials	5,000	10,000				
Wages	7,500	15,000	80p ×	80p ×		
Depreciation	12,000	12,000	25,000	50,000		
Rent	8,000	8,000				
To process Y	32,500	45,000	20,000	40,000		
					180p ×	180p ×
Process Y					25,000	50,000
Materials	2,500	5,000	2,500	5,000		
Wages	10,000	20,000	10,000	20,000		
Depreciation	12,000	12,000	12,000	12,000		
Rent	8,000	8,000	8,000	8,000		
Cost of production	65,000	90,000	52,500	85,000	45,000	90,000
General expenses	2,000	4,000	2,000	4,000	2,000	4,000
Net profit (loss)	(17,000)	6,000	(4,500)	11,000	3,000	6,000
Sales	50,000	100,000	50,000	100,000	50,000	100,000

Question 14.2

(a)

	£	£	£	£	£	£
Sales		46,000		92,000		138,000
Variable cost	25,300		50,600		75,900	
Depreciation	3,600		7,200		10,800	
General expenses	10,000		14,000		18,000	
Interest*	3,900		9,300		14,700	
		42,800		81,100		119,400
Profit		3,200		10,900		18,600

* Calculation:

		£		£		£
Cost of plant		36,000		72,000		108,000
Available for investment		10,000		10,000		10,000
Balance to be borrowed		26,000		62,000		98,000
Borrowings at 15%		3,900		9,300		14,700

(b) Eagles can either retain ownership of the business or sell it to Troon Ltd and remain as manager. Under either of these options his income varies according to the level of sales, and is calculated as follows:

	£ Existing	£ + 46,000	£ + 92,000	£ +138,000
Sales				
Retain ownership:				
Existing profit	20,000	20,000	20,000	20,000
Profit from exports	—	3,200	10,900	18,600
Total income	20,000	23,200	30,900	38,600
Sell to Troon Ltd:				
Invest proceeds of sale to earn annual interest	12,000	12,000	12,000	12,000
Salary as manager	14,000	14,000	14,000	14,000
Bonus for additional sales	—	3,000	6,000	9,000
Total	26,000	29,000	32,000	35,000

It can be seen that Eagles is better off to sell the business and work as manager unless the largest increase in sales under consideration can be achieved. He must consider whether this is likely. Also, the relief of no longer having the responsibility of both owning and managing the business may be attractive together with the possession of personal capital in the form of cash. These considerations may induce him to sell the business even if he considers the higher income from retention can probably be achieved.

Question 14.3(a)

Summary profit and loss account 19X4

	£000
Sales (60,000 × £5)	300
Variable costs (60,000 × £3*)	180
Total contribution	120
Fixed costs†	100
Net profit	20

Notes
*£5 (Selling price) − £2 (Contribution) = £3 (Variable cost).
† Balancing figure.

(b)

$$\frac{\text{Fixed costs}}{\text{Contribution}} = \frac{£100,000}{£2} = 50,000 \text{ units}$$

$$50,000 \times £5 = £250,000$$

(c) **Summary profit and loss account 19X5**

	£000
Sales (90,000 × £4.50)	405
Variable costs (90,000 × £2)	180
Total contribution	225
Fixed costs (£100,000+£80,000)	180
Net profit	45

(d)

$$\frac{\text{Fixed costs}}{\text{Contribution}} = \frac{£180,000}{(£4.50 - £2)} = 72,000 \text{ units}$$

$$72,000 \times £4.50 = £324,000$$

Question 14.4

Workings

	Output = 0	Output = 100,000
19X4		
Revenue	0	£500,000
Variable cost	0	£300,000
Fixed cost	£100,000	£100,000
Total cost	£100,000	£400,000
19X5		
Revenue	0	£450,000
Variable cost	0	£200,000
Fixed cost	£180,000	£180,000
Total cost	£180,000	£380,000

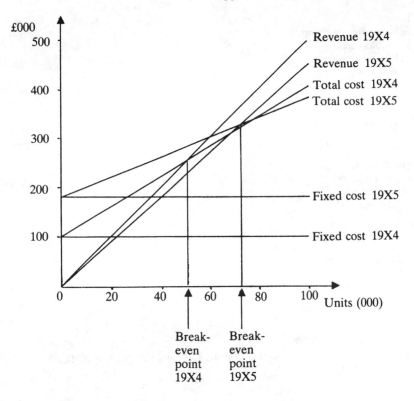

£000

Question 14.5

(a)

	£	£
Sales		400,000
Raw materials	100,000	
Wages	200,000	
Depreciation	20,000	
		320,000
Gross profit		80,000
General expenses (20,000 + 15,000*)	35,000	
Interest	10,000	
		45,000
Net profit		35,000

(b)

	£	£
Selling price per unit		2.00
Variable costs:		
Raw materials	.50	
Wages	.30	
		.80
Contribution		1.20
Fixed costs:		
Depreciation		20,000
Interest		20,000
Expenses*		15,000
		55,000
Additional profit:		
Profit under plan 1		35,000
Existing profit		20,000
		15,000

$$\text{Sales} = \frac{55,000 + 15,000}{1.20} = 58,333 \text{ units OR } 58,333 \times £2 = £116,667$$

Note
* The increase in sales is greater than £100,000 and so the full additional general expenses are incurred.

(c) The condition necessary for the company as a whole to make the same profit as in 19X6 is that the extra sales break even. This point is calculated as follows:

	£
Fixed costs of plan 2:	
Depreciation	20,000
Interest	20,000
Expenses†	5,000
	45,000

$$\text{Break even sales} = \frac{45,000}{1.2} = 37,500 \text{ units OR } 37,500 \times 2 = £75,000$$

Note
† As the increase in sales is less than £100,000, the additional expenses are limited to £5,000.

Question 14.6 (£000)

(a) Payback period: Zero 1.75 years
Nemo 2.75 years

(b) Average annual profit: Zero $(140-80)/4 = 15$
Nemo $(160-90)/4 = 17.5$
Average capital employed: Zero $80/2 = 40$
Nemo $90/2 = 45$
ROCE: Zero $15/40 = 37.5\%$
Nemo $17.5/45 = 38.9\%$

(c)

	20% Discount factor	Project Zero Cash flow	Present value	Project Nemo Cash flow	Present value
Year 1	0.833	50	41.65	30	24.99
2	0.694	40	27.76	30	20.82
3	0.579	30	17.37	40	23.16
4	0.482	20	9.64	60	28.92
			96.42		97.89
Less: Initial investment			80.00		90.00
NPV			16.42		7.89

(d) Profitability index: Zero $96.42/80 = 1.21$
Nemo $97.89/90 = 1.09$

(e) Zero has a better payback period, NPV and profitability index, while Nemo gives a better return on capital employed. These results are consistent with the fact that Nemo's cash flow increases towards the end of its life, and these flows are given less weight by the former methods of appraisal. Zero appears to be the better investment.

Question 14.7

	Jan. £	Feb. £	March £	April £	May £	June £
Receipts:						
Sales	—	—	12,000	12,000	12,000	12,000
Capital	20,000					
Loan	8,000					
	28,000	—	12,000	12,000	12,000	12,000
Payments:						
Fixed assets	20,000					
Purchases	—	16,000	8,000	8,000	8,000	8,000
Expenses	800	800	800	800	800	800
Drawings	200	200	200	200	200	200
Interest	—	—	—	—	—	400
	21,000	17,000	9,000	9,000	9,000	9,400
Opening balance	—	7,000	(10,000)	(7,000)	(4,000)	(1,000)
+ Receipts	28,000	—	12,000	12,000	12,000	12,000
− Payments	21,000	17,000	9,000	9,000	9,000	9,400
Closing balance	7,000	(10,000)	(7,000)	(4,000)	(1,000)	1,600

Question 14.8

Forecast Trading and Profit and Loss Account

	£	£
Sales(W2)		72,000
Less: Cost of goods sold (W3)		48,000
Gross profit		24,000
Expenses (W1)	4,800	
Loan interest (.5 × 8,000 × 10%)	400	
Overdraft interest	300	
Depreciation (.5 × 20,000 × 20%)	2,000	
		7,500
Net profit		16,500

Forecast balance sheet

	£	£
Fixed assets		
Cost		20,000
Less: Depreciation		2,000
		18,000
Current assets		
Stock (W3)	8,000	
Debtors (May + June sales)	24,000	
Cash (W1)	1,600	
	33,600	
Current liabilities		
Trade creditors (June purchases)	8,000	
Accrued interest	300	
	8,300	
Working capital		25,300
		43,300
Capital		
Capital introduced		20,000
Profit		16,500
		36,500
Less: Drawings (W1)		1,200
Closing capital		35,300
Loan		8,000
		43,300

Workings
W1. Forecast cash account produced by adding across the individual columns in the solution to Question 11.7.

Cash Account

	£		£
Capital	20,000	Plant	20,000
Loan	8,000	Creditors	48,000
Debtors	48,000	Expenses	4,800
		Drawings	1,200
		Loan interest	400
		Balance c/d	1,600
	76,000		76,000

W2. Sales can be calculated in two alternative ways:

(a) Sales = Cash from debtors + Closing debtors*
= £48,000(W1) + £24,000 (May + June sales) = £72,000

or

(b) £12,000 (Monthly sales) × 6 (Number of months) = £72,000

W3. Cost of goods sold
Purchases can be calculated in two alternative ways:

(a) Purchases = Payments to creditors + closing creditors*

= £48,000 (W1) + £8,000 (June purchases) = £56,000

or

(b) £16,000 (January purchases) + (5 × £8,000) = £56,000

Cost of goods sold = Purchases − Closing stock*
= £56,000 − £8,000† = £48,000

Note
* As this is the first period of trading, there are no opening debtors, creditors or stocks.
†

		£
Purchases		56,000
Less: Cost of goods sold:		
$\frac{100}{150}$ × £72,000 (sales)		48,000
Closing stock		8,000

Question 14.9

Statement of Funds for the Six Months to 30 June 19X6

	£	£
Sources of funds		
Profit		16,500
Add: Depreciation		2,000
		———
Funds generated from operations		18,500
Funds from other sources:		
Capital introduced	20,000	
Loan	8,000	
	———	
		28,000
		———
		46,500
Application of funds		
Purchase of fixed assets	20,000	
Drawings	1,200	
	———	
		21,200
		———
		25,300
*Increase/(decrease) in working capital**		
Increase in stock	8,000	
Increase in debtors	24,000	
Increase in cash	1,600	
Increase in creditors	(8,000)	
Increase in accruals	(300)	
	———	
		25,300
		———

Note
* As the statement of funds covers the first six months of the firm's life, the opening balances of the working capital items are zero.

Index